Dabar Yahuah – Yahuah Scriptures

Apókryfos – Hidden Away

Edited and restored by
Dr. Yeral E. Ogando

© 2025, DYYS: Dr. Yeral. E. Ogando

www.yahuahbible.com

Paperback:
ISBN: 978-1-946249-31-9

Hardcover:
ISBN: 978-1-946249-32-6

Dabar Yahuah – Yahuah Scriptures

Apókryfos (απόκρυφοσ) – Hidden Away

The Hidden Books of the Bible—Now Restored with the Sacred Name of Yahuah | Yahusha.

For centuries, believers have only known a **Bible missing key books**—the sacred writings labeled *Apocrypha* (from the Greek *Apokryfos*, meaning "hidden away or concealed"). Far from being "forbidden" or "occult," these **lost books of the Bible** were concealed to keep humanity in spiritual blindness, away from the fullness of **true biblical knowledge** and **restored faith in Yahuah**.

The world has read an incomplete Bible. Entire books, once cherished and guarded by the priests of Zadok at Qumran, were concealed—labeled as *Apokryfos* (ἀπόκρυφος), meaning *"hidden away.* These writings were intentionally obscured to keep humanity in spiritual blindness, away from the fullness of truth and the true practices of Yahuah's people.

Now, in the **Dabar Yahuah – Yahuah Scriptures**, these **ancient hidden scriptures** return. Restored from the **Dead Sea Scrolls found at Qumran**— the very texts preserved by the **priests of Zadok** and used by **Yahusha Ha'Mashiyach** and His followers—you will experience the Bible as the first believers knew it. Yahusha Himself quoted and taught from these inspired books, and now they are once again revealed for Yahuah's people.

This restored collection draws from the **King James 1611 edition** (public domain), together with the ancient **Books of Jubilees and Enoch** translated by R.H. Charles from the Ethiopic text (public domain). Every page has been reverently prepared to **restore the true Name of Yahuah**—erased by tradition yet preserved by prophecy for such a time as this.

As Daniel 12 foretold, *"knowledge shall increase"* in the last days. What was once hidden is no longer hidden. What was concealed is now revealed.

Inside **Dabar Yahuah – Yahuah Scriptures**, you will find:

- The restored Apokryfos books, once part of the biblical canon at Qumran
- The Name of Yahuah restored in every passage for authentic worship
- Writings and teachings used across both Old and New Testament times
- A deepened understanding of Yahusha's words through the texts He Himself knew

This is not just another Bible. It is a **restoration of the ancient inspired Word**, guarded for centuries, revealed now for Yahuah's people.

👉 Open the pages of truth. Step into the age of knowledge. And walk in the restored light of Yahuah.

Study Guide: Why Study the Hidden/Apocryphal Books of the Bible

Introduction

The hidden or apocryphal books—including Enoch, Jubilees, Sirach, Wisdom of Solomon, Tobit, Baruch, Prayer of Azariah, Bel and the Dragon, and others—provide deep insights into biblical history, theology, ethics, and prophecy. Studying them enhances understanding of Êlôhîym's Word, His plan, and His relationship with humanity.

1. Historical and Cultural Context

- **Cultural Insight:** The Apokryphos reveal Yahûdîy customs, law interpretation, eschatological expectations, and spiritual practices during the exile, post-exile, and pre-Messianic eras. They provide context for the religious and societal frameworks that shaped the first-century world of the Messiah and early apostles.

- **Custodianship:** Many of these writings were preserved and safeguarded in Qumram by the temple priests, particularly the sons of Zadok and the line of Aaron, recognized as the true custodians of the biblical canon. They maintained these texts as inspired scripture, ensuring their careful transmission across generations.

- **Messianic and Apostolic Use:** Evidence suggests that the Messiah (Yahusha) and His apostles were familiar with, and at times referenced, these writings. For example, the Epistle of Jude directly quotes Enoch (Jude 14–15 referencing 1 Enoch 1:9), indicating the authoritative status these texts held in early Messianic teaching. Yahusha's use of the Son of Man title.

- **Canonical and Spiritual Value:** Texts such as Enoch, Jubilees, and Sirach not only shaped religious thought but also provided ethical guidance and prophetic insight. Their preservation by the temple priests underscores their perceived divine inspiration and the spiritual authority attributed to them within the broader corpus of Yahûdîy sacred literature.

2. Theological Insights

- **Divine Justice and Mercy:** Books like the Prayer of Azariah and Bel and the Dragon emphasize Êlôhîym's justice and deliverance (Daniel 3:24–30; Isa 44:9–20).

- **Wisdom Literature:** Wisdom of Solomon and Sirach teach virtues, ethics, and practical guidance.

- **Prophecy and Eschatology:** Enoch, Jubilees, and 2 Esdras contain visions and prophecies about judgment, angels, and the Messiah.

3. Scriptural Parallels and Proofs

Apocryphal Book	Canonical References / Parallels	Importance
Enoch	Jude 14–15; 2 Peter 2:4; Genesis 6	Angelic rebellion, Nephilim, prophecy of judgment
Jubilees	Genesis; Exodus	Fills in genealogical and chronological details; clarifies the law
Sirach	Proverbs, Ecclesiastes	Moral instruction and wisdom ethics
Wisdom of Solomon	Psalms; Proverbs; New Testament references	Explores immortality, righteousness, and divine wisdom
Tobit	Genesis; Judges	Faithfulness, angelic guidance, divine intervention
Prayer of Azariah	Daniel 3:24–30	Prayer in persecution and communal repentance
Bel and the Dragon	Daniel 3; Isaiah 44	Êlôhîym's supremacy over idols, punishing idolaters

4. Moral and Spiritual Lessons

- **Faithfulness under persecution:** Daniel, Azariah, Shadrach, Meshach, Abednego (trust in Yahuah).
- **Repentance and Intercession:** Enoch, Azariah, Jubilees.
- **Wisdom for Daily Life:** Sirach, Wisdom of Solomon.
- **Rejection of Idolatry:** Bel and the Dragon, Prayer of Azariah.

5. Academic and Scholarly Value

- **Textual Studies:** Comparing apocryphal to canonical texts shows how Scripture was transmitted and preserved.
- **New Testament Context:** Ideas in Jude, 2 Peter, Matthew echo apocryphal texts.
- **Cultural Insight:** Yahûdîy beliefs, angelology, demonology, eschatology.
- **Archaeological Evidence:** Dead Sea Scrolls include fragments of Enoch, Jubilees, confirming early use.

6. Custodianship and Preservation

- Many apocryphal and canonical texts were found in **Qumran and Bethavara**, carefully guarded by the temple priests.
- The **sons of Zadok**, descendants of Aaron, were the true custodians of the biblical canon and scriptures.
- Only the **sons of Aaron** had the authority to preserve and validate the true biblical canon, ensuring the integrity of Scripture over generations.

7. Practical Reasons for Study

1. Deepens Bible Literacy
2. Strengthens Faith
3. Expands Moral and Spiritual Insight
4. Prepares for Theological Study
5. Reveals Lost Wisdom (genealogies, angelic hierarchies, covenant explanations)

Table of Major Apokryphos

Apokryphos	Period / Origin	Custodianship	Use by Messiah / Apostles	New Testament References / Echoes	Notes on Significance	Evidence of Inspiration / Why Study Today
1 Enoch (The Book of Enoch)	3rd–1st century BCE	Preserved in Qumram; guarded by sons of Zadok and temple priest	Cited as authoritative by early Messianic teachers	Jude 14–15 directly quotes 1 Enoch 1:9; parallels in Revelation and Matthew (angels, judgment)	Offers apocalyptic visions, angelology, and prophecy; demonstrates early Yahûdîy eschatology	Quoted in NT, preserved faithfully, provides insight into angelic and cosmic order; validates early Yahûdîy-Messianic worldview
Jubilees	2nd century BCE	Kept by priestly line in Qumram	Used for instruction in law and history	Echoed in Acts 7:42–43 (themes of covenant faithfulness)	Rewrites Genesis and Exodus with angelic mediation; emphasizes covenant obedience	Shows divine guidance of history, reinforces covenantal laws, aligns with NT teachings; studied for historical-theological continuity

Apokryphos	Period / Origin	Custodianship	Use by Messiah / Apostles	New Testament References / Echoes	Notes on Significance	Evidence of Inspiration / Why Study Today
Sirach (Ecclesiasticus)	2nd century BCE	Transmitted by temple scribes	Ethical teachings used in instruction	James 3:13–18 echoes its wisdom principles; parallels in Matthew 23	Wisdom literature bridging Torah ethics and practical guidance for Messianic community	Offers timeless ethical instruction; integrated into early Yahûdîy and Messianic teachings; highlights Êlôhîym's wisdom in everyday life
Tobit	3rd–2nd century BCE	Preserved in priestly Qumram libraries	Used as moral exemplar	Themes of divine guidance and angelic assistance reflected in Luke 1:19	Emphasizes righteousness, prayer, and angelic intervention	Demonstrates Yahuah's providence and intervention; teaches moral and spiritual perseverance
Wisdom of Solomon	1st century BCE	Maintained among temple custodians	Guidance for righteous living; anticipates Messianic wisdom	1 Corinthians 1:24 reflects Messiah as "wisdom of Êlôhîym"	Connects Hellenistic Yahûdîy thought to Messianic expectation	Presents divine wisdom as guiding principle; foreshadows Messianic revelation; inspires righteous living
Bel and the Dragon / Daniel Additions	2nd–1st century BCE	Preserved and studied in Qumram	Used to illustrate true worship and prophetic insight	Parallels in Matthew 4:10 (true worship of Yahuah)	Demonstrates divine authority over idolatry and spiritual discernment	Highlights the supremacy of Yahuah over idols; encourages spiritual discernment; reinforces faith in divine justice
Baruch	2nd century BCE	Guarded in priestly libraries	Used for reflection on repentance and covenant	Hebrews 11:32 (themes of exile and faithfulness)	Encourages faithfulness and hope during oppression	Provides encouragement and reflection on repentance; preserves prophetic voice aligning with canonical scriptures

References

1. 1 Enoch 1:9; Jude 14–15
2. Acts 7:42–43
3. James 3:13–18; Matthew 23
4. Luke 1:19
5. 1 Corinthians 1:24
6. Matthew 4:10
7. Hebrews 11:32

Conclusion

The Apokrypha are not forgotten or forbidden—they are **divinely inspired scriptures**, hidden for centuries to conceal Yahuah's true wisdom from humanity. "Apókryfos" means **hidden away**, not occult, and these texts carry the authentic teachings and practices Êlôhîym intended from the very first man.

For too long, we have been misled, denied access to the knowledge of what has happened, what is happening, and what will happen in humanity. But now, in this **age of knowledge**, the hidden scriptures are resurfacing. They offer the path to truth, righteousness, and divine insight that has always been reserved for the faithful.

To embrace the Apókryfos is to step into the light, reclaim the wisdom of Yahuah, and connect with the eternal knowledge meant for those who seek Him. The time has come—the hidden is now revealed.

The hidden/apocryphal books enrich understanding of Êlôhîym's Word, provide historical and theological insights, offer moral and spiritual lessons, and reveal continuity of faith, wisdom, and righteousness. Studying them equips believers, scholars, and students with a fuller picture of Êlôhîym's plan and strengthens faith under trials. They are the inspired scriptures that have been hidden from us for century, taking us away from the real teachings and biblical practices in Yahuah.

Book of Chănôk (Enoch) & Bible Parallels (Dabar Yahuah Scriptures Study Guide)

This study guide presents a comparison between the Book of Chănôk (Enoch) and the books of the Bible (Old and New Testament). It includes summaries of each section of Chănôk (Enoch), as well as a chapter-by-chapter comparison table showing parallels with biblical texts.

Comparison Table

Enoch Chapter(s)	Summary	OT Parallels	NT Parallels
1	Yahuah comes with His holy ones to execute judgment.	Deut 33:2, Isa 66:15–16	Jude 14–15 (direct quote)
6–7	The Watchers descend, take wives, produce Nephilim.	Gen 6:1–4	1 Pet 3:19–20
8	Watchers teach forbidden knowledge (sorcery, weapons, astrology).	Gen 4:22, Deut 18:10–12	Rev 9:21
9–10	Angels intercede; judgment decreed; Azazel bound.	Dan 10:13, Isa 24:21–22	2 Pet 2:4, Jude 6
12–16	Enoch intercedes; visions of Watchers' fate.	Gen 6:5–7	Heb 11:5
17–19	Enoch shown prison of angels.	Isa 14:12–15	Rev 20:1–3
20	List of archangels and duties.	Dan 10:13, 12:1	Rev 12:7
22	Four hollow places of Sheol (for souls).	Job 21:30, Ps 9:17	Luke 16:19–31
25	Vision of Tree of Life on holy mountain.	Gen 2:9, Ezek 47:12	Rev 22:2
36	End of first vision: judgment & paradise.	Isa 65:17–25	Rev 21
37–71	Son of Man/Chosen One revealed; throne of glory; judgment of kings.	Dan 7:9–14	Matt 25:31, Rev 20:11–15
40	Angels around the throne.	Isa 6:2–3	Rev 4:6–8
46–48	Son of Man pre-existent, sits on throne.	Dan 7:13–14	John 1:1–3, Rev 1:13
54–56	Chains prepared for kings, judgment of fallen angels.	Ps 149:8–9	Rev 20:1–3
60	Judgment of flood; Leviathan & Behemoth.	Job 40–41	Rev 13:1
62–63	Nations bow before the Son of Man; kings terrified.	Ps 2:10–12	Phil 2:10–11, Rev 6:15–17
69	Fallen angels named; Son of Man exalted.	Gen 6:1–4	Rev 12:9
72–82	Laws of sun, moon, stars; 364-day calendar.	Gen 1:14–18	Rev 21:23

Enoch Chapter(s)	Summary	OT Parallels	NT Parallels
83–84	Dream of flood judgment.	Gen 7	2 Pet 2:5
85–90	History of Yasharel as animals, Messiah as White Bull.	Ezek 34	John 10:11
91–93	History in 10 weeks (epochs).	Lev 25	Acts 1:7
94–105	Woes to sinners, blessings to righteous.	Ps 1, Prov 10	Matt 5–7
106–107	Birth of Noah miraculous, shining like an angel.	Gen 5:29, 6:8–9	Luke 3:36
108	Final reward for righteous, punishment for sinners.	Isa 66:24	Rev 21–22

Section Summaries

Book of the Watchers (1–36)

Watchers' fall, Nephilim, judgment, Sheol divisions, Tree of Life.

Book of Parables (37–71)

Son of Man, throne visions, final judgment of kings and sinners.

Astronomical Book (72–82)

Heavenly luminaries, calendar system.

Dream Visions (83–90)

Flood vision + Yasharel's history as animals (Animal Apocalypse).

Epistle of Enoch (91–108)

Exhortations, Apocalypse of Weeks, blessings/curses, vision of Noah, final judgment.

Chănôk (חֲנוֹךְ) - Enoch

Part One
Chapters 1-36

Chapter 1

1. The words of the blessing of Chănôk, where he blessed the elect and righteous, who will be living in the day of tribulation, when all the wicked and ungodless are to be removed.

2. And he took up his parable and said: Chănôk a righteous man, whose eyes were opened by Êlôhîym (אֱלֹהִים), saw the vision of the Qâdôsh (קָדוֹשׁ) in the shâmayim that the angels showed me, and from them I heard everything, and from them I understood as I saw, but not for this generation, but for a remote one which is for to come.

3. Concerning the elect I said, and took up my parable concerning them: The Qâdôsh Gibbôr (גִּבּוֹר) ÊL (אֵל) will come forth from His dwelling,

4. And the Êlôhîym Ôlâm (עוֹלָם) will tread upon the earth, even on Mount Sîynay (סִינַי), and appear from his camp and appear in the strength of His might from the shâmayim of shâmayim.

5. And all shall be smitten with fear and the Watchers shall quake, and great fear and trembling shall seize them unto the ends of the earth.

6. And the high mountains shall be shaken, and the high hills shall be made low, and shall melt like wax before the flame.

7. And the earth shall be wholly rent in sunder, and all that is upon the earth shall perish, and there shall be a judgement upon all men.

8. But with the righteous he will make peace. And will protect the elect, and mercy shall be upon them. And they shall all belong to Êlôhîym, and they shall be prospered, and they shall all be blessed. And he will help them all, and light shall appear unto them, and he will make peace with them.

9. And behold! He comes with ten thousands of his qâdôsh ones, to execute judgement upon all, and to destroy all the ungodly: And to convict all flesh of all the works of their ungodliness which they have ungodly committed, and of all the hard things which ungodly sinners have spoken against him.

Chapter 2

1. Observe you everything that takes place in the shâmayim, how they do not change their orbits, and the luminaries which are in the shâmayim, how they all rise and set in order each in its season, and do not transgress against their appointed order.

2. Behold you the earth, and give heed to the things which take place upon it from first to last, how steadfast they are, how none of the things upon earth change, but all the works of Êlôhîym appear to you.

3. Behold the summer and the winter, how the whole earth is filled with water, and clouds and dew and rain lie upon it.

Chapter 3

1. Observe and see how in the winter all the trees seem as though they had withered and shed all their leaves, except fourteen trees, which do not lose their foliage but retain the old foliage from two to three years till the new comes.

Chapter 4

1. And again, observe you the days of summer how the sun is above the earth over against it. And you seek shade and shelter because of the heat of the sun, and the earth also burns with growing heat, and so you cannot tread on the earth, or on a rock because of its heat.

Chapter 5

1. Observe you how the trees cover themselves with green leaves and bear fruit: wherefore give you heed and know with regard to all his works, and recognize how he that lives forever has made them so.

2. And all his works go on thus from year to year forever, and all the tasks which they accomplish for him, and their tasks do not change, but according as Êlôhîym has ordained so is it done.

3. And behold how the sea and the rivers in like manner accomplish and do not change their tasks from his commandments.

4. But you have not been steadfast, nor done the commandments of Yahuah, but you have turned away and spoken proud and hard words with your impure mouths against his greatness. Oh, you hard hearted, you shall find no peace.

5. Therefore shall you execrate your days, and the years of your life shall perish, and the years of your destruction shall be multiplied in eternal execration, and you shall find no mercy.

6. In those days you shall make your names an eternal execration unto all the righteous, and by you shall all who curse, curse, and all the sinners and ungodless shall imprecate by you, and for you the ungodless there shall be a curse.

7. And all the {. . .} shall rejoice, and there shall be forgiveness of sins, and every mercy and peace and forbearance: There shall be salvation unto them, a goodly light. And for all of you sinners there shall be no salvation, but on you all shall abide a curse. But for the elect there shall be light and joy and peace, and they shall inherit the earth.

8. And then there shall be bestowed upon the elect wisdom, and they shall all live and never sin again, either through ungodliness or through pride: But they who are wise shall be humble.

9. And they shall not transgress again, nor shall they sin all the days of their life, nor shall they die of the divine anger or wrath, but they shall complete the number of the days of their life. And their lives shall be increased in peace, and the years of their joy shall be multiplied, in eternal gladness and peace, all the days of their life.

Chapter 6

1. And it came to pass when the children of men had multiplied that in those days were born unto them beautiful and comely daughters.

2. And the angels, the children of the shâmayim, saw and lusted after them, and said to one another: Come, let us choose us women from among the children of men and beget us children.

3. And Semyaza, who was their leader, said unto them: I fear you will not indeed agree to do this deed, and I alone shall have to pay the penalty of a great sin.

4. And they all answered him and said: Let us all swear an oath, and all bind ourselves by mutual spoken curse not to abandon this plan but to do this thing.

5. Then they all swore together and bound themselves by mutual spoken curse upon it.

6. And they were in all two hundred; who descended in the days of Yârad (יָרַד) on the summit of Mount Chermôn (חֶרְמוֹן), and they called it Mount Chermôn, because they had sworn and bound themselves by mutual spoken curse upon it.

7. And these are the names of their leaders: Semiazas, their leader, Arakiba, Rameel, Kokabiel, Tamiel, Ramiel, Danel, Ezeqeel, Baraqiyal, Ăśâhêl, Armaros, Batarel, Ananel, Zaqiel, Samsapeel, Satarel, Turel, Yomyael, Sariel.

8. These are their chiefs of tens.

Chapter 7

1. And all the others together with them took unto themselves women, and each chose for himself one, and they began to go in unto them and to defile themselves with them, and they taught them charms and enchantments, and the cutting of roots, and made them acquainted with plants.

2. And they became pregnant, and they bare great nephîyl (נְפִיל), whose height was three thousand ells:

3. Who consumed all the acquisitions of men. And when men could no longer sustain them,

4. The nephîyl turned against them and devoured mankind.

5. And they began to sin against birds, and beasts, and reptiles, and fish, and to devour one another's flesh, and drink the blood.

6. Then the earth laid accusation against the lawless ones.

Chapter 8

1. And Ăzâzêl taught men to make swords, and knives, and shields, and breastplates, and made known to them the metals of the earth and the art of working them, and bracelets, and ornaments, and the use of antimony, and the beautifying of the eyelids, and all kinds of costly stones, and all coloring tinctures.

2. And there arose much ungodliness, and they committed fornication, and they were led astray, and became corrupt in all their ways.

3. Semyaza taught enchantments, and root cuttings, Armaros the resolving of enchantments, Baraqiyal taught astrology, Kokhebel the constellations, Ezeqeel the knowledge of the clouds, Araqiel the signs of the earth, Shamsiel the signs of the sun, and Sariel the course of the moon.

4. And as men perished, they cried, and their cry went up to shâmayim . . .

Chapter 9

1. And then Mîykâêl (מִיכָאֵל), Ûrîyêl (אוּרִיאֵל), Râphâêl, and Gabrîyêl (גַּבְרִיאֵל) looked down from shâmayim and saw much blood being shed upon the earth, and all lawlessness being wrought upon the earth.

2. And they said one to another: The earth made without inhabitant cries the voice of their crying up to the gates of shâmayim.

3. And now to you, the qâdôsh ones of shâmayim, the souls of men make their suit, saying, "Bring our cause before Elyôn (עֶלְיוֹן) Êl (אֵל)."

4. And they said to the Yahuah of the ages: Âdôn (אָדוֹן) of âdôn (אָדוֹן), Êl of Êlôhîym, Melek

of Melakim, and Êlôhîym of the ages, the throne of your glory stands unto all the generations of the ages, and your name Qâdôsh and glorious and blessed unto all the ages!

5. You have made all things, and you have power over all things: And all things are naked and open in your sight, and you see all things, and nothing can hide itself from you.

6. You see what Ăzâzêl has done, who has taught all unrighteousness on earth and revealed the eternal secrets which were preserved in shâmayim, which men were striving to learn:

7. And Semyaza, to whom you have given authority to bear rule over his associates.

8. And they have gone to the daughters of men upon the earth, and have slept with the women, and have defiled themselves, and revealed to them all kinds of sins.

9. And the women have borne nephîyl, and the whole earth has thereby been filled with blood and unrighteousness.

10. And now, behold, the souls of those who have died are crying and making their suit to the gates of shâmayim, and their lamentations have ascended: and cannot cease because of the lawless deeds which are wrought on the earth.

11. And you know all things before they come to pass, and you see these things and you do suffer them, and you do not say to us what we are to do to them in regard to these.

Chapter 10

1. Then Elyôn Êl said, the Qâdôsh and Gibbôr Êl spoke, and sent Ûrîyêl to the son of Lemek (לֶמֶךְ), and said to him:

2. Go to Nôach (נֹחַ) and tell him in my name "Hide yourself" and reveal to him the end that is approaching: that the whole earth will be destroyed, and a deluge is about to come upon the whole earth, and will destroy all that is on it.

3. And now instruct him that he may escape and his seed may be preserved for all the generations of the world.

4. And Yahuah said to Râphâêl again: Bind Ăzâzêl hand and foot, and cast him into the darkness: And make an opening in the desert, which is in Dudael, and cast him therein.

5. And place upon him rough and jagged rocks, and cover him with darkness, and let him abide there forever, and cover his face that he may not see light.

6. And on the day of the great judgement he shall be cast into the fire.

7. And heal the earth which the angels have corrupted, and proclaim the healing of the earth, that they may heal the plague, and that all the children of men may not perish through all the secret things that the Watchers have disclosed and have taught their sons.

8. And the whole earth has been corrupted through the works that were taught by Ăzâzêl: To him ascribe all sin.

9. And Yahuah said to Gabrîyêl: Proceed against the bastards and the reprobates, and against the children of fornication: and destroy the children of fornication and the children of the Watchers from among men and cause them to go forth: send them one against the other that they may destroy each other in battle: for length of days they shall not have.

10. And no request that they (i.e. their fathers) make of you shall be granted unto their fathers on their behalf; for they hope to live an eternal life, and that each one of them will live five hundred years.

11. And Yahuah said unto Mîykâêl: Go, bind Semyaza and his associates who have united themselves with women so as to have defiled themselves with them in all their uncleanness.

12. And when their sons have slain one another, and they have seen the destruction of their beloved ones, bind them fast for seventy generations in the valleys of the earth, till the day of their judgement and of their consummation, till the judgement that is forever and ever is consummated.

13. In those days they shall be led off to the abyss of fire: And to the torment and the prison in which they shall be confined forever.

14. And whosoever shall be condemned and destroyed will from thenceforth be bound together with them to the end of all generations.

15. And destroy all the spirits of the reprobate and the children of the Watchers, because they have wronged mankind.

16. Destroy all wrong from the face of the earth and let every evil work come to an end: And let the plant of righteousness and truth appear: And it shall prove a blessing; the works of righteousness and truth shall be planted in truth and joy forevermore.

17. And then shall all the righteous escape, and shall live till they beget thousands of children, and all the days of their youth and their old age, shall they complete in peace.

18. And then shall the whole earth be tilled in righteousness, and shall all be planted with trees and be full of blessing.

19. And all desirable trees shall be planted on it, and they shall plant vines on it: And the vine which they plant thereon shall yield wine in abundance, and as for all the seed which is sown thereon each measure of it shall bear a thousand, and each measure of olives shall yield ten presses of oil.

20. And you cleanse the earth from all oppression, and from all unrighteousness, and from all sin, and from all ungodlessness: And all the uncleanness that is wrought upon the earth destroy from off the earth.

21. And all the children of men shall become righteous, and all nations shall offer adoration and shall praise me, and all shall worship me.

22. And the earth shall be cleansed from all defilement, and from all sin, and from all punishment, and from all torment, and I will never again send them upon it from generation to generation and forever.

Chapter 11

1. And in those days I will open the store chambers of blessing which are in the shâmayim, so as to send them down upon the earth over the work and labor of the children of men.

2. And truth and peace shall be associated together throughout all the days of the world and throughout all the generations of men.

Chapter 12

1. Before these things Chănôk was hidden, and no one of the children of men knew where he was hidden, and where he abode, and what had become of him.

2. And his activities had to do with the Watchers, and his days were with the qâdôsh ones.

3. And I Chănôk was blessing Yahuah of majesty and the King of the ages, and lo! The Watchers called me Chănôk the scribe and said to me:

4. Chănôk, you scribe of righteousness, go, declare to the Watchers of the shâmayim who have left the high shâmayim, the Qâdôsh eternal place, and have defiled themselves with women, and have done as the children of earth do, and have taken unto themselves women: You have wrought great destruction on the earth:

5. And you shall have no peace nor forgiveness of sin: And inasmuch as they delight themselves in their children,

6. The murder of their beloved ones shall they see, and over the destruction of their children shall they lament, and shall make supplication unto eternity, but mercy and peace you shall not attain.

Chapter 13

1. And Chănôk went and said: Ăzâzêl, you shall have no peace: A severe sentence has gone forth against you to put you in bonds:

2. And you shall not have toleration nor request granted to you, because of the unrighteousness which you have taught, and because of all the works of ungodliness and unrighteousness and sin which you have shown to men.

3. Then I went and spoke to them all together, and they were all afraid, and fear and trembling seized them.

4. And they besought me to draw up a petition for them that they might find forgiveness, and to read their petition in the presence of Yahuah of shâmayim.

5. For from thenceforward they could not speak with him nor lift up their eyes to shâmayim for shame of their sins for which they had been condemned.

6. Then I wrote out their petition, and the prayer in regard to their spirits and their deeds individually and in regard to their requests that they should have forgiveness and length.

7. And I went off and sat down at the waters of Dan, in the land of Dan, to the south of the west of Chermôn: I read their petition till I fell asleep.

8. And behold a dream came to me, and visions fell down upon me, and I saw visions of chastisement, and a voice came bidding me to tell it to the sons of shâmayim, and reprimand them.

9. And when I awoke, I came unto them, and they were all sitting gathered together, weeping in Hebelsyail, which is between Lebânôn and Seneser, with their faces covered.

10. And I recounted before them all the visions which I had seen in sleep, and I began to speak the words of righteousness, and to reprimand the shâmayimly Watchers.

Chapter 14

1. The book of the words of righteousness, and of the reprimand of the eternal Watchers in accordance with the command of the Qâdôsh Gibbôr Êl in that vision.

2. I saw in my sleep what I will now say with a tongue of flesh and with the breath of my mouth: Which the Gibbôr Êl has given to men to converse therewith and understand with the heart.

3. As he has created and given to man the power of understanding the word of wisdom, so he has created me also and given me the power of reprimanding the Watchers, the children of shâmayim.

4. I wrote out your petition, and in my vision it appeared thus, that your petition will not be granted unto you throughout all the days

of eternity, and that judgement has been finally passed upon you: Yeah your petition will not be granted unto you.

5. And from henceforth you shall not ascend into shâmayim unto all eternity, and in bonds of the earth the decree has gone forth to bind you for all the days of the world.

6. And that previously you shall have seen the destruction of your beloved sons and you shall have no pleasure in them, but they shall fall before you by the sword.

7. And your petition on their behalf shall not be granted, nor yet on your own: Even though you weep and pray and speak all the words contained in the writing which I have written.

8. And the vision was shown to me thus: Behold, in the vision clouds invited me and a mist summoned me, and the course of the stars and the lightnings sped and hastened me, and the winds in the vision caused me to fly and lifted me upward, and bore me into shâmayim.

9. And I went in till I drew nigh to a wall which is built of crystals and surrounded by tongues of fire: And it began to affright me.

10. And I went into the tongues of fire and drew nigh to a large house which was built of crystals: And the walls of the house were like a tessellated floor made of crystals, and its groundwork was of crystal.

11. Its ceiling was like the path of the stars and the lightnings, and between them were fiery Kerûb (כְּרוּב), and their shâmayim was clear as water.

12. A flaming fire surrounded the walls, and its portals blazed with fire.

13. And I entered into that house, and it was hot as fire and cold as ice: There were no delights of life therein: Fear covered me, and trembling got hold upon me.

14. And as I quaked and trembled, I fell upon my face.

15. And I beheld a vision, And lo! There was a second house, greater than the former, and the entire portal stood open before me, and it was built of flames of fire.

16. And in every respect it so excelled in splendor and magnificence and extent that I cannot describe to you its splendor and its extent.

17. And its floor was of fire, and above it were lightnings and the path of the stars, and its ceiling also was flaming fire.

18. And I looked and saw therein a lofty throne: Its appearance was as crystal, and the wheels thereof as the shining sun, and there was the vision of Kerûb.

19. And from underneath the throne came streams of flaming fire so that I could not look thereon.

20. And the Gibbôr (גִּבּוֹר) Kâbôd (כָּבוֹד) sat thereon, and his raiment shone more brightly than the sun and was whiter than any snow.

21. None of the angels could enter and could behold his face because of the magnificence and glory and no flesh could behold him.

22. The flaming fire was round about him, and a great fire stood before him, and none around could draw nigh him: Ten thousand times ten thousand stood before him, yet he needed no counselor.

23. And the most qâdôsh ones who were nigh to him did not leave by night nor depart from him.

24. And until then I had been prostrate on my face, trembling: and Yahuah called me

with his own mouth, and said to me: Come hither, Chănôk, and hear my word.

25. And one of the qâdôsh ones came to me and woke me, and he made me rise up and approach the door: And I bowed my face downwards.

Chapter 15

1. And he answered and said to me, and I heard his voice: Do not fear, Chănôk, you righteous man and scribe of righteousness: Approach hither and hear my voice.

2. And go, say to the Watchers of shâmayim, who have sent you to intercede for them: You should intercede for men, and not men for you:

3. Wherefore you have left the high, qâdôsh, and eternal shâmayim, and lain with women, and defiled yourselves with the daughters of men and taken to yourselves women, and done like the children of earth, and begotten nephîyl as your sons?

4. And though you were qâdôsh, spiritual, living the eternal life, you have defiled yourselves with the blood of women, and have begotten children with the blood of flesh, and, as the children of men, have lusted after flesh and blood as those also do who die and perish.

5. Therefore I have given them women also that they might impregnate them, and beget children by them, that thus nothing might be wanting to them on earth.

6. But you were formerly spiritual, living the eternal life, and immortal for all generations of the world.

7. And therefore I have not appointed women for you; for as for the spiritual ones of the shâmayim, in shâmayim is their dwelling.

8. And now, the nephîyl, who are produced from the spirits and flesh, shall be called evil spirits upon the earth, and on the earth shall be their dwelling.

9. Evil spirits have proceeded from their bodies; because they are born from men and from the qâdôsh Watchers is their beginning and primal origin; they shall be evil spirits on earth, and evil spirits shall they be called.

10. As for the spirits of shâmayim, in shâmayim shall be their dwelling, but as for the spirits of the earth which were born upon the earth, on the earth shall be their dwelling.

11. And the spirits of the nephîyl afflict, oppress, destroy, attack, do battle, and work destruction on the earth, and cause trouble: They take no food, but nevertheless hunger and thirst, and cause offences.

12. And these spirits shall rise up against the children of men and against the women, because they have proceeded from them.

Chapter 16

1. From the days of the slaughter and destruction and death of the nephîyl, from the souls of whose flesh the spirits, having gone forth, shall destroy without incurring judgement thus shall they destroy until the day of the consummation, the great judgement in which the age shall be consummated, over the Watchers and the ungodless, yeah, shall be wholly consummated.

2. And now as to the watchers who have sent you to intercede for them, who had been before time in shâmayim, say to them:

3. You have been in shâmayim, but all the mysteries had not yet been revealed to you, and you knew worthless ones, and these in the hardness of your hearts you have made known to the women, and through these

mysteries women and men work much evil on earth.

4. Say to them therefore: "You have no peace."

Chapter 17

1. And they took and brought me to a place in which those who were there were like flaming fire, and, when they wished, they appeared as men.

2. And they brought me to the place of darkness, and to a mountain the point of whose summit reached to shâmayim.

3. And I saw the places of the luminaries and the treasuries of the stars and of the thunder and in the uttermost depths, where were a fiery bow and arrows and their quiver, and a fiery sword and all the lightnings.

4. And they took me to the living waters, and to the fire of the west, which receives every setting of the sun.

5. And I came to a river of fire in which the fire flows like water and discharges itself into the great sea towards the west.

6. I saw the great rivers and came to the great river and to the great darkness, and went to the place where no flesh walks.

7. I saw the mountains of the darkness of winter and the place whence all the waters of the deep flow.

8. I saw the mouths of all the rivers of the earth and the mouth of the deep.

Chapter 18

1. I saw the treasuries of all the winds: I saw how he had furnished with them the whole creation and the firm foundations of the earth.

2. And I saw the corner stone of the earth: I saw the four winds which bear the earth and the firmament of the shâmayim.

3. And I saw how the winds stretch out the vaults of shâmayim, and have their station between shâmayim and earth: These are the pillars of the shâmayim.

4. I saw the winds of shâmayim which turn and bring the circumference of the sun and all the stars to their setting.

5. I saw the winds on the earth carrying the clouds: I saw the paths of the angels. I saw at the end of the earth the firmament of the shâmayim above.

6. And I proceeded and saw a place which burns day and night, where there are seven mountains of magnificent stones, three towards the east, and three towards the south.

7. And as for those towards the east, was of colored stone, and one of pearl, and one of jacinth, and those towards the south of red stone.

8. But the middle one reached to shâmayim like the throne of Êlôhîym, of alabaster, and the summit of the throne was of sapphire.

9. And I saw a flaming fire.

10. And beyond these mountains is a region the end of the great earth: There the shâmayim were completed.

11. And I saw a deep abyss, with columns of shâmayim fire, and among them I saw columns of fire fall, which were beyond measure alike towards the height and towards the depth.

12. And beyond that abyss I saw a place which had no firmament of the shâmayim above, and no firmly founded earth beneath it: There was no water upon it, and no birds, but it was a waste and horrible place.

13. I saw there seven stars like great burning mountains, and to me, when I inquired regarding them,

14. The angel said: This place is the end of shâmayim and earth: This has become a prison for the stars and the host of shâmayim.

15. And the stars which roll over the fire are they which have transgressed the commandment of Yahuah in the beginning of their rising, because they did not come forth at their appointed times.

16. And he was wroth with them, and bound them till the time when their guilt should be consummated even for ten thousand years.

Chapter 19

1. And Ûrîyêl said to me: Here shall stand the angels who have connected themselves with women, and their spirits assuming many different forms are defiling mankind and shall lead them astray into sacrificing to demons as gods, here they shall stand, till the day of the great judgement in which they shall be judged till they are made an end of.

2. And the women also of the angels who went astray shall become sirens.

3. And I, Chănôk, alone saw the vision, the ends of all things: And no man shall see as I have seen.

Chapter 20

1. And these are the names of the qâdôsh angels who watch.

2. Ûrîyêl, one of the qâdôsh angels, who is over the world and over Tartaróo (ταρταρόω).

3. Râphâêl, one of the qâdôsh angels, who is over the spirits of men.

4. Reûêl, one of the qâdôsh angels who takes vengeance on the world of the luminaries.

5. Mîykâêl, one of the qâdôsh angels, to wit, he that is set over the best part of mankind and over chaos.

6. Śarâhqael, one of the qâdôsh angels, who is set over the spirits, who sin in the spirit.

7. Gabrîyêl, one of the qâdôsh angels, who is over paradise and the nâchâsh and the Kerûb.

8. Remiêl, one of the qâdôsh angels, whom Êlôhîym set over those who rise.

Chapter 21

1. And I proceeded to where things were chaotic.

2. And I saw there something horrible: I saw neither a shâmayim above nor a firmly founded earth, but a place chaotic and horrible.

3. And there I saw seven stars of the shâmayim bound together in it, like great mountains and burning with fire.

4. Then I said: For what sin are they bound, and on what account have they been cast in hither?

5. Then Ûrîyêl said, one of the qâdôsh angels, who was with me, and was chief over them, and said: Chănôk, why do you ask, and why are you eager for the truth?

6. These are of the number of the stars of shâmayim, which have transgressed the commandment of Yahuah, and are bound here till ten thousand years, the time entailed by their sins, are consummated.

7. And from thence I went to another place, which was still more horrible than the former, and I saw a horrible thing: A great fire there which burnt and blazed, and the place was cleft as far as the abyss, being full of great descending columns of fire: Neither its extent or magnitude I could see, nor I could conjecture.

8. Then I said: How fearful is the place and how terrible to look upon!

9. Then Ûrîyêl answered me, one of the qâdôsh angels who was with me, and said unto me: Chănôk, why you have such fear and affright? And I answered: Because of this fearful place, and because of the spectacle of the pain.

10. And he said unto me: This place is the prison of the angels, and here they will be imprisoned forever.

Chapter 22

1. And thence I went to another place, and he showed me in the west another great and high mountain and of hard rock.

2. And there were four hollow places in it, deep and very smooth: Three of them were dark and one bright; and there was a fountain of water in its midst. And I said: How smooth are the hollow places and deep and dark to view.

3. Then Râphâêl answered, one of the qâdôsh angels who was with me, and said unto me: These hollow places have been created for this very purpose that the spirits of the souls of the dead should assemble therein, yea that all the souls of the children of men should assemble here.

4. And these places have been made to receive them till the day of their judgement and till their appointed period till the period appointed, till the great judgement comes upon them.

5. I saw the spirit of a dead man making suit, and his voice went forth to shâmayim and made suit.

6. And I asked Râphâêl the angel who was with me, and I said unto him: This spirit which makes suit, whose is it, whose voice goes forth and makes suit to shâmayim?

7. And he answered me saying: This is the spirit which went forth from Hebel (הֶבֶל), whom his brother Qayin (קַיִן) slew, and he makes his suit against him till his seed is destroyed from the face of the earth, and his seed is annihilated from among the seed of men.

8. Then I asked regarding all the hollow places: Why is one separated from the other?

9. Then he answered me saying: These three have been made that the spirits of the dead might be separated. And this division has bas been made for the spirits of the righteous, in which there is a bright spring of water.

10. And this has been made for sinners when they die and are buried in the earth and judgement has not been executed upon them in their lifetime.

11. Here their spirits shall be set apart in this great pain, till the great day of judgement, scourgings, and torments of the accursed forever, so that there may be retribution for their spirits. There he shall bind them forever.

12. And this division has been made for the spirits of those who make their suit, who make disclosures concerning their destruction, when they were slain in the days of the sinners.

13. And this has been made for the spirits of men who shall not be righteous but sinners, who are ungodly, and of the lawless they shall be companions: But their spirits shall not be punished in the day of judgement nor shall they be raised from thence.

14. Then I blessed Yahuah Kâbôd and said: Blessed are you, Yahuah Tsedâqâh (צְדָקָה), who rule over the world.

Chapter 23

1. From thence I went to another place to the west of the ends of the earth.

2. And I saw a burning fire which ran without resting, and did not pause from its course day or night but ran regularly.

3. And I asked saying: What is this which does not rest?

4. Then Reûêl, one of the qâdôsh angels who was with me, answered me and said unto me: This course of fire which you have seen is the fire in the west which persecutes all the luminaries of shâmayim.

Chapter 24

1. And from thence I went to another place of the earth, and he showed me a mountain range of fire which burnt day and night.

2. And I went beyond it and saw seven magnificent mountains all differing each from the other, and the stones thereof were magnificent and beautiful, magnificent as a whole, of glorious appearance and fair exterior: Three towards the east, one founded on the other, and three towards the south, one upon the other, and deep rough ravines, no one of which joined with any other.

3. And the seventh mountain was in the midst of these, and it excelled them in height, resembling the seat of a throne: And fragrant trees encircled the throne.

4. And among them was a tree such as I had never yet smelt, neither was any among them nor were others like it: It had a fragrance beyond all fragrance, and its leaves and blooms and wood do not wither forever: And its fruit is beautiful, and its fruit resembles the dates of a palm.

5. Then I said: How beautiful is this tree, and fragrant, and its leaves are fair, and its blooms very delightful in appearance.

6. Then Mîykâêl answered, one of the qâdôsh and honored angels who was with me, and was their leader.

Chapter 25

1. And he said unto me: Chănôk, why do you ask me regarding the fragrance of the tree, and why do you wish to learn the truth?

2. Then I answered him saying: I wish to know about everything, but especially about this tree.

3. And he answered saying: This high mountain which you have seen, whose summit is like the throne of Êlôhîym, is his throne, where the Qâdôsh Gibbôr Êl, Yahuah Kâbôd, the Melek Ôlâm, will sit, when he shall come down to visit the earth with goodness.

4. And as for this fragrant tree no mortal is permitted to touch it till the great judgement, when he shall take vengeance on all and bring everything to its consummation forever. It shall then be given to the righteous and qâdôsh.

5. Its fruit shall be for food to the elect: It shall be transplanted to the qâdôsh place, to the temple of Yahuah, the Melek Ôlâm.

6. Then they shall rejoice with joy and be glad, and into the qâdôsh place shall they enter; and its fragrance shall be in their bones, and they shall live a long life on earth, such as your fathers lived: And in their days shall no sorrow or plague or torment or calamity touch them.

7. Then I blessed Êlôhîym Kâbôd, the Melek Ôlâm, who has prepared such things for the righteous, and has created them and promised to give to them.

Chapter 26

1. And I went from thence to the middle of the earth, and I saw a blessed place in which there were trees with branches abiding and blooming of a dismembered tree.

2. And there I saw a qâdôsh mountain, and underneath the mountain to the east there

was a stream and it flowed towards the south.

3. And I saw towards the east another mountain higher than this, and between them a deep and narrow ravine: In it also ran a stream underneath the mountain.

4. And to the west thereof there was another mountain, lower than the former and of small elevation, and a ravine deep and dry between them: And another deep and dry ravine was at the extremities of the three mountains.

5. And all the ravines were deep and narrow, being formed of hard rock, and trees were not planted upon them.

6. And I marveled at the rocks, and I marveled at the ravine, yea, I marveled very much.

Chapter 27

1. Then I said: For what object is this blessed land, which is entirely filled with trees, and this accursed valley between?

2. Then Ûrîyêl, one of the qâdôsh angels who was with me, answered and said: This accursed valley is for those who are accursed forever: Here shall all the accursed be gathered together who utter with their lips against Yahuah unseemly words and of his glory speak hard things. Here they shall be gathered together, and here shall be the place of their habitation.

3. In the last times, in the days of true judgement, in the presence of the righteous forever: Here shall the godly bless Yahuah Kâbôd, the Melek Ôlâm.

4. In the days of judgement over the former, they shall bless him for the mercy in accordance with which he has assigned them their lot.

5. Then I blessed Yahuah Kâbôd and set forth his glory and lauded him gloriously.

Chapter 28

1. And thence I went towards the east, into the midst of the mountain range of the desert, and I saw a wilderness and it was solitary, full of trees and plants.

2. And water gushed forth from above.

3. Rushing like a copious watercourse which flowed towards the north west it caused clouds and dew to ascend on every side.

Chapter 29

1. And thence I went to another place in the desert, and approached to the east of this mountain range.

2. And there I saw aromatic trees exhaling the fragrance of lebônâh (לְבוֹנָה) and myrrh, and the trees also were similar to the almond tree.

Chapter 30

1. And beyond these, I went afar to the east, and I saw another place, a valley full of water.

2. And therein there was a tree, the color (?) of fragrant trees such as the mastic.

3. And on the sides of those valleys I saw fragrant cinnamon.

4. And beyond these I proceeded to the east.

Chapter 31

1. And I saw other mountains, and among them were ăshêrâh of trees, and there flowed forth from them nectar, which is named Śârâhra and galbanum.

2. And beyond these mountains I saw another mountain to the east of the ends of the earth, whereon aloe trees, and all the trees were full of stacte, being like almond trees.

3. And when one burnt it, it smelt sweeter than any fragrant odor.

Chapter 32

1. To the north east I beheld seven mountains full of choice nard and mastic and cinnamon and pepper.

2. And thence I went over the summits of all these mountains, far towards the east of the earth, and passed above the Red sea and went far from it, and passed over the angel Zotiêl.

3. And I came to the Garden of Tsedâqâh, and from afar off trees more numerous than these trees and great two trees there, very great, beautiful, and glorious, and magnificent, and the tree of knowledge, whose qâdôsh fruit they eat and know great wisdom.

4. That tree is in height like the fir, and its leaves are like those of the Carob tree: And its fruit is like the clusters of the vine, very beautiful: And the fragrance of the tree penetrates afar.

5. Then I said: How beautiful is the tree, and how attractive is its look!

6. Then Râphâêl the qâdôsh angel, who was with me, answered me and said: This is the tree of wisdom, of which your father old in years and your aged mother, who were before you, have eaten, and they learnt wisdom and their eyes were opened, and they knew that they were naked and they were driven out of the Garden.

Chapter 33

1. And from thence I went to the ends of the earth and saw there great beasts, and each differed from the other; and I saw birds also differing in appearance and beauty and voice, the one differing from the other.

2. And to the east of those beasts I saw the ends of the earth whereon the shâmayim rests, and the portals of the shâmayim open.

3. And I saw how the stars of shâmayim come forth, and I counted the portals out of which they proceed, and wrote down all their outlets, of each individual star by itself, according to their number and their names, their courses and their positions, and their times and their months, as Ûrîyêl the qâdôsh angel who was with me showed me.

4. He showed all things to me and wrote them down for me: Also their names he wrote for me, and their laws and their companies.

Chapter 34

1. And from thence I went towards the north to the ends of the earth, and there I saw a great and glorious device at the ends of the whole earth.

2. And here I saw three portals of shâmayim open in the shâmayim: Through each of them proceed north winds: When they blow there is cold, hail, frost, snow, dew, and rain.

3. And out of one portal they blow for good: But when they blow through the other two portals, it is with violence and affliction on the earth, and they blow with violence.

Chapter 35

1. And from thence I went towards the west to the ends of the earth, and saw there three portals of the shâmayim open such as I had seen in the east, the same number of portals, and the same number of outlets.

Chapter 36

1. And from thence I went to the south to the ends of the earth, and saw there three open

portals of the shâmayim: And thence there come dew, rain, and wind.

2. And from thence I went to the east to the ends of the shâmayim, and saw here the three eastern portals of shâmayim open and small portals above them.

3. Through each of these small portals pass the stars of shâmayim and run their course to the west on the path which is shown to them.

4. And as often as I saw I blessed always Yahuah Kâbôd, and I continued to bless Yahuah Kâbôd who has wrought great and glorious wonders, to show the greatness of his work to the angels and to spirits and to men, that they might praise his work and all his creation: That they might see the work of his might and praise the great work of his hands and bless him forever.

Part Two - The Parables
Chapters 37-71

Chapter 37

1. The second vision which he saw, the vision of wisdom which Chănôk the son of Yârad, the son of Mahălalêl, the son of Qêynân (קֵינָן), the son of Ĕnôsh (אֱנוֹשׁ), the son of Shêth (שֵׁת), the son of Âdâm, saw.

2. And this is the beginning of the words of wisdom which I lifted up my voice to speak and say to those which dwell on earth: Hear, you men of old time, and see, you that come after, the words of the Qâdôsh which I will speak before Yahuah of Rûach.

3. It were better to declare them only to the men of old time, but even from those that come after we will not withhold the beginning of wisdom.

4. Till the present day such wisdom has never been given by Yahuah of Rûach as I have received according to my insight, according to the good pleasure of Yahuah of Rûach by whom the lot of eternal life has been given to me.

5. Now three parables were imparted to me, and I lifted up my voice and recounted them to those that dwell on the earth.

Chapter 38
The First Parable.

1. When the congregation of the righteous shall appear, and sinners shall be judged for their sins, and shall be driven from the face of the earth:

2. And when the Tsedâqâh Êl shall appear before the eyes of the righteous, whose elect works hang upon Yahuah of Rûach, and light shall appear to the righteous and the elect who dwell on the earth. Where then will be the dwelling of the sinners, and where the resting place of those who have denied Yahuah of Rûach? It had been good for them if they had not been born.

3. When the secrets of the righteous shall be revealed and the sinners judged, and the ungodless driven from the presence of the righteous and elect.

4. From that time those that possess the earth shall no longer be powerful and exalted: And they shall not be able to behold the face of the qâdôsh, for Yahuah of Rûach has caused his light to appear on the face of the qâdôsh, righteous, and elect.

5. Then shall the kings and the mighty perish and be given into the hands of the righteous and qâdôsh. And thenceforward none shall seek for themselves mercy from Yahuah of Rûach, for their life is at an end.

Chapter 39

1. And it shall come to pass in those days that elect and qâdôsh children will descend from the high shâmayim, and their seed will become one with the children of men.

2. And in those days Chănôk received books of zeal and wrath, and books of disquiet and expulsion. And mercy shall not be accorded to them, says Yahuah of Rûach.

3. And in those days a whirlwind carried me off from the earth, and set me down at the end of the shâmayim.

4. And there I saw another vision, the dwelling places of the qâdôsh, and the resting places of the righteous.

5. Here my eyes saw their dwellings with his righteous angels, and their resting places with the qâdôsh. And they petitioned and interceded and prayed for the children of men, and righteousness flowed before them as water, and mercy like dew upon the earth: Thus it is among them forever and ever.

6. And in that place my eyes saw the Bâchîyr Êl of righteousness and of faith,

7. And I saw his dwelling place under the wings of Yahuah of Rûach. And righteousness shall prevail in his days, and the righteous and elect shall be without number before him forever and ever. And all the righteous and elect before him shall be strong as fiery lights, and their mouth shall be full of blessing, and their lips extol the name of Yahuah of Rûach, and righteousness before him shall never fail, and uprightness shall never fail before Him.

8. There I wished to dwell, and my spirit longed for that dwelling place: And there heretofore has been my portion, for so has it been established concerning me before Yahuah of Rûach.

9. In those days I praised and extolled the name of Yahuah of Rûach with blessings and praises, because he has destined me for blessing and glory according to the good pleasure of Yahuah of Rûach.

10. For a long time my eyes regarded that place, and I blessed him and praised him, saying: Blessed is he, and may he be blessed from the beginning and forevermore.

11. And before him there is no ceasing. He knows before the world was created what is forever and what will be from generation unto generation.

12. Those who do not sleep bless you: They stand before your glory and bless, praise, and extol, saying: "Qâdôsh, Qâdôsh, Qâdôsh, is Yahuah of Rûach: He fills the earth with spirits."'

13. And here my eyes saw all those who do not sleep: They stand before him and bless and say: Blessed be you, and blessed be the name of Yahuah forever and ever.

14. And my face was changed; for I could no longer behold.

Chapter 40

1. And after that I saw thousands of thousands and ten thousand times ten thousand, I saw a multitude beyond number and reckoning, who stood before Yahuah of Rûach.

2. And on the four sides of Yahuah of Rûach I saw four presences, different from those that do not sleep, and I learnt their names: For the angel that went with me made known to me their names, and showed me all the hidden things.

3. And I heard the voices of those four presences as they uttered praises before Yahuah Kâbôd.

4. The first voice blesses Yahuah of Rûach forever and ever.

5. And the second voice I heard blessing the Bâchîyr Êl and the elect ones who hang upon Yahuah of Rûach.

6. And the third voice I heard pray and intercede for those who dwell on the earth and supplicate in the name of Yahuah of Rûach.

7. And I heard the fourth voice fending off the adversaries and forbidding them to come before Yahuah of Rûach to accuse them who dwell on the earth.

8. After that I asked the angel of peace who went with me, who showed me everything that is hidden: Who are these four presences which I have seen and whose words I have heard and written down?

9. And he said to me: This first is Mîykâêl, the merciful and long suffering: and the second, who is set over all the diseases and all the wounds of the children of men, is Râphâêl: And the third, who is set over all the powers, is Gabrîyêl: And the fourth, who is set over the repentance unto hope of those who inherit eternal life, is named Phanuêl.

10. And these are the four angels of Yahuah of Rûach and the four voices I heard in those days.

Chapter 41

1. And after that I saw all the secrets of the shâmayim, and how the kingdom is divided, and how the actions of men are weighed in the balance.

2. And there I saw the mansions of the elect and the mansions of the qâdôsh, and my eyes saw there all the sinners being driven from thence which deny the name of Yahuah of Rûach, and being dragged off: And they could not abide because of the punishment which proceeds from Yahuah of Rûach.

3. And there my eyes saw the secrets of the lightning and of the thunder, and the secrets of the winds, how they are divided to blow over the earth, and the secrets of the clouds and dew, and there I saw from whence they proceed in that place and from whence they saturate the dusty earth.

4. And there I saw closed chambers out of which the winds are divided, the chamber of the hail and winds, the chamber of the mist, and of the clouds, and the cloud thereof hovers over the earth from the beginning of the world.

5. And I saw the chambers of the sun and moon, whence they proceed and whither they come again, and their glorious return, and how one is superior to the other, and their stately orbit, and how they do not leave their orbit, and they add nothing to their orbit and they take nothing from it, and they keep faith with each other, in accordance with the oath by which they are bound together.

6. And first the sun goes forth and traverses his path according to the commandment of Yahuah of Rûach, and mighty is his name forever and ever.

7. And after that I saw the hidden and the visible path of the moon, and she accomplishes the course of her path in that place by day and by night, the one holding a position opposite to the other before Yahuah of Rûach. And they give thanks and praise and do not rest; for unto them their thanksgiving is rest.

8. For the sun changes oft for a blessing or a curse, and the course of the path of the moon

is light to the righteous and darkness to the sinners in the name of Yahuah, who made a separation between the light and the darkness, and divided the spirits of men, and strengthened the spirits of the righteous, in the name of his righteousness.

9. For no angel hinders and no power is able to hinder; for he appoints a judge for them all and he judges them all before him.

Chapter 42

1. Wisdom found no place where she might dwell; then a dwelling place was assigned to her in the shâmayim.

2. Wisdom went forth to make her dwelling among the children of men, and found no dwelling place: Wisdom returned to her place, and took her seat among the angels.

3. And unrighteousness went forth from her chambers: Whom she did not seek, she found, and dwelt with them, as rain in a desert and dew on a thirsty land.

Chapter 43

1. And I saw other lightnings and the stars of shâmayim, and I saw how he called them all by their names and they hearkened unto him.

2. And I saw how they are weighed in a righteous balance according to their proportions of light: I saw the width of their spaces and the day of their appearing, and how their revolution produces lightning: And I saw their revolution according to the number of the angels, and how they keep faith with each other.

3. And I asked the angel who went with me who showed me what was hidden: What are these?

4. And he said to me: Yahuah of Rûach has showed you their parabole's meaning: These are the names of the qâdôsh who dwell on the earth and believe in the name of Yahuah of Rûach forever and ever.

Chapter 44

1. Also another phenomenon I saw in regard to the lightnings: How some of the stars arise and become lightnings and cannot part with their new form.

Chapter 45

1. And this is the second Parable concerning those who deny the name of the dwelling of the qâdôsh ones and Yahuah of Rûach.

2. And into the shâmayim they shall not ascend, and on the earth they shall not come: Such shall be the lot of the sinners, who have denied the name of Yahuah of Rûach, who are thus preserved for the day of suffering and tribulation.

3. On that day my Bâchîyr Êl shall sit on the throne of glory and shall try their works, and their places of rest shall be innumerable. And their souls shall grow strong within them when they see my elect ones, and those who have called upon my glorious name:

4. Then I will cause my Bâchîyr Êl to dwell among them. And I will transform the shâmayim and make it an eternal blessing and light.

5. And I will transform the earth and make it a blessing: And I will cause my elect ones to dwell upon it: But the sinners and evil doers shall not set foot thereon.

6. For I have provided and satisfied with peace my righteous ones and have caused them to dwell before me: But for the sinners there is judgement impending with me, so that I shall destroy them from the face of the earth.

Chapter 46

1. And there I saw One who had a head of days, and his head was white like wool, and with him was another being whose countenance had the appearance of a man, and his face was full of graciousness, like one of the qâdôsh angels.

2. And I asked the angel who went with me and showed me all the hidden things, concerning that Bên *(בֶּן)* Âdâm (אָדָם), who he was, and whence he was, and why he went with the Attîyq (עַתִּיק) Yôm (יוֹם)?

3. And he answered and said unto me: This is the Bên Âdâm who has righteousness, with whom dwells righteousness, and who reveals all the treasures of that which is hidden, because Yahuah of Rûach has chosen him, and whose lot has the preeminence before Yahuah of Rûach in uprightness forever.

4. And this Bên Âdâm whom you have seen, shall raise up the kings and the mighty from their seats, and the strong from their thrones and shall loosen the reins of the strong, and break the teeth of the sinners.

5. And he shall put down the kings from their thrones and kingdoms because they do not extol and praise him, nor humbly acknowledge whence the kingdom was bestowed upon them.

6. And he shall put down the countenance of the strong, and shall fill them with shame. And darkness shall be their dwelling, and worms shall be their bed, and they shall have no hope of rising from their beds, because they do not extol the name of Yahuah of Rûach.

7. And these are they who judge the stars of shâmayim, and raise their hands against Elyôn Êl, and tread upon the earth and dwell upon it. And all their deeds manifest unrighteousness, and their power rests upon their riches, and their faith is in the gods which they have made with their hands, and they deny the name of Yahuah of Rûach,

8. And they persecute the houses of his congregations, and the faithful who hang upon the name of Yahuah of Rûach.

Chapter 47

1. And in those days shall have ascended the prayer of the righteous, and the blood of the righteous from the earth before Yahuah of Rûach.

2. In those days the qâdôsh ones who dwell above in the shâmayim, shall unite with one voice and supplicate and pray and praise, and give thanks and bless the name of Yahuah of Rûach on behalf of the blood of the righteous which has been shed, and that the prayer of the righteous may not be in vain before Yahuah of Rûach, that judgement may be done unto them, and that they may not have to suffer forever.

3. In those days I saw the Attîyq Yôm when he seated himself upon the throne of his glory, and the books of the living were opened before him: And all his host which is in shâmayim above and his counselors stood before him,

4. And the hearts of the qâdôsh were filled with joy; because the number of the righteous had been offered, and the prayer of the righteous had been heard, and the blood of the righteous been required before Yahuah of Rûach.

Chapter 48

1. And in that place I saw the fountain of righteousness which was inexhaustible: And around it were many fountains of wisdom:

And all the thirsty drank of them, and were filled with wisdom, and their dwellings were with the righteous and qâdôsh and elect.

2. And at that hour that Bên Âdâm was named in the presence of Yahuah of Rûach, and his name before the Attîyq Yôm.

3. Yea, before the sun and the signs were created, before the stars of the shâmayim were made, his name was named before Yahuah of Rûach.

4. He shall be a staff to the righteous whereon to stay themselves and not fall, and he shall be the light of the Gentiles, and the hope of those who are troubled of heart.

5. All who dwell on earth shall fall down and worship before him, and will praise and bless and celebrate with song Yahuah of Rûach.

6. And for this reason he has been chosen and hidden before him, before the creation of the world and forevermore.

7. And the wisdom of Yahuah of Rûach has revealed him to the qâdôsh and righteous; for he has preserved the lot of the righteous, because they have hated and despised this world of unrighteousness, and have hated all its works and ways in the name of Yahuah of Rûach: For in his name they are saved, and according to his good pleasure it has been in regard to their life.

8. In these days downcast in countenance shall the kings of the earth have become, and the strong who possess the land because of the works of their hands, for on the day of their anguish and affliction they shall not be able to save themselves.

9. And I will give them over into the hands of Bâchîyr Êl: As straw in the fire so shall they burn before the face of the qâdôsh: As lead in the water shall they sink before the face of the righteous, and no trace of them shall be found any more.

10. And on the day of their affliction there shall be rest on the earth, and before them they shall fall and not rise again: And there shall be no one to take them with his hands and raise them: For they have denied Yahuah of Rûach and his Mâshîyach (מָשִׁיחַ). The name of Yahuah of Rûach be blessed.

Chapter 49

1. For wisdom is poured out like water, and glory does not fail before him forevermore.

2. For he is mighty in all the secrets of righteousness, and unrighteousness shall disappear as a shadow, and have no continuance; because the Bâchîyr Êl stands before Yahuah of Rûach, and his glory is forever and ever, and his might unto all generations.

3. And in him dwells the spirit of wisdom, and the spirit which gives insight, and the spirit of understanding and of might, and the spirit of those who have fallen asleep in righteousness.

4. And he shall judge the secret things, and none shall be able to utter a lying word before him; for he is the Bâchîyr Êl before Yahuah of Rûach according to his good pleasure.

Chapter 50

1. And in those days a change shall take place for the qâdôsh and elect, and the Bâchîyr Êl shall abide upon them, and glory and honor shall turn to the qâdôsh,

2. On the day of affliction on which evil shall have been treasured up against the sinners. And the righteous shall be victorious in the name of Yahuah of Rûach: And he will cause the others to witness this that they may repent and forgo the works of their hands.

3. They shall have no honor through the name of Yahuah of Rûach, yet through his name shall they be saved, and Yahuah of Rûach will have compassion on them, for his compassion is great.

4. And he is righteous also in his judgement, and in the presence of his glory unrighteousness also shall not maintain itself: At his judgement the unrepentant shall perish before him.

5. And from henceforth I will have no mercy on them, says Yahuah of Rûach.

Chapter 51

1. And in those days the earth shall also give back that which has been entrusted to it, and Sheôl also shall give back that which it has received, and Tartaróo shall give back that which it owes. For in those days the Bâchîyr Êl shall arise,

2. And he shall choose the righteous and qâdôsh from among them: For the day has drawn nigh that they should be saved.

3. And the Bâchîyr Êl shall in those days sit on my throne, and his mouth shall pour forth all the secrets of wisdom and counsel: For Yahuah of Rûach has given them to him and has glorified him.

4. And in those days shall the mountains leap like rams, and the hills also shall skip like lambs satisfied with milk, and the faces of all the angels in shâmayim shall be lighted up with joy.

5. And the earth shall rejoice, and the righteous shall dwell upon it, and the elect shall walk thereon.

Chapter 52

1. And after those days in that place where I had seen all the visions of that which is hidden, for I had been carried off in a whirlwind and they had borne me towards the west.

2. There my eyes saw all the secret things of shâmayim that shall be, a mountain of iron, and a mountain of copper, and a mountain of silver, and a mountain of gold, and a mountain of soft metal, and a mountain of lead.

3. And I asked the angel who went with me, saying, what are these things which I have seen in secret?

4. And he said unto me: All these things which you have seen shall serve the dominion of his Mâshîyach that he may be potent and mighty on the earth.

5. And that angel of peace answered, saying unto me: Wait a little, and there shall be revealed unto you all the secret things which surround Yahuah of Rûach.

6. And these mountains which your eyes have seen, the mountain of iron, and the mountain of copper, and the mountain of silver, and the mountain of gold, and the mountain of soft metal, and the mountain of lead, all these shall be in the presence of the Bâchîyr Êl as wax: Before the fire, and like the water which streams down from above upon those mountains, and they shall become powerless before his feet.

7. And it shall come to pass in those days that none shall be saved, either by gold or by silver, and none be able to escape.

8. And there shall be no iron for war, nor shall one clothe oneself with a breastplate. Bronze shall be of no service, and tin shall be of no service and shall not be esteemed, and lead shall not be desired.

9. And all these things shall be denied and destroyed from the surface of the earth, when the Bâchîyr Êl shall appear before the face of Yahuah of Rûach.

Chapter 53

1. There my eyes saw a deep valley with open mouths, and all who dwell on the earth and sea and islands shall bring to him gifts and presents and tokens of homage, but that deep valley shall not become full.

2. And their hands commit lawless deeds, and the sinners devour all whom they lawlessly oppress: Yet the sinners shall be destroyed before the face of Yahuah of Rûach, and they shall be banished from off the face of his earth, and they shall perish forever and ever.

3. For I saw all the angels of punishment abiding there and preparing all the instruments of adversary.

4. And I asked the angel of peace who went with me: For whom are they preparing these Instruments?

5. And he said unto me: They prepare these for the kings and the mighty of this earth, that they may thereby be destroyed.

6. And after this the Tsaddîyq (צַדִּיק) Êl and Bâchîyr Êl shall cause the house of his congregation to appear: Henceforth they shall be no more hindered in the name of Yahuah of Rûach.

7. And these mountains shall not stand as the earth before his righteousness, but the hills shall be as a fountain of water, and the righteous shall have rest from the oppression of sinners.

Chapter 54

1. And I looked and turned to another part of the earth, and saw there a deep valley with burning fire.

2. And they brought the kings and the mighty, and began to cast them into this deep valley.

3. And there my eyes saw how they made these their instruments, iron chains of immeasurable weight.

4. And I asked the angel of peace who went with me, saying: For whom are these chains being prepared?

5. And he said unto me: These are being prepared for the hosts of Ăzâzêl, so that they may take them and cast them into the abyss of complete condemnation, and they shall cover their jaws with rough stones as Yahuah of Rûach commanded.

6. And Mîykâêl, and Gabrîyêl, and Râphâêl, and Phanuêl shall take hold of them on that great day, and cast them on that day into the burning furnace, that Yahuah of Rûach may take vengeance on them for their unrighteousness in becoming subject to the adversary and leading astray those who dwell on the earth.

7. And in those days shall punishment come from Yahuah of Rûach, and he will open all the chambers of waters which are above the shâmayim, and of the fountains which are beneath the earth.

8. And all the waters shall be joined with the waters: That which is above the shâmayim is the masculine, and the water which is beneath the earth is the feminine.

9. And they shall destroy all who dwell on the earth and those who dwell under the ends of the shâmayim.

10. And when they have recognized their unrighteousness which they have wrought on the earth, then by these shall they perish.

Chapter 55

1. And after that the Attîyq Yôm repented and said: In vain I have destroyed all who dwell on the earth.

2. And he swore by his great name: Henceforth I will not do so to all who dwell on the earth, and I will set a sign in the shâmayim: And this shall be a pledge of good faith between me and them forever, so long as shâmayim is above the earth. And this is in accordance with my command.

3. When I have desired to take hold of them by the hand of the angels on the day of tribulation and pain because of this, I will cause my chastisement and my wrath to abide upon them, says Êlôhîym, Yahuah of Rûach.

4. You mighty kings who dwell on the earth, you shall have to behold my Bâchîyr Êl, how he sits on the throne of glory and judges Ăzâzêl, and all his associates, and all his hosts in the name of Yahuah of Rûach.

Chapter 56

1. And I saw there the hosts of the angels of punishment going, and they held scourges and chains of iron and bronze.

2. And I asked the angel of peace who went with me, saying: To whom are these who hold the scourges going?

3. And he said unto me: To their elect and beloved ones, that they may be cast into the chasm of the abyss of the valley.

4. And then that valley shall be filled with their elect and beloved, and the days of their lives shall be at an end, and the days of their leading astray shall not thenceforward be reckoned.

5. And in those days the angels shall return and hurl themselves to the east upon the Parthos (Πάρθος) and Mâday (מָדַי): They shall stir up the kings, so that a spirit of unrest shall come upon them, and they shall rouse them from their thrones, that they may break forth as lions from their lairs, and as hungry wolves among their flocks.

6. And they shall go up and tread under foot the land of his elect ones and the land of his elect ones shall be before them a threshing-floor and a highway:

7. But the city of my righteous shall be a hindrance to their horses. And they shall begin to fight among themselves, and their right hand shall be strong against themselves, and a man shall not know his brother, nor a son his father or his mother, till there'll be no number of the corpses through their slaughter, and their punishment do not be in vain.

8. In those days Sheôl shall open its jaws, and they shall be swallowed up therein and their destruction shall be at an end; Sheôl shall devour the sinners in the presence of the elect.

Chapter 57

1. And it came to pass after this that I saw another host of wagons, and men riding thereon, and coming on the winds from the east, and from the west to the south.

2. And the noise of their wagons was heard, and when this turmoil took place the qâdôsh ones from shâmayim remarked it, and the pillars of the earth were moved from their place, and the sound thereof was heard from the one end of shâmayim to the other, in one day.

3. And they shall all fall down and worship Yahuah of Rûach. And this is the end of the second Parable.

Chapter 58

1. And I began to speak the Third Parable concerning the righteous and elect.

2. Blessed are you, you righteous and elect, for glorious shall be your lot.

3. And the righteous shall be in the light of the sun. And the elect in the light of eternal life: The days of their life shall be unending, and the days of the qâdôsh without number.

4. And they shall seek the light and find righteousness with Yahuah of Rûach: There shall be peace to the righteous in the name of Yahuah Ôlâm (עוֹלָם).

5. And after this it shall be said to the qâdôsh in shâmayim that they should seek out the secrets of righteousness, the heritage of faith: For it has become bright as the sun upon earth, and the darkness is past.

6. And there shall be a light that never end, and to a number of days they shall not come, for the darkness shall first have been destroyed, and the light established before Yahuah of Rûach and the light of uprightness established forever before Yahuah of Rûach.

Chapter 59

1. In those days my eyes saw the secrets of the lightnings, and of the lights, and their judgements they execute: And they lighten for a blessing or a curse as Yahuah of Rûach will.

2. And there I saw the secrets of the thunder, and how when it resounds above in the shâmayim, the sound thereof is heard, and he caused me to see the judgements executed on the earth, whether they are for wellbeing and blessing, or for a curse according to the word of Yahuah of Rûach.

3. And after that all the secrets of the lights and lightnings were shown to me, and they lighten for blessing and for satisfying.

Chapter 60
A Fragment of the Book of Nôach

1. In the year 500, in the seventh month, on the fourteenth day of the month in the life of Nôach. In that Parable I saw how a mighty quaking made the shâmayim of shâmayim to quake, and the host of Elyôn Êl, and the angels, a thousand thousands and ten thousand times ten thousand, were disquieted with a great disquiet.

2. And the Attîyq Yôm sat on the throne of his glory, and the angels and the righteous stood around him.

3. And a great trembling seized me, and fear took hold of me, and my loins gave way, and dissolved were my reins, and I fell upon my face.

4. And Mîykâêl sent another angel from among the qâdôsh ones and he raised me up, and when he had raised me up my spirit returned; for I had not been able to endure the look of this host, and the commotion and the quaking of the shâmayim.

5. And Mîykâêl said unto me: Why are you disquieted with such a vision? Until this day lasted the day of his mercy; and he has been merciful and longsuffering towards those who dwell on the earth.

6. And when the day, and the power, and the punishment, and the judgement come, which Yahuah of Rûach has prepared for those who worship not the righteous law, and for those who deny the righteous judgement, and for those who take his name in vain, that day is prepared, for the elect a covenant, but for sinners an inquisition.

25. When the punishment of Yahuah of Rûach shall rest upon them, it shall rest in order that the punishment of Yahuah of Rûach may not come, in vain, and it shall

slay the children with their mothers and the children with their fathers. Afterwards the judgement shall take place according to his mercy and his patience.

7. And on that day were two monsters parted, a female monster named Liwyâthân (לִוְיָתָן), to dwell in the abysses of the ocean over the fountains of the waters.

8. But the male is named Behêmôth, who occupied with his breast a waste wilderness named Duidain, on the east of the Garden where the elect and righteous dwell, where my grandfather was taken up, the seventh from Âdâm, the first man whom Yahuah of Rûach created.

9. And I besought the other angel that he should show me the might of those monsters, how they were parted on one day and cast, the one into the abysses of the sea, and the other unto the dry land of the wilderness.

10. And he said to me: You Bên Âdâm, herein you do seek to know what is hidden.

11. And the other angel who went with me and showed me what was hidden told me what is first and last in the shâmayim in the height, and beneath the earth in the depth, and at the ends of the shâmayim, and on the foundation of the shâmayim.

12. And the chambers of the winds, and how the winds are divided, and how they are weighed, and how the portals of the winds are reckoned, each according to the power of the wind, and the power of the lights of the moon, and according to the power that is fitting: And the divisions of the stars according to their names, and how all the divisions are divided.

13. And the thunders according to the places where they fall, and all the divisions that are made among the lightnings that it may lighten, and their host that they may at once obey.

14. For the thunder has places of rest which are assigned to it while it is waiting for its peal; and the thunder and lightning are inseparable, and although not one and undivided, they both go together through the spirit and do not separate.

15. For when the lightning lightens, the thunder utters its voice, and the spirit enforces a pause during the peal, and divides equally between them; for the treasury of their peals is like the sand, and each one of them as it peals is held in with a bridle, and turned back by the power of the spirit, and pushed forward according to the many quarters of the earth.

16. And the spirit of the sea is masculine and strong, and according to the might of his strength he draws it back with a rein, and in like manner it is driven forward and disperses amid all the mountains of the earth.

17. And the spirit of the hoar frost is his own angel, and the spirit of the hail is a good angel.

18. And the spirit of the snow has forsaken his chambers on account of his strength, there is a special spirit therein, and that which ascends from it is like smoke, and its name is frost.

19. And the spirit of the mist is not united with them in their chambers, but it has a special chamber; for its course is glorious both in light and in darkness, and in winter and in summer, and in its chamber is an angel.

20. And the spirit of the dew has its dwelling at the ends of the shâmayim, and is connected with the chambers of the rain, and its course is in winter and summer: And its

clouds and the clouds of the mist are connected, and the one gives to the other.

21. And when the spirit of the rain goes forth from its chamber, the angels come and open the chamber and lead it out, and when it is diffused over the whole earth it unites with the water on the earth. And whenever it unites with the water on the earth {...}

22. For the waters are for those who dwell on the earth; for they are nourishment for the earth from Elyôn Êl who is in shâmayim: Therefore there is a measure for the rain, and the angels take it in charge.

23. And these things I saw towards the Garden of the Tsaddîyq.

24. And the angel of peace who was with me said to me: These two monsters, prepared conformably to the greatness of Êlôhîym, shall feed ...

Chapter 61

1. And I saw in those days how long cords were given to those angels, and they took to themselves wings and flew, and they went towards the north.

2. And I asked the angel, saying unto him: Why have those angels taken these cords and gone off? And he said unto me: They have gone to measure.

3. And the angel who went with me said unto me: These shall bring the measures of the righteous, and the ropes of the righteous to the righteous, that they may stay themselves on the name of Yahuah of Rûach forever and ever.

4. The elect shall begin to dwell with the elect, and those are the measures which shall be given to faith and which shall strengthen righteousness.

5. And these measures shall reveal all the secrets of the depths of the earth, and those who have been destroyed by the desert, and those who have been devoured by the beasts, and those who have been devoured by the fish of the sea, that they may return and stay themselves on the day of the Bâchîyr Êl; For none shall be destroyed before Yahuah of Rûach, and none can be destroyed.

6. And all who dwell above in the shâmayim received a command and power and one voice and one light like unto fire.

7. And that One with their first words they blessed, and extolled and lauded with wisdom, and they were wise in utterance and in the spirit of life.

8. And Yahuah of Rûach placed the Bâchîyr Êl on the throne of glory. And he shall judge all the works of the qâdôsh above in the shâmayim, and in the balance shall their deeds be weighed.

9. And when he shall lift up his countenance to judge their secret ways according to the word of the name of Yahuah of Rûach, and their path according to the way of the righteous judgement of Yahuah of Rûach, then they all shall with one voice speak and bless, and glorify and extol and sanctify the name of Yahuah of Rûach.

10. And he will summon all the host of the shâmayim, and all the qâdôsh ones above, and the host of Êlôhîym, the Kerûb, Śârâph (שְׂרָף) and Ôphân (אוֹפָן), and all the angels of power, and all the angels of principalities, and the Bâchîyr Êl, and the other powers on the earth and over the water.

11. On that day shall raise one voice, and bless and glorify and exalt in the spirit of faith, and in the spirit of wisdom, and in the spirit of patience, and in the spirit of mercy, and in the spirit of judgement and of peace,

and in the spirit of goodness, and shall all say with one voice: Blessed is he, and may the name of Yahuah of Rûach be blessed forever and ever.

12. All who do not sleep above in shâmayim shall bless him: All the qâdôsh ones who are in shâmayim shall bless him, and all the elect who dwell in the Garden of life: And every spirit of light who is able to bless, and glorify, and extol, and hallow your blessed name, and all flesh shall beyond measure glorify and bless your name forever and ever.

13. For great is the mercy of Yahuah of Rûach, and he is longsuffering, and all his works and all that he has created he has revealed to the righteous and elect in the name of Yahuah of Rûach.

Chapter 62

1. And thus Yahuah commanded the kings and the mighty and the exalted, and those who dwell on the earth, and said: Open your eyes and lift up your horns if you are able to recognize the Bâchîyr Êl.

2. And Yahuah of Rûach seated him on the throne of his glory, and the spirit of righteousness was poured out upon him, and the word of his mouth slays all the sinners, and all the unrighteous are destroyed from before his face.

3. And there shall stand up in that day all the kings and the mighty, and the exalted and those who hold the earth, and they shall see and recognize how he sits on the throne of his glory, and righteousness is judged before him, and no lying word is spoken before him.

4. Then shall pain come upon them as on a woman in travail, and she has pain in bringing forth when her child enters the mouth of the womb, and she has pain in bringing forth.

5. And one portion of them shall look on the other, and they shall be terrified, and they shall be downcast of countenance, and pain shall seize them, when they see that Bên Âdâm sitting on the throne of his glory.

6. And the kings and the mighty and all who possess the earth shall bless and glorify and extol him who rules over all, who was hidden.

7. For from the beginning the Bên Âdâm was hidden, and Elyôn Êl preserved him in the presence of his might, and revealed him to the elect.

8. And the congregation of the elect and qâdôsh shall be sown, and all the elect shall stand before him on that day.

9. And all the kings and the mighty and the exalted and those who rule the earth shall fall down before him on their faces, and worship and set their hope upon that Bên Âdâm, and petition him and supplicate for mercy at his hands.

10. Nevertheless that Yahuah of Rûach will so press them that they shall hastily go forth from his presence, and their faces shall be filled with shame, and the darkness grow deeper on their faces.

11. And he will deliver them to the angels for punishment, to execute vengeance on them because they have oppressed his children and his elect.

12. And they shall be a spectacle for the righteous and for his elect: They shall rejoice over them, because the wrath of Yahuah of Rûach rests upon them, and his sword is drunk with their blood.

13. And the righteous and elect shall be saved on that day, and they shall never thenceforward see the face of the sinners and unrighteous.

14. And Yahuah of Rûach will abide over them, and with that Bên Âdâm they shall eat and lie down and rise up forever and ever.

15. And the righteous and elect shall have risen from the earth, and ceased to be of downcast countenance. And they shall have been clothed with garments of glory,

16. And these shall be the garments of life from Yahuah of Rûach: And your garments shall not grow old, nor your glory pass away before Yahuah of Rûach.

Chapter 63

1. In those days shall the mighty and the kings who possess the earth implore him to grant them a little respite from his angels of punishment to whom they were delivered, that they might fall down and worship before Yahuah of Rûach, and confess their sins before him.

2. And they shall bless and glorify Yahuah of Rûach, and say: Blessed is Yahuah of Rûach and Yahuah of Melāķīm, and Yahuah of the Gibbôr and Yahuah of the Kâbêd (כָּבֵד), and Yahuah of Kâbôd and Yahuah of Chokmâh (חָכְמָה),

3. And splendid in every secret thing is your power from generation to generation, and your glory forever and ever: Deep are all your secrets and innumerable, and your righteousness is beyond reckoning.

4. We have now learnt that we should glorify and bless Yahuah of Melāķīm and him who is king over all kings.

5. And they shall say: Would that we had rest to glorify and give thanks and confess our faith before his glory!

6. And now we long for a little rest but find it not: We follow hard upon and do not obtain it: And light has vanished from before us, and darkness is our dwelling place forever and ever:

7. For we have not believed before him nor glorified the name of Yahuah of Rûach, nor glorified our Yahuah, but our hope was in the sceptre of our kingdom, and in our glory.

8. And in the day of our suffering and tribulation he does not save us, and we find no respite for confession, that our Yahuah is true in all his works, and in his judgements and his justice, and his judgements have no respect of persons.

9. And we pass away from before his face on account of our works, and all our sins are reckoned up in righteousness.

10. Now they shall say unto themselves: Our souls are full of unrighteous gain, but it does not prevent us from descending from the midst thereof into the burden of Sheôl.

11. And after that their faces shall be filled with darkness and shame before that Bên Âdâm, and they shall be driven from his presence, and the sword shall abide before his face in their midst.

12. Thus spoke Yahuah of Rûach: This is the ordinance and judgement with respect to the mighty and the kings and the exalted and those who possess the earth before Yahuah of Rûach.

Chapter 64

1. And other forms I saw hidden in that place.

2. I heard the voice of the angel saying: These are the angels who descended to the earth, and revealed what was hidden to the children of men and seduced the children of men into committing sin.

Chapter 65

1. And in those days Nôach saw the earth that it had sunk down and its destruction was nigh.

2. And he arose from thence and went to the ends of the earth, and cried aloud to his grandfather Chănôk: And Nôach said three times with an embittered voice: Hear me, hear me, hear me.

3. And I said unto him: Tell me what it is that is falling out on the earth that the earth is in such evil plight and shaken, lest perchance I shall perish with it?

4. And thereupon there was a great commotion, on the earth, and a voice was heard from shâmayim, and I fell on my face.

5. And Chănôk my grandfather came and stood by me, and said unto me: Why you have cried unto me with a bitter cry and weeping?

6. And a command has gone forth from the presence of Yahuah concerning those who dwell on the earth that their ruin is accomplished because they have learnt all the secrets of the angels, and all the violence of the adversaries, and all their powers, the most secret ones and all the power of those who practice sorcery, and the power of witchcraft, and the power of those who make molten images for the whole earth:

7. And how silver is produced from the dust of the earth, and how soft metal originates in the earth.

8. For lead and tin are not produced from the earth like the first: It is a fountain that produces them, and an angel stands therein, and that angel is preeminent.

9. And after that my grandfather Chănôk took hold of me by my hand and raised me up, and said unto me: Go, for I have asked Yahuah of Rûach as touching this commotion on the earth.

10. And he said unto me: Because of their unrighteousness, their judgement has been determyd upon and shall not be withheld by me forever. Because of the sorceries which they have searched out and learnt, the earth and those who dwell upon it shall be destroyed.

11. And these, they have no place of repentance forever, because they have shown them what was hidden, and they are the damned: But as for you, my son, Yahuah of Rûach knows that you are pure, and guiltless of this reproach concerning the secrets.

12. And he has destined your name to be among the qâdôsh, and will preserve you among those who dwell on the earth, and has destined your righteous seed both for kingship and for great honors, and from your seed shall proceed a fountain of the righteous and qâdôsh without number forever.

Chapter 66

1. And after that he showed me the angels of punishment who are prepared to come and let loose all the powers of the waters which are beneath in the earth in order to bring judgement and destruction on all who abide and dwell on the earth.

2. And Yahuah of Rûach gave commandment to the angels who were going forth, that they should not cause the waters to rise but should hold them in check; for those angels were over the powers of the waters.

3. And I went away from the presence of Chănôk.

Chapter 67

1. And in those days the word of Êlôhîym came unto me, and he said unto me: Nôach,

your lot has come up before me, a lot without blame, a lot of love and uprightness.

2. And now the angels are making a wooden building, and when they have completed that task I will place my hand upon it and preserve it, and there shall come forth from it the seed of life, and a change shall set in so that the earth will not remain without inhabitant.

3. And I will make fast your seed before me forever and ever, and I will spread abroad those who dwell with you: It shall not be unfruitful on the face of the earth, but it shall be blessed and multiply on the earth in the name of Yahuah.

4. And he will imprison those angels, who have shown unrighteousness, in that burning valley which my grandfather Chănôk had formerly shown to me in the west among the mountains of gold and silver and iron and soft metal and tin.

5. And I saw that valley in which there was a great convulsion and a convulsion of the waters.

6. And when all this took place, from that fiery molten metal and from the convulsion thereof in that place, there was produced a smell of sulphur, and it was connected with those waters, and that valley of the angels who had led astray mankind burned beneath that land.

7. And through its valleys proceed streams of fire, where these angels are punished who had led astray those who dwell upon the earth.

8. But those waters shall in those days serve for the kings and the mighty and the exalted, and those who dwell on the earth, for the healing of the body, but for the punishment of the spirit; now their spirit is full of lust, that they may be punished in their body, for they have denied Yahuah of Rûach and see their punishment daily, and yet did not believe in his name.

9. And in proportion as the burning of their bodies becomes severe, a corresponding change shall take place in their spirit forever and ever; for before Yahuah of Rûach none shall utter an idle word.

10. For the judgement shall come upon them, because they believe in the lust of their body and deny the Rûach of Yahuah.

11. And those same waters will undergo a change in those days; for when those angels are punished in these waters, these water springs shall change their temperature, and when the angels ascend, this water of the springs shall change and become cold.

12. And I heard Mîykâêl answering and saying: This judgement wherewith the angels are judged is a testimony for the kings and the mighty who possess the earth.

13. Because these waters of judgement minister to the healing of the body of the kings and the lust of their body; therefore they will not see and will not believe that those waters will change and become a fire which burns forever.

Chapter 68

1. And after that my grandfather Chănôk gave me the teaching of all the secrets in the book in the Parables which had been given to him, and he put them together for me in the words of the book of the Parables.

2. And on that day Mîykâêl answered Râphâêl and said: The power of the spirit transports and makes me to tremble because of the severity of the judgement of the secrets, the judgement of the angels: Who can endure

the severe judgement which has been executed, and before which they melt away?

3. And Mîykâêl answered again, and said to Râphâêl: Who is he whose heart is not softened concerning it, and whose reins are not troubled by this word of judgement that has gone forth upon them because of those who have thus led them out?

4. And it came to pass when he stood before Yahuah of Rûach, Mîykâêl said thus to Râphâêl: I will not take their part under the eye of Yahuah; for Yahuah of Rûach has been angry with them because they do as if they were Yahuah.

5. Therefore all that is hidden shall come upon them forever and ever; for neither angel nor man shall have his portion in it, but alone they have received their judgement forever and ever.

Chapter 69

1. And after this judgement they shall terrify and make them to tremble because they have shown this to those who dwell on the earth.

2. And behold the names of those angels and these are their names: The first of them is Samyaza, the second Artaqifa, and the third Armen, the fourth Kokaebel, the fifth Turael, the sixth Rumyal, the seventh Danyal, the eighth Neqael, the ninth Baraqel, the tenth Ăzâzêl, the eleventh Armaros, the twelfth Bataryal, the thirteenth Busaseyal, the fourteenth Hananel, the fifteenth Turel, and the sixteenth Simapesiel, the seventeenth Yetrel, the eighteenth Tumael, the nineteenth Turel, the twentieth Rumael, the twenty first Ăzâzêl.

3. And these are the chiefs of their angels and their names, and their chief ones over hundreds and over fifties and over tens.

4. The name of the first Yeqon: That is, the one who led astray all the sons of Êlôhîym, and brought them down to the earth, and led them astray through the daughters of men.

5. And the second was named Asbeel: He imparted to the qâdôsh sons of Êlôhîym evil counsel, and led them astray so that they defiled their bodies with the daughters of men.

6. And the third was named Gadreel: He it is who showed the children of men all the blows of death, and he led astray Chawwâh (חַוָּה), and showed the weapons of death to the sons of men, the shield and the coat of mail, and the sword for battle, and all the weapons of death to the children of men.

7. And from his hand they have proceeded against those who dwell on the earth from that day and forevermore.

8. And the fourth was named Penemuel: He taught the children of men the bitter and the sweet, and he taught them all the secrets of their wisdom.

9. And he instructed mankind in writing with ink and paper, and thereby many sinned from eternity to eternity and until this day.

10. For men were not created for such a purpose, to give confirmation to their good faith with pen and ink.

11. For men were created exactly like the angels, to the intent that they should continue pure and righteous, and death, which destroys everything, could not have taken hold of them, but through this their knowledge they are perishing, and through this power it is consuming me.

12. And the fifth was named Kasdeya: This is he who showed the children of men all the wicked smitings of spirits and demons, and

the smitings of the embryo in the womb, that it may pass away, and the smitings of the soul the bites of the serpent, and the smitings which befall through the noontide heat, the son of the serpent named Tabaêt.

13. And this is the task of Kasbeel, the chief of the oath which he showed to the qâdôsh ones when he dwelt high above in glory, and its name is Biqa.

14. This angel requested Mîykâêl to show him the hidden name that he might enunciate it in the oath, so that those might quake before that name and oath who revealed all that was in secret to the children of men.

15. And this is the power of this oath, for it is powerful and strong, and he placed this oath Akae in the hand of Mîykâêl.

16. And these are the secrets of this oath {. . .} and they are strong through his oath: And the shâmayim was suspended before the world was created, and forever.

17. And through it the earth was founded upon the water, and from the secret recesses of the mountains come beautiful waters, from the creation of the world and unto eternity.

18. And through that oath the sea was created, and as its foundation he set for it the sand against the time of its anger, and it does not dare to pass beyond it from the creation of the world unto eternity.

19. And through that oath are the depths made fast, and abide and do not stir from their place from eternity to eternity.

20. And through that oath the sun and moon complete their course, and do not deviate from their ordinance from eternity to eternity.

21. And through that oath the stars complete their course, and he calls them by their names, and they answer him from eternity to eternity.

22. And in like manner the spirits of the water, and of the winds, and of all zephyrs, and their paths from all the quarters of the winds.

23. And there are preserved the voices of the thunder and the light of the lightnings: And there are preserved the chambers of the hail and the chambers of the hoarfrost, and the chambers of the mist, and the chambers of the rain and the dew.

24. And all these believe and give thanks before Yahuah of Rûach, and glorify him with all their power, and their food is in every act of thanksgiving: They thank and glorify and extol the name of Yahuah of Rûach forever and ever.

25. And this oath is mighty over them and through it they are preserved and their paths are preserved, and their course is not destroyed.

26. And there was great joy among them, and they blessed and glorified and extolled, because the name of that Bên Âdâm had been revealed unto them.

27. And he sat on the throne of his glory, and the sum of judgement was given unto the Bên Âdâm, and he caused the sinners to pass away and be destroyed from off the face of the earth, and those who have led the world astray.

28. With chains shall they be bound, and in their assemblage place of destruction shall they be imprisoned, and all their works vanish from the face of the earth.

29. And from henceforth there shall do not behing corruptible; for that Bên Âdâm has appeared, and has seated himself on the throne of his glory, and all evil shall pass

away before his face, and the word of that Bên Âdâm shall go forth and be strong before Yahuah of Rûach.

Chapter 70

1. And it came to pass after this that his name during his lifetime was raised aloft to that Bên Âdâm and to Yahuah of Rûach from among those who dwell on the earth.

2. And he was raised aloft on the chariots of the spirit and his name vanished among them.

3. And from that day I was no longer numbered among them: And he set me between the two winds, between the north and the west, where the angels took the cords to measure for me the place for the elect and righteous.

4. And there I saw the first fathers and the righteous who from the beginning dwell in that place.

Chapter 71

1. And it came to pass after this that my spirit was translated and it ascended into the shâmayim: And I saw the qâdôsh sons of Êlôhîym. They were stepping on flames of fire: Their garments were white and their raiment, and their faces shone like snow.

2. And I saw two streams of fire, and the light of that fire shone like hyacinth, and I fell on my face before Yahuah of Rûach.

3. And the angel Mîykâêl one of the archangels seized me by my right hand, and lifted me up and led me forth into all the secrets, and he showed me all the secrets of righteousness.

4. And he showed me all the secrets of the ends of the shâmayim, and all the chambers of all the stars, and all the luminaries, whence they proceed before the face of the qâdôsh ones.

5. And he translated my spirit into the shâmayim of shâmayim, and I saw there as it were a structure built of crystals, and between those crystals tongues of living fire.

6. And my spirit saw the girdle which girt that house of fire, and on its four sides were streams full of living fire, and they girt that house.

7. And roundabout were Śârâph, Kerûb, and Ôphân: And these are they who do not sleep and guard the throne of his glory.

8. And I saw angels who could not be counted, a thousand thousands, and ten thousand times ten thousand, encircling that house. And Mîykâêl, and Râphâêl, and Gabrîyêl, and Phanuêl, and the qâdôsh angels who are above the shâmayim, go in and out of that house.

9. And they came forth from that house, and Mîykâêl and Gabrîyêl, Râphâêl and Phanuêl, and many qâdôsh angels without number.

10. And with them the Attîyq Yôm, his head white and pure as wool, and his raiment indescribable.

11. And I fell on my face, and my whole body became relaxed, and my spirit was transfigured; and I cried with a loud voice . . . with the spirit of power, and blessed and glorified and extolled.

12. And these blessings which went forth out of my mouth were well pleasing before that Attîyq Yôm.

13. And that Attîyq Yôm came with Mîykâêl and Gabrîyêl, Râphâêl and Phanuêl, thousands and ten thousands of angels without number. [*Lost passage wherein the Bên Âdâm was described as accompanying the Attîyq Yôm, and Chănôk asked one of the angels (as*

in xlvi. 3) concerning the Bên Âdâm as to who he was.]

14. And he (the angel) came to me and greeted me with his voice, and said unto me. This is the Bên Âdâm who is born unto righteousness, and righteousness abides over him, and the righteousness of the Attîyq Yôm does not forsake him.

15. And he said unto me: He proclaims unto you peace in the name of the world to come; for from hence has proceeded peace since the creation of the world, and so shall it be unto you forever and forever and ever.

16. And all shall walk in his ways since righteousness never forsakes him: With him will be their dwelling places, and with him their heritage, and they shall not be separated from him forever and ever and ever.

17. And so there shall be length of days with that Bên Âdâm, and the righteous shall have peace and an upright way in the name of Yahuah of Rûach forever and ever.

Part Three
The Book of the Courses of the Shâmayim Luminaries.
Chapters 72-82

Chapter 72

1. The Book of the Courses of the Luminaries of the shâmayim, the relations of each, according to their classes, their dominion and their seasons, according to their names and places of origin, and according to their months, which Ûrîyêl, the qâdôsh angel, who was with me, who is their guide, showed me; and he showed me all their laws exactly as they are, and how it is with regard to all the years of the world and unto eternity, till the new creation is accomplished which endures till eternity.

2. And this is the first law of the luminaries: The luminary the sun has its rising in the eastern portals of the shâmayim, and its setting in the western portals of the shâmayim.

3. And I saw six portals in which the sun rises, and six portals in which the sun sets and the moon rises and sets in these portals, and the leaders of the stars and those whom they lead: Six in the east and six in the west, and all following each other in accurately corresponding order: Also many windows to the right and left of these portals.

4. And first there goes forth the great luminary, named the sun, and his circumference is like the circumference of the shâmayim, and he is quite filled with illuminating and heating fire.

5. The chariot on which he ascends, the wind drives, and the sun goes down from the shâmayim and returns through the north in order to reach the east, and is so guided that he comes to the appropriate that portal and shines in the face of the shâmayim.

6. In this way he rises in the first month in the great portal, which is the fourth those six portals in the cast.

7. And in that fourth portal from which the sun rises in the first month are twelve window openings, from which proceed a flame when they are opened in their season.

8. When the sun rises in the shâmayim, he comes forth through that fourth portal

thirty, mornings in succession, and sets accurately in the fourth portal in the west of the shâmayim.

9. And during this period the day becomes daily longer and the night nightly shorter to the thirtieth morning.

10. On that day the day is longer than the night by a ninth part, and the day amounts exactly to ten parts and the night to eight parts.

11. And the sun rises from that fourth portal, and sets in the fourth and returns to the fifth portal of the east thirty mornings, and rises from it and sets in the fifth portal.

12. And then the day becomes longer by two parts and amounts to eleven parts, and the night becomes shorter and amounts to seven parts.

13. And it returns to the east and enters into the sixth portal, and rises and sets in the sixth portal one and thirty mornings on account of its sign.

14. On that day the day becomes longer than the night, and the day becomes double the night, and the day becomes twelve parts, and the night is shortened and becomes six parts.

15. And the sun mounts up to make the day shorter and the night longer, and the sun returns to the east and enters into the sixth portal, and rises from it and sets thirty mornings.

16. And when thirty mornings are accomplished, the day decreases by exactly one part, and becomes eleven parts, and the night seven.

17. And the sun goes forth from that sixth portal in the west, and goes to the east and rises in the fifth portal for thirty mornings, and sets in the west again in the fifth western portal.

18. On that day the day decreases by two parts, and amounts to ten parts and the night to eight parts.

19. And the sun goes forth from that fifth portal and sets in the fifth portal of the west, and rises in the fourth portal for one and thirty mornings on account of its sign, and sets in the west.

20. On that day the day is equalized with the night, and becomes of equal length, and the night amounts to nine parts and the day to nine parts.

21. And the sun rises from that portal and sets in the west, and returns to the east and rises thirty mornings in the third portal and sets in the west in the third portal.

22. And on that day the night becomes longer than the day, and night becomes longer than night, and day shorter than day till the thirtieth morning, and the night amounts exactly to ten parts and the day to eight parts.

23. And the sun rises from that third portal and sets in the third portal in the west and returns to the east, and for thirty mornings rises in the second portal in the east, and in like manner sets in the second portal in the west of the shâmayim.

24. And on that day the night amounts to eleven parts and the day to seven parts.

25. And the sun rises on that day from that second portal and sets in the west in the second portal, and returns to the east into the first portal for one and thirty mornings, and sets in the first portal in the west of the shâmayim.

26. And on that day the night becomes longer and amounts to the double of the day: And the night amounts exactly to twelve parts and the day to six.

27. And the sun has therewith traversed the divisions of his orbit and turns again on those divisions of his orbit, and enters that portal thirty mornings and sets also in the west opposite to it.

28. And on that night has the night decreased in length by a ninth part, and the night has become eleven parts and the day seven parts.

29. And the sun has returned and entered into the second portal in the east, and returns on those his divisions of his orbit for thirty mornings, rising and setting.

30. And on that day the night decreases in length, and the night amounts to ten parts and the day to eight.

31. And on that day the sun rises from that portal, and sets in the west, and returns to the east, and rises in the third portal for one and thirty mornings, and sets in the west of the shâmayim.

32. On that day the night decreases and amounts to nine parts, and the day to nine parts, and the night is equal to the day and the year is exactly as to its days three hundred and sixty four.

33. And the length of the day and of the night, and the shortness of the day and of the night arise through the course of the sun these distinctions are made (lit. they are separated).

34. So it comes that its course becomes daily longer, and its course nightly shorter.

35. And this is the law and the course of the sun, and his return as often as he returns sixty times and rises, the great luminary which is named the sun, forever and ever.

36. And that which thus rises is the great luminary, and is so named according to its appearance, according as Yahuah commanded.

37. As he rises, so he sets and does not decrease, and does not rest, but runs day and night, and his light is sevenfold brighter than that of the moon; but as regards size they are both equal.

Chapter 73

1. And after this law I saw another law dealing with the smaller luminary, which is named the moon.

2. And her circumference is like the circumference of the shâmayim, and her chariot in which she rides is driven by the wind, and light is given to her in definite measure.

3. And her rising and setting change every month: and her days are like the days of the sun, and when her light is uniform (full) it amounts to the seventh part of the light of the sun.

4. And thus she rises. And her first phase in the east comes forth on the thirtieth morning: And on that day she becomes visible, and constitutes for you the first phase of the moon on the thirtieth day together with the sun in the portal where the sun rises.

5. And the one half of her goes forth by a seventh part, and her whole circumference is empty, without light, with the exception of one seventh part of it, and the fourteenth part of her light.

6. And when she receives one seventh part of the half of her light, her light amounts to one seventh part and the half thereof.

7. And she sets with the sun, and when the sun rises the moon rises with him and receives the half of one part of light, and in that night in the beginning of her morning the moon sets with the sun, and is invisible

that night with the fourteen parts and the half of one of them.

8. And she rises on that day with exactly a seventh part, and comes forth and recedes from the rising of the sun, and in her remaining days she becomes bright in the remaining thirteen parts.

Chapter 74

1. And I saw another course, a law for her, and how according to that law she performs her monthly revolution.

2. And all these Ûrîyêl, the qâdôsh angel who is the leader of them all, showed to me, and their positions, and I wrote down their positions as he showed them to me, and I wrote down their months as they were, and the appearance of their lights till fifteen days were accomplished.

3. In single seventh parts she accomplishes all her light in the east, and in single seventh parts accomplishes all her darkness in the west.

4. And in certain months she alters her settings, and in certain months she pursues her own peculiar course.

5. In two months the moon sets with the sun: In those two middle portals the third and the fourth.

6. She goes forth for seven days, and turns about and returns again through the portal where the sun rises, and accomplishes all her light: And she recedes from the sun, and in eight days enters the sixth portal from which the sun goes forth.

7. And when the sun goes forth from the fourth portal she goes forth seven days, until she goes forth from the fifth and turns back again in seven days into the fourth portal and accomplishes all her light: And she recedes and enters into the first portal in eight days.

8. And she returns again in seven days into the fourth portal from which the sun goes forth.

9. Thus I saw their position how the moons rose and the sun set in those days.

10. And if five years are added together the sun has an over plus of thirty days, and all the days which accrue to it for one of those five years, when they are full, amount to 364 days.

11. And the over plus of the sun and of the stars amounts to six days: In 5 years 6 days every year come to 30 days: And the moon falls behind the sun and stars to the number of 30 days.

12. And the sun and the stars bring in all the years exactly, so that they do not advance or delay their position by a single day unto eternity; but complete the years with perfect justice in 364 days.

13. In 3 years there are 1,092 days, and in 5 years 1,820 days, so that in 8 years there are 2,912 days.

14. For the moon alone the days amount in 3 years to 1,062 days, and in 5 years she falls 50 days behind: To the sum (of 1,770) there is to be added (1,000 and) 62 days.

15. And in 5 years there are 1,770 days, so that for the moon the days in 8 years amount to 21,832 days.

16. For in 8 years she falls behind to the amount of 80 days, all the days she falls behind in 8 years are 80.

17. And the year is accurately completed in conformity with their world stations and the stations of the sun, which rise from the portals through which it the sun rises and sets 30 days.

Chapter 75

1. And the leaders of the heads of the thousands, who are placed over the whole creation and over all the stars, have also to do with the four intercalary days, being inseparable from their office, according to the reckoning of the year, and these render service on the four days which are not reckoned in the reckoning of the year.

2. And owing to them men go wrong therein, for those luminaries truly render service on the world stations, one in the first portal, one in the third portal of the shâmayim, one in the fourth portal, and one in the sixth portal, and the exactness of the year is accomplished through its separate three hundred and sixty four stations.

3. For the signs and the times and the years and the days the angel Ûrîyêl showed to me, whom Yahuah Kâbôd has set forever over all the luminaries of the shâmayim, in the shâmayim and in the world, that they should rule on the face of the shâmayim and be seen on the earth, and be leaders for the day and the night, the sun, moon, and stars, and all the ministering creatures which make their revolution in all the chariots of the shâmayim.

4. In like manner Ûrîyêl showed me twelve doors, open in the circumference of the sun's chariot in the shâmayim, through which the rays of the sun break forth: And from them is warmth diffused over the earth, when they are opened at their appointed seasons.

5. And for the winds and the spirit of the dew when they are opened, standing open in the shâmayim at the ends.

6. As for the twelve portals in the shâmayim, at the ends of the earth, out of which go forth the sun, moon, and stars, and all the works of shâmayim in the east and in the west.

7. There are many windows open to the left and right of them, and one window at its appointed season produces warmth, corresponding as these do to those doors from which the stars come forth according as he has commanded them, and wherein they set corresponding to their number.

8. And I saw chariots in the shâmayim, running in the world, above those portals in which revolve the stars that never set.

9. And one is larger than all the rest, and it is that that makes its course through the entire world.

Chapter 76

1. And at the ends of the earth I saw twelve portals open to all the quarters of the shâmayim, from which the winds go forth and blow over the earth.

2. Three of them are open on the face the east of the shâmayim, and three in the west, and three on the right the south of the shâmayim, and three on the left the north.

3. And the three first are those of the east, and three are of the north, and three after those on the left of the south, and three of the west.

4. Through four of these come winds of blessing and prosperity, and from those eight come hurtful winds: When they are sent, they bring destruction on all the earth and on the water upon it, and on all who dwell thereon, and on everything which is in the water and on the land.

5. And the first wind from those portals, called the east wind, comes forth through the first portal which is in the east, inclining towards the south: From it come forth desolation, drought, heat, and destruction.

6. And through the second portal in the middle comes what is fitting, and from it there

come rain and fruitfulness and prosperity and dew; and through the third portal which lies toward the north come cold and drought.

7. And after these come forth the south winds through three portals: Through the first portal of them inclining to the east comes forth a hot wind.

8. And through the middle portal next to it there come forth fragrant smells, and dew and rain, and prosperity and health.

9. And through the third portal lying to the west come forth dew and rain, locusts and desolation.

10. And after these the north winds: From the seventh portal in the east come dew and rain, locusts and desolation.

11. And from the middle portal come in a direct direction health and rain and dew and prosperity; and through the third portal in the west come cloud and hoar frost, and snow and rain, and dew and locusts.

12. And after these four are the west winds: Through the first portal adjoining the north come forth dew and hoar frost, and cold and snow and frost.

13. And from the middle portal come forth dew and rain, and prosperity and blessing; and through the last portal which adjoins the south come forth drought and desolation, and burning and destruction.

14. And the twelve portals of the four quarters of the shâmayim are therewith completed, and all their laws and all their plagues and all their benefactions I have shown to you, my son Methûshelach (מְתוּשֶׁלַח).

Chapter 77

1. And the first quarter is called the east, because it is the first: And the second, the south, because Elyôn Êl will descend there, yea, there in quite a special sense he who is blessed forever will descend.

2. And the west quarter is named the diminished, because there all the luminaries of the shâmayim wane and go down.

3. And the fourth quarter, named the north, is divided into three parts: The first of them is for the dwelling of men: And the second contains seas of water, and the abysses and forests and rivers, and darkness and clouds; and the third part contains the Garden of righteousness.

4. I saw seven high mountains, higher than all the mountains which are on the earth: And thence comes forth hoar frost, and days, seasons, and years pass away.

5. I saw seven rivers on the earth larger than all the rivers: One of them coming from the west pours its waters into the Great Sea.

6. And these two come from the north to the sea and pour their waters into the Red Sea in the east.

7. And the remaining, four come forth on the side of the north to their own sea, two of them to the Red Sea, and two into the Great Sea and discharge themselves there and some say: Into the desert.

8. Seven great islands I saw in the sea and in the mainland: Two in the mainland and five in the Great Sea.

Chapter 78

1. And the names of the sun are the following: The first Oryares, and the second Tâôm (תָּאוֹם).

2. And the moon has four names: The first name is Asonya, the second Ebla, the third Benase, and the fourth Erae.

3. These are the two great luminaries: Their circumference is like the circumference of the shâmayim, and the size of the circumference of both is alike.

4. In the circumference of the sun there are seven portions of light which are added to it more than to the moon, and in definite measures it is transferred till the seventh portion of the sun is exhausted.

5. And they set and enter the portals of the west, and make their revolution by the north, and come forth through the eastern portals on the face of the shâmayim.

6. And when the moon rises one fourteenth part appears in the shâmayim: The light becomes full in her: On the fourteenth day she accomplishes her light.

7. And fifteen parts of light are transferred to her till the fifteenth day when her light is accomplished, according to the sign of the year, and she becomes fifteen parts, and the moon grows by the addition of fourteenth parts.

8. And in her waning the moon decreases on the first day to fourteen parts of her light, on the second to thirteen parts of light, on the third to twelve, on the fourth to eleven, on the fifth to ten, on the sixth to nine, on the seventh to eight, on the eighth to seven, on the ninth to six, on the tenth to five, on the eleventh to four, on the twelfth to three, on the thirteenth to two, on the fourteenth to the half of a seventh, and all her remaining light disappears wholly on the fifteenth.

9. And in certain months the month has twenty nine days and once twenty eight.

10. And Ûrîyêl showed me another law: When light is transferred to the moon, and on which side it is transferred to her by the sun.

11. During all the period during which the moon is growing in her light, she is transferring it to herself when opposite to the sun during fourteen days her light is accomplished in the shâmayim, and when she is illumined throughout, her light is accomplished full in the shâmayim.

12. And on the first day she is called the new moon, for on that day the light rises upon her.

13. She becomes full moon exactly on the day when the sun sets in the west, and from the east she rises at night, and the moon shines the whole night through till the sun rises over against her and the moon is seen over against the sun.

14. On the side whence the light of the moon comes forth, there again she wanes till all the light vanishes and all the days of the month are at an end, and her circumference is empty, void of light.

15. And three months she makes of thirty days, and at her time she makes three months of twenty nine days each, in which she accomplishes her waning in the first period of time, and in the first portal for one hundred and seventy seven days.

16. And in the time of her going out she appears for three months of thirty days each, and for three months she appears of twenty nine each.

17. At night she appears like a man for twenty days each time, and by day she appears like the shâmayim, and there is nothing else in her save her light.

Chapter 79

1. And now, my son, I have shown you everything, and the law of all the stars of the shâmayim is completed.

2. And he showed me all the laws of these for every day, and for every season of bearing rule, and for every year, and for its going forth, and for the order prescribed to it every month and every week:

3. And the waning of the moon which takes place in the sixth portal: For in this sixth portal her light is accomplished, and after that there is the beginning of the waning:

4. And the waning which takes place in the first portal in its season, till one hundred and seventy seven days are accomplished: Reckoned according to weeks, twenty five weeks and two days.

5. She falls behind the sun and the order of the stars exactly five days in the course of one period, and when this place which you see has been traversed.

6. Such is the picture and sketch of every luminary which Ûrîyêl the archangel, who is their leader, showed unto me.

Chapter 80

1. And in those days the angel Ûrîyêl answered and said to me: Behold, I have shown you everything, Chănôk, and I have revealed everything to you that you should see this sun and this moon, and the leaders of the stars of the shâmayim and all those who turn them, their tasks and times and departures.

2. And in the days of the sinners the years shall be shortened, and their seed shall be tardy on their lands and fields, and all things on the earth shall alter, and shall not appear in their time: And the rain shall be kept back and the shâmayim shall withhold it.

3. And in those times the fruits of the earth shall be backward, and shall not grow in their time, and the fruits of the trees shall be withheld in their time.

4. And the moon shall alter her order, and not appear at her time.

5. And in those days the sun shall be seen and he shall journey in the evening on the extremity of the great chariot in the west And shall shine more brightly than accords with the order of light.

6. And many chiefs of the stars shall transgress the order prescribed. And these shall alter their orbits and tasks, and not appear at the seasons prescribed to them.

7. And the whole order of the stars shall be concealed from the sinners, and the thoughts of those on the earth shall err concerning them, and they shall be altered from all their ways, yea, they shall err and take them to be gods.

8. And evil shall be multiplied upon them, and punishment shall come upon them so as to destroy all.

Chapter 81

1. And he said unto me: Observe, Chănôk, these shâmayim tablets, and read what is written thereon, and mark every individual fact.

2. And I observed the shâmayim tablets, and read everything which was written thereon and understood everything, and read the book of all the deeds of mankind, and of all the children of flesh that shall be upon the earth to the remotest generations.

3. And forthwith I blessed Yahuah Gibbôr Êl, the Melek Kâbôd forever, in that he has made all the works of the world, and I extolled Yahuah because of his patience, and blessed him because of the children of men.

4. And after that I said: Blessed is the man who dies in righteousness and goodness,

concerning whom there is no book of unrighteousness written, and against whom no day of judgement shall be found.

5. And those seven qâdôsh ones brought me and placed me on the earth before the door of my house, and said to me: Declare everything to your son Methûshelach, and show to all your children that no flesh is righteous in the sight of Yahuah, for he is their Bârâ (בְּרָא).

6. One year we will leave you with your son, till you give your last commands, that you may teach your children and record it for them, and testify to all your children; and in the second year they shall take you from their midst.

7. Let your heart be strong, for the good shall announce righteousness to the good; the righteous with the righteous shall rejoice, and shall offer congratulation to one another.

8. But the sinners shall die with the sinners, and the apostate go down with the apostate.

9. And those who practice righteousness shall die on account of the deeds of men, and be taken away on account of the doings of the ungodly.

10. And in those days they ceased to speak to me, and I came to my people, blessing Yahuah of the Têbêl (תֵּבֵל).

Chapter 82

1. And now, my son Methûshelach, all these things I am recounting to you and writing down for you! And I have revealed to you everything, and given you books concerning all these: So preserve, my son Methûshelach, the books from your father's hand, and see that you deliver them to the generations of the world.

2. I have given wisdom to you and to your children, and your children that shall be to you, that they may give it to their children for generations, this wisdom namely that passes their thought.

3. And those who understand it shall not sleep, but shall listen with the ear that they may learn this wisdom, and it shall please those that eat thereof better than good food.

4. Blessed are all the righteous, blessed are all those who walk in the way of righteousness and do not sin as the sinners, in the reckoning of all their days in which the sun traverses the shâmayim, entering into and departing from the portals for thirty days with the heads of thousands of the order of the stars, together with the four which are intercalated which divide the four portions of the year, which lead them and enter with them four days.

5. Owing to them men shall be at fault and not reckon them in the whole reckoning of the year: Yea, men shall be at fault, and not recognize them accurately.

6. For they belong to the reckoning of the year and are truly recorded thereon forever, one in the first portal and one in the third, and one in the fourth and one in the sixth, and the year is completed in three hundred and sixty four days.

7. And the account thereof is accurate and the recorded reckoning thereof exact; for the luminaries, and months and festivals, and years and days, has Ûrîyêl shown and revealed to me, to whom Yahuah of the whole creation of the world has subjected the host of shâmayim.

8. And he has power over night and day in the shâmayim to cause the light to give light

to men sun, moon, and stars, and all the powers of the shâmayim which revolve in their circular chariots.

9. And these are the orders of the stars, which set in their places, and in their seasons and festivals and months.

10. And these are the names of those who lead them, who watch that they enter at their times, in their orders, in their seasons, in their months, in their periods of dominion, and in their positions.

11. Their four leaders who divide the four parts of the year enter first; and after them the twelve leaders of the orders who divide the months; and for the three hundred and sixty days there are heads over thousands who divide the days; and for the four intercalary days there are the leaders which sunder the four parts of the year.

12. And these heads over thousands are intercalated between leader and leader, each behind a station, but their leaders make the division.

13. And these are the names of the leaders who divide the four parts of the year which are ordained: Milkiêl, Helêmmelek, and Melêyal, and Narêl.

14. And the names of those who lead them: Adnarêl, and Iyasusaêl, and Elomeêl, these three follow the leaders of the orders, and there is one that follows the three leaders of the orders which follow those leaders of stations that divide the four parts of the year.

15. In the beginning of the year Melkeyal rises first and rules, who is named Tamâini and sun, and all the days of his dominion while he bears rule are ninety one days.

16. And these are the signs of the days which are to be seen on earth in the days of his dominion: Sweat, and heat, and calms; and all the trees bear fruit, and leaves are produced on all the trees, and the harvest of wheat, and the rose flowers, and all the flowers which come forth in the field, but the trees of the winter season become withered.

17. And these are the names of the leaders which are under them: Berkaêl, Zelebsêl, and another who is added a head of a thousand, called Hiluyaseph: And the days of the dominion of this leader are at an end.

18. The next leader after him is Helêmmelek, whom one names the shining sun, and all the days of his light are ninety one days.

19. And these are the signs of his days on the earth: Glowing heat and dryness, and the trees ripen their fruits and produce all their fruits ripe and ready, and the sheep pair and become pregnant, and all the fruits of the earth are gathered in, and everything that is in the fields, and the winepress: These things take place in the days of his dominion.

20. These are the names, and the orders, and the leaders of those heads of thousands: Gidâlyal, Keêl, and Heêl, and the name of the head of a thousand which is added to them, Asfaêl: And the days of his dominion are at an end.

Part Four
The Dream-Visions
Chapters 83-90

Chapter 83

1. And now, my son Methûshelach, I will show you all my visions which I have seen, recounting them before you.

2. Two visions I saw before I took a woman, and the one was quite unlike the other: The first when I was learning to write: the second before I took your mother, when I saw a terrible vision. And regarding them I prayed to Yahuah.

3. I had laid me down in the house of my grandfather Mahălalêl, when I saw in a vision how the shâmayim collapsed and was borne off and fell to the earth.

4. And when it fell to the earth I saw how the earth was swallowed up in a great abyss, and mountains were suspended on mountains, and hills sank down on hills, and high trees were rent from their stems, and hurled down and sunk in the abyss.

5. And thereupon a word fell into my mouth, and I lifted up my voice to cry aloud, and said: The earth is destroyed.

6. And my grandfather Mahălalêl woke me as I lay near him, and said unto me: Why do you cry so, my son, and why do you make such lamentation?

7. And I recounted to him the whole vision which I had seen, and he said unto me: A terrible thing you have seen, my son, and of grave moment is your dream vision as to the secrets of all the sin of the earth: It must sink into the abyss and be destroyed with a great destruction.

8. And now, my son, arise and make petition to Yahuah Kâbôd, since you are a believer, that a remnant may remain on the earth, and that he may not destroy the whole earth.

9. My son, from shâmayim all this will come upon the earth, and upon the earth there will be great destruction.

10. After that I arose and prayed and implored and besought, and wrote down my prayer for the generations of the world, and I will show everything to you, my son Methûshelach.

11. And when I had gone forth below and seen the shâmayim, and the sun rising in the east, and the moon setting in the west, and a few stars, and the whole earth, and everything as he had known it in the beginning, then I blessed Yahuah of judgement and extolled him because he had made the sun to go forth from the windows of the east, and he ascended and rose on the face of the shâmayim, and set out and kept traversing the path shown unto him.

Chapter 84

1. And I lifted up my hands in righteousness and blessed the Qâdôsh and Gibbôr Êl, and spoke with the breath of my mouth, and with the tongue of flesh, which Êlôhîym has made for the children of the flesh of men, that they should speak therewith, and he gave them breath and a tongue and a mouth that they should speak therewith:

2. Blessed are you, O Yahuah, Melek, great and mighty in your greatness, Yahuah of the whole creation of the shâmayim, Âdôn

of âdôn and Êlôhîym of the whole world. And your power and kingship and greatness abide forever and ever, and throughout all generations your dominion; and all the shâmayim are your throne forever, and the whole earth your footstool forever and ever.

3. For you have made and you rule all things, and nothing is too hard for you, wisdom does not depart from the place of your throne, nor turns away from your presence. And you know and see and hear everything, and there is nothing hidden from you for you see everything.

4. And now the angels of your shâmayim are guilty of trespass, and upon the flesh of men abides your wrath until the great day of judgement.

5. And now, O Êlôhîym and Yahuah and Gibbôr Melek, I implore and beseech you to fulfil my prayer, to leave me a posterity on earth, and do not destroy all the flesh of man, and make the earth without inhabitant, so that there should be an eternal destruction.

6. And now, my Yahuah, destroy from the earth the flesh which has aroused your wrath, but the flesh of righteousness and uprightness establish as a plant of the eternal seed, and do not hide your face from the prayer of your servant, O Yahuah.

Chapter 85

1. And after this I saw another dream, and I will show the whole dream to you, my son.

2. And Chănôk lifted up his voice and spoke to his son Methûshelach: To you, my son, I will speak: Hear my words, incline your ear to the dream vision of your father.

3. Before I took your mother Edna, I saw in a vision on my bed, and behold a bull came forth from the earth, and that bull was white; and after it came forth a heifer, and along with this latter came forth two bulls, one of them black and the other red.

4. And that black bull gored the red one and pursued him over the earth, and thereupon I could no longer see that red bull.

5. But that black bull grew and that heifer went with him, and I saw that many oxen proceeded from him which resembled and followed him.

6. And that cow, that first one, went from the presence of that first bull in order to seek that red one, but did not find him, and lamented with a great lamentation over him and sought him.

7. And I looked till that first bull came to her and quieted her, and from that time onward she cried no more.

8. And after that she bore another white bull, and after him she bore many bulls and black cows.

9. And I saw in my sleep that white bull likewise grow and become a great white bull, and from him proceeded many white bulls, and they resembled him. And they began to beget many white bulls, which resembled them, one following the other, even many.

Chapter 86

1. And again I saw with my eyes as I slept, and I saw the shâmayim above, and behold a star fell from shâmayim, and it arose and eat and pastured among those oxen.

2. And after that I saw the large and the black oxen, and behold they all changed

their stalls and pastures and their cattle, and began to live with each other.

3. And again I saw in the vision, and looked towards the shâmayim, and behold I saw many stars descend and cast themselves down from shâmayim to that first star, and they became bulls among those cattle and pastured with them among them.

4. And I looked at them and saw, and behold they all let out their privy members, like horses, and began to cover the cows of the oxen, and they all became pregnant and bare elephants, camels, and asses.

5. And all the oxen feared them and were affrighted at them, and began to bite with their teeth and to devour, and to gore with their horns.

6. And they began, moreover, to devour those oxen; and behold all the children of the earth began to tremble and quake before them and to flee from them.

Chapter 87

1. And again I saw how they began to gore each other and to devour each other, and the earth began to cry aloud.

2. And I raised my eyes again to shâmayim, and I saw in the vision, and behold there came forth from shâmayim beings who were like white men: and four went forth from that place and three with them.

3. And those three that had last come forth grasped me by my hand and took me up, away from the generations of the earth, and raised me up to a lofty place, and showed me a tower raised high above the earth, and all the hills were lower.

4. And one said unto me: Remain here till you see everything that befalls those elephants, camels, and asses, and the stars and the oxen, and all of them.

Chapter 88

1. And I saw one of those four who had come forth first, and he seized that first star which had fallen from the shâmayim, and bound it hand and foot and cast it into an abyss: now that abyss was narrow and deep, and horrible and dark.

2. And one of them drew a sword, and gave it to those elephants and camels and asses: Then they began to smite each other, and the whole earth quaked because of them.

3. And as I was beholding in the vision, lo, one of those four who had come forth stoned them from shâmayim, and gathered and took all the great stars whose privy members were like those of horses, and bound them all hand and foot, and cast them in an abyss of the earth.

Chapter 89

1. And one of those four went to that white bull and instructed him in a secret, without his being terrified: He was born a bull and became a man, and built for himself a great vessel and dwelt thereon; and three bulls dwelt with him in that vessel and they were covered in.

2. And again I raised my eyes towards shâmayim and saw a lofty roof, with seven water torrents thereon, and those torrents flowed with much water into an enclosure.

3. And I saw again, and behold fountains were opened on the surface of that great enclosure, and that water began to swell and rise upon the surface, and I saw that enclosure till all its surface was covered with water.

4. And the water, the darkness, and mist increased upon it; and as I looked at the height of that water, that water had risen above the height of that enclosure, and was streaming over that enclosure, and it stood upon the earth.

5. And all the cattle of that enclosure were gathered together until I saw how they sank and were swallowed up and perished in that water.

6. But that vessel floated on the water, while all the oxen and elephants and camels and asses sank to the bottom with all the animals, so that I could no longer see them, and they were not able to escape, but perished and sank into the depths.

7. And again I saw in the vision till those water torrents were removed from that high roof, and the chasms of the earth were leveled up and other abysses were opened.

8. Then the water began to run down into these, till the earth became visible; but that vessel settled on the earth, and the darkness retired and light appeared.

9. But that white bull which had become a man came out of that vessel, and the three bulls with him, and one of those three was white like that bull, and one of them was red as blood, and one black: And that white bull departed from them.

10. And they began to bring forth beasts of the field and birds, so that there arose different genera: Lions, tigers, wolves, dogs, hyenas, wild boars, foxes, squirrels, swine, falcons, vultures, kites, eagles, and ravens; and among them was born a white bull.

11. And they began to bite one another; but that white bull which was born among them begat a wild ass and a white bull with it, and the wild asses multiplied.

12. But that bull which was born from him begat a black wild boar and a white sheep; and the former begat many boars, but that sheep begat twelve sheep.

13. And when those twelve sheep had grown, they gave up one of them to the asses, and those asses again gave up that sheep to the wolves, and that sheep grew up among the wolves.

14. And Yahuah brought the eleven sheep to live with it and to pasture with it among the wolves: And they multiplied and became many flocks of sheep.

15. And the wolves began to fear them, and they oppressed them until they destroyed their little ones, and they cast their young into a river of much water: But those sheep began to cry aloud on account of their little ones, and to complain unto their Yahuah.

16. And a sheep which had been saved from the wolves fled and escaped to the wild asses; and I saw the sheep how they lamented and cried, and besought their Yahuah with all their might, till that Âdônây of the sheep descended at the voice of the sheep from a lofty abode, and came to them and pastured them.

17. And he called that sheep which had escaped the wolves, and spoke with it concerning the wolves that it should admonish them not to touch the sheep.

18. And the sheep went to the wolves according to the word of Yahuah, and another sheep met it and went with it, and the two went and entered together into the assembly of those wolves, and spoke with them and admonished them not to touch the sheep from henceforth.

19. And thereupon I saw the wolves, and how they oppressed the sheep exceedingly with all their power; and the sheep cried aloud.

20. And Yahuah came to the sheep and they began to smite those wolves: And the wolves began to make lamentation; but the sheep became quiet and forthwith ceased to cry out.

21. And I saw the sheep till they departed from among the wolves; but the eyes of the wolves were blinded, and those wolves departed in pursuit of the sheep with all their power.

22. And Âdônây of the sheep went with them, as their leader, and all his sheep followed him: And his face was dazzling and glorious and terrible to behold.

23. But the wolves began to pursue those sheep till they reached a sea of water.

24. And that sea was divided, and the water stood on this side and on that before their face, and their Yahuah led them and placed himself between them and the wolves.

25. And as those wolves did not yet see the sheep, they proceeded into the midst of that sea, and the wolves followed the sheep, and those wolves ran after them into that sea.

26. And when they saw Âdônây of the sheep, they turned to flee before his face, but that sea gathered itself together, and became as it had been created, and the water swelled and rose till it covered those wolves.

27. And I saw till all the wolves who pursued those sheep perished and were drowned.

28. But the sheep escaped from that water and went forth into a wilderness, where there was no water and no grass; and they began to open their eyes and to see; and I saw Âdônây of the sheep pasturing them and giving them water and grass, and that sheep going and leading them.

29. And that sheep ascended to the summit of that lofty rock, and Âdônây of the sheep sent it to them.

30. And after that I saw Âdônây of the sheep who stood before them, and his appearance was great and terrible and majestic, and all those sheep saw him and were afraid before his face.

31. And they all feared and trembled because of him, and they cried to that sheep with them which was among them: We are not able to stand before our Yahuah or to behold him.

32. And that sheep which led them again ascended to the summit of that rock, but the sheep began to be blinded and to wander from the way which he had showed them, but that sheep won't not thereof.

33. And Âdônây of the sheep was wrathful exceedingly against them, and that sheep discovered it, and went down from the summit of the rock, and came to the sheep, and found the greatest part of them blinded and fallen away.

34. And when they saw it they feared and trembled at its presence, and desired to return to their folds.

35. And that sheep took other sheep with it, and came to those sheep which had fallen away, and began to slay them; and the sheep feared its presence, and thus that sheep brought back those sheep that had fallen away, and they returned to their folds.

36. And I saw in this vision till that sheep became a man and built a house for Âdônây of the sheep, and placed all the sheep in that house.

37. And I saw till this sheep which had met that sheep which led them fell asleep: And I saw till all the great sheep perished and little ones arose in their place, and they came to a pasture, and approached a stream of water.

38. Then that sheep, their leader which had become a man, withdrew from them and fell asleep, and all the sheep sought it and cried over it with a great crying.

39. And I saw till they left off crying for that sheep and crossed that stream of water, and there arose the two sheep as leaders in the place of those which had fallen asleep and led them.

40. And I saw till the sheep came to a goodly place, and a pleasant and glorious land, and I saw till those sheep were satisfied; and that house stood among them in the pleasant land.

41. And sometimes their eyes were opened, and sometimes blinded, till another sheep arose and led them and brought them all back, and their eyes were opened.

42. And the dogs and the foxes and the wild boars began to devour those sheep till Âdônây of the sheep raised up another sheep a ram from their midst, which led them.

43. And that ram began to butt on either side those dogs, foxes, and wild boars till he had destroyed them all.

44. And that sheep whose eyes were opened saw that ram, which was among the sheep, till it forsook its glory and began to butt those sheep, and trampled upon them, and behaved itself unseemly.

45. And Âdônây of the sheep sent the lamb to another lamb and raised it to being a ram and leader of the sheep instead of that ram which had forsaken its glory.

46. And it went to it and spoke to it alone, and raised it to being a ram, and made it the prince and leader of the sheep; but during all these things those dogs oppressed the sheep.

47. And the first ram pursued that second ram, and that second ram arose and fled before it; and I saw till those dogs pulled down the first ram.

48. And that second ram arose and led the little sheep.

49. And those sheep grew and multiplied; but all the dogs, and foxes, and wild boars feared and fled before it, and that ram butted and killed the wild beasts, and those wild beasts had no longer any power among the sheep and robbed them no more of ought. And that ram begat many sheep and fell asleep; and a little sheep became ram in its stead, and became prince and leader of those sheep.

50. And that house became great and broad, and it was built for those sheep: And a tower lofty and great was built on the house for Âdônây of the sheep, and that house was low, but the tower was elevated and lofty, and Âdônây of the sheep stood on that tower and they offered a full table before him.

51. And again I saw those sheep that they again erred and went many ways, and forsook that their house, and Âdônây of the sheep called some from among the sheep and sent them to the sheep, but the sheep began to slay them.

52. And one of them was saved and was not slain, and it sped away and cried aloud over the sheep; and they sought to slay it, but Âdônây of the sheep saved it from the sheep, and brought it up to me, and caused it to dwell there.

53. And many other sheep he sent to those sheep to testify unto them and lament over them.

54. And after that I saw that when they forsook the house of Yahuah and his tower they fell away entirely, and their eyes were

blinded; and I saw Âdônây of the sheep how he wrought much slaughter among them in their herds until those sheep invited that slaughter and betrayed his place.

55. And he gave them over into the hands of the lions and tigers, and wolves and hyenas, and into the hand of the foxes, and to all the wild beasts, and those wild beasts began to tear in pieces those sheep.

56. And I saw that he forsook that their house and their tower and gave them all into the hand of the lions, to tear and devour them, into the hand of all the wild beasts.

57. And I began to cry aloud with all my power, and to appeal to Âdônây of the sheep, and to represent to him in regard to the sheep that they were devoured by all the wild beasts.

58. But he remained unmoved, though he saw it, and rejoiced that they were devoured and swallowed and robbed, and left them to be devoured in the hand of all the beasts.

59. And he called seventy shepherds, and cast those sheep to them that they might pasture them, and he spoke to the shepherds and their companions: Let each individual of you pasture the sheep henceforward, and everything that I shall command you that do you.

60. And I will deliver them over unto you duly numbered, and tell you which of them are to be destroyed and them you destroy.

61. And he gave over unto them those sheep. And he called another and spoke unto him: Observe and mark everything that the shepherds will do to those sheep; for they will destroy more of them than I have commanded them.

62. And every excess and the destruction which will be wrought through the shepherds, namely how many they destroy according to my command, and how many according to their own caprice: Record against every individual shepherd all the destruction he effects.

63. And read out before me by number how many they destroy, and how many they deliver over for destruction, that I may have this as a testimony against them, and know every deed of the shepherds, that I may comprehend and see what they do, whether or not they abide by my command which I have commanded them.

64. But they shall not know it, and you shall not declare it to them, nor admonish them, but only record against each individual all the destruction which the shepherds effect each in his time and lay it all before me.

65. And I saw till those shepherds pastured in their season, and they began to slay and to destroy more than they were bidden, and they delivered those sheep into the hand of the lions.

66. And the lions and tigers eat and devoured the greater part of those sheep, and the wild boars eat along with them; and they burnt that tower and demolished that house.

67. And I became exceedingly sorrowful over that tower because that house of the sheep was demolished, and afterwards I was unable to see if those sheep entered that house.

68. And the shepherds and their associates delivered over those sheep to all the wild beasts, to devour them, and each one of them received in his time a definite number: It was written by the other in a book how many each one of them destroyed of them.

69. And each one slew and destroyed many more than was prescribed; and I began to weep and lament on account of those sheep.

70. And thus in the vision I saw that one who wrote, how he wrote down every one that was destroyed by those shepherds, day by day, and carried up and laid down and showed actually the whole book to Âdônây of the sheep even everything that they had done, and all that each one of them had made away with, and all that they had given over to destruction.

71. And the book was read before Âdônây of the sheep, and he took the book from his hand and read it and sealed it and laid it down.

72. And forthwith I saw how the shepherds pastured for twelve hours, and behold three of those sheep turned back and came and entered and began to build up all that had fallen down of that house; but the wild boars tried to hinder them, but they were not able.

73. And they began again to build as before, and they reared up that tower, and it was named the high tower; and they began again to place a table before the tower, but all the bread on it was polluted and not pure.

74. And as touching all this the eyes of those sheep were blinded so that they did not see, and the eyes of their shepherds likewise; and they delivered them in large numbers to their shepherds for destruction, and they trampled the sheep with their feet and devoured them.

75. And Âdônây of the sheep remained unmoved till all the sheep were dispersed over the field and mingled with them, the beasts, and they, the shepherds did not save them out of the hand of the beasts.

76. And this one who wrote the book carried it up, and showed it and read it before Âdônây of the sheep, and implored him on their account, and besought him on their account as he showed him all the doings of the shepherds, and gave testimony before him against all the shepherds.

77. And he took the actual book and laid it down beside him and departed.

Chapter 90

1. And I saw till that in this manner thirty five shepherds undertook the pasturing of the sheep, and they severally completed their periods as did the first; and others received them into their hands, to pasture them for their period, each shepherd in his own period.

2. And after that I saw in my vision all the birds of shâmayim coming, the eagles, the vultures, the kites, the ravens; but the eagles led all the birds; and they began to devour those sheep, and to pick out their eyes and to devour their flesh.

3. And the sheep cried out because their flesh was being devoured by the birds, and as for me I looked and lamented in my sleep over that shepherd who pastured the sheep.

4. And I saw until those sheep were devoured by the dogs and eagles and kites, and they left neither flesh nor skin nor sinew remaining on them till only their bones stood there: and their bones too fell to the earth and the sheep became few.

5. And I saw until that twenty three had undertaken the pasturing and completed in their several periods fifty eight times.

6. But behold lambs were borne by those white sheep, and they began to open their eyes and to see, and to cry to the sheep.

7. Yea, they cried to them, but they did not hearken to what they said to them, but were exceedingly deaf, and their eyes were very exceedingly blinded.

8. And I saw in the vision how the ravens flew upon those lambs and took one of those lambs, and dashed the sheep in pieces and devoured them.

9. And I saw till horns grew upon those lambs, and the ravens cast down their horns; and I saw till there sprouted a great horn of one of those sheep, and their eyes were opened.

10. And it looked at them and their eyes opened, and it cried to the sheep, and the rams saw it and all ran to it.

11. And notwithstanding all this those eagles and vultures and ravens and kites still kept tearing the sheep and swooping down upon them and devouring them: Still the sheep remained silent, but the rams lamented and cried out.

12. And those ravens fought and battled with it and sought to lay low its horn, but they had no power over it.

13. And I saw till the shepherds and eagles and those vultures and kites came, and they cried to the ravens that they should break the horn of that ram, and they battled and fought with it, and it battled with them and cried that its help might come.

14. And I saw till that man, who wrote down the names of the shepherds and carried up unto the presence of Âdônây of the sheep came and helped it and showed it everything: He had come down for the help of that ram.

15. And I saw till Âdônây of the sheep came unto them in wrath, and all who saw him fled, and they all fell into his shadow from before his face.

16. All the eagles and vultures and ravens and kites were gathered together, and there came with them all the sheep of the field, yea, they all came together, and helped each other to break that horn of the ram.

17. And I saw that man, who wrote the book according to the command of Yahuah, till he opened that book concerning the destruction which those twelve last shepherds had wrought, and showed that they had destroyed much more than their predecessors, before Âdônây of the sheep.

18. And I saw till Âdônây of the sheep came unto them and took in his hand the staff of his wrath, and smote the earth, and the earth clave asunder, and all the beasts and all the birds of the shâmayim fell from among those sheep, and were swallowed up in the earth and it covered them.

19. And I saw till a great sword was given to the sheep, and the sheep proceeded against all the beasts of the field to slay them, and all the beasts and the birds of the shâmayim fled before their face.

20. And I saw till a throne was erected in the pleasant land, and Âdônây of the sheep sat himself thereon, and the other took the sealed books and opened those books before Âdônây of the sheep.

21. And Yahuah called those men the seven first white ones, and commanded that they should bring before Him, beginning with the first star which led the way, all the stars whose privy members were like those of horses, and they brought them all before him.

22. And he said to that man who wrote before him, being one of those seven white ones, and said unto him: Take those seventy shepherds to whom I delivered the sheep, and who taking them on their own authority slew more than I commanded them.

23. And behold they were all bound, I saw, and they all stood before him.

24. And the judgement was held first over the stars, and they were judged and found

guilty, and went to the place of condemnation, and they were cast into an abyss, full of fire and flaming, and full of pillars of fire.

25. And those seventy shepherds were judged and found guilty, and they were cast into that fiery abyss.

26. And I saw at that time how a like abyss was opened in the midst of the earth, full of fire, and they brought those blinded sheep, and they were all judged and found guilty and cast into this fiery abyss, and they burned; now this abyss was to the right of that house.

27. And I saw those sheep burning and their bones burning.

28. And I stood up to see till they folded up that old house; and carried off all the pillars, and all the beams and ornaments of the house were at the same time folded up with it, and they carried it off and laid it in a place in the south of the land.

29. And I saw till Âdônây of the sheep brought a new house greater and loftier than that first, and set it up in the place of the first which had beer folded up: all its pillars were new, and its ornaments were new and larger than those of the first, the old one which He had taken away, and all the sheep were within it.

30. And I saw all the sheep which had been left, and all the beasts on the earth, and all the birds of the shâmayim, falling down and doing homage to those sheep and making petition to and obeying them in everything.

31. And thereafter those three who were clothed in white and had seized me by my hand, who had taken me up before, and the hand of that ram also seizing hold of me, they took me up and set me down in the midst of those sheep before the judgement took place.

32. And those sheep were all white, and their wool was abundant and clean.

33. And all that had been destroyed and dispersed, and all the beasts of the field, and all the birds of the shâmayim, assembled in that house, and Âdônây of the sheep rejoiced with great joy because they were all good and had returned to his house.

34. And I saw till they laid down that sword, which had been given to the sheep, and they brought it back into the house, and it was sealed before the presence of Yahuah, and all the sheep were invited into that house, but it did not hold them.

35. And the eyes of them all were opened, and they saw the good, and there was not one among them that did not see.

36. And I saw that that house was large and broad and very full.

37. And I saw that a white bull was born, with large horns and all the beasts of the field and all the birds of the air feared him and made petition to him all the time.

38. And I saw till all their generations were transformed, and they all became white bulls; and the first among them became a lamb, and that lamb became a great animal and had great black horns on its head; and Âdônây of the sheep rejoiced over it and over all the oxen.

39. And I slept in their midst: And I awoke and saw everything.

40. This is the vision which I saw while I slept, and I awoke and blessed Yahuah Tsedâqâh and gave him glory.

41. Then I wept with a great weeping and my tears did not stay till I could no longer endure it: When I saw, they flowed on account of what I had seen; for everything

shall come and be fulfilled, and all the deeds of men in their order were shown to me.

42. On that night I remembered the first dream, and because of it I wept and was troubled, because I had seen that vision.

Part Five

Chapters 91-105

Chapter 91

1. And now, my son Methûshelach, call to me all your brothers and gather together to me all the sons of your mother; for the word calls me, and the spirit is poured out upon me, that I may show you everything that shall befall you forever.

2. And there upon Methûshelach went and summoned to him all his brothers and assembled his relatives.

3. And he spoke unto all the children of righteousness and said: Hear, you sons of Chănôk, all the words of your father, and hearken right to the voice of my mouth; for I exhort you and say unto you, beloved:

4. Love uprightness and walk therein. And do not draw nigh to uprightness with a double heart, and do not associate with those of a double heart, but walk in righteousness, my sons. And it shall guide you on good paths, and righteousness shall be your companion.

5. For I know that violence must increase on the earth, and a great chastisement be executed on the earth, and all unrighteousness come to an end: Yea, it shall be cut off from its roots, and its whole structure be destroyed.

6. And unrighteousness shall again be consummated on the earth, and all the deeds of unrighteousness and of violence and transgression shall prevail in a twofold degree.

7. And when sin and unrighteousness and blasphemy and violence in all kinds of deeds increase, and apostasy and transgression and uncleanness increase, a great chastisement shall come from shâmayim upon all these, and Yahuah Qâdôsh will come forth with wrath and chastisement to execute judgement on earth.

8. In those days violence shall be cut off from its roots, and the roots of unrighteousness together with deceit, and they shall be destroyed from under shâmayim.

9. And all the idols of the heathen shall be abandoned, and the temples burned with fire, and they shall remove them from the whole earth, and they, the heathen shall be cast into the judgement of fire, and shall perish in wrath and in grievous judgement forever.

10. And the righteous shall arise from their sleep, and wisdom shall arise and be given unto them.

11. And after that the roots of unrighteousness shall be cut off, and the sinners shall be destroyed by the sword {. . .} shall be cut off from the blasphemers in every place, and those who plan violence and those who commit blasphemy shall perish by the sword.

12. And after that there shall be another, the eighth week that of righteousness, and a sword shall be given to it that a righteous judgement may be executed on the

oppressors, and sinners shall be delivered into the hands of the righteous.

13. And at its close they shall acquire houses through their righteousness, and a house shall be built for the Gibbôr Melek in glory forevermore, and all mankind shall look to the path of uprightness.

14. And after that, in the ninth week, the righteous judgement shall be revealed to the whole world, and all the works of the ungodless shall vanish from all the earth, and the world shall be written down for destruction. And all mankind shall look to the path of uprightness,

15. And after this, in the tenth week in the seventh part, there shall be the great eternal judgement, in which he will execute vengeance among the angels.

16. And the first shâmayim shall depart and pass away, and a new shâmayim shall appear, and all the powers of the shâmayim shall give sevenfold light.

17. And after that there will be many weeks without number forever, and all shall be in goodness and righteousness, and sin shall no more be mentioned forever.

18. And now I tell you, my sons, and show you the paths of righteousness and the paths of violence. Yea, I will show them to you again that you may know what will come to pass.

19. And now, hearken unto me, my sons, and walk in the paths of righteousness, and walk not in the paths of violence; for all who walk in the paths of unrighteousness shall perish forever.

Chapter 92

1. The book written by Chănôk: Chănôk indeed wrote this complete doctrine of wisdom, which is praised of all men and a judge of all the earth, for all my children who shall dwell on the earth. And for the future generations who shall observe uprightness and peace.

2. Do not let your spirit be troubled on account of the times; for the Qâdôsh and Gibbôr Êl has appointed days for all things.

3. And the Tsedâqâh Êl shall arise from sleep, shall arise and walk in the paths of righteousness, and all his path and conversation shall be in eternal goodness and grace.

4. He will be gracious to the righteous and give him eternal uprightness, and he will give him power so that he shall be endowed with goodness and righteousness. And he shall walk in eternal light.

5. And sin shall perish in darkness forever, and shall no more be seen from that day forevermore.

Chapter 93

1. And after that Chănôk both gave and began to recount from the books.

2. And Chănôk said: Concerning the children of righteousness and concerning the elect of the world, and concerning the plant of uprightness, I will speak these things, Yea, I Chănôk will declare them unto you, my sons: According to that which appeared to me in the shâmayim vision, and which I have known through the word of the qâdôsh angels, and have learnt from the shâmayim tablets.

3. And Chănôk began to recount from the books and said: I was born the seventh in the first week, while judgement and righteousness still endured.

4. And after me there shall arise in the second week great wickedness, and deceit shall

have sprung up; and in it there shall be the first end. And in it a man shall be saved; and after it is ended unrighteousness shall grow up, and a law shall be made for the sinners.

5. And after that in the third week at its close, a man shall be elected as the plant of righteous judgement, and his posterity shall become the plant of righteousness forevermore.

6. And after that in the fourth week, at its close, visions of the qâdôsh and righteous shall be seen, and a law for all generations and an enclosure shall be made for them.

7. And after that in the fifth week, at its close, the house of glory and dominion shall be built forever.

8. And after that in the sixth week all who live in it shall be blinded, and the hearts of all of them shall ungodlessly forsake wisdom. And in it a man shall ascend; and at its close the house of dominion shall be burnt with fire, and the whole race of the chosen root shall be dispersed.

9. And after that in the seventh week shall an apostate generation arise, and many shall be its deeds, and all its deeds shall be apostate.

10. And at its close shall be elected, the elect righteous of the eternal plant of righteousness, to receive sevenfold instruction concerning all his creation.

11. For who is there of all the children of men that is able to hear the voice of the Qâdôsh without being troubled? And who can think his thoughts? And who is there that can behold all the works of shâmayim?

12. And how should there be one who could behold the shâmayim, and who is there that could understand the things of shâmayim and see a soul or a spirit and could tell thereof, or ascend and see all their ends and think them or do like them?

13. And who is there of all men that could know what is the breadth and the length of the earth, and to whom has been shown the measure of all of them?

14. Or is there anyone who could discern the length of the shâmayim and how great is its height, and upon what it is founded, and how great is the number of the stars, and where all the luminaries rest?

Chapter 94

1. And now I say unto you, my sons, love righteousness and walk therein; for the paths of righteousness are worthy of acceptance, but the paths of unrighteousness shall suddenly be destroyed and vanish.

2. And to certain men of a generation shall the paths of violence and of death be revealed, and they shall hold themselves afar from them, and shall not follow them.

3. And now I say unto you the righteous: Do not walk in the paths of wickedness, nor in the paths of death, and do not draw nigh to them, lest you are destroyed.

4. But seek and choose for yourselves righteousness and an elect life, and walk in the paths of peace, and you shall live and prosper.

5. And hold fast my words in the thoughts of your hearts, and do not suffer them to be effaced from your hearts; for I know that sinners will tempt men to evilly entreat wisdom, so that no place may be found for her, and no manner of temptation may diminish.

6. Woe to those who build unrighteousness and oppression and lay deceit as a foundation; for they shall be suddenly overthrown, and they shall have no peace.

7. Woe to those who build their houses with sin; for from all their foundations shall they be overthrown, and by the sword shall they fall. And those who acquire gold and silver in judgement suddenly shall perish.

8. Woe to you, you rich, for you have trusted in your riches, and from your riches shall you depart, because you have not remembered Elyôn Êl in the days of your riches.

9. You have committed blasphemy and unrighteousness, and have become ready for the day of slaughter, and the day of darkness and the day of the great judgement.

10. Thus I speak and declare unto you: He who has created you will overthrow you, and for your fall there shall be no compassion, and your Bârâ will rejoice at your destruction.

11. And your righteous ones in those days shall be a reproach to the sinners and the ungodless.

Chapter 95

1. Oh that my eyes were a cloud of waters that I might weep over you, and pour down my tears as a cloud of waters: That so I might rest from my trouble of heart!

2. Who has permitted you to practice reproaches and wickedness? And so judgement shall overtake you, sinners.

3. Do not fear the sinners, you righteous; for again will Yahuah deliver them into your hands, that you may execute judgement upon them according to your desires.

4. Woe to you who fulminate anathemas which cannot be reversed: Healing shall therefore be far from you because of your sins.

5. Woe to you who requite your neighbor with evil; for you shall be requited according to your works.

6. Woe to you, lying witnesses, and to those who weigh out injustice, for suddenly you shall perish.

7. Woe to you, sinners, for you persecute the righteous; for you shall be delivered up and persecuted because of injustice, and heavy shall its yoke be upon you.

Chapter 96

1. Be hopeful, you righteous; for suddenly shall the sinners perish before you, and you shall have dominion over them according to your desires.

2. And in the day of the tribulation of the sinners, your children shall mount and rise as eagles, and higher than the vultures will be your nest, and you shall ascend and enter the crevices of the earth, and the clefts of the rock forever as coneys before the unrighteous, and the sirens shall sigh because of you and weep.

3. Wherefore do not fear, you that have suffered; for healing shall be your portion, and a bright light shall enlighten you, and the voice of rest you shall hear from shâmayim.

4. Woe unto you, you sinners, for your riches make you appear like the righteous, but your hearts convict you of being sinners, and this fact shall be a testimony against you for a memorial of your evil deeds.

5. Woe to you who devour the finest of the wheat, and drink wine in large bowls, and tread underfoot the lowly with your might.

6. Woe to you who drink water from every fountain, for suddenly you shall be consumed and wither away, because you have forsaken the fountain of life.

7. Woe to you who work unrighteousness and deceit and blasphemy: It shall be a memorial against you for evil.

8. Woe to you, you mighty, who with might oppress the righteous; for the day of your destruction is coming. In those days many and good days shall come to the righteous, in the day of your judgement.

Chapter 97

1. Believe, you righteous, that the sinners will become a shame and perish in the day of unrighteousness.

2. Be it known unto you sinners that Elyôn Êl is mindful of your destruction, and the angels of shâmayim rejoice over your destruction.

3. What will you do, you sinners, and whither will you flee on that day of judgement, when you hear the voice of the prayer of the righteous?

4. Yea, you shall fare like unto them, against whom this word shall be a testimony: You have been companions of sinners.

5. And in those days the prayer of the righteous shall reach unto Yahuah, and for you the days of your judgement shall come.

6. And all the words of your unrighteousness shall be read out before the Gibbôr Qâdôsh Êl, and your faces shall be covered with shame, and he will reject every work which is grounded on unrighteousness.

7. Woe to you, you sinners, who live on the mid ocean and on the dry land, whose remembrance is evil against you.

8. Woe to you who acquire silver and gold in unrighteousness and say: We have become rich with riches and have possessions; and have acquired everything we have desired.

9. And now let us do what we purposed: For we have gathered silver, and many are the husbandmen in our houses. And our granaries are brim full as with water.

10. Yea and like water your lies shall flow away; for your riches shall not abide but speedily ascend from you; for you have acquired it all in unrighteousness, and you shall be given over to a great curse.

Chapter 98

1. And now I swear unto you, to the wise and to the foolish, for you shall have manifold experiences on the earth.

2. For you men shall put on more adornments than a woman, and colored garments more than a virgin: In royalty and in grandeur and in power, and in silver and in gold and in purple, and in splendor and in food they shall be poured out as water.

3. Therefore they shall be wanting in doctrine and wisdom, and they shall perish thereby together with their possessions; and with all their glory and their splendor, and in shame and in slaughter and in great destitution, their spirits shall be cast into the furnace of fire.

4. I have sworn unto you, you sinners, as a mountain has not become a slave, and a hill does not become the handmaid of a woman, even so sin has not been sent upon the earth, but man of himself has created it, and under a great curse shall they fall who commit it.

5. And barrenness has not been given to the woman, but on account of the deeds of her own hands she dies without children.

6. I have sworn unto you, you sinners, by the Qâdôsh Gibbôr Êl that all your evil deeds are revealed in the shâmayim, and that none of your deeds of oppression are covered and hidden.

7. And do not think in your spirit nor say in your heart that you do not know and that you do not see that every sin is every day

recorded in shâmayim in the presence of Elyôn Êl.

8. From henceforth you know that all your oppression wherewith you oppress is written down every day till the day of your judgement.

9. Woe to you, you fools, for through your folly you shall perish: And you transgress against the wise, and so good hap shall not be your portion.

10. And now, you know that you are prepared for the day of destruction: Wherefore do not hope to live, you sinners, but you shall depart and die; for you know no ransom; for you are prepared for the day of the great judgement, for the day of tribulation and great shame for your spirits.

11. Woe to you, you obstinate of heart, who work wickedness and eat blood: Whence have you good things to eat and to drink and to be filled? From all the good things which Yahuah Elyôn Êl has placed in abundance on the earth; therefore you shall have no peace.

12. Woe to you who love the deeds of unrighteousness: Wherefore do you hope for good hap unto yourselves? Know that you shall be delivered into the hands of the righteous, and they shall cut off your necks and slay you, and have no mercy upon you.

13. Woe to you who rejoice in the tribulation of the righteous; for no grave shall be dug for you.

14. Woe to you who set at nothing the words of the righteous; for you shall have no hope of life.

15. Woe to you who write down lying and ungodless words; for they write down their lies that men may hear them and act ungodlessly towards their neighbor.

16. Therefore they shall have no peace but die a sudden death.

Chapter 99

1. Woe to you who work ungodlessness, and glory in lying and extol them: You shall perish, and no happy life shall be yours.

2. Woe to them who pervert the words of uprightness, and transgress the eternal law, and transform themselves into what they were not into sinners: They shall be trodden under foot upon the earth.

3. In those days make ready, you righteous, to raise your prayers as a memorial, and place them as a testimony before the angels, that they may place the sin of the sinners for a memorial before Elyôn Êl.

4. In those days the nations shall be stirred up, and the families of the nations shall arise on the day of destruction.

5. And in those days the destitute shall go forth and carry off their children, and they shall abandon them, so that their children shall perish through them: Yea, they shall abandon their children that are still sucklings, and do not return to them, and shall have no pity on their beloved ones.

6. And again I swear to you, you sinners that sin is prepared for a day of unceasing bloodshed.

7. And they who worship stones, and grave images of gold and silver and wood and stone and clay, and those who worship impure spirits and demons, and all kinds of idols not according to knowledge, shall get no manner of help from them.

8. And they shall become ungodless because of the folly of their hearts, and their eyes shall be blinded through the fear of their hearts and through visions in their dreams.

9. Through these they shall become ungodless and fearful; for they shall have wrought all their work in a lie, and shall have worshiped a stone: Therefore in an instant shall they perish.

10. But in those days blessed are all they who accept the words of wisdom, and understand them, and observe the paths of Elyôn Êl, and walk in the path of his righteousness, and do not become ungodless with the ungodless; for they shall be saved.

11. Woe to you who spread evil to your neighbors; for you shall be slain in Sheôl.

12. Woe to you who make deceitful and false measures, and to them who cause bitterness on the earth; for they shall thereby be utterly consumed.

13. Woe to you who build your houses through the grievous toil of others, and all their building materials are the bricks and stones of sin; I tell you, you shall have no peace.

14. Woe to them who reject the measure and eternal heritage of their fathers and whose souls follow after idols; for they shall have no rest.

15. Woe to them who work unrighteousness and help oppression, and slay their neighbors until the day of the great judgement.

16. For he shall cast down your glory, and bring affliction on your hearts, and shall arouse his fierce indignation and destroy you all with the sword; and all the qâdôsh and righteous shall remember your sins.

Chapter 100

1. And in those days in one place the fathers together with their sons shall be smitten and brothers, one with another shall fall in death till the streams flow with their blood.

2. For a man shall not withhold his hand from slaying his sons and his sons' sons, and the sinner shall not withhold his hand from his honored brother: From dawn till sunset they shall slay one another.

3. And the horse shall walk up to the breast in the blood of sinners, and the chariot shall be submerged to its height.

4. In those days the angels shall descend into the secret places and gather together into one place all those who brought down sin and Elyôn Êl will arise on that day of judgement to execute great judgement among sinners.

5. And over all the righteous and qâdôsh, he will appoint guardians from among the qâdôsh angels to guard them as the apple of an eye, until he makes an end of all wickedness and all sin, and though the righteous sleep a long sleep, they have nothing to fear.

6. And then the children of the earth shall see the wise in security, and shall understand all the words of this book, and recognize that their riches shall not be able to save them in the overthrow of their sins.

7. Woe to you, sinners, on the day of strong anguish, you who afflict the righteous and burn them with fire: You shall be requited according to your works.

8. Woe to you, you obstinate of heart, who watch in order to devise wickedness: Therefore shall fear come upon you and there shall be none to help you.

9. Woe to you, you sinners, on account of the words of your mouth, and on account of the deeds of your hands which your ungodlessness as wrought, in blazing flames burning worse than fire you shall burn.

10. And now, you know that from the angels he will inquire as to your deeds in shâmayim, from the sun and from the moon

and from the stars in reference to your sins because upon the earth you execute judgement on the righteous.

11. And he will summon to testify against you every cloud and mist and dew and rain; for they shall all be withheld because of you from descending upon you, and they shall be mindful of your sins.

12. And now give presents to the rain that it do not be withheld from descending upon you, nor yet the dew, when it has received gold and silver from you that it may descend.

13. When the hoar frost and snow with their chilliness, and all the snow storms with all their plagues fall upon you, in those days you shall not be able to stand before them.

Chapter 101

1. Observe the shâmayim, you children of shâmayim, and every work of Elyôn Êl, and you fear him and work no evil in his presence.

2. If he closes the windows of shâmayim, and withholds the rain and the dew from descending on the earth on your account, what will you do then?

3. And if he sends his anger upon you because of your deeds, you cannot petition him; for you spoke proud and insolent words against his righteousness: Therefore you shall have no peace.

4. And you do not see the sailors of the ships, how their ships are tossed to and fro by the waves, and are shaken by the winds, and are in sore trouble?

5. And therefore do they fear because all their goodly possessions go upon the sea with them, and they have evil forebodings of heart that the sea will swallow them and they will perish therein.

6. Are not the entire sea and all its waters, and all its movements, the work of Elyôn Êl, and he has not set limits to its doings, and confined it throughout by the sand?

7. And at his reproof it is afraid and dries up, and all its fish die and all that is in it; but you sinners that are on the earth do not fear him.

8. He has not made the shâmayim and the earth, and all that is therein? Who has given understanding and wisdom to everything that moves on the earth and in the sea?

9. Do not the sailors of the ships fear the sea? Yet sinners do not fear Elyôn Êl.

Chapter 102

1. In those days when he has brought a grievous fire upon you, whither will you flee, and where will you find deliverance? And when he launches forth his word against you, will you not be affrighted and fear?

2. And all the luminaries shall be affrighted with great fear, and all the earth shall be affrighted and tremble and be alarmed.

3. And all the angels shall execute their commands and shall seek to hide themselves from the presence of the Gibbôr Kâbôd, and the children of earth shall tremble and quake; and you sinners shall be cursed forever, and you shall have no peace.

4. You do not fear, you souls of the righteous, and be hopeful you that have died in righteousness.

5. And do not grieve if your soul has descended into Sheôl in grief, and that in your life your body did not fare according to your goodness, but wait for the day of the judgement of sinners and for the day of cursing and chastisement.

6. And yet when you die the sinners speak over you: As we die, so die the righteous, and what benefit do they reap for their deeds?

7. Behold, even as we, so do they die in grief and darkness, and what have they more than we? From henceforth we are equal.

8. And what will they receive and what will they see forever? Behold, they too have died, and henceforth forever shall they see no light.

9. I tell you, you sinners, you are content to eat and drink, and rob and sin, and strip men naked, and acquire wealth and see good days.

10. Have you seen the righteous how their end falls out, that no manner of violence is found in them till their death?

11. Nevertheless they perished and became as though they had not been, and their spirits descended into Sheôl in tribulation.

Chapter 103

1. Now, therefore, I swear to you, the righteous, by the glory of the Gibbôr and Hădar (הֶדֶר) and Gâbar (גְּבַר) Êl in dominion, and by his greatness I swear to you.

2. I know a mystery and have read the shâmayim tablets, and have seen the qâdôsh books, and have found written therein and inscribed regarding them:

3. That all goodness and joy and glory are prepared for them, and written down for the spirits of those who have died in righteousness, and that manifold good shall be given to you in recompense for your labors, and that your lot is abundantly beyond the lot of the living.

4. And the spirits of you who have died in righteousness shall live and rejoice, and their spirits shall not perish, nor their memorial from before the face of the Gibbôr Êl unto all the generations of the world: Wherefore no longer fear their contumely.

5. Woe to you, you sinners, when you have died, if you die in the wealth of your sins, and those who are like you say regarding you: Blessed are the sinners: They have seen all their days.

6. And how they have died in prosperity and in wealth, and have not seen tribulation or murder in their life; and they have died in honor, and judgement has not been executed on them during their life.

7. Know you that their souls will be made to descend into Sheôl and they shall be wretched in their great tribulation.

8. And into darkness and chains and a burning flame where there is grievous judgement shall your spirits enter; and the great judgement shall be for all the generations of the world. Woe to you, for you shall have no peace.

9. Do not say in regard to the righteous and good who are in life: In our troubled days we have toiled laboriously and experienced every trouble, and met with much evil and been consumed, and have become few and our spirit small.

10. And we have been destroyed and have not found any to help us even with a word: We have been tortured and destroyed, and not hoped to see life from day today.

11. We hoped to be the head and have become the tail: We have toiled laboriously and had no satisfaction in our toil; and we have become the food of the sinners and the unrighteous, and they have laid their yoke heavily upon us.

12. They have had dominion over us that hated us and smote us; and to those that

hated us we have bowed our necks but they did not pity us.

13. We desired to get away from them that we might escape and be at rest, but found no place whereunto we should flee and be safe from them.

14. And are complained to the rulers in our tribulation, and cried out against those who devoured us, but they did not attend to our cries and would not hearken to our voice.

15. And they helped those who robbed us and devoured us and those who made us few; and they concealed their oppression, and they did not remove from us the yoke of those that devoured us and dispersed us and murdered us, and they concealed their murder, and did not remember that they had lifted up their hands against us.

Chapter 104

1. I swear unto you, that in shâmayim the angels remember you for good before the glory of the Gibbôr Êl: And your names are written before the glory of the Gibbôr Êl.

2. Be hopeful; for beforetime you were put to shame through ill and affliction; but now you shall shine as the lights of shâmayim, you shall shine and you shall be seen, and the portals of shâmayim shall be opened to you.

3. And in your cry, cry for judgement, and it shall appear to you; for all your tribulation shall be visited on the rulers, and on all who helped those who plundered you.

4. Be hopeful, and do not cast away your hopes for you shall have great joy as the angels of shâmayim.

5. What shall you are obliged to do? You shall not have to hide on the day of the great judgement and you shall not be found as sinners, and the eternal judgement shall be far from you for all the generations of the world.

6. And now do not fear, you righteous, when you see the sinners growing strong and prospering in their ways: Do not be companions with them, but keep afar from their violence; for you shall become companions of the hosts of shâmayim.

7. And, although you sinners say: All our sins shall not be searched out and be written down, nevertheless they shall write down all your sins every day.

8. And now I show unto you that light and darkness, day and night, see all your sins.

9. Do not be ungodless in your hearts, and do not lie and do not alter the words of uprightness, nor charge with lying the words of the Qâdôsh Gibbôr Êl, nor take account of your idols; for all your lying and all your ungodlessness do not issue in righteousness but in great sin.

10. And now I know this mystery, that sinners will alter and pervert the words of righteousness in many ways, and will speak wicked words, and lie, and practice great deceits, and write books concerning their words.

11. But when they write down truthfully all my words in their languages, and do not change or diminish ought from my words but write them all down truthfully, all that I first testified concerning them.

12. Then, I know another mystery, that books will be given to the righteous and the wise to become a cause of joy and uprightness and much wisdom.

13. And to them shall the books be given, and they shall believe in them and rejoice

over them, and then shall all the righteous who have learnt therefrom all the paths of uprightness be recompensed.

Chapter 105

1. In those days Yahuah bid them to summon and testify to the children of earth concerning their wisdom: Show it unto them; for you are their guides, and a recompense over the whole earth.

2. For I and my son will be united with them forever in the paths of uprightness in their lives; and you shall have peace: Rejoice, you children of uprightness. Âmên.

Part Six
Chapters 106-107
Fragment of the Book of Nôach

Chapter 106

1. And after some days my son Methûshelach took a woman for his son Lemek, and she became pregnant by him and bore a son.

2. And his body was white as snow and red as the blooming of a rose, and the hair of his head and his long locks were white as wool, and his eyes beautiful. And when he opened his eyes, he lighted up the whole house like the sun, and the whole house was very bright.

3. And thereupon he arose in the hands of the midwoman, opened his mouth, and conversed with Yahuah Tsedâqâh.

4. And his father Lemek was afraid of him and fled, and came to his father Methûshelach.

5. And he said unto him: I have begotten a strange son, diverse from and unlike man, and resembling the sons of the Êlôhîym of shâmayim; and his nature is different and he is not like us, and his eyes are as the rays of the sun, and his countenance is glorious.

6. And it seems to me that he is not sprung from me but from the angels, and I fear that in his days a wonder may be wrought on the earth.

7. And now, my father, I am here to petition you and implore you that you may go to Chănôk, our father, and learn from him the truth, for his dwelling place is among the angels.

8. And when Methûshelach heard the words of his son, he came to me to the ends of the earth; for he had heard that I was there, and he cried aloud, and I heard his voice and I came to him. And said unto him: Behold, here am I, my son, wherefore you have come to me?

9. And he answered and said: Because of a great cause of anxiety I have come to you, and because of a disturbing vision I have approached.

10. And now, my father, hear me: Unto Lemek my son there has been born a son, the like of whom there is none, and his nature is not like man's nature, and the color of his body is whiter than snow and redder than the bloom of a rose, and the hair of his head is whiter than white wool, and his eyes are like the rays of the sun, and he opened his eyes and thereupon lighted up the whole house.

11. And he arose in the hands of the midwoman, and opened his mouth and blessed Yahuah of shâmayim.

12. And his father Lemek became afraid and fled to me, and did not believe that he was sprung from him, but that he was in the likeness of the angels of shâmayim; and behold I have come to you that you may make known to me the truth.

13. And I, Chănôk, answered and said unto him: Yahuah will do a new thing on the earth, and this I have already seen in a vision, and make known to you that in the generation of my father Yârad some of the angels of shâmayim transgressed the word of Yahuah.

14. And behold they commit sin and transgress the law, and have united themselves with women and commit sin with them, and have married some of them, and have begot children by them.

15. Yea, there shall come a great destruction over the whole earth, and there shall be a deluge and a great destruction for one year.

16. And this son who has been born unto you shall be left on the earth, and his three children shall be saved with him: When all mankind that are on the earth shall die, he and his sons shall be saved.

17. And they shall produce on the earth nephîyl not according to the spirit, but according to the flesh, and there shall be a great punishment on the earth, and the earth shall be cleansed from all impurity.

18. And now make known to your son Lemek that he who has been born is in truth his son, and call his name Nôach; for he shall be left to you, and he and his sons shall be saved from the destruction, which shall come upon the earth on account of all the sin and all the unrighteousness, which shall be consummated on the earth in his days.

19. And after that there shall be still more unrighteousness than that which was first consummated on the earth; for I know the mysteries of the qâdôsh ones; for he, Yahuah, has showed me and informed me, and I have read them in the shâmayim tablets.

Chapter 107

1. And I saw written on them that generation upon generation shall transgress, till a generation of righteousness arises, and transgression is destroyed and sin passes away from the earth, and all manner of good comes upon it.

2. And now, my son, go and make known to your son Lemek that this son, which has been born, is in truth his son, and that this is no lie.

3. And when Methûshelach had heard the words of his father Chănôk, for he had shown to him everything in secret, he returned and showed them to him and called the name of that son Nôach; for he will comfort the earth after all the destruction.

Part Seven

Chapters 108, An Appendix to the Book of Chănôk

Chapter 108

1. Another book which Chănôk wrote for his son Methûshelach and for those who will come after him, and keep the law in the last days.

2. You who have done good shall wait for those days till an end is made of those who work evil; and an end of the might of the transgressors.

3. And wait you indeed till sin has passed away, for their names shall be blotted out of the book of life and out of the qâdôsh books, and their seed shall be destroyed forever, and their spirits shall be slain, and they shall cry and make lamentation in a place that is a chaotic wilderness, and in the fire shall they burn; for there is no earth there.

4. And I saw there something like an invisible cloud; for because of its depth I could not look over, and I saw a flame of fire blazing brightly, and things like shining mountains circling and sweeping to and fro.

5. And I asked one of the qâdôsh angels who was with me and said unto him: What is this shining thing? For it is not a shâmayim but only the flame of a blazing fire, and the voice of weeping and crying and lamentation and strong pain.

6. And he said unto me: This place which you see here are cast the spirits of sinners and blasphemers, and of those who work wickedness, and of those who pervert everything that Yahuah has spoken through the mouth of the Nâbîy, even the things that shall be.

7. For some of them are written and inscribed above in the shâmayim, in order that the angels may read them and know that which shall befall the sinners, and the spirits of the humble, and of those who have afflicted their bodies, and been recompensed by Êlôhîym; and of those who have been put to shame by wicked men:

8. Who love Êlôhîym and loved neither gold nor silver nor any of the good things which are in the world, but gave over their bodies to torture.

9. Who, since they came into being, longed not after earthly food, but regarded everything as a passing breath, and lived accordingly, and Yahuah tried them much, and their spirits were found pure so that they should bless his name.

10. And all the blessings destined for them I have recounted in the books. And he has assigned them their recompense, because they have been found to be such as loved shâmayim more than their life in the world, and though they were trodden under foot of wicked men, and experienced abuse and reviling from them and were put to shame, yet they blessed me.

11. And now I will summon the spirits of the good who belong to the generation of light, and I will transform those who were born in darkness, who in the flesh were not recompensed with such honor as their faithfulness deserved.

12. And I will bring forth in shining light those who have loved my Qâdôsh name, and I will seat each on the throne of his honor.

13. And they shall be resplendent for times without number; for righteousness is the judgement of Êlôhîym; for to the faithful he will give faithfulness in the habitation of upright paths.

14. And they shall see those who were, born in darkness led into darkness, while the righteous shall be resplendent.

15. And the sinners shall cry aloud and see them resplendent, and they indeed will go where days and seasons are prescribed for them.

Translated by R. H. Charles, D.Litt., D.D.

Book of Jubilees & Berēshīth (Genesis) Parallels (Missing and Clarified Sections)

This study guide highlights the sections in the Book of Jubilees that clarify, expand, or provide missing details from the Book of Berēshīth (Genesis). The Book of Jubilees, sometimes called 'Little Berēshīth (Genesis),' retells Berēshīth (Genesis) with additional details about angels, covenants, laws, chronology, and patriarchal stories that are not found in Berēshīth (Genesis).

Comparison Table: Jubilees vs. Berēshīth (Genesis)

Jubilees Section	Berēshīth (Genesis) Parallel	Clarification / Expansion in Jubilees
Jub. 2	Gen 1–2	Angels created on Day 1; Shabbath sanctified from creation.
Jub. 3	Gen 2–3	Adam & Chawwâh stayed in Eden 7 years before sin; angels taught Adam farming.
Jub. 4	Gen 4–5	Precise dates for Qayin, **Shêth**; detailed genealogy.
Jub. 5	Gen 6–9	Watchers sinned with women; giants caused corruption leading to Flood.
Jub. 6	Gen 9	**Nôach's** covenant linked to Feast of Weeks (Shâbûa).
Jub. 7	Gen 9–10	Nôach gave laws: dietary rules, blood prohibition, morality.
Jub. 8–9	Gen 10	Nôach divided earth among **Shêm, Châm, Yepheth** with boundaries.
Jub. 8	Gen 11	Qeynan found writings of Watchers; forbidden knowledge.
Jub. 11–12	Gen 11–12	Abraham rejected idolatry, destroyed idols, prayed to Yahuah.
Jub. 14	Gen 15	Clarifies 400-year prophecy starts with Abraham, not just Mitsrayim.
Jub. 16–17	Gen 18–21	Details on Sarah's laughter; covenant of circumcision reaffirmed.
Jub. 17–18	Gen 22	Mastema (satanic figure) tested Abraham with Yitschâq's sacrifice.
Jub. 19–20	Gen 23	Abraham's farewell commands and ethical instructions.
Jub. 21–22	Gen 25	Abraham instructs Yitschâq/ Yaăqôb on offerings and priesthood.
Jub. 28–29	Gen 29–30	**Dîynâh's** story expanded; **Lêwîy** consecrated to priesthood.
Jub. 32	Gen 35	Yaăqôb's Bêythêl vision expanded; tithing and priesthood instructions.
Jub. 33–34	Gen 34	Lêwîy's priesthood justified through Dîynâh's avenging.
Jub. 44–45	Gen 37–50	Adds dates/timing of famine years; angelic help in Yôsêph's rise.
Jub. 50	Exod 20	Shabbâth laws expanded; Jubilee cycles (49 years) explained.

Key Themes of Jubilees Clarifications

1. Angels were present from the first day of creation, guiding humanity.

2. Jubilees provides precise chronology (years, jubilees, weeks) absent in Berēshīth (Genesis).

3. Watchers and giants are integrated into the Berēshīth (Genesis) flood story.

4. Covenants expanded: Nôach's covenant tied to Shâbûa; Abraham's clarified with exact years.

5. Mastema introduced as an adversary influencing sin and testing Abraham.

6. Laws (Shabbâth, circumcision, sacrifices, purity, and tithes) revealed before Sîynay.

7. Extra patriarchal stories: Abraham destroys idols, Yaăqôb consecrates **Lêwîy**, Nôach divides earth.

8. History structured by 49-year jubilee cycles, giving a calendar framework to Berēshīth (Genesis) events.

This is the history of the division of the days of the law and of the testimony, of the events of the years, of their (year) weeks, of their Jubilees throughout all the years of the world, as Yahuah spoke to Môsheh (מֹשֶׁה) on Mount Sîynay when he went up to receive the tables of the law and of the commandment, according to the voice of Êlôhîym as he said unto him: Go up to the top of the Mount.

Sêpher (סֵפֶר) Yôbêl (יוֹבֵל) – Book of Jubilee

(The Book of Jubilees - by R.H. Charles, Oxford: Clarendon Press, 1913)

Chapter 1

1. And it came to pass in the first year of the exodus of the children of Yâshârêl (יִשְׂרָאֵל) out of Mitsrayim (מִצְרַיִם), in the third month, on the sixteenth day of the month, that Êlôhîym spoke to Môsheh, saying: Come up to me on the Mount, and I will give you two tables of stone of the law and of the commandment, which I have written, that you may teach them.

2. And Môsheh went up into the mount of Êlôhîym, and the glory of Yahuah abode on Mount Sîynay, and a cloud overshadowed it six days.

3. And he called to Môsheh on the seventh day out of the midst of the cloud, and the appearance of the glory of Yahuah was like a flaming fire on the top of the mount.

4. And Môsheh was on the Mount forty days and forty nights, and Êlôhîym taught him the earliest and the later history of the division of all the days of the law and of the testimony.

5. And he said: Incline your heart to every word which I shall speak to you on this mount, and write them in a book in order that their generations may see how I have not forsaken them for all the evil which they have wrought in transgressing the covenant which I establish between me and you for their generations this day on Mount Sîynay.

6. And thus it will come to pass when all these things come upon them, that they will recognize that I am more righteous than they in all their judgments and in all their actions, and they will recognize that I have been truly with them.

7. And you do write for yourself all these words which I declare unto you this day, for I know their rebellion and their stiff neck, before I bring them into the land of which I swore to their fathers, to Abrâhâm and to Yitschâq (צְחָק) and to Yaăqôb (יַעֲקֹב), saying: Unto your seed I will give a land flowing with milk and honey.

8. And they will eat and be satisfied, and they will turn to strange gods, to gods which cannot deliver them from aught of their tribulation: And this witness shall be heard for a witness against them.

9. For they will forget all my commandments, all that I command them, and they will walk after the Gentiles, and after their uncleanness, and after their shame, and will serve their gods, and these will prove unto them an offence and a tribulation and an affliction and a snare.

10. And many will perish and they will be taken captive, and will fall into the hands of the enemy, because they have forsaken my ordinances and my commandments, and the festivals of my covenant, and my Shabbâth (שַׁבָּת), and my qâdôsh place which I have hallowed for myself in their midst, and my tabernacle, and my sanctuary, which I have hallowed for myself in the midst of the land,

that I should set my name upon it, and that it should dwell there.

11. And they will make to themselves high places and ăshêrâh (אֲשֵׁרָה) and graven images, and they will worship, each his own graven image, so as to go astray, and they will sacrifice their children to demons, and to all the works of the error of their hearts.

12. And I will send witnesses unto them that I may witness against them but they will not hear, and will slay the witnesses also, and they will persecute those who seek the law, and they will abrogate and change everything so as to work evil before my eyes.

13. And I will hide my face from them, and I will deliver them into the hand of the Gentiles for captivity, and for a prey, and for devouring, and I will remove them from the midst of the land, and I will scatter them among the Gentiles.

14. And they will forget all my law and all my commandments and all my judgments, and will go astray as to new moons, and Shabbâth, and festivals, and jubilees, and ordinances.

15. And after this they will turn to me from among the Gentiles with all their heart and with all their soul and with all their strength, and I will gather them from among all the Gentiles, and they will seek me, so that I shall be found of them, when they seek me with all their heart and with all their soul.

16. And I will disclose to them abounding peace with righteousness, and I will remove them, the plant of uprightness, with all my heart and with all my soul, and they shall be for a blessing and not for a curse, and they shall be the head and not the tail.

17. And I will build my sanctuary in their midst, and I will dwell with them, and I will be their Êlôhîym and they shall be my people in truth and righteousness.

18. And I will not forsake them nor fail them; for I am Yahuah their Êlôhîym.

19. And Môsheh fell on his face and prayed and said, O Yahuah my Êlôhîym, do not forsake your people and your inheritance, so that they should wander in the error of their hearts, and do not deliver them into the hands of their enemies, the Gentiles, lest they should rule over them and cause them to sin against you.

20. Let your mercy, O Yahuah, be lifted up upon your people, and create in them an upright spirit, and do not let the spirit of Belîyaal (בְּלִיַּעַל) rule over them to accuse them before you, and to ensnare them from all the paths of righteousness, so that they may perish from before your face.

21. But they are your people and your inheritance, which you have delivered with your great power from the hands of the Mitsrîy (מִצְרִי): Create in them a clean heart and a qâdôsh spirit, and let them not be ensnared in their sins from henceforth until eternity.

22. And Yahuah said unto Môsheh: I know their contrariness and their thoughts and their stiffneckedness, and they will not be obedient till they confess their own sin and the sin of their fathers.

23. And after this they will turn to me in all uprightness and with all their heart and with all their soul, and I will circumcise the foreskin of their heart and the foreskin of the heart of their seed, and I will create in them a qâdôsh spirit, and I will cleanse them so that they shall not turn away from me from that day unto eternity.

24. And their souls will cleave to me and to all my commandments, and they will

fulfil my commandments, and I will be their father and they shall be my children.

25. And they all shall be called children of the living Êlôhîym, and every angel and every spirit shall know, yea, they shall know that these are my children, and that I am their father in uprightness and righteousness, and that I love them.

26. And you do write down for yourself all these words which I declare unto you on this mountain, the first and the last, which shall come to pass in all the divisions of the days in the law and in the testimony and in the weeks and the jubilees unto eternity, until I descend and dwell with them throughout eternity.

27. And he said to the angel of the presence: Write for Môsheh from the beginning of creation till my sanctuary has been built among them for all eternity.

28. And Yahuah will appear to the eyes of all, and all shall know that I am the Êlôhîym of Yâshârêl and the father of all the children of Yaăqôb, and Melek on Mount Tsîyôn (צִיּוֹן) for all eternity. And Tsîyôn and Yerûshâlaim (יְרוּשָׁלַםִ) shall be qâdôsh.

29. And the angel of the presence who went before the camp of Yâshârêl took the tables of the divisions of the years from the time of the creation of the law and of the testimony of the weeks of the jubilees, according to the individual years, according to all the number of the jubilees, from the day of the creation when the shâmayim and the earth shall be renewed and all their creation according to the powers of the shâmayim, and according to all the creation of the earth, until the sanctuary of Yahuah shall be made in Yarûshâlaim on Mount Tsîyôn, and all the luminaries be renewed for healing and for peace and for blessing for all the elect of Yâshârêl, and that thus it may be from that day and unto all the days of the earth.

Chapter 2

1. And the angel of the presence spoke to Môsheh according to the word of Yahuah, saying: Write the complete history of the creation, how in six days Yahuah Êlôhîym finished all his works and all that he created, and kept Shabbâth on the seventh day and hallowed it for all ages, and appointed it as a sign for all his works.

2. For on the first day he created the shâmayim which are above and the earth and the waters and all the spirits which serve before him, the angels of the presence, and the angels of sanctification, and the angels of the spirit of fire and the angels of the spirit of the winds, and the angels of the spirit of the clouds, and of darkness, and of snow and of hail and of hoar frost, and the angels of the voices and of the thunder and of the lightning, and the angels of the spirits of cold and of heat, and of winter and of spring and of autumn and of summer and of all the spirits of his creatures which are in the shâmayim and on the earth, he created the abysses and the darkness, eventide and night, and the light, dawn and day, which he has prepared in the knowledge of his heart.

3. And thereupon we saw his works, and praised him, and lauded before him on account of all his works; for seven great works he did create on the first day.

4. And on the second day he created the firmament in the midst of the waters, and the waters were divided on that day, half of them went up above and half of them went down below the firmament that was in the midst over the face of the whole earth. And this was the only work Êlôhîym created on the second day.

5. And on the third day he commanded the waters to pass from off the face of the whole

earth into one place, and the dry land to appear.

6. And the waters did so as he commanded them, and they retired from off the face of the earth into one place outside of this firmament, and the dry land appeared.

7. And on that day he created for them all the seas according to their separate gathering places, and all the rivers, and the gatherings of the waters in the mountains and on all the earth, and all the lakes, and all the dew of the earth, and the seed which is sown, and all sprouting things, and fruit bearing trees, and trees of the wood, and the Garden of Eden, in Eden and all *plants after their kind*.

8. These four great works Êlôhîym created on the third day. And on the fourth day he created the sun and the moon and the stars, and set them in the firmament of the shâmayim, to give light upon all the earth, and to rule over the day and the night, and divide the light from the darkness.

9. And Êlôhîym appointed the sun to be a great sign on the earth for days and for Shabbâth and for months and for feasts and for years and for Shabbâth of years and for jubilees and for all seasons of the years.

10. And it divides the light from the darkness and for prosperity, that all things may prosper which shoot and grow on the earth.

11. These three kinds he made on the fourth day. And on the fifth day he created great sea monsters in the depths of the waters, for these were the first things of flesh that were created by his hands, the fish and everything that moves in the waters, and everything that flies, the birds and all their kind.

12. And the sun rose above them to prosper them, and above everything that was on the earth, everything that shoots out of the earth, and all fruit bearing trees, and all flesh.

13. These three kinds he created on the fifth day. And on the sixth day he created all the animals of the earth, and all cattle, and everything that moves on the earth.

14. And after all this he created man, a man and a woman he created them, and gave him dominion over all that is upon the earth, and in the seas, and over everything that flies, and over beasts and over cattle, and over everything that moves on the earth, and over the whole earth, and over all this he gave him dominion.

15. And these four kinds he created on the sixth day. And there were altogether two and twenty kinds.

16. And he finished all his work on the sixth day, all that is in the shâmayim and on the earth, and in the seas and in the abysses, and in the light and in the darkness, and in everything.

17. And he gave us a great sign, the Shabbâth day, that we should work six days, but keep Shabbâth on the seventh day from all work.

18. And all the angels of the presence, and all the angels of sanctification, these two great classes, he has bidden us to keep the Shabbâth with him in shâmayim and on earth.

19. And he said unto us: Behold, I will separate unto myself a people from among all the peoples, and these shall keep the Shabbâth day, and I will sanctify them unto myself as my people, and will bless them; as I have sanctified the Shabbâth day and do sanctify it unto myself, even so I will bless them, and they shall be my people and I will be their Êlôhîym.

20. And I have chosen the seed of Yaăqôb from among all that I have seen, and have written

him down as my first born son, and have sanctified him unto myself forever and ever; and I will teach them the Shabbâth day, that they may keep Shabbâth thereon from all work.

21. And thus he created therein a sign in accordance with which they should keep Shabbâth with us on the seventh day, to eat and to drink, and to bless him who has created all things as he has blessed and sanctified unto himself a peculiar people above all peoples, and that they should keep Shabbâth together with us.

22. And he caused his commands to ascend as a sweet savor acceptable before him all the days.

23. There were two and twenty heads of mankind from Âdâm to Yaăqôb, and two and twenty kinds of work were made until the seventh day; this is blessed and qâdôsh; and the former also is blessed and qâdôsh; and this one serves with that one for sanctification and blessing.

24. And to this, Yaăqôb and his seed, it was granted that they should always be the blessed and qâdôsh of the first testimony and law, even as he had sanctified and blessed the Shabbâth day on the seventh day.

25. He created shâmayim and earth and everything that he created in six days, and Êlôhîym made the seventh day qâdôsh, for all his works; therefore he commanded on its behalf that, whoever does any work thereon shall die, and that he who defiles it shall surely die.

26. Wherefore you do command the children of Yâshârêl to observe this day that they may keep it qâdôsh and not do thereon any work, and not to defile it, as it is holier than all other days.

27. And whoever profanes it shall surely die, and whoever does thereon any work shall surely die eternally, that the children of Yâshârêl may observe this day throughout their generations, and not be rooted out of the land; for it is a qâdôsh day and a blessed day.

28. And every one who observes it and keeps Shabbâth thereon from all his work, will be qâdôsh and blessed throughout all days like unto us.

29. Declare and say to the children of Yâshârêl the law of this day both that they should keep Shabbâth thereon, and that they should not forsake it in the error of their hearts; and that it is not lawful to do any work thereon which is unseemly, to do thereon their own pleasure, and that they should not prepare thereon anything to be eaten or drunk, and that it is not lawful to draw water, or bring in or take out thereon through their gates any burden, which they had not prepared for themselves on the sixth day in their dwellings.

30. And they shall not bring in nor take out from house to house on that day; for that day is more qâdôsh and blessed than any jubilee day of the jubilees; on this we kept Shabbâth in the shâmayim before it was made known to any flesh to keep Shabbâth thereon on the earth.

31. And the Bârâ of all things blessed it, but he did not sanctify all peoples and nations to keep Shabbâth thereon, but Yâshârêl alone: Them alone he permitted to eat and drink and to keep Shabbâth thereon on the earth.

32. And the Bârâ (בְּרָא) of all things blessed this day which he had created for blessing and qôdesh and glory above all days.

33. This law and testimony was given to the children of Yâshârêl as a law forever unto their generations.

Chapter 3

1. And on the six days of the second week we brought, according to the word of Êlôhîym, unto Âdâm all the beasts, and all the cattle, and all the birds, and everything that moves on the earth, and everything that moves in the water, according to their kinds, and according to their types: the beasts on the first day; the cattle on the second day; the birds on the third day; and all that which moves on the earth on the fourth day; and that which moves in the water on the fifth day.

2. And Âdâm named them all by their respective names, and as he called them, so was their name.

3. And on these five days Âdâm saw all these, male and female, according to every kind that was on the earth, but he was alone and found no helpmeet for him.

4. And Yahuah said unto us: It is not good that the man should be alone: Let us make a helpmeet for him.

5. And Yahuah our Êlôhîym caused a deep sleep to fall upon him, and he slept, and he took for the woman one rib from among his ribs, and this rib was the origin of the woman from among his ribs, and he built up the flesh in its stead, and built the woman.

6. And he awoke Âdâm out of his sleep and on awaking he rose on the sixth day, and he brought her to him, and he knew her, and said unto her: This is now bone of my bones and flesh of my flesh; she shall be called my woman; because she was taken from her husband.

7. Therefore shall man and woman be one and therefore shall a man leave his father and his mother, and cleave unto his woman, and they shall be one flesh.

8. In the first week was Âdâm created, and the rib, his woman, in the second week he showed her unto him: And for this reason the commandment was given to keep in their defilement, for a male seven days, and for a female twice seven days.

9. And after Âdâm had completed forty days in the land where he had been created, we brought him into the Garden of Eden to till and keep it, but his woman they brought in on the eightieth day, and after this she entered into the Garden of Eden.

10. And for this reason the commandment is written on the shâmayim tablets in regard to her that gives birth: If she bears a male, she shall remain in her uncleanness seven days according to the first week of days, and thirty and three days she shall remain in the blood of her purifying, and she shall not touch any hallowed thing, nor enter into the sanctuary, until she accomplishes these days which are enjoined in the case of a male child.

11. But in the case of a female child she shall remain in her uncleanness two weeks of days, according to the first two weeks, and sixty six days in the blood of her purification, and they will be in all eighty days.

12. And when she had completed these eighty days we brought her into the Garden of Eden, for it is holier than all the earth besides and every tree that is planted in it is qâdôsh.

13. Therefore, there was ordained regarding her who bears a male or a female child the statute of those days that she should touch no hallowed thing, nor enter into the sanctuary until these days for the male or female child are accomplished.

14. This is the law and testimony which was written down for Yâshârêl, in order that they should observe it all the days.

15. And in the first week of the first jubilee, Âdâm and his woman were in the Garden of Eden for seven years tilling and keeping it, and we gave him work and we instructed him to do everything that is suitable for tillage.

16. And he tilled, and was naked and did not know it, and was not ashamed, and he protected the Garden from the birds and beasts and cattle, and gathered its fruit, and eat, and put aside the residue for himself and for his woman and put aside that which was being kept.

17. And after the completion of the seven years, which he had completed there, seven years exactly, and in the second month, on the seventeenth day of the month, the Nâchâsh (נָחָשׁ) came and approached the woman, and the Nâchâsh said to the woman, has Êlôhîym commanded you, saying, you shall not eat of every tree of the Garden?

18. And she said to it, of all the fruit of the trees of the Garden Êlôhîym has said unto us, eat; but of the fruit of the tree which is in the midst of the Garden Êlôhîym has said unto us, shall not eat thereof, neither shall you touch it, lest you die.

19. And the Nâchâsh said unto the woman, you shall not surely die: For Êlôhîym does know that on the day you shall eat thereof, your eyes will be opened, and you will be as gods, and you will know good and evil.

20. And the woman saw the tree that it was agreeable and pleasant to the eye, and that its fruit was good for food, and she took thereof and ate.

21. And when she had first covered her shame with fig leaves, she gave thereof to Âdâm and he ate, and his eyes were opened, and he saw that he was naked.

22. And he took fig leaves and sewed them together, and made an apron for himself, and covered his shame.

23. And Êlôhîym cursed the Nâchâsh, and was wroth with it forever.

24. And he was wroth with the woman, because she harkened to the voice of the Nâchâsh, and did eat; and he said unto her: I will greatly multiply your sorrow and your pains: In sorrow you shall bring forth children, and your return shall be unto your husband, and he will rule over you.

25. And to Âdâm also he said, because you have harkened unto the voice of your woman, and have eaten of the tree of which I commanded you that you should not eat thereof, cursed be the ground for your sake: thorns and thistles shall it bring forth to you, and you shall eat your bread in the sweat of your face, till you return to the earth from whence you were taken; for earth you are, and unto earth you shall return.

26. And he made for them coats of skin, and clothed them, and sent them forth from the Garden of Eden.

27. And on that day on which Âdâm went forth from the Garden, he offered as a sweet savor an offering, lebônâh, galbanum, and stacte, and spices in the morning with the rising of the sun from the day when he covered his shame.

28. And on that day was closed the mouth of all beasts, and of cattle, and of birds, and of whatever walks, and of whatever moves, so that they could no longer speak: For they had all spoken one with another with one lip and with one tongue.

29. And he sent out of the Garden of Eden all flesh that was in the Garden of Eden, and all flesh was scattered according to its kinds,

and according to its types unto the places which had been created for them.

30. And to Âdâm alone he did give the wherewithal to cover his shame, of all the beasts and cattle.

31. On this account, it is prescribed on the shâmayim tablets as touching all those who know the judgment of the law that they should cover their shame, and should not uncover themselves as the Gentiles uncover themselves.

32. And on the beginning of the fourth month, Âdâm and his woman went forth from the Garden of Eden, and they dwelt in the land of Eldâ in the land of their creation.

33. And Âdâm called the name of his women Chawwâh (חַוָּה).

34. And they had no son till the first jubilee, and after this he knew her.

35. Now he tilled the land as he had been instructed in the Garden of Eden.

Chapter 4

1. And in the third week in the second jubilee she gave birth to Qayin, and in the fourth she gave birth to Hebel, and in the fifth she gave birth to her daughter Âwân.

2. And in the first year of the third jubilee, Qayin slew Hebel because Êlôhîym accepted the sacrifice of Hebel, and did not accept the offering of Qayin.

3. And he slew him in the field: And his blood cried from the ground to shâmayim, complaining because he had slain him.

4. And Yahuah reproved Qayin because of Hebel, because he had slain him, and he made him a fugitive on the earth because of the blood of his brother, and he cursed him upon the earth.

5. And on this account it is written on the shâmayim tables, cursed is he who smites his neighbor treacherously, and let all who have seen and heard say, so be it; and the man who has seen and not declared it, let him be accursed as the other.

6. And for this reason we announce when we come before Yahuah our Êlôhîym all the sin which is committed in shâmayim and on earth, and in light and in darkness, and everywhere.

7. And Âdâm and his woman mourned for Hebel four weeks of years, and in the fourth year of the fifth week they became joyful, and Âdâm knew his woman again, and she bare him a son, and he called his name Shêth; for he said Êlôhîym has raised up a second seed unto us on the earth instead of Hebel; for Qayin slew him.

8. And in the sixth week he begat his daughter Azûrâ.

9. And Qayin took Âwân his sister to be his woman and she bare him Chănôk at the close of the fourth jubilee. And in the first year of the first week of the fifth jubilee, houses were built on the earth, and Qayin built a city, and called its name after the name of his son Chănôk.

10. And Âdâm knew Chawwâh his woman and she bare yet nine sons.

11. And in the fifth week of the fifth jubilee Shêth took Azûrâ his sister to be his woman, and in the fourth year of the sixth week she bare him Ĕnôsh (אֱנוֹשׁ).

12. He began to call on the name of Yahuah on the earth.

13. And in the seventh jubilee in the third week Ĕnôsh took Nôâm his sister to be his woman, and she bare him a son in the third year of the fifth week, and he called his name Qêynân (קֵינָן).

14. And at the close of the eighth jubilee Qêynân took Mûalêlêth his sister to be his woman, and she bare him a son in the ninth jubilee, in the first week in the third year of this week, and he called his name Mahălalêl.

15. And in the second week of the tenth jubilee Mahălalêl took unto him to woman Dîynâh (דִינָה), the daughter of Barâkîêl, the daughter of his father's brother, and she bare him a son in the third week in the sixth year, and he called his name Yârad, for in his days the angels of Yahuah descended on the earth, those who are named the Watchers, that they should instruct the children of men, and that they should do judgment and uprightness on the earth.

16. And in the eleventh jubilee Yârad took to himself a woman, and her name was Bâraka, the daughter of Râsûyâl, a daughter of his father's brother, in the fourth week of this jubilee, and she bare him a son in the fifth week, in the fourth year of the jubilee, and he called his name Chănôk.

17. And he was the first among men that are born on earth who learnt writing and knowledge and wisdom and who wrote down the signs of shâmayim according to the order of their months in a book that men might know the seasons of the years according to the order of their separate months.

18. And he was the first to write a testimony and he testified to the sons of men among the generations of the earth, and recounted the weeks of the jubilees, and made known to them the days of the years, and set in order the months and recounted the Shabbâth of the years as we made them, known to him.

19. And what was and what will be he saw in a vision of his sleep, as it will happen to the children of men throughout their generations until the Day of Judgment; he saw and understood everything, and wrote his testimony, and placed the testimony on earth for all the children of men and for their generations.

20. And in the twelfth jubilee, in the seventh week thereof, he took to himself a woman, and her name was Ednî, the daughter of Dânêl, the daughter of his father's brother, and in the sixth year in this week she bare him a son and he called his name Methûshelach.

21. And he was moreover with the angels of Êlôhîym these six jubilees of years, and they showed him everything which is on earth and in the shâmayim, the rule of the sun, and he wrote down everything.

22. And he testified to the Watchers, who had sinned with the daughters of men; for these had begun to unite themselves, so as to be defiled, with the daughters of men, and Chănôk testified against them all.

23. And he was taken from among the children of men, and we conducted him into the Garden of Eden in majesty and honor, and behold there he writes down the condemnation and judgment of the world, and all the wickedness of the children of men.

24. And on account of it, Êlôhîym brought the waters of the flood upon all the land of Eden; for there he was set as a sign and that he should testify against all the children of men, that he should recount all the deeds of the generations until the day of condemnation.

25. And he burnt the incense of the sanctuary, even sweet spices acceptable before Yahuah on the Mount.

26. For Yahuah has four places on the earth, the Garden of Eden, and the Mount of the East, and this mountain on which you are this day, Mount Sîynay, and Mount Tsîyôn which will be sanctified in the new creation

for a sanctification of the earth; through it will the earth be sanctified from all its guilt and its uncleanness throughout the generations of the world.

27. And in the fourteenth jubilee Methûshelach took unto himself a woman, Ednâ the daughter of Azrîyêl (עֲזְרִיאֵל), the daughter of his father's brother, in the third week, in the first year of this week, and he begat a son and called his name Lemek.

28. And in the fifteenth jubilee in the third week Lemek took to himself a woman, and her name was Bêtênôs the daughter of Bârâki'îl, the daughter of his father's brother, and in this week she bare him a son and he called his name Nôach, saying, this one will comfort me for my trouble and all my work, and for the ground which Yahuah has cursed.

29. And at the close of the nineteenth jubilee, in the seventh week in the sixth year thereof, Âdâm died, and all his sons buried him in the land of his creation, and he was the first to be buried in the earth.

30. And he lacked seventy years of one thousand years; for one thousand years are as one day in the testimony of the shâmayim and therefore was it written concerning the tree of knowledge: On the day that you eat thereof you shall die. For this reason he did not complete the years of this day; for he died during it.

31. At the close of this jubilee Qayin was killed after him in the same year; for his house fell upon him and he died in the midst of his house, and he was killed by its stones; for with a stone he had killed Hebel, and by a stone was he killed in righteous judgment.

32. For this reason it was ordained on the shâmayim tablets: With the instrument with which a man kills his neighbor with the same shall he be killed; after the manner that he wounded him, in like manner shall they deal with him.

33. And in the twenty fifth jubilee Nôach took to himself a woman, and her name was Emzârâ, the daughter of Râkêêl, the daughter of his father's brother, in the first year in the fifth week: and in the third year thereof she bare him Shêm, in the fifth year thereof she bare him Châm (חָם), and in the first year in the sixth week she bare him Yapheth (יֶפֶת).

Chapter 5

1. And it came to pass when the children of men began to multiply on the face of the earth and daughters were born unto them, that the angels of Êlôhîym saw them on a certain year of this jubilee, that they were beautiful to look upon; and they took themselves women of all whom they chose, and they bare unto them sons and they were nephîyl.

2. And lawlessness increased on the earth and all flesh corrupted its way, alike men and cattle and beasts and birds and everything that walks on the earth, all of them corrupted their ways and their orders, and they began to devour each other, and lawlessness increased on the earth and every imagination of the thoughts of all men was thus evil continually.

3. And Êlôhîym looked upon the earth, and behold it was corrupt, and all flesh had corrupted its orders, and all that were upon the earth had wrought all manner of evil before his eyes.

4. And he said that he would destroy man and all flesh upon the face of the earth which he had created.

5. But Nôach found grace before the eyes of Yahuah.

6. And against the angels whom he had sent upon the earth, he was exceedingly wroth, and he gave commandment to root them out of all their dominion, and he bid us to bind them in the depths of the earth, and behold they are bound in the midst of them, and are kept separate.

7. And against their sons went forth a command from before his face that they should be smitten with the sword, and be removed from under shâmayim.

8. And he said: My spirit shall not always abide on man; for they also are flesh and their days shall be one hundred and twenty years.

9. And he sent his sword into their midst that each should slay his neighbor, and they began to slay each other till they all fell by the sword and were destroyed from the earth.

10. And their fathers were witnesses of their destruction, and after this they were bound in the depths of the earth forever, until the day of the great condemnation, when judgment is executed on all those who have corrupted their ways and their works before Yahuah.

11. And he destroyed all from their places, and there was not left one of them whom he did not judge according to all their wickedness.

12. And he made for all his works a new and righteous nature, so that they should not sin in their whole nature forever, but should be all righteous each in his kind always.

13. And the judgment of all is ordained and written on the shâmayim tablets in righteousness, even the judgment of all who depart from the path which is ordained for them to walk in; and if they walk not therein, judgment is written down for every creature and forevery kind.

14. And there is nothing in shâmayim or on earth, or in light or in darkness, or in Sheôl or in the depth, or in the place of darkness which is not judged; and all their judgments are ordained and written and engraved.

15. In regard to all he will judge, the great according to his greatness, and the small according to his smallness, and each according to his way.

16. And he is not one who will regard the person of any, nor is he one who will receive gifts, if he says that he will execute judgment on each: If one gave everything that is on the earth, he will not regard the gifts or the person of any, nor accept anything at his hands, for he is a righteous judge.

17. And of the children of Yâshârêl it has been written and ordained: If they turn to him in righteousness he will forgive all their transgressions and pardon all their sins.

18. It is written and ordained that he will show mercy to all who turn from all their guilt once each year.

19. And as for all those who corrupted their ways and their thoughts before the flood, no man's person was accepted save that of Nôach alone; for his person was accepted in behalf of his sons, whom Êlôhîym saved from the waters of the flood on his account; for his heart was righteous in all his ways, according as it was commanded regarding him, and he had not departed from nothing that was ordained for him.

20. And Yahuah said that he would destroy everything which was upon the earth, both men and cattle, and beasts, and fowls of the air, and that which moves on the earth.

21. And he commanded Nôach to make him an ark that he might save himself from the waters of the flood.

22. And Nôach made the ark in all respects as he commanded him, in the twenty seventh jubilee of years, in the fifth week in the fifth year on the beginning of the first month.

23. And he entered in the sixth year thereof, in the second month, on the beginning of the second month, till the sixteenth; and he entered, and all that we brought to him, into the ark, and Yahuah closed it from without on the seventeenth evening.

24. And Yahuah opened seven flood gates of shâmayim, and the mouths of the fountains of the great deep, seven mouths in number.

25. And the flood gates began to pour down water from the shâmayim forty days and forty nights, and the fountains of the deep also sent up waters, until the whole world was full of water.

26. And the waters increased upon the earth: Fifteen cubits did the waters rise above all the high mountains, and the ark was lift up above the earth, and it moved upon the face of the waters.

27. And the water prevailed on the face of the earth five months, one hundred and fifty days.

28. And the ark went and rested on the top of Lûbâr, one of the mountains of Ărâraṭ.

29. And on the beginning in the fourth month the fountains of the great deep were closed and the flood gates of shâmayim were restrained; and on the beginning of the seventh month all the mouths of the abysses of the earth were opened, and the water began to descend into the deep below.

30. And on the beginning of the tenth month the tops of the mountains were seen, and on the beginning of the first month the earth became visible.

31. And the waters disappeared from above the earth in the fifth week in the seventh year thereof, and on the seventeenth day in the second month the earth was dry.

32. And on the twenty seventh thereof he opened the ark, and sent forth from it beasts, and cattle, and birds, and every moving thing.

Chapter 6

1. And on the beginning of the third month he went forth from the ark, and built an altar on that mountain.

2. And he made atonement for the earth, and took a kid and made atonement by its blood for all the guilt of the earth; for everything that had been on it had been destroyed, save those that were in the ark with Nôach.

3. And he placed the fat thereof on the altar, and he took an ox, and a goat, and a sheep and kids, and salt, and a turtle dove, and the young of a dove, and placed a burnt sacrifice on the altar, and poured thereon an offering mingled with oil, and sprinkled wine and strewed lebônâh over everything, and caused a goodly savor to arise, acceptable before Yahuah.

4. And Yahuah smelt the goodly savor, and he made a covenant with him that there should not be any more a flood to destroy the earth; that all the days of the earth seed time and harvest should never cease; cold and heat, and summer and winter, and day and night should not change their order, nor cease forever.

5. And you, you increase and multiply upon the earth, and become many upon it, and be a blessing upon it. The fear of you and the dread of you I will inspire in everything that is on earth and in the sea.

6. And behold I have given unto you all beasts, and all winged things, and everything that moves on the earth, and the fish in the waters, and all things for food; as the green herbs, I have given you all things to eat.

7. But flesh, with the life thereof, with the blood, you shall not eat; for the life of all flesh is in the blood, lest your blood of your lives be required. At the hand of every man, at the hand of every beast I will require the blood of man.

8. Whoso sheds man's blood by man shall his blood be shed, for in the image of Êlôhîym, he made man.

9. And you, you increase, and multiply on the earth.

10. And Nôach and his sons swore that they would not eat any blood that was in any flesh, and he made a covenant before Yahuah Êlôhîym forever throughout all the generations of the earth in this month.

11. On this account he spoke to you that you should make a covenant with the children of Yâshârêl in this month upon the mountain with an oath, and that you should sprinkle blood upon them because of all the words of the covenant, which Yahuah made with them forever.

12. And this testimony is written concerning you that you should observe it continually, so that you should not eat on any day any blood of beasts or birds or cattle during all the days of the earth, and the man who eats the blood of beast or of cattle or of birds during all the days of the earth, he and his seed shall be rooted out of the land.

13. And you do command the children of Yâshârêl to eat no blood, so that their names and their seed may be before Yahuah our Êlôhîym continually.

14. And for this law there is no limit of days, for it is forever. They shall observe it throughout their generations, so that they may continue supplicating on your behalf with blood before the altar; every day and at the time of morning and evening they shall seek forgiveness on your behalf perpetually before Yahuah that they may keep it and not be rooted out.

15. And he gave to Nôach and his sons a sign that there should not be again a flood on the earth.

16. He set his bow in the cloud for a sign of the eternal covenant that there should not be again a flood on the earth to destroy it all the days of the earth.

17. For this reason it is ordained and written on the shâmayim tablets, that they should celebrate the feast of weeks in this month once a year, to renew the covenant every year.

18. And this whole festival was celebrated in shâmayim from the day of creation till the days of Nôach, twenty six jubilees and five weeks of years: and Nôach and his sons observed it for seven jubilees and one week of years, till the day of Nôach's death, and from the day of Nôach's death his sons did away with it until the days of Abrâhâm, and they ate blood.

19. But Abrâhâm observed it, and Yitschâq and Yaăqôb and his children observed it up to your days, and in your days the children of Yâshârêl forgot it until you celebrated it anew on this mountain.

20. And you do command the children of Yâshârêl to observe this festival in all their generations for a commandment unto them: One day in the year in this month they shall celebrate the festival.

21. For it is the Feast of weeks and the feast of first fruits: This feast is twofold and of a

double nature: According to what is written and engraved concerning it, celebrate it.

22. For I have written in the book of the first law, in that which I have written for you, that you should celebrate it in its season, one day in the year, and I explained to you its sacrifices that the children of Yâshârêl should remember and should celebrate it throughout their generations in this month, one day in every year.

23. And on the beginning of the first month, and on the beginning of the fourth month, and on the beginning of the seventh month, and on the beginning of the tenth month are the days of remembrance, and the days of the seasons in the four divisions of the year. These are written and ordained as a testimony forever.

24. And Nôach ordained them for himself as feasts for the generations forever, so that they have become thereby a memorial unto him.

25. And on the beginning of the first month he was bidden to make for himself an ark, and on that day the earth became dry and he opened the ark and saw the earth.

26. And on the beginning of the fourth month the mouths of the depths of the abyss beneath were closed. And on the beginning of the seventh month all the mouths of the abysses of the earth were opened, and the waters began to descend into them.

27. And on the beginning of the tenth month the tops of the mountains were seen, and Nôach was glad.

28. And on this account he ordained them for himself as feasts for a memorial forever, and thus are they ordained.

29. And they placed them on the shâmayim tablets, each had thirteen weeks; from one to another passed their memorial, from the first to the second, and from the second to the third, and from the third to the fourth.

30. And all the days of the commandment will be two and fifty weeks of days, and these will make the entire year complete. Thus it is engraved and ordained on the shâmayim tablets.

31. And there is no neglecting this commandment for a single year or from year to year.

32. And you command the children of Yâshârêl that they observe the years according to this reckoning, three hundred and sixty four days, and these will constitute a complete year, and they will not disturb its time from its days and from its feasts; for everything will fall out in them according to their testimony, and they will not leave out any day nor disturb any feasts.

33. But if they do neglect and do not observe them according to his commandment, then they will disturb all their seasons and the years will be dislodged from this order, and they will disturb the seasons and the years will be dislodged and they will neglect their ordinances.

34. And all the children of Yâshârêl will forget and will not find the path of the years, and will forget the new months, and seasons, and Shabbâth and they will go wrong as to all the order of the years.

35. For I know and from henceforth I will declare it unto you, and it is not of my own devising; for the book lies written before me, and on the shâmayim tablets the division of days is ordained, lest they forget the feasts of the covenant and walk according to the feasts of the Gentiles after their error and after their ignorance.

36. For there will be those who will assuredly make observations of the moon, how it disturbs the seasons and comes in from year to year ten days too soon.

37. For this reason the years will come upon them when they will disturb the order, and make an abominable day, the day of testimony, and an unclean day a feast day, and they will confound all the days, the qâdôsh with the unclean, and the unclean day with the qâdôsh; for they will go wrong as to the months and Shabbâth and feasts and jubilees.

38. For this reason I command and testify to you that you may testify to them; for after your death your children will disturb them, so that they will not make the year three hundred and sixty four days only, and for this reason they will go wrong as to the new months and seasons and Shabbâth and festivals, and they will eat all kinds of blood with all kinds of flesh.

Chapter 7

1. And in the seventh week in the first year thereof, in this jubilee, Nôach planted vines on the mountain on which the ark had rested, named Lûbâr, one of the Ărârat Mountains, and they produced fruit in the fourth year, and he guarded their fruit, and gathered it in this year in the seventh month.

2. And he made wine therefrom and put it into a vessel, and kept it until the fifth year, until the first day, on the beginning of the first month.

3. And he celebrated with joy the day of this feast, and he made a burnt sacrifice unto Yahuah, one young ox and one ram, and seven sheep, each a year old, and a kid of male goats, that he might make atonement thereby for himself and his sons.

4. And he prepared the kid first, and placed some of its blood on the flesh that was on the altar which he had made, and all the fat he laid on the altar where he made the burnt sacrifice, and the ox and the ram and the sheep, and he laid all their flesh upon the altar.

5. And he placed all their offerings mingled with oil upon it, and afterwards he sprinkled wine on the fire which he had previously made on the altar, and he placed incense on the altar and caused a sweet savor to ascend acceptable before Yahuah his Êlôhîym.

6. And he rejoiced and drank of this wine, he and his children with joy.

7. And it was evening, and he went into his tent, and being drunken he lay down and slept, and was uncovered in his tent as he slept.

8. And Châm saw Nôach his father naked, and went forth and told his two brethren without.

9. And Shêm took his garment and arose, he and Yapheth, and they placed the garment on their shoulders and went backward and covered the shame of their father, and their faces were backward.

10. And Nôach awoke from his sleep and knew all that his younger son had done unto him, and he cursed his son and said: Cursed be Kenaan (כְּנַעַן); an enslaved servant shall he be unto his brethren.

11. And he blessed Shêm, and said: Blessed be Yahuah Êlôhîym of Shêm, and Kenaan shall be his servant.

12. Êlôhîym shall enlarge Yapheth, and Êlôhîym shall dwell in the dwelling of Shêm, and Kenaan shall be his servant.

13. And Châm knew that his father had cursed his younger son, and he was displeased that he had cursed his son. And he parted from his father, he and his sons with him, Kûsh (כוש) and Mitsrayim and Pût and Kenaan.

14. And he built for himself a city and called its name after the name of his woman Nêêlâtâmâûk.

15. And Yapheth saw it, and became envious of his brother, and he too built for himself a city, and he called its name after the name of his woman Âdatanêsês.

16. And Shêm dwelt with his father Nôach, and he built a city close to his father on the mountain, and he too called its name after the name of his woman Sêdêqêtêlêbâb.

17. And behold these three cities are near Mount Lûbâr; Sêdêqêtêlêbâb fronting the mountain on its east; and Nêêlâtâmâûk on the south; Âdatanêsês towards the west.

18. And these are the sons of Shêm: Êylâm (עֵילָם), and Ashshûr, and Arpakshad, this son was born two years after the flood and Lûd, and Ărâm.

19. The sons of Yapheth: Gômer and Mâgôg and Mâday and Yâwân (יָוָן), Tûbal and Meshek and Tîyrâs: These are the sons of Nôach.

20. And in the twenty eighth jubilee Nôach began to enjoin upon his sons' sons the ordinances and commandments, and all the judgments that he knew, and he exhorted his sons to observe righteousness, and to cover the shame of their flesh, and to bless their Bârâ, and honor father and mother, and love their neighbor, and guard their souls from fornication and uncleanness and all iniquity.

21. For owing to these three things came the flood upon the earth, namely, owing to the fornication wherein the Watchers against the law of their ordinances went a whoring after the daughters of men, and took themselves women of all which they chose: and they made the beginning of uncleanness.

22. And they begat sons the Nâphîdîm, and they were all unlike, and they devoured one another: and the Nephîyl slew the Nâphîl, and the Nâphîl slew the Elyô, and the Elyô mankind, and one man another.

23. And every one sold himself to work iniquity and to shed much blood, and the earth was filled with iniquity.

24. And after this they sinned against the beasts and birds, and all that moves and walks on the earth: And much blood was shed on the earth, and every imagination and desire of men imagined vanity and evil continually.

25. And Yahuah destroyed everything from off the face of the earth; because of the wickedness of their deeds, and because of the blood which they had shed in the midst of the earth he destroyed everything.

26. And we were left, I and you, my sons, and everything that entered with us into the ark, and behold I see your works before me that you do not walk in righteousness: for in the path of destruction you have begun to walk, and you are parting one from another, and are envious one of another, and so it comes that you are not in harmony, my sons, each with his brother.

27. For I see, and behold the demons have begun their seductions against you and against your children and now I fear on your behalf, that after my death you will shed the blood of men upon the earth, and that you, too, will be destroyed from the face of the earth.

28. For whoso sheds man's blood, and whoso eats the blood of any flesh, shall all be destroyed from the earth.

29. And there shall not be left any man that eats blood, or that sheds the blood of man

on the earth, nor shall there be left to him any seed or descendants living under shâmayim; for into Sheôl they shall go, and into the place of condemnation they shall descend, and into the darkness of the deep they shall all be removed by a violent death.

30. There shall be no blood seen upon you of all the blood there shall be all the days in which you have killed any beasts or cattle or whatever flies upon the earth, and work you a good work to your souls by covering that which has been shed on the face of the earth.

31. And you shall not be like him who eats with blood, but guard yourselves that none may eat blood before you: Cover the blood, for thus I have been commanded to testify to you and your children, together with all flesh.

32. And do not suffer the soul to be eaten with the flesh, that your blood, which is your life, may not be required at the hand of any flesh that sheds it on the earth.

33. For the earth will not be clean from the blood which has been shed upon it; for only through the blood of him that shed it will the earth be purified throughout all its generations.

34. And now, my children, harken: Work judgment and righteousness that you may be planted in righteousness over the face of the whole earth, and your glory lifted up before my Êlôhîym, who saved me from the waters of the flood.

35. And behold, you will go and build for yourselves cities, and plant in them all the plants that are upon the earth, and moreover all fruit bearing trees.

36. For three years the fruit of everything that is eaten will not be gathered: and in the fourth year its fruit will be accounted qâdôsh and they will offer the first fruits, acceptable before Êlôhîym Elyôn Êl, who created shâmayim and earth and all things. Let them offer in abundance the first of the wine and oil as first fruits on the altar of Yahuah, who receives it, and what is left let the servants of the house of Yahuah eat before the altar which receives it.

37. And in the fifth year you make the release so that you release it in righteousness and uprightness, and you shall be righteous, and all that you plant shall prosper.

38. For thus did Chănôk, the father of your father command Methûshelach, his son, and Methûshelach his son Lemek, and Lemek commanded me all the things which his fathers commanded him.

39. And I also will give you commandment, my sons, as Chănôk commanded his son in the first jubilees: while still living, the seventh in his generation, he commanded and testified to his son and to his son's sons until the day of his death.

Chapter 8

1. In the twenty ninth jubilee, in the first week, in the beginning thereof Arpakshad took to himself a woman and her name was Râsûêyâ, the daughter of Shûshan (שׁוּשָׁן), the daughter of Êylâm, and she bare him a son in the third year in this week, and he called his name Qêynân.

2. And the son grew, and his father taught him writing, and he went to seek for himself a place where he might seize for himself a city.

3. And he found a writing which former generations had carved on the rock, and he read what was thereon, and he transcribed it and sinned owing to it; for it contained the teaching of the Watchers in accordance with which they used to observe the omens of the sun and moon and stars in all the signs of shâmayim.

4. And he wrote it down and said nothing regarding it; for he was afraid to speak to Nôach about it lest he should be angry with him on account of it.

5. And in the thirtieth jubilee, in the second week, in the first year thereof, he took to himself a woman, and her name was Mêlkâ, the daughter of Mâday, the son of Yapheth, and in the fourth year he begat a son, and called his name Shêlâh; for he said: Truly I have been sent.

6. And in the fourth year he was born, and Shêlâh grew up and took to himself a woman, and her name was Mûak, the daughter of Keśed, his father's brother, in the one and thirtieth jubilee, in the fifth week, in the first year thereof.

7. And she bare him a son in the fifth year thereof, and he called his name Êber: And he took unto himself a woman, and her name was Azûrâd, the daughter of Nêbrôd, in the thirty second jubilee, in the seventh week, in the third year thereof.

8. And in the sixth year thereof, she bare him son, and he called his name Peleg; for in the days when he was born the children of Nôach began to divide the earth among themselves: For this reason he called his name Peleg.

9. And they divided it secretly among themselves, and told it to Nôach.

10. And it came to pass in the beginning of the thirty third jubilee that they divided the earth into three parts, for Shêm and Châm and Yapheth, according to the inheritance of each, in the first year in the first week, when one of us who had been sent, was with them.

11. And he called his sons, and they drew nigh to him, they and their children, and he divided the earth into the lots, which his three sons were to take in possession, and they reached forth their hands, and took the writing out of the bosom of Nôach, their father.

12. And there came forth on the writing as Shêm's lot the middle of the earth which he should take as an inheritance for himself and for his sons for the generations of eternity, from the middle of the mountain range of Râphâ (רְפָא), from the mouth of the water from the river Tînâ, and his portion goes towards the west through the midst of this river, and it extends till it reaches the water of the abysses, out of which this river goes forth and pours its waters into the sea Mêat, and this river flows into the great sea. And all that is towards the north is Yapheth's, and all that is towards the south belongs to Shêm.

13. And it extends till it reaches Kârâsô: This is in the bosom of the tongue which looks towards the south.

14. And his portion extends along the great sea, and it extends in a straight line till it reaches the west of the tongue which looks towards the south: For this sea is named the tongue of the Mitsrîy Sea.

15. And it turns from here towards the south towards the mouth of the great sea on the shore of its waters, and it extends to the west to Afrâ, and it extends till it reaches the waters of the river Gîychôn (גִּיחוֹן), and to the south of the waters of Gîychôn, to the banks of this river.

16. And it extends towards the east, till it reaches the Garden of Eden, to the south thereof, to the south and from the east of the whole land of Eden and of the whole east, it turns to the east and proceeds till it reaches the east of the mountain named Râphâ, and

it descends to the bank of the mouth of the river Tînâ.

17. This portion came forth by lot for Shêm and his sons, that they should possess it forever unto his generations forevermore.

18. And Nôach rejoiced that this portion came forth for Shêm and for his sons, and he remembered all that he had spoken with his mouth in prophecy; for he had said: Blessed be Yahuah Êlôhîym of Shêm and may Yahuah dwell in the dwelling of Shêm.

19. And he knew that the Garden of Eden is the Qâdôsh Qâdôsh, and the dwelling of Yahuah, and Mount Sîynay the center of the desert, and Mount Tsîyôn, the center of the navel of the earth: These three were created as Qâdôsh places facing each other.

20. And he blessed the Êl of Êlôhîym, who had put the word of Yahuah into his mouth, and Yahuah forevermore.

21. And he knew that a blessed portion and a blessing had come to Shêm and his sons unto the generations forever, the whole land of Eden and the whole land of the Red Sea, and the whole land of the east and India, and on the Red Sea and the mountains thereof, and all the land of Bâshân, and all the land of Lebânôn and the islands of Kaftûr, and all the mountains of Sanîr and Amânâ, and the mountains of Ashshûr in the north, and all the land of Êylâm, Ashshûr, and Bâbel, and Shûshan and Mâêdâi, and all the mountains of Ărâraṭ, and all the region beyond the sea, which is beyond the mountains of Ashshûr towards the north, a blessed and spacious land, and all that is in it is very good.

22. And for Châm came forth the second portion, beyond the Gîychôn towards the south to the right of the Garden, and it extends towards the south and it extends to all the mountains of fire, and it extends towards the west to the sea of Atel and it extends towards the west till it reaches the sea of Mâûk, that sea into which everything which is not destroyed descends.

23. And it goes forth towards the north to the limits of Gâdîr, and it goes forth to the coast of the waters of the sea to the waters of the great sea till it draws near to the river Gîychôn, and goes along the river Gîychôn till it reaches the right of the Garden of Eden.

24. And this is the land which came forth for Châm as the portion which he was to occupy forever for himself and his sons unto their generations forever.

25. And for Yapheth came forth the third portion beyond the river Tînâ to the north of the outflow of its waters, and it extends north easterly to the whole region of Gôg, and to all the country east thereof.

26. And it extends northerly to the north, and it extends to the mountains of Qêlt towards the north, and towards the sea of Mâûk, and it goes forth to the east of Gâdîr as far as the region of the waters of the sea.

27. And it extends until it approaches the west of Fârâ and it returns towards Afêrâg, and it extends easterly to the waters of the sea of Mêat.

28. And it extends to the region of the river Tînâ in a north easterly direction until it approaches the boundary of its waters towards the mountain Râphâ, and it turns round towards the north.

29. This is the land which came forth for Yapheth and his sons as the portion of his inheritance which he should possess for himself and his sons, for their generations forever; five great islands, and a great land in the north.

30. But it is cold, and the land of Châm is hot, and the land of Shêm is neither hot nor cold, but it is of blended cold and heat.

Chapter 9

1. And Châm divided among his sons, and the first portion came forth for Kûsh towards the east, and to the west of him for Mitsrayim, and to the west of him for Pût, and to the west of him and to the west thereof on the sea for Kenaan.

2. And Shêm also divided among his sons, and the first portion came forth for Châm and his sons, to the east of the river Chiddeqel (חִדֶּקֶל) till it approaches the east, the whole land of India, and on the Red Sea on its coast, and the waters of Dedân, and all the mountains of Mêbrî and Êlâa, and all the land of Shûshan and all that is on the side of Pharnâk to the Red Sea and the river Tînâ.

3. And for Ashshûr came forth the second portion, all the land of Ashshûr and Nîyneweh (נִינְוֵה) and Shinâr and to the border of India, and it ascends and skirts the river.

4. And for Arpakshad came forth the third portion, all the land of the region of the Kaśdîy (כַּשְׂדִּי) to the east of the Perâth (פְּרָת), bordering on the Red Sea, and all the waters of the desert close to the tongue of the sea which looks towards Mitsrayim, all the land of Lebânôn and Sânîr and Amânâ to the border of the Perâth.

5. And for Ărâm there came forth the fourth portion, all the land of Ăram Nahărayim (אֲרַם נַהֲרַיִם) between the Chiddeqel and the Perâth to the north of the Kaśdîy to the border of the mountains of Ashshûr and the land of Arârâ.

6. And there came forth for Lûd the fifth portion, the mountains of Ashshûr and all appertaining to them till it reaches the Great Sea, and till it reaches the east of Ashshûr his brother.

7. And Yapheth also divided the land of his inheritance among his sons.

8. And the first portion came forth for Gômer to the east from the north side to the river Tînâ; and in the north there came forth for Mâgôg all the inner portions of the north until it reaches to the sea of Mêat.

9. And for Mâday came forth as his portion that he should possess from the west of his two brothers to the islands, and to the coasts of the islands.

10. And for Yâwân came forth the fourth portion every island and the islands which are towards the border of Lûd.

11. And for Tûbal there came forth the fifth portion in the midst of the tongue which approaches towards the border of the portion of Lûd to the second tongue, to the region beyond the second tongue unto the third tongue.

12. And for Meshek came forth the sixth portion, all the region beyond the third tongue till it approaches the east of Gâdîr.

13. And for Tîyrâs there came forth the seventh portion, four great islands in the midst of the sea, which reach to the portion of Châm and the islands of Kâmâtûrî came out by lot for the sons of Arpakshad as his inheritance.

14. And thus the sons of Nôach divided unto their sons in the presence of Nôach their father, and he bound them all by an oath, imprecating a curse on every one that sought to seize the portion which had not fallen to him by his lot.

15. And they all said, "So be it; so be it" for themselves and their sons forever throughout

their generations till the day of judgment, on which Yahuah Êlôhîym shall judge them with a sword and with fire for all the unclean wickedness of their errors, wherewith they have filled the earth with transgression and uncleanness and fornication and sin.

Chapter 10

1. And in the third week of this jubilee the unclean demons began to lead astray the children of the sons of Nôach, and to make to err and destroy them.

2. And the sons of Nôach came to Nôach their father, and they told him concerning the demons which were leading astray and blinding and slaying his sons' sons.

3. And he prayed before Yahuah his Êlôhîym, and said: Êlôhîym of the spirits of all flesh, who have shown mercy unto me and have saved me and my sons from the waters of the flood, and have not caused me to perish as you did the sons of perdition; for your grace has been great towards me, and great has been your mercy to my soul; let your grace be lift up upon my sons, and do not let wicked spirits rule over them lest they should destroy them from the earth.

4. But you do bless me and my sons, that we may increase and multiply and replenish the earth.

5. And you know how your Watchers, the fathers of these spirits, acted in my day: and as for these spirits which are living, imprison them and hold them fast in the place of condemnation, and do not let them bring destruction on the sons of your servant, my Êlôhîym; for these are malignant, and created in order to destroy.

6. And do not let them rule over the spirits of the living; for you alone can exercise dominion over them. And do not let them have power over the sons of the righteous from henceforth and forevermore.

7. And Yahuah our Êlôhîym bid us to bind all.

8. And the chief of the spirits, Mastêmâ, came and said: Yahuah, Bârâ, let some of them remain before me, and let them harken to my voice, and do all that I shall say unto them; for if some of them are not left to me, I shall not be able to execute the power of my will on the sons of men; for these are for corruption and leading astray before my judgment, for great is the wickedness of the sons of men.

9. And he said: Let the tenth part of them remain before him, and let nine parts descend into the place of condemnation.

10. And one of us he commanded that we should teach Nôach all their remedies; for he knew that they would not walk in uprightness, nor strive in righteousness.

11. And we did according to all his words: All the malignant evil ones we bound in the place of condemnation and a tenth part of them we left that they might be subject before the Adversary on the earth.

12. And we explained to Nôach all the remedies of their diseases, together with their seductions, how he might heal them with herbs of the earth.

13. And Nôach wrote down all things in a book as we instructed him concerning every kind of remedy. Thus the evil spirits were precluded from hurting the sons of Nôach.

14. And he gave all that he had written to Shêm, his eldest son; for he loved him exceedingly above all his sons.

15. And Nôach slept with his fathers, and was buried on Mount Lûbâr in the land of Ărâraṭ.

16. Nine hundred and fifty years he completed in his life, nineteen jubilees and two weeks and five years.

17. And in his life on earth he excelled the children of men save Chănôk because of the righteousness, wherein he was perfect. For Chănôk's office was ordained for a testimony to the generations of the world, so that he should recount all the deeds of generation unto generation, till the Day of Judgment.

18. And in the three and thirtieth jubilee, in the first year in the second week, Peleg took to himself a woman, whose name was Lômnâ the daughter of Shinâr, and she bare him a son in the fourth year of this week, and he called his name Rêû; for he said: Behold the children of men have become evil through the wicked purpose of building for themselves a city and a tower in the land of Shinâr.

19. For they departed from the land of Ărâraṭ eastward to Shinâr; for in his days they built the city and the tower, saying, go to, let us ascend thereby into shâmayim.

20. And they began to build, and in the fourth week they made brick with fire, and the bricks served them for stone, and the clay with which they cemented them together was asphalt which comes out of the sea, and out of the fountains of water in the land of Shinâr.

21. And they built it: forty and three years were they building it; its breadth was 203 bricks, and the height of a brick was the third of one; its height amounted to 5433 cubits and 2 palms, and the extent of one wall was thirteen stades and of the other thirty stades.

22. And Yahuah our Êlôhîym said unto us: Behold, they are one people, and this they begin to do, and now nothing will be withheld from them. Go to, let us go down and confound their language that they may not understand one another's speech, and they may be dispersed into cities and nations, and one purpose will no longer abide with them till the Day of Judgment.

23. And Yahuah descended, and we descended with him to see the city and the tower which the children of men had built.

24. And he confounded their language, and they no longer understood one another's speech, and they ceased then to build the city and the tower.

25. For this reason the whole land of Shinâr is called Bâbel, because Yahuah did there confound all the language of the children of men, and from thence they were dispersed into their cities, each according to his language and his nation.

26. And Yahuah sent a mighty wind against the tower and overthrew it upon the earth, and behold it was between Ashshûr and Bâbel (בֶּל) in the land of Shinâr, and they called its name "Overthrow".

27. In the fourth week in the first year in the beginning thereof in the four and thirtieth jubilee, were they dispersed from the land of Shinâr.

28. And Châm and his sons went into the land which he was to occupy, which he acquired as his portion in the land of the south.

29. And Kenaan saw the land of Lebânôn to the river of Mitsrayim, that it was very good, and he went not into the land of his inheritance to the west, that is to the sea, and he dwelt in the land of Lebânôn, eastward and westward from the border of Yardên (יַרְדֵּן) and from the border of the sea.

30. And Châm, his father, and Kûsh and Mitsrayim his brothers said unto him: You

have settled in a land which is not yours, and which did not fall to us by lot: do not do so; for if you do so, you and your sons will fall in the land and be accursed through sedition; for by sedition you have settled, and by sedition will your children fall, and you shall be rooted out forever.

31. Do not dwell in the dwelling of Shêm; for to Shêm and to his sons it did come by their lot.

32. Cursed are you, and cursed you shall be beyond all the sons of Nôach, by the curse by which we bound ourselves by an oath in the presence of the Qâdôsh judge, and in the presence of Nôach our father.

33. But he did not harken unto them, and dwelt in the land of Lebânôn from Chămâth (חֲמָת) to the entering of Mitsrayim, he and his sons until this day.

34. And for this reason that land is named Kenaan.

35. And Yapheth and his sons went towards the sea and dwelt in the land of their portion, and Mâday saw the land of the sea and it did not please him, and he begged a portion from Châm and Ashshûr and Arpakshad, his woman's brother, and he dwelt in the land of Mâday (מָדַי), near to his woman's brother until this day.

36. And he called his dwelling place, and the dwelling place of his sons, Mâday, after the name of their father Mâday.

Chapter 11

1. And in the thirty fifth jubilee, in the third week, in the first year thereof, Rêû took to himself a woman, and her name was Ôrâ, the daughter of Ûr, the son of Keśed, and she bare him a son, and he called his name Sêrôh, in the seventh year of this week in this jubilee.

2. And the sons of Nôach began to war on each other, to take captive and to slay each other, and to shed the blood of men on the earth, and to eat blood, and to build strong cities, and walls, and towers, and individuals began to exalt themselves above the nation, and to found the beginnings of kingdoms, and to go to war, people against people, and nation against nation, and city against city, and all began to do evil, and to acquire arms, and to teach their sons war, and they began to capture cities, and to sell male and female slaves.

3. And Ûr, the son of Keśed, built the city of Ărâ of the Kaśdîy, and called its name after his own name and the name of his father.

4. And they made for themselves molten images, and they worshipped each the idol, the molten image which they had made for themselves, and they began to make graven images and unclean simulacra, and malignant spirits assisted and seduced them into committing transgression and uncleanness.

5. And the prince Mastêmâ exerted himself to do all this, and he sent forth other spirits, those which were put under his hand, to do all manner of wrong and sin, and all manner of transgression, to corrupt and destroy, and to shed blood upon the earth.

6. For this reason he called the name of Sêrôh, Śerûg, for every one turned to do all manner of sin and transgression.

7. And he grew up, and dwelt in Ûr of the Kaśdîy, near to the father of his woman's mother, and he worshipped idols, and he took to himself a woman in the thirty sixth jubilee, in the fifth week, in the first year thereof and her name was Mêlkâ, the daughter of Kâbêr, the daughter of his father's brother.

8. And she bare him Nâchôr (נָחוֹר), in the first year of this week, and he grew and

dwelt in Ûr of the Kaśdîy, and his father taught him the researches of the Kaśdîy to divine and augur, according to the signs of shâmayim.

9. And in the thirty seventh jubilee in the sixth week, in the first year thereof, he took to himself a woman, and her name was Iyâskâ, the daughter of Nêstâg of the Kaśdîy.

10. And she bare him Terach in the seventh year of this week.

11. And the prince Mastêmâ sent ravens and birds to devour the seed which was sown in the land, in order to destroy the land, and rob the children of men of their labors. Before they could plough in the seed, the ravens picked it from the surface of the ground.

12. And for this reason he called his name Terach because the ravens and the birds reduced them to destitution and devoured their seed.

13. And the years began to be barren, owing to the birds, and they devoured all the fruit of the trees from the trees: It was only with great effort that they could save a little of all the fruit of the earth in their days.

14. And in this thirty ninth jubilee, in the second week in the first year, Terach took to himself a woman, and her name was Ednâ, the daughter of Abrâm, the daughter of his father's sister.

15. And in the seventh year of this week she bare him a son, and he called his name Abrâm, by the name of the father of his mother; for he had died before his daughter had conceived a son.

16. And the child began to understand the errors of the earth that all went astray after graven images and after uncleanness, and his father taught him writing, and he was two weeks of years old, and he separated himself from his father, that he might not worship idols with him.

17. And he began to pray to the Bârâ of all things that he might save him from the errors of the children of men, and that his portion should not fall into error after uncleanness and vileness.

18. And the seed time came for the sowing of seed upon the land, and they all went forth together to protect their seed against the ravens, and Abrâm went forth with those that went, and the child was a lad of fourteen years.

19. And a cloud of ravens came to devour the seed, and Abrâm ran to meet them before they settled on the ground, and cried to them before they settled on the ground to devour the seed, and said, do not descend: return to the place whence you came, and they proceeded to turn back.

20. And he caused the clouds of ravens to turn back that day seventy times, and of all the ravens throughout all the land where Abrâm was there settled there not so much as one.

21. And all who were with him throughout all the land saw him cry out, and all the ravens turn back, and his name became great in all the land of the Kaśdîy.

22. And there came to him this year all those that wished to sow, and he went with them until the time of sowing ceased: And they sowed their land, and that year they brought enough grain home and eat and were satisfied.

23. And in the first year of the fifth week Abrâm taught those who made implements for oxen, the artificers in wood, and they made a vessel above the ground, facing the frame of the plough, in order to put the seed

thereon, and the seed fell down therefrom upon the share of the plough, and was hidden in the earth, and they no longer feared the ravens.

24. And after this manner they made vessels above the ground on all the frames of the ploughs, and they sowed and tilled all the land, according as Abrâm commanded them, and they no longer feared the birds.

Chapter 12

1. And it came to pass in the sixth week, in the seventh year thereof, that Abrâm said to Terach his father, saying: Father.

2. And he said, behold, here am I, my son. And he said, what help and profit do we have from those idols which you do worship, and before which you do bow yourself?

3. For there is no spirit in them, for they are dumb forms, and a misleading of the heart. Do not worship them:

4. Worship the Êlôhîym of shâmayim, who causes the rain and the dew to descend on the earth and does everything upon the earth, and has created everything by his word, and all life is from before his face.

5. Why do you worship things that have no spirit in them? For they are the work of men's hands, and on your shoulders you do bear them, and you have no help from them, but they are a great cause of shame to those who make them, and a misleading of the heart to those who worship them: Do not worship them.

6. And his father said unto him, I also know it, my son, but what shall I do with a people who have made me to serve before them?

7. And if I tell them the truth, they will slay me; for their soul cleaves to them to worship them and honor them.

8. Keep silent, my son, lest they slay you. And these words he spoke to his two brothers, and they were angry with him and he kept silent.

9. And in the fortieth jubilee, in the second week, in the seventh year thereof, Abrâm took to himself a woman, and her name was Śaray, the daughter of his father, and she became his woman.

10. And Chârân, his brother, took to himself a woman in the third year of the third week, and she bare him a son in the seventh year of this week, and he called his name Lôt.

11. And Nâchôr, his brother, took to himself a woman.

12. And in the sixtieth year of the life of Abrâm, that is, in the fourth week, in the fourth year thereof, Abrâm arose by night, and burned the house of the idols, and he burned all that was in the house and no man knew it.

13. And they arose in the night and sought to save their gods from the midst of the fire.

14. And Chârân hasted to save them, but the fire flamed over him, and he was burnt in the fire, and he died in Ûr of the Kaśdîy before Terach his father, and they buried him in Ûr of the Kaśdîy.

15. And Terach went forth from Ûr of the Kaśdîy, he and his sons, to go into the land of Lebânôn and into the land of Kenaan, and he dwelt in the land of Chârân, and Abrâm dwelt with Terach his father in Chârân two weeks of years.

16. And in the sixth week, in the fifth year thereof, Abrâm sat up throughout the night on the beginning of the seventh month to observe the stars from the evening to the morning, in order to see what would be the character of the year with regard to

the rains, and he was alone as he sat and observed.

17. And a word came into his heart and he said: All the signs of the stars, and the signs of the moon and of the sun are all in the hand of Yahuah. Why do I search them out?

18. If he desires, he causes it to rain, morning and evening; and if he desires, he withholds it, and all things are in his hand.

19. And he prayed that night and said, my Êlôhîym, Êlôhîym Elyôn Êl, you alone are my Êlôhîym, and you and your dominion I have chosen. And you have created all things, and all things that are the work of your hands.

20. Deliver me from the hands of evil spirits who have dominion over the thoughts of men's hearts, and do not let them lead me astray from you, my Êlôhîym. And you establish me and my seed forever that we do not go astray from henceforth and forevermore.

21. And he said, shall I return unto Ûr of the Kaśdîy who seek my face that I may return to them, am I to remain here in this place? The right path before you prosper it in the hands of your servant that he may fulfil it and that I may not walk in the deceitfulness of my heart, O my Êlôhîym.

22. And he made an end of speaking and praying, and behold the word of Yahuah was sent to him through me, saying: You get up from your country, and from your kindred and from the house of your father unto a land which I will show you, and I shall make you a great and numerous nation.

23. And I will bless you and I will make your name great, and you shall be blessed in the earth, and in you shall all families of the earth be blessed, and I will bless them that bless you, and curse them that curse you.

24. And I will be an Êlôhîym to you and your son, and to your son's son, and to all your seed: Do not fear, from henceforth and unto all generations of the earth I am your Êlôhîym.

25. And Yahuah Êlôhîym said: Open his mouth and his ears that he may hear and speak with his mouth, with the language which has been revealed; for it had ceased from the mouths of all the children of men from the day of the overthrow of Bâbel.

26. And I opened his mouth, and his ears and his lips, and I began to speak with him in Êber (עֵבֶר) in the tongue of the creation.

27. And he took the books of his fathers, and these were written in Êber, and he transcribed them, and he began from henceforth to study them, and I made known to him that which he could not understand, and he studied them during the six rainy months.

28. And it came to pass in the seventh year of the sixth week that he spoke to his father and informed him, that he would leave Chârân to go into the land of Kenaan to see it and return to him.

29. And Terach his father said unto him; go in peace: May Êlôhîym Ôlâm make your path straight. And Yahuah be with you, and protect you from all evil, and grant unto you grace, mercy and favor before those who see you, and may none of the children of men have power over you to harm you; go in peace.

30. And if you see a land pleasant to your eyes to dwell in, then arise and take me to you and take Lôt with you, the son of Chârân your brother as your own son: Yahuah be with you.

31. And Nâchôr your brother leave with me till you return in peace, and we go with you all together.

Chapter 13

1. And Abrâm journeyed from Chârân, and he took Śâray, his woman, and Lôt, his brother Chârân's son, to the land of Kenaan, and he came into Ashshûr, and proceeded to Shekem, and dwelt near a lofty oak.

2. And he saw, and, behold, the land was very pleasant from the entering of Chămâth to the lofty oak.

3. And Yahuah said to him: To you and to your seed will I give this land.

4. And he built an altar there, and he offered thereon a burnt sacrifice to Yahuah, who had appeared to him.

5. And he removed from thence unto the mountain . . . Bêythêl on the west and Ay on the east, and pitched his tent there.

6. And he saw and behold, the land was very wide and good, and everything grew thereon, vines and figs and pomegranates, oaks and ilexes, and terebinths and oil trees, and cedars and cypresses and date trees, and all trees of the field, and there was water on the mountains.

7. And he blessed Yahuah who had led him out of Ûr of the Kaśdîy, and had brought him to this land.

8. And it came to pass in the first year, in the seventh week, on the beginning of the first month, that he built an altar on this mountain, and called on the name of Yahuah: You, Êlôhîym Ôlâm, are my Êlôhîym.

9. And he offered on the altar a burnt sacrifice unto Yahuah that he should be with him and not forsake him all the days of his life.

10. And he removed from thence and went towards the south, and he came to Chebrôn and Chebrôn was built at that time, and he dwelt there two years, and he went thence into the land of the south, to Beâlôth, and there was a famine in the land.

11. And Abrâm went into Mitsrayim in the third year of the week, and he dwelt in Mitsrayim five years before his woman was torn away from him.

12. Now Tanais in Mitsrayim was at that time built, seven years after Chebrôn.

13. And it came to pass when Parôh (פַּרְעֹה) seized Śâray, the woman of Abrâm that Yahuah plagued Parôh and his house with great plagues because of Śâray, Abrâm's woman.

14. And Abrâm was very glorious because of possessions in sheep, and cattle, and asses, and horses, and camels, and menservants, and maidservants, and in silver and gold exceedingly. And Lôt also his brother's son, was wealthy.

15. And Parôh gave back Śâray, the woman of Abrâm, and he sent him out of the land of Mitsrayim, and he journeyed to the place where he had pitched his tent at the beginning, to the place of the altar, with Ay on the east, and Bêythêl on the west, and he blessed Yahuah his Êlôhîym who had brought him back in peace.

16. And it came to pass in the forty first jubilee in the third year of the first week that he returned to this place and offered thereon a burnt sacrifice, and called on the name of Yahuah, and said: You, Êlôhîym Elyôn Êl, are my Êlôhîym forever and ever.

17. And in the fourth year of this week Lôt parted from him, and Lôt dwelt in Sedôm (סְדֹם), and the men of Sedôm were sinners exceedingly.

18. And it grieved him in his heart that his brother's son had parted from him; for he had no children.

19. In that year when Lôt was taken captive, Yahuah said unto Abrâm, after that Lôt had parted from him, in the fourth year of this week: Lift up your eyes from the place where you are dwelling, northward and southward, and westward and eastward.

20. For all the land which you see I will give to you and to your seed forever, and I will make your seed as the sand of the sea: Though a man may number the dust of the earth, yet your seed shall not be numbered.

21. Arise, walk through the land in the length of it and the breadth of it, and see it all; for to your seed I will give it. And Abrâm went to Chebrôn, and dwelt there.

22. And in this year came Kedorlâômer, king of Êylâm, and Amrâphel, king of Shinâr, and Ăryôk king of Ellâsâr, and Tidâl (תִדְעָל), king of nations, and slew the king of Ămôrâh (עֲמֹרָה), and the king of Sedôm fled, and many fell through wounds in the vale of Śiddîym, by the Salt Sea.

23. And they took captive Sedôm and Âdâm and Tsebôîym, and they took captive Lôt also, the son of Abrâm's brother, and all his possessions, and they went to Dân.

24. And one who had escaped came and told Abrâm that his brother's son had been taken captive and Abrâm armed his household servants . . .

25. . . . for Abrâm, and for his seed, a tenth of the first fruits to Yahuah, and Yahuah ordained it as an ordinance forever that they should give it to the Kôhên (כֹּהֵן) who served before him, that they should possess it forever.

26. And to this law there is no limit of days; for he has ordained it for the generations forever that they should give to Yahuah the tenth of everything, of the seed and of the wine and of the oil and of the cattle and of the sheep.

27. And he gave it unto his Kôhên to eat and to drink with joy before him.

28. And the king of Sedôm came to him and bowed himself before him, and said: Our master Abrâm, give unto us the souls which you have rescued, but let the booty be yours.

29. And Abrâm said unto him: I lift up my hands to Êlôhîym Elyôn Êl, that from a thread to a shoe latchet I shall not take aught that is yours lest you should say, I have made Abrâm rich; save only what the young men have eaten, and the portion of the men who went with me, Ânêr, Eshkôl, and Mamrê. These shall take their portion.

Chapter 14

1. After these things, in the fourth year of this week, on the beginning of the third month, the word of Yahuah came to Abrâm in a dream, saying: Do not fear, Abrâm; I am your defender, and your reward will be exceeding great.

2. And he said: Yahuah, Yahuah, what you will give me, seeing I go hence childless, and the son of Mâsêq, the son of my handmaid, is the Dammeśeq Ĕlîyezer: He will be my heir, and to me you have given no seed.

3. And he said unto him: This man will not be your heir, but one that will come out of your own bowels; he will be your heir.

4. And he brought him forth abroad, and said unto him: Look toward shâmayim and number the stars if you are able to number them.

5. And he looked toward shâmayim, and beheld the stars. And he said unto him: So shall your seed be.

6. And he believed in Yahuah, and it was counted to him for righteousness.

7. And he said unto him: I am Yahuah that brought you out of Ûr of the Kaśdîy, to give you the land of the Kenaanîy to possess it forever; and I will be Êlôhîym unto you and to your seed after you.

8. And he said: Yahuah, Yahuah, whereby shall I know that I shall inherit it?

9. And he said unto him: Take me a heifer of three years, and a goat of three years, and a sheep of three years, and a turtle dove, and a pigeon.

10. And he took all these in the middle of the month and he dwelt at the oak of Mamrê, which is near Chebrôn.

11. And he built there an altar, and sacrificed all these; and he poured their blood upon the altar, and divided them in the midst, and laid them over against each other; but the birds he did not divide.

12. And birds came down upon the pieces, and Abrâm drove them away, and did not suffer the birds to touch them.

13. And it came to pass, when the sun had set, that an ecstasy fell upon Abrâm, and lo! A horror of great darkness fell upon him, and it was said unto Abrâm: Know of a surety that your seed shall be a stranger in a land that is not theirs, and they shall bring them into bondage, and afflict them four hundred years.

14. And the nation also to whom they will be in bondage I will judge, and after that they shall come forth thence with much substance.

15. And you shall go to your fathers in peace, and be buried in a good old age.

16. But in the fourth generation they shall return hither; for the iniquity of the Ěmôrîy (אֱמֹרִי) is not yet full.

17. And he awoke from his sleep, and he arose, and the sun had set; and there was a flame, and behold! A furnace was smoking, and a flame of fire passed between the pieces.

18. And on that day Yahuah made a covenant with Abrâm, saying: To your seed I will give this land, from the river of Mitsrayim unto the great river, the river Perâth, the Qêynîy (קֵינִי), the Qenizzîy (קְנִזִּי), the Qadmônîy (קַדְמֹנִי), the Perizzîy (פְּרִזִּי), and the Râphâ (רְפָא), the Phakorites, and the Chiwwîy (חִוִּי), and the Ěmôrîy, and the Kenaanîy, and the Girgâshîy (גִּרְגָּשִׁי), and the Yebûsîy (יְבוּסִי).

19. And the day passed, and Abrâm offered the pieces, and the birds, and their fruit offerings, and their drink offerings, and the fire devoured them.

20. And on that day we made a covenant with Abrâm, according as we had covenanted with Nôach in this month; and Abrâm renewed the festival and ordinance for himself forever.

21. And Abrâm rejoiced, and made all these things known to Śâray his woman; and he believed that he would have seed, but she did not bear.

22. And Śâray advised her husband Abrâm, and said unto him: Go in unto Hâgâr, my Mitsrîy maid: It may be that I shall build up seed unto you by her.

23. And Abrâm harkened unto the voice of Śâray his woman, and said unto her, do so. And Śâray took Hâgâr, her maid, the Mitsrîy, and he gave her to Abrâm, her husband, to be his woman.

24. And he went in unto her, and she conceived and bare him a son, and he called his name Yishmâêl (יִשְׁמָעֵאל), in the fifth year of this week; and this was the eighty sixth year in the life of Abrâm.

Chapter 15

1. And in the fifth year of the fourth week of this jubilee, in the third month, in the middle of the month, Abrâm celebrated the feast of the first fruits of the grain harvest.

2. And he offered new offerings on the altar, the first fruits of the produce, unto Yahuah, a heifer and a goat and a sheep on the altar as a burnt sacrifice unto Yahuah; their fruit offerings and their drink offerings he offered upon the altar with lebônâh.

3. And Yahuah appeared to Abrâm, and said unto him: I am Êlôhîym Shadday Êl; approve yourself before me and you are perfect.

4. And I will make my covenant between me and you, and I will multiply you exceedingly.

5. And Abrâm fell on his face, and Êlôhîym talked with him, and said:

6. Behold my ordinance is with you, and you shall be the father of many nations.

7. Neither shall your name any more be called Abrâm, but your name from henceforth, even forever, shall be Abrâhâm. For the father of many nations I have made you.

8. And I will make you very great, and I will make you into nations, and kings shall come forth from you.

9. And I shall establish my covenant between me and you, and your seed after you, throughout their generations, for an eternal covenant, so that I may be an Êlôhîym unto you, and to your seed after you.

10. And I will give to you and to your seed after you, the land where you have been a sojourner, the land of Kenaan, that you may possess it forever, and I will be their Êlôhîym.

11. And Yahuah said unto Abrâhâm: And as for you, you do keep my covenant, you and your seed after you: And you circumcise every male among you, and circumcise your foreskins, and it shall be a token of an eternal covenant between me and you.

12. And the child on the eighth day you shall circumcise, every male throughout your generations, him that is born in the house, or whom you have bought with money from any stranger, whom you have acquired who is not of your seed.

13. He that is born in your house shall surely be circumcised, and those whom you have bought with money shall be circumcised, and my covenant shall be in your flesh for an eternal ordinance.

14. And the uncircumcised male who is not circumcised in the flesh of his foreskin on the eighth day, that soul shall be cut off from his people, for he has broken my covenant.

15. And Êlôhîym said unto Abrâhâm: As for Śâray your woman, her name shall no more be called Śâray, but Śârâh shall be her name.

16. And I will bless her, and give you a son by her, and I will bless him, and he shall become a nation, and kings of nations shall proceed from him.

17. And Abrâhâm fell on his face, and rejoiced, and said in his heart: Shall a son be born to him that is a hundred years old, and shall Śârâh, who is ninety years old, bring forth?

18. And Abrâhâm said unto Êlôhîym: O that Yishmâêl might live before you.

19. And Êlôhîym said: Yea, and Śârâh also shall bear you a son, and you shall call his name Yitschâq, and I will establish my covenant with him, an everlasting covenant, and for his seed after him.

20. And as for Yishmâêl I have also heard you, and behold I will bless him, and make

him great, and multiply him exceedingly, and he shall beget twelve princes, and I will make him a great nation.

21. But my covenant I will establish with Yitschâq, whom Śârâh shall bear to you, in these days, in the next year.

22. And he left off speaking with him, and Êlôhîym went up from Abrâhâm.

23. And Abrâhâm did according as Êlôhîym had said unto him, and he took Yishmâêl his son, and all that were born in his house, and whom he had bought with his money, every male in his house, and circumcised the flesh of their foreskin.

24. And on the selfsame day was Abrâhâm circumcised, and all the men of his house, and those born in the house, and all those, whom he had bought with money from the children of the stranger, were circumcised with him.

25. This law is for all the generations forever, and there is no circumcision of the days, and no omission of one day out of the eight days; for it is an eternal ordinance, ordained and written on the shâmayim tablets.

26. And every one that is born, the flesh of whose foreskin is not circumcised on the eighth day, does not belong to the children of the covenant which Yahuah made with Abrâhâm, but to the children of destruction; nor is there, moreover, any sign on him that he is Yahuah's, but he is destined to be destroyed and slain from the earth, and to be rooted out of the earth, for he has broken the covenant of Yahuah our Êlôhîym.

27. For all the angels of the presence and all the angels of sanctification have been so created from the day of their creation, and before the angels of the presence and the angels of sanctification he has sanctified Yâshârêl, that they should be with him and with his qâdôsh angels.

28. And you do command the children of Yâshârêl and let them observe the sign of this covenant for their generations as an eternal ordinance, and they will not be rooted out of the land.

29. For the command is ordained for a covenant, that they should observe it forever among all the children of Yâshârêl.

30. For Yishmâêl and his sons and his brothers and Êśâw, Yahuah did not cause to approach him, and he did not choose them because they are the children of Abrâhâm, because he knew them, but he chose Yâshârêl to be his people.

31. And he sanctified it, and gathered it from among all the children of men; for there are many nations and many peoples, and all are his, and over all he has placed spirits in authority to lead them astray from him.

32. But over Yâshârêl he did not appoint any angel or spirit, for he alone is their ruler, and he will preserve them and require them at the hand of his angels and his spirits, and at the hand of all his powers in order that he may preserve them and bless them, and that they may be his and he may be theirs from henceforth forever.

33. And now I announce unto you that the children of Yâshârêl will not keep true to this ordinance, and they will not circumcise their sons according to all this law; for in the flesh of their circumcision they will omit this circumcision of their sons, and all of them, sons of Belîyaal, will leave their sons uncircumcised as they were born.

34. And there will be great wrath from Yahuah against the children of Yâshârêl. because they have forsaken his covenant

and turned aside from his word, and provoked and blasphemed, inasmuch as they do not observe the ordinance of this law; for they have treated their members like the Gentiles, so that they may be removed and rooted out of the land. And there will no more be pardon or forgiveness unto them so that there should be forgiveness and pardon for all the sin of this eternal error.

Chapter 16

1. And on the beginning of the fourth month we appeared unto Abrâhâm, at the oak of Mamrê, and we talked with him, and we announced to him that a son would be given to him by Śârâh his woman.

2. And Śârâh laughed, for she heard that we had spoken these words with Abrâhâm, and we admonished her, and she became afraid, and denied that she had laughed on account of the words.

3. And we told her the name of her son, as his name is ordained and written in the shâmayim tablets, Yitschâq,

4. And that when we returned to her at a set time, she would have conceived a son.

5. And in this month Yahuah executed his judgments on Sedôm, and Ămôrâh, and Tsebôîym, and all the region of the Yardên, and he burned them with fire and brimstone, and destroyed them until this day, even as lo I have declared unto you all their works, that they are wicked and sinners exceedingly, and that they defile themselves and commit fornication in their flesh, and work uncleanness on the earth.

6. And, in like manner, Êlôhîym will execute judgment on the places where they have done according to the uncleanness of the Sedôm, like unto the judgment of Sedôm.

7. But we saved Lôt; for Êlôhîym remembered Abrâhâm, and sent him out from the midst of the overthrow.

8. And he and his daughters committed sin upon the earth, such as had not been on the earth since the days of Âdâm till his time; for the man lay with his daughters.

9. And, behold, it was commanded and engraved concerning all his seed, on the shâmayim tablets, to remove them and root them out, and to execute judgment upon them like the judgment of Sedôm, and to leave no seed of the man on earth on the day of condemnation.

10. And in this month Abrâhâm moved from Chebrôn, and departed and dwelt between Qâdêsh and Shûr in the mountains of Gerâr.

11. And in the middle of the fifth month he moved from thence, and dwelt at the Well of the Oath.

12. And in the middle of the sixth month Yahuah visited Śârâh and did unto her as he had spoken and she conceived.

13. And she bare a son in the third month, and in the middle of the month, at the time of which Yahuah had spoken to Abrâhâm, on the festival of the first fruits of the harvest, Yitschâq was born.

14. And Abrâhâm circumcised his son on the eighth day: He was the first that was circumcised according to the covenant which is ordained forever.

15. And in the sixth year of the fourth week we came to Abrâhâm, to the Well of the Oath, and we appeared unto him as we had told Śârâh that we should return to her, and she would have conceived a son.

16. And we returned in the seventh month, and found Śârâh with child before us and

we blessed him, and we announced to him all the things which had been decreed concerning him, that he should not die till he should beget six sons more, and should see them before he died; but that in Yitschâq should his name and seed be called:

17. And that all the seed of his sons should be Gentiles, and be reckoned with the Gentiles; but from the sons of Yitschâq one should become a qâdôsh seed, and should not be reckoned among the Gentiles.

18. For he should become the portion of Elyôn Êl, and all his seed had fallen into the possession of Êlôhîym, that it should be unto Yahuah a people for his possession above all nations and that it should become a kingdom and Kôhên and a qâdôsh nation.

19. And we went our way, and we announced to Sârâh all that we had told him, and they both rejoiced with exceeding great joy.

20. And he built there an altar to Yahuah who had delivered him, and who was making him rejoice in the land of his sojourning, and he celebrated a festival of joy in this month seven days, near the altar which he had built at the Well of the Oath.

21. And he built booths for himself and for his servants on this festival, and he was the first to celebrate the feast of Sûkkâh (סָכָּה) on the earth.

22. And during these seven days he brought each day to the altar a burnt offering to Yahuah, two oxen, two rams, seven sheep, one male goat, for a sin offering, that he might atone thereby for himself and for his seed.

23. And, as a thank offering, seven rams, seven kids, seven sheep, and seven male goats, and their fruit offerings and their drink offerings; and he burnt all the fat thereof on the altar, a chosen offering unto Yahuah for a sweet smelling savor.

24. And he burnt morning and evening fragrant substances, lebônâh and galbanum, and stackte, and nard, and myrrh, and spice, and costum; all these seven he offered, crushed, mixed together in equal parts and pure.

25. And he celebrated this feast during seven days, rejoicing with all his heart and with all his soul, he and all those who were in his house, and there was no stranger with him, nor any that was uncircumcised.

26. And he blessed his Bârâ who had created him in his generation, for he had created him according to his good pleasure; for he knew and perceived that from him would arise the plant of righteousness for the eternal generations, and from him a qâdôsh seed, so that it should become like him who had made all things.

27. And he blessed and rejoiced, and he called the name of this festival the Feast of Yahuah, a joy acceptable to Êlôhîym Elyôn Êl.

28. And we blessed him forever, and all his seed after him throughout all the generations of the earth, because he celebrated this festival in its season, according to the testimony of the shâmayim tablets.

29. For this reason it is ordained on the shâmayim tablets concerning Yâshârêl, that they shall celebrate the feast of tabernacles seven days with joy, in the seventh month, acceptable before Yahuah, a statute forever throughout their generations every year.

30. And to this there is no limit of days; for it is ordained forever regarding Yâshârêl that they should celebrate it and dwell in booths, and set wreaths upon their heads, and take leafy boughs, and willows from the brook.

31. And Abrâhâm took branches of palm trees, and the fruit of goodly trees, and every day going round the altar with the branches seven times a day in the morning, he praised and gave thanks to his Êlôhîym for all things in joy.

Chapter 17

1. And in the first year of the fifth week Yitschâq was weaned in this jubilee, and Abrâhâm made a great banquet in the third month, on the day his son Yitschâq was weaned.

2. And Yishmâêl, the son of Hâgâr, the Mitsrîy, was before the face of Abrâhâm, his father, in his place, and Abrâhâm rejoiced and blessed Êlôhîym because he had seen his sons and had not died childless.

3. And he remembered the words which he had spoken to him on the day on which Lôt had parted from him, and he rejoiced because Yahuah had given him seed upon the earth to inherit the earth, and he blessed with all his mouth the Bârâ of all things.

4. And Śârâh saw Yishmâêl playing and dancing, and Abrâhâm rejoicing with great joy, and she became jealous of Yishmâêl and said to Abrâhâm, cast out this bondwoman and her son; for the son of this bondwoman will not be heir with my son, Yitschâq.

5. And the thing was grievous in Abrâhâm's sight, because of his maidservant and because of his son, that he should drive them from him.

6. And Êlôhîym said to Abrâhâm, let it not be grievous in your sight, because of the child and because of the bondwoman; in all that Śârâh has said unto you, harken to her words and do them; for in Yitschâq shall your name and seed be called.

7. But as for the son of this bondwoman I will make him a great nation, because he is of your seed.

8. And Abrâhâm rose up early in the morning, and took bread and a bottle of water, and placed them on the shoulders of Hâgâr and the child, and sent her away.

9. And she departed and wandered in the wilderness of Beêrsheba, and the water in the bottle was spent, and the child thirsted, and was not able to go on, and fell down.

10. And his mother took him and cast him under an olive tree, and went and sat her down over against him, at the distance of a bow shot; for she said, let me not see the death of my child, and as she sat she wept.

11. And an angel of Êlôhîym, one of the qâdôsh, said unto her, why do you weep, Hâgâr? Arise take the child, and hold him in your hand; for Êlôhîym has heard your voice, and has seen the child.

12. And she opened her eyes, and she saw a well of water, and she went and filled her bottle with water, and she gave her child to drink, and she arose and went towards the wilderness of Pârân.

13. And the child grew and became an archer, and Êlôhîym was with him, and his mother took him a woman from among the daughters of Mitsrayim.

14. And she bare him a son, and he called his name Nebâyôth; for she said, Yahuah was nigh to me when I called upon him.

15. And it came to pass in the seventh week, in the first year thereof, in the first month in this jubilee, on the twelfth of this month, there were voices in shâmayim regarding Abrâhâm, that he was faithful in all that he told him, and that he loved Yahuah, and that in every affliction he was faithful.

16. And the prince Mastêmâ came and said before Êlôhîym, behold, Abrâhâm loves Yitschâq his son, and he delights in him above all things else; bid him to offer him as a burnt offering on the altar, and you will see if he will do this command, and you will know if he is faithful in everything wherein you do try him.

17. And Yahuah knew that Abrâhâm was faithful in all his afflictions; for he had tried him through his country and with famine, and had tried him with the wealth of kings, and had tried him again through his woman, when she was torn from him, and with circumcision; and had tried him through Yishmâêl and Hâgâr, his maid servant, when he sent them away.

18. And in everything wherein he had tried him, he was found faithful, and his soul was not impatient, and he was not slow to act; for he was faithful and a lover of Yahuah.

Chapter 18

1. And Êlôhîym said to him, Abrâhâm, Abrâhâm; and he said, behold, here I am.

2. And he said, take your beloved son whom you love, even Yitschâq, and go unto the high country, and offer him on one of the mountains which I will point out unto you.

3. And he rose early in the morning and saddled his ass, and took his two young men with him, and Yitschâq his son, and clave the wood of the burnt offering, and he went to the place on the third day, and he saw the place afar off.

4. And he came to a well of water, and he said to his young men, you abide here with the ass, and I and the lad shall go yonder, and when we have worshipped we shall come again to you.

5. And he took the wood of the burnt offering and laid it on Yitschâq his son, and he took in his hand the fire and the knife, and they went both of them together to that place.

6. And Yitschâq said to his father, father; and he said, here I am, my son. And he said unto him, behold the fire, and the knife, and the wood; but where is the sheep for the burnt offering, father?

7. And he said, Êlôhîym will provide for himself a sheep for a burnt offering, my son. And he drew near to the place of the mount of Êlôhîym.

8. And he built an altar, and he placed the wood on the altar, and bound Yitschâq his son, and placed him on the wood which was upon the altar, and stretched forth his hand to take the knife to slay Yitschâq his son.

9. And I stood before him, and before the prince Mastêmâ, and Yahuah said, do not bid him to lay his hand on the lad, nor to do anything to him, for I have shown that he fears Yahuah.

10. And I called to him from shâmayim, and said unto him: Abrâhâm, Abrâhâm; and he was terrified and said: Behold, here I am.

11. And I said unto him: Do not lay your hand upon the lad, neither you do nothing to him; for now I have shown that you fear Yahuah, and have not withheld your son, your first born son, from me.

12. And the prince Mastêmâ was put to shame; and Abrâhâm lifted up his eyes and looked, and, behold a ram caught . . . by his horns, and Abrâhâm went and took the ram and offered it for a burnt offering in the stead of his son.

13. And Abrâhâm called that place "Yahuah Yireh (הֹוָה יְרְאֶה)", so that it is said in the mount Yahuah has seen: That is Mount Tsîyôn.

14. And Yahuah called Abrâhâm by his name a second time from shâmayim, as he caused us to appear to speak to him in the name of Yahuah.

15. And he said: By myself I have sworn, says Yahuah, because you have done this thing, and have not withheld your son, your beloved son, from me, that in blessing I will bless you, and in multiplying I will multiply your seed as the stars of shâmayim, and as the sand which is on the seashore. And your seed shall inherit the cities of its enemies,

16. And in your seed shall all nations of the earth be blessed; because you have obeyed my voice, and I have shown to all that you are faithful unto me in all that I have said unto you: Go in peace.

17. And Abrâhâm went to his young men, and they arose and went together to Beêrsheba, and Abrâhâm dwelt by the Well of the Oath.

18. And he celebrated this festival every year, seven days with joy, and he called it the Feast of Yahuah according to the seven days during which he went and returned in peace.

19. And accordingly has it been ordained and written on the shâmayim tablets regarding Yâshârêl and its seed that they should observe this festival seven days with the joy of festival.

Chapter 19

1. And in the first year of the first week in the forty second jubilee, Abrâhâm returned and dwelt opposite Chebrôn that is Qiryath Arba, two weeks of years.

2. And in the first year of the third week of this jubilee the days of the life of Śârâh were accomplished, and she died in Chebrôn.

3. And Abrâhâm went to mourn over her and bury her, and we tried him to see if his spirit were patient and he was not indignant in the words of his mouth; and he was found patient in this, and was not disturbed.

4. For in patience of spirit he conversed with the children of Chêth (חֵת), to the intent that they should give him a place in which to bury his dead.

5. And Yahuah gave him grace before all who saw him, and he besought in gentleness the sons of Chêth, and they gave him the land of the double cave over against Mamrê that is Chebrôn, for four hundred pieces of silver.

6. And they besought him saying, we shall give it to you for nothing; but he would not take it from their hands for nothing, for he gave the price of the place, the money in full, and he bowed down before them twice, and after this he buried his dead in the double cave.

7. And all the days of the life of Śârâh were one hundred and twenty seven years that is, two jubilees and four weeks and one year: these are the days of the years of the life of Śârâh.

8. This is the tenth trial wherewith Abrâhâm was tried, and he was found faithful, patient in spirit.

9. And did not say a single word regarding the rumor in the land how that Êlôhîym had said that he would give it to him and to his seed after him, and he begged a place there to bury his dead; for he was found faithful, and was recorded on the shâmayim tablets as the friend of Êlôhîym.

10. And in the fourth year thereof he took a woman for his son Yitscḥâq and her name was Ribqâh (רִבְקָה), the daughter of Bethûêl, the son of Nâchôr, the brother of Abrâhâm,

the sister of Lâbân and daughter of Bethûêl; and Bethûêl was the son of Milkâh (מִלְכָּה), who was the woman of Nâchôr, the brother of Abrâhâm.

11. And Abrâhâm took to himself a third woman, and her name was Qeṭûrâh, from among the daughters of his household servants, for Hâgâr had died before Śârâh.

12. And she bare him six sons, Zimrân, and Yoqshân, and Medân, and Midyân, and Yishbâq, and Shûach, in the two weeks of years.

13. And in the sixth week, in the second year thereof, Ribqâh bare to Yitschâq two sons, Yaăqôb and Êśâw, and Yaăqôb was a smooth and upright man, and Êśâw was fierce, a man of the field, and hairy, and Yaăqôb dwelt in tents.

14. And the youths grew, and Yaăqôb learned to write; but Êśâw did not learn, for he was a man of the field and a hunter, and he learnt war, and all his deeds were fierce.

15. And Abrâhâm loved Yaăqôb, but Yitschâq loved Êśâw.

16. And Abrâhâm saw the deeds of Êśâw, and he knew that in Yaăqôb should his name and seed be called; and he called Ribqâh and gave commandment regarding Yaăqôb, for he knew that she too loved Yaăqôb much more than Êśâw.

17. And he said unto her: My daughter, watch over my son Yaăqôb, for he shall be in my stead on the earth, and for a blessing in the midst of the children of men, and for the glory of the whole seed of Shêm.

18. For I know that Yahuah will choose him to be a people for possession unto himself, above all peoples that are upon the face of the earth.

19. And behold, Yitschâq my son loves Êśâw more than Yaăqôb, but I see that you truly love Yaăqôb.

20. Add still further to your kindness to him, and let your eyes be upon him in love; for he shall be a blessing unto us on the earth from henceforth unto all generations of the earth.

21. Let your hands be strong and let your heart rejoice in your son Yaăqôb; for I have loved him far beyond all my sons. He shall be blessed forever, and his seed shall fill the whole earth.

22. If a man can number the sand of the earth, his seed also shall be numbered.

23. And all the blessings wherewith Yahuah has blessed me and my seed shall belong to Yaăqôb and his seed always.

24. And in his seed shall my name be blessed, and the name of my fathers, Shêm, and Nôach, and Chănôk, and Mahălalêl, and Ĕnôsh, and Shêth, and Âdâm.

25. And these shall serve to lay the foundations of the shâmayim, and to strengthen the earth, and to renew all the luminaries which are in the firmament.

26. And he called Yaăqôb before the eyes of Ribqâh his mother, and kissed him, and blessed him, and said:

27. Yaăqôb, my beloved son, whom my soul loves, may Êlôhîym bless you from above the firmament, and may he give you all the blessings wherewith he blessed Âdâm, and Chănôk, and Nôach, and Shêm; and all the things of which he told me, and all the things which he promised to give me, may he cause to cleave to you and to your seed forever, according to the days of shâmayim above the earth.

28. And the spirits of Mastêmâ shall not rule over you or over your seed to turn you from Yahuah, who is your Êlôhîym from henceforth forever.

29. And may Yahuah Êlôhîym be an Âb (אָב) to you and you the first born son, and to the people always.

30. Go in peace, my son. And they both went forth together from Abrâhâm.

31. And Ribqâh loved Yaăqôb, with all her heart and with all her soul, very much more than Êśâw; but Yitschâq loved Êśâw much more than Yaăqôb.

Chapter 20

1. And in the forty second jubilee, in the first year of the seventh week, Abrâhâm called Yishmâêl, and his twelve sons, and Yitschâq and his two sons, and the six sons of Qeţûrâh, and their sons.

2. And he commanded them that they should observe the way of Yahuah; that they should work righteousness, and love each his neighbor, and act on this manner among all men; that they should each so walk with regard to them as to do judgment and righteousness on the earth.

3. That they should circumcise their sons, according to the covenant which he had made with them, and not deviate to the right hand or the left of all the paths which Yahuah had commanded us; and that we should keep ourselves from all fornication and uncleanness, and renounce from among us all fornication and uncleanness.

4. And if any woman or maid commit fornication among you, burn her with fire and do not let them commit fornication with her after their eyes and their heart; and do not let them take to themselves women from the daughters of Kenaan; for the seed of Kenaan will be rooted out of the land.

5. And he told them of the judgment of the nephîyl, and the judgment of the Sedôm, how they had been judged on account of their wickedness, and had died on account of their fornication, and uncleanness, and mutual corruption through fornication.

6. And guard yourselves from all fornication and uncleanness, and from all pollution of sin, lest you make our name a curse, and your whole life a hissing, and all your sons to be destroyed by the sword, and you become accursed like Sedôm, and all your remnant as the sons of Ămôrâh.

7. I implore you, my sons, love the Êlôhîym of shâmayim and you cleave to all his commandments. And do not walk after their idols, and after their uncleannesses,

8. And do not make for yourselves molten or graven gods; for they are vanity, and there is no spirit in them; for they are work of men's hands, and all who trust in them, trust in nothing.

9. Do not serve them, nor worship them, but you serve Êlôhîym Elyôn Êl, and worship him continually: And hope for his countenance always, and work uprightness and righteousness before him, that he may have pleasure in you and grant you his mercy, and send rain upon you morning and evening, and bless all your works which you have wrought upon the earth, and bless your bread and your water, and bless the fruit of your womb and the fruit of your land, and the herds of your cattle, and the flocks of your sheep.

10. And you will be for a blessing on the earth, and all nations of the earth will desire you, and bless your sons in my name, that they may be blessed as I am.

11. And he gave to Yishmâêl and to his sons, and to the sons of Qeṭûrâh, gifts, and sent them away from Yitschâq his son, and he gave everything to Yitschâq his son.

12. And Yishmâêl and his sons, and the sons of Qeṭûrâh and their sons, went together and dwelt from Parân to the entering in of Bâbel in all the land which is towards the East facing the desert.

13. And these mingled with each other, and their name was called Ărâb, and Yishmâêlîy.

Chapter 21

1. And in the sixth year of the seventh week of this jubilee Abrâhâm called Yitschâq his son, and commanded him: Saying, I have become old, and do not know the day of my death, and am full of my days.

2. And behold, I am one hundred and seventy five years old, and throughout all the days of my life I have remembered Yahuah, and sought with all my heart to do his will, and to walk uprightly in all his ways.

3. My soul has hated idols, and I have despised those that served them, and I have given my heart and spirit that I might observe to do the will of him who created me.

4. For he is the living Êlôhîym, and he is Qâdôsh and faithful, and he is righteous beyond all, and there is with him no accepting of men's and no accepting of gifts; for Êlôhîym is righteous, and executes judgment on all those who transgress his commandments and despise his covenant.

5. And you do, my son, observe his commandments and his ordinances and his judgments, and do not walk after the abominations and after the graven images and after the molten images.

6. And eat no blood at all of animals or cattle, or of any bird which flies in the shâmayim.

7. And if you do slay a victim as an acceptable peace offering, you slay it, and pour out its blood upon the altar, and all the fat of the offering offer on the altar with fine flour and the meat offering mingled with oil, with its drink offering, offer them all together on the altar of burnt offering; it is a sweet savor before Yahuah.

8. And you will offer the fat of the sacrifice of thank offerings on the fire which is upon the altar, and the fat which is on the belly, and all the fat on the inwards and the two kidneys, and all the fat that is upon them, and upon the loins and liver you shall remove, together with the kidneys.

9. And offer all these for a sweet savor acceptable before Yahuah, with its meat offering and with its drink offering, for a sweet savor, the bread of the offering unto Yahuah.

10. And eat its meat on that day and on the second day, and do not let the sun on the second day go down upon it till it is eaten, and let nothing be left over for the third day; for it is not acceptable and let it no longer be eaten, and all who eat thereof will bring sin upon themselves; for thus I have found it written in the books of my forefathers, and in the words of Chănôk, and in the words of Nôach.

11. And on all your offerings you shall strew salt, and do not let the salt of the covenant be lacking in all your offerings before Yahuah.

12. And as regards the wood of the sacrifices, beware lest you bring other wood for the altar in addition to these: Cypress, defran, sagad, fir, pine, cedar, savin, palm, olive, myrrh, laurel, citron, juniper and balsam.

13. And of these kinds of wood lay upon the altar under the sacrifice, such as have been tested as to their appearance, and do not lay

thereon any split or dark wood, but hard and clean, without fault, a sound and new growth; and do not lay thereon old wood, for its fragrance is gone for there is no longer fragrance in it as before.

14. Besides these kinds of wood there is none other that you shall place on the altar, for the fragrance is dispersed, and the smell of its fragrance does not goes up to shâmayim.

15. Observe this commandment and do it, my son, that you may be upright in all your deeds.

16. And at all times be clean in your body, and wash yourself with water before you approach to offer on the altar, and wash your hands and your feet before you draw near to the altar; and when you are done sacrificing, wash again your hands and your feet.

17. And let no blood appear upon you nor upon your clothes; be on your guard, my son, against blood, be on your guard exceedingly; cover it with dust.

18. And do not eat any blood for it is the soul; do not eat no blood whatever.

19. And take no gifts for the blood of man, lest it be shed with impunity, without judgment; for it is the blood that is shed that causes the earth to sin, and the earth cannot be cleansed from the blood of man save by the blood of him who shed it.

20. And take no present or gift for the blood of man: Blood for blood, that you may be accepted before Yahuah, Êlôhîym Elyôn Êl; for he is the defense of the good: And that you may be preserved from all evil, and that he may save you from every kind of death.

21. I see, my son that all the works of the children of men are sin and wickedness, and all their deeds are uncleanness and an abomination and a pollution, and there is no righteousness with them.

22. Beware, lest you should walk in their ways and tread in their paths, and sin a sin unto death before Êlôhîym Elyôn Êl. Else he will hide his face from you and give you back into the hands of your transgression, and root you out of the land, and your seed likewise from under shâmayim, and your name and your seed shall perish from the whole earth.

23. Turn away from all their deeds and all their uncleanness, and observe the ordinance of Êlôhîym Elyôn Êl, and do his will and be upright in all things.

24. And he will bless you in all your deeds, and will raise up from you a plant of righteousness through all the earth, throughout all generations of the earth, and my name and your name shall not be forgotten under shâmayim forever.

25. Go, my son in peace. May Êlôhîym Elyôn Êl, my Êlôhîym and your Êlôhîym, strengthen you to do his will, and may he bless all your seed and the residue of your seed for the generations forever, with all righteous blessings, that you may be a blessing on all the earth.

26. And he went out from him rejoicing.

Chapter 22

1. And it came to pass in the first week in the forty fourth jubilee, in the second year, that is, the year in which Abrâhâm died, that Yitschâq and Yishmâêl came from the Well of the Oath to celebrate the feast of weeks that is, the feast of the first fruits of the harvest to Abrâhâm, their father, and Abrâhâm rejoiced because his two sons had come.

2. For Yitschâq had many possessions in Beêrsheba, and Yitschâq was wont to go and see his possessions and to return to his father.

3. And in those days Yishmâêl came to see his father, and they both came together, and Yitschâq offered a sacrifice for a burnt offering, and presented it on the altar of his father which he had made in Chebrôn.

4. And he offered a thank offering and made a feast of joy before Yishmâêl, his brother: and Ribqâh made new cakes from the new grain, and gave them to Yaăqôb, her son, to take them to Abrâhâm, his father, from the first fruits of the land, that he might eat and bless the Bârâ of all things before he died.

5. And Yitschâq, too, sent by the hand of Yaăqôb to Abrâhâm a best thank offering, that he might eat and drink.

6. And he eat and drank, and blessed Êlôhîym Elyôn Êl, who has created shâmayim and earth, who has made all the fat things of the earth, and given them to the children of men that they might eat and drink and bless their Bârâ.

7. And now I give thanks unto you, my Êlôhîym, because you have caused me to see this day: Behold, I am one hundred three score and fifteen years, an old man and full of days, and all my days have been unto me peace.

8. The sword of the adversary has not overcome me in all that you have given me and my children all the days of my life until this day.

9. My Êlôhîym, may your mercy and your peace be upon your servant, and upon the seed of his sons, that they may be to you a chosen nation and an inheritance from among all the nations of the earth from henceforth unto all the days of the generations of the earth, unto all the ages.

10. And he called Yaăqôb and said: My son Yaăqôb, may the Êlôhîym of all bless you and strengthen you to do righteousness, and his will before him, and may he choose you and your seed that you may become a people for his inheritance according to his will always.

11. And you do, my son, Yaăqôb, draw near and kiss me. And he drew near and kissed him, and he said: Blessed be my son Yaăqôb and all the sons of Êlôhîym Elyôn Êl, unto all the ages: May Êlôhîym give unto you a seed of righteousness; and some of your sons may he sanctify in the midst of the whole earth; may nations serve you, and all the nations bow themselves before your seed.

12. Be strong in the presence of men, and exercise authority over all the seed of Shêth. Then your ways and the ways of your sons will be justified, so that they shall become a qâdôsh nation.

13. May Êlôhîym Elyôn Êl give you all the blessings wherewith he has blessed me and wherewith he blessed Nôach and Âdâm; may they rest on the sacred head of your seed from generation to generation forever.

14. And may he cleanse you from all unrighteousness and impurity that you may be forgiven all the transgressions; which you have committed ignorantly. And may he strengthen you, and bless you. And may you inherit the whole earth,

15. And may he renew his covenant with you. That you may be to him a nation for his inheritance for all the ages, and that he may be to you and to your seed an Êlôhîym in truth and righteousness throughout all the days of the earth.

16. And you do, my son Yaăqôb, remember my words, and observe the commandments of Abrâhâm, your father: Separate yourself from the nations, and do not eat with them: And do not do according to their works, and do not become their associate; for their works are unclean, and all their

ways are a pollution and an abomination and uncleanness.

17. They offer their sacrifices to the dead and they worship evil spirits, and they eat over the graves, and all their works are vanity and nothingness.

18. They have no heart to understand and their eyes do not see what their works are, and how they err in saying to a piece of wood: You are my Êlôhîym, and to a stone: You are my Yahuah and you are my deliverer. And they have no heart.

19. And as for you, my son Yaăqôb, may Êlôhîym Elyôn Êl help you and the Êlôhîym of shâmayim bless you and remove you from their uncleanness and from all their error.

20. You are ware, my son Yaăqôb, of taking a woman from any seed of the daughters of Kenaan; for all his seed is to be rooted out of the earth.

21. For, owing to the transgression of Châm, Kenaan erred, and all his seed shall be destroyed from off the earth and all the residue thereof, and none springing from him shall be saved on the Day of Judgment.

22. And as for all the worshippers of idols and the profane. There shall be no hope for them in the land of the living. And there shall be no remembrance of them on the earth; for they shall descend into Sheôl. And into the place of condemnation shall they go, as the children of Sedôm were taken away from the earth so will all those who worship idols be taken away.

23. Do not fear, my son Yaăqôb, and do not be dismayed, O son of Abrâhâm: May Êlôhîym Elyôn Êl preserve you from destruction, and from all the paths of error may he deliver you.

24. This house I have built for myself that I might put my name upon it in the earth: It is given to you and to your seed forever, and it will be named the house of Abrâhâm; it is given to you and to your seed forever; for you will build my house and establish my name before Êlôhîym forever: Your seed and your name will stand throughout all generations of the earth.

25. And he ceased commanding him and blessing him.

26. And the two lay together on one bed, and Yaăqôb slept in the bosom of Abrâhâm, his father's father and he kissed him seven times, and his affection and his heart rejoiced over him.

27. And he blessed him with all his heart and said: Êlôhîym Elyôn Êl, the Êlôhîym of all, and Bârâ of all, who brought me forth from Ûr of the Kaśdîy that he might give me this land to inherit it forever, and that I might establish a qâdôsh seed, blessed be Elyôn Êl forever.

28. And he blessed Yaăqôb and said: My son, over whom with all my heart and my affection I rejoice, may your grace and your mercy be lift up upon him and upon his seed always.

29. And do not forsake him, nor set him at nothing from henceforth unto the days of eternity, and may your eyes be opened upon him and upon his seed, that you may preserve him, and bless him, and may sanctify him as a nation for your inheritance;

30. And bless him with all your blessings from henceforth unto all the days of eternity, and renew your covenant and your grace with him and with his seed according to all your good pleasure unto all the generations of the earth.

Chapter 23

1. And he placed two fingers of Yaăqôb on his eyes, and he blessed the Êlôhîym of Êlôhîym,

and he covered his face and stretched out his feet and slept the sleep of eternity, and was gathered to his fathers.

2. And notwithstanding all this Yaăqôb was lying in his bosom, and he did not know that Abrâhâm, his father's father, was dead.

3. And Yaăqôb awoke from his sleep, and behold Abrâhâm was cold as ice, and he said: Father, father; but there was none that spoke, and he knew that he was dead.

4. And he arose from his bosom and ran and told Ribqâh, his mother; and Ribqâh went to Yitschâq in the night, and told him; and they went together, and Yaăqôb with them, and a lamp was in his hand, and when they had gone in they found Abrâhâm lying dead.

5. And Yitschâq fell on the face of his father and wept and kissed him.

6. And the voices were heard in the house of Abrâhâm, and Yishmâêl his son arose, and went to Abrâhâm his father, and wept over Abrâhâm his father, he and all the house of Abrâhâm, and they wept with a great weeping.

7. And his sons Yitschâq and Yishmâêl buried him in the double cave, near Śârâh his woman, and they wept for him forty days, all the men of his house, and Yitschâq and Yishmâêl, and all their sons, and all the sons of Qeṭûrâh in their places; and the days of weeping for Abrâhâm were ended.

8. And he lived three jubilees and four weeks of years, one hundred and seventy five years, and completed the days of his life, being old and full of days.

9. For the days of the forefathers, of their life, were nineteen jubilees; and after the Flood they began to grow less than nineteen jubilees, and to decrease in jubilees, and to grow old quickly, and to be full of their days because of manifold tribulation and the wickedness of their ways, with the exception of Abrâhâm.

10. For Abrâhâm was perfect in all his deeds with Yahuah, and well pleasing in righteousness all the days of his life; and behold, he did not complete four jubilees in his life, when he had grown old because of the wickedness, and was full of his days.

11. And all the generations which shall arise from this time until the day of the great judgment shall grow old quickly, before they complete two jubilees, and their knowledge shall forsake them because of their old age and all their knowledge shall vanish away.

12. And in those days, if a man live a jubilee and a half of years, they shall say regarding him: He has lived long, and the greater part of his days are pain and sorrow and tribulation, and there is no peace:

13. For calamity follows on calamity, and wound on wound, and tribulation on tribulation, and evil tidings on evil tidings, and illness on illness, and all evil judgments such as these, one with another, illness and overthrow, and snow and frost and ice, and fever, and chills, and torpor, and famine, and death, and sword, and captivity, and all kinds of calamities and pains.

14. And all these shall come on an evil generation, which transgresses on the earth: Their works are uncleanness and fornication, and pollution and abominations.

15. Then they shall say: The days of the forefathers were many even, unto a thousand years, and were good; but behold, the days of our life, if a man has lived many, are three score years and ten, and, if he is strong, four score years, and those evil, and there is no peace in the days of this evil generation.

16. And in that generation the sons shall convict their fathers and their elders of sin and unrighteousness, and of the words of their mouth and the great wickednesses which they perpetrate, and concerning their forsaking the covenant which Yahuah made between them and him, that they should observe and do all his commandments and his ordinances and all his laws, without departing either to the right hand or the left.

17. For all have done evil, and every mouth speaks iniquity and all their works are an uncleanness and an abomination, and all their ways are pollution, uncleanness and destruction.

18. Behold the earth shall be destroyed on account of all their works, and there shall be no seed of the vine, and no oil; for their works are altogether faithless, and they shall all perish together, beasts and cattle and birds, and all the fish of the sea, on account of the children of men.

19. And they shall strive one with another, the young with the old, and the old with the young, the poor with the rich, the lowly with the great, and the beggar with the prince, on account of the law and the covenant; for they have forgotten commandment, and covenant, and feasts, and months, and Shabbâth, and jubilees, and all judgments.

20. And they shall stand with bows and swords and war to turn them back into the way; but they shall not return until much blood has been shed on the earth, one by another.

21. And those who have escaped shall not return from their wickedness to the way of righteousness, but they shall all exalt themselves to deceit and wealth, that they may each take all that is his neighbor's, and they shall name the great name, but not in truth and not in righteousness, and they shall defile the qâdôsh of qâdôsh with their uncleanness and the corruption of their pollution.

22. And a great punishment shall befall the deeds of this generation from Yahuah, and he will give them over to the sword and to judgment and to captivity, and to be plundered and devoured.

23. And he will wake up against them the sinners of the Gentiles, who have neither mercy nor compassion, and who shall respect the person of none, neither old nor young, nor any one, for they are more wicked and strong to do evil than all the children of men. And they shall use violence against Yâshârêl and transgression against Yaăqôb, and much blood shall be shed upon the earth, and there shall be none to gather and none to bury.

24. In those days they shall cry aloud, and call and pray that they may be saved from the hand of the sinners, the Gentiles; but none shall be saved.

25. And the heads of the children shall be white with grey hair, and a child of three weeks shall appear old like a man of one hundred years, and their stature shall be destroyed by tribulation and oppression.

26. And in those days the children shall begin to study the laws, and to seek the commandments, and to return to the path of righteousness.

27. And the days shall begin to grow many and increase among those children of men till their days draw nigh to one thousand years. And to a greater number of years than before was the number of the days.

28. And there shall be no old man nor one who is not satisfied with his days, for all shall be as children and youths.

29. And all their days they shall complete and live in peace and in joy, and there shall be no adversary nor any evil destroyer; for all their days shall be days of blessing and healing.

30. And at that time Yahuah will heal his servants, and they shall rise up and see great peace, and drive out their adversaries. And the righteous shall see and be thankful, and rejoice with joy forever and ever, and shall see all their judgments and all their curses on their enemies.

31. And their bones shall rest in the earth, and their spirits shall have much joy, and they shall know that it is Yahuah who executes judgment, and shows mercy to hundreds and thousands and to all that love him.

32. And you do, Môsheh, write down these words; for thus are they written, and they record them on the shâmayim tablets for a testimony for the generations forever.

Chapter 24

1. And it came to pass after the death of Abrâhâm that Yahuah blessed Yitschâq his son, and he arose from Chebrôn and went and dwelt at the Well of the Vision in the first year of the third week of this jubilee, seven years.

2. And in the first year of the fourth week a famine began in the land, besides the first famine, which had been in the days of Abrâhâm.

3. And Yaăqôb sod lentil pottage, and Êśâw came from the field hungry. And he said to Yaăqôb his brother: Give me of this red pottage. And Yaăqôb said to him: Sell to me your primogeniture, this birthright and I will give you bread, and also some of this lentil pottage.

4. And Êśâw said in his heart: I shall die; of what profit to me is this birthright?

5. And he said to Yaăqôb: I give it to you. And Yaăqôb said: Swear to me, this day, and he swore unto him.

6. And Yaăqôb gave his brother Êśâw bread and pottage, and he ate till he was satisfied, and Êśâw despised his birthright; for this reason was Êśâw's name called Ědôm, on account of the red pottage which Yaăqôb gave him for his birthright.

7. And Yaăqôb became the elder, and Êśâw was brought down from his dignity.

8. And the famine was over the land, and Yitschâq departed to go down into Mitsrayim in the second year of this week, and went to the king of the Pelishtîy (פְּלִשְׁתִּי) to Gerâr, unto Ăbîymelek.

9. And Yahuah appeared unto him and said unto him: Do not go down into Mitsrayim; dwell in the land that I shall tell you of, and sojourn in this land, and I will be with you and bless you.

10. For to you and to your seed I will give all this land, and I will establish my oath which I swore unto Abrâhâm your father, and I will multiply your seed as the stars of shâmayim, and will give unto your seed all this land.

11. And in your seed shall all the nations of the earth be blessed, because your father obeyed my voice, and kept my charge and my commandments, and my laws, and my ordinances, and my covenant; and now obey my voice and dwell in this land.

12. And he dwelt in Gerâr three weeks of years.

13. And Ăbîymelek charged concerning him, and concerning all that was his, saying: Any man that shall touch him or aught that is his shall surely die.

14. And Yitschâq waxed strong among the Pelishtîy, and he got many possessions, oxen and sheep and camels and asses and a great household.

15. And he sowed in the land of the Pelishtîy and brought in a hundred fold, and Yitschâq became exceedingly great, and the Pelishtîy envied him.

16. Now all the wells which the servants of Abrâhâm had dug during the life of Abrâhâm, the Pelishtîy had stopped them after the death of Abrâhâm, and filled them with earth.

17. And Ăbîymelek said unto Yitschâq: Go from us, for you are much mightier than we, and Yitschâq departed thence in the first year of the seventh week, and sojourned in the valleys of Gerâr.

18. And they dug again the wells of water which the servants of Abrâhâm, his father, had dug, and which the Pelishtîy had closed after the death of Abrâhâm his father, and he called their names as Abrâhâm his father had named them.

19. And the servants of Yitschâq dug a well in the valley, and found living water, and the shepherds of Gerâr strove with the shepherds of Yitschâq, saying: The water is ours; and Yitschâq called the name of the well "Êśeq (עֵשֶׂק)", because they had been perverse with us.

20. And they dug a second well, and they strove for that also, and he called its name "Śiṭnâh (שִׂטְנָה)". And he arose from thence and they dug another well, and for that they strove not, and he called the name of it "Rechôbôth (רְחֹבוֹת)", and Yitschâq said: Now Yahuah has made room for us, and we have increased in the land.

21. And he went up from thence to the Well of the Oath in the first year of the first week in the forty fourth jubilee.

22. And Yahuah appeared to him that night, on the beginning of the first month, and said unto him: I am the Êlôhîym of Abrâhâm your father; do not fear, for I am with you, and shall bless you and shall surely multiply your seed as the sand of the earth, for the sake of Abrâhâm my servant.

23. And he built an altar there, which Abrâhâm his father had first built, and he called upon the name of Yahuah, and he offered sacrifice to the Êlôhîym of Abrâhâm his father.

24. And they dug a well and they found living water.

25. And the servants of Yitschâq dug another well and did not find water, and they went and told Yitschâq that they had not found water, and Yitschâq said: I have sworn this day to the Pelishtîy and this thing has been announced to us.

26. And he called the name of that place the Well of the Oath; for there he had sworn to Ăbîymelek and Ăchûzzath his friend and Pîykôl the prefect Ôr his host.

27. And Yitschâq knew that day that under constraint he had sworn to them to make peace with them.

28. And Yitschâq on that day cursed the Pelishtîy and said: Cursed be the Pelishtîy unto the day of wrath and indignation from the midst of all nations; may Êlôhîym make them a derision and a curse and an object of wrath and indignation in the hands of the sinners the Gentiles and in the hands of the Kittîy.

29. And whoever escapes the sword of the enemy and the Kittîy, may the righteous nation root out in judgment from under shâmayim; for they shall be the enemies and foes of my children throughout their generations upon the earth.

30. And no remnant shall be left to them, nor one that shall be saved on the day of the wrath of judgment; for destruction and rooting out and expulsion from the earth is the whole seed of the Pelishtîy reserved, and there shall no longer be left for these Kaphtôrîy a name or a seed on the earth.

31. For though he ascend unto shâmayim, thence he shall be brought down, and though he make himself strong on earth, thence he shall be dragged forth, and though he hide himself among the nations, even from thence he shall be rooted out; and though he descend into Sheôl, there also shall his condemnation be great, and there also he shall have no peace.

32. And if he goes into captivity, by the hands of those that seek his life they shall slay him on the way, and neither name nor seed shall be left to him on all the earth; for into eternal malediction he shall depart.

33. And thus is it written and engraved concerning him on the shâmayim tablets, to do unto him on the Day of Judgment, so that he may be rooted out of the earth.

Chapter 25

1. And in the second year of this week in this jubilee, Ribqâh called Yaăqôb her son, and spoke unto him, saying: My son, do not take you a woman of the daughters of Kenaan, as Êsâw, your brother, who took him two women of the daughters of Kenaan, and they have embittered my soul with all their unclean deeds: For all their deeds are fornication and lust, and there is no righteousness with them, for their deeds are evil.

2. And I, my son, love you exceedingly, and my heart and my affection bless you every hour of the day and watch of the night.

3. And now, my son, hearken to my voice, and do the will of your mother, and do not take you a woman of the daughters of this land, but only of the house of my father, and of my father's kindred. You shall take you a woman of the house of my father, and Êlôhîym Elyôn Êl will bless you, and your children shall be a righteous generation and a qâdôsh seed.

4. And then spoke Yaăqôb to Ribqâh, his mother, and said unto her: Behold, mother, I am nine weeks of years old, and I neither know nor I have touched any woman, nor I have betrothed myself to any, nor even think of taking me a woman of the daughters of Kenaan.

5. For I remember, mother, the words of Abrâhâm, our father, for he commanded me not to take a woman of the daughters of Kenaan, but to take me a woman from the seed of my father's house and from my kindred.

6. I have heard before that daughters have been born to Lâbân, your brother, and I have set my heart on them to take a woman from among them.

7. And for this reason I have guarded myself in my spirit against sinning or being corrupted in all my ways throughout all the days of my life; for with regard to lust and fornication, Abrâhâm, my father, gave me many commands.

8. And, despite all that he has commanded me, these two and twenty years my brother has striven with me, and spoken frequently to me and said: My brother, take to woman a sister of my two women; but I refuse to do as he has done.

9. I swear before you, mother that all the days of my life I will not take me a woman from the daughters of the seed of Kenaan, and I will not act wickedly as my brother has done.

10. Do not fear, mother; be assured that I shall do your will and walk in uprightness, and not corrupt my ways forever.

11. And thereupon she lifted up her face to shâmayim and extended the fingers of her hands, and opened her mouth and blessed Êlôhîym Elyôn Êl, who had created the shâmayim and the earth, and she gave him thanks and praise.

12. And she said: Blessed be Yahuah Êlôhîym, and may his qâdôsh name be blessed forever and ever, who has given me Yaăqôb as a pure son and a qâdôsh seed; for he is yours, and yours shall his seed be continually and throughout all the generations forevermore.

13. Bless him, O Yahuah, and place in my mouth the blessing of righteousness, that I may bless him.

14. And at that hour, when the spirit of righteousness descended into her mouth, she placed both her hands on the head of Yaăqôb, and said:

15. Blessed are you, Yahuah Tsedâqâh and Êlôhîym of the ages and may he bless you beyond all the generations of men. May he give you, my son, the path of righteousness, and reveal righteousness to your seed.

16. And may he make your sons many during your life, and may they arise according to the number of the months of the year. And may their sons become many and great beyond the stars of shâmayim, and their numbers be more than the sand of the sea.

17. And may he give them this goodly land as he said he would give it to Abrâhâm and to his seed after him always. And may they hold it as a possession forever.

18. And may I see born unto you, my son, blessed children during my life, and a blessed and qâdôsh seed may all your seed be.

19. And as you have refreshed your mother's spirit during her life, the womb of her that bare you blesses you thus, my affection and my breasts bless you and my mouth and my tongue praise you greatly.

20. Increase and spread over the earth, and may your seed be perfect in the joy of shâmayim and earth forever; and may your seed rejoice, and on the great day of peace may it have peace.

21. And may your name and your seed endure to all the ages, and may Êlôhîym Elyôn Êl be their Êlôhîym, and may the Êlôhîym of righteousness dwell with them, and by them may his sanctuary be built unto all the ages.

22. Blessed be he that blesses you, and all flesh that curses you falsely, may it be cursed.

23. And she kissed him, and said to him; may Yahuah of the world love you as the heart of your mother and her affection rejoice in you and bless you. And she ceased from blessing.

Chapter 26

1. And in the seventh year of this week Yitschâq called Êśâw, his elder son, and said unto him: I am old, my son, and behold my eyes are dim in seeing, and I do not know the day of my death.

2. And now take your hunting weapons your quiver and your bow, and go out to the field, and hunt and catch me a venison, my son, and make me savory meat, such as my soul loves, and bring it to me that I may eat, and that my soul may bless you before I die.

3. But Ribqâh heard Yitschâq speaking to Êśâw.

4. And Êśâw went forth early to the field to hunt and catch and bring home to his father.

5. And Ribqâh called Yaăqôb, her son, and said unto him: Behold, I heard Yitschâq, your father, speak unto Êśâw, your brother, saying: Hunt for me, and make me savory meat, and bring it to me that I may eat and bless you before Yahuah before I die.

6. And now, my son, obey my voice in that which I command you: Go to your flock and fetch me two good kids of male goats, and I will make them savory meat for your father, such as he loves, and you shall bring it to your father that he may eat and bless you before Yahuah before he die, and that you may be blessed.

7. And Yaăqôb said to Ribqâh his mother: Mother, I shall not withhold anything which my father would eat, and which would please him: I only fear, my mother, that he will recognise my voice and wish to touch me.

8. And you know that I am smooth, and Êśâw, my brother, is hairy, and I shall appear before his eyes as an evildoer, and shall do a deed which he had not commanded me, and he will be wroth with me, and I shall bring upon myself a curse, and not a blessing.

9. And Ribqâh, his mother, said unto him: Upon me be your curse, my son, only obey my voice.

10. And Yaăqôb obeyed the voice of Ribqâh, his mother, and went and fetched two good and fat kids of male goats, and brought them to his mother, and his mother made them savory meat such as he loved.

11. And Ribqâh took the goodly rainment of Êśâw, her elder son, which was with her in the house, and she clothed Yaăqôb with them, her younger son, and she put the skins of the kids upon his hands and on the exposed parts of his neck.

12. And she gave the meat and the bread which she had prepared into the hand of her son Yaăqôb.

13. And Yaăqôb went in to his father and said: I am your son: I have done according as you bid me: Arise and sit and eat of that which I have caught, father, that your soul may bless me.

14. And Yitschâq said to his son: How you have found it so quickly, my son?

15. And Yaăqôb said: Because Yahuah your Êlôhîym caused me to find it.

16. And Yitschâq said unto him: Come near, that I may feel you, my son, if you are my son Êśâw or not.

17. And Yaăqôb went near to Yitschâq, his father, and he felt him and said: The voice is Yaăqôb's voice, but the hands are the hands of Êśâw,

18. And he did not discern him, because it was a dispensation from shâmayim to remove his power of perception and Yitschâq did not discern it, for his hands were hairy as his brother Êśâw's, so that he blessed him.

19. And he said: Are you my son Êśâw? And he said: I am your son: And he said, bring near to me that I may eat of that which you have caught, my son, that my soul may bless you.

20. And he brought near to him, and he did eat, and he brought him wine and he drank.

21. And Yitschâq, his father, said unto him: Come near and kiss me, my son.

22. And he came near and kissed him. And he smelled the smell of his raiment, and he blessed him and said: Behold, the smell of my son is as the smell of a full field which Yahuah has blessed.

23. And may Yahuah give you of the dew of shâmayim and of the dew of the earth, and plenty of corn and oil: Let nations serve you, and peoples bow down to you.

24. Be master over your brethren, and let your mother's sons bow down to you; and may all the blessings wherewith Yahuah has blessed me and blessed Abrâhâm, my father; be imparted to you and to your seed forever: Cursed be he that curses you, And blessed be he that blesses you.

25. And it came to pass as soon as Yitschâq had made an end of blessing his son Yaăqôb, and Yaăqôb had gone forth from Yitschâq his father he hid himself and Êśâw, his brother, came in from his hunting.

26. And he also made savory meat, and brought it to his father, and said unto his father: Let my father arise, and eat of my venison that your soul may bless me.

27. And Yitschâq, his father, said unto him: Who are you? And he said unto him: I am your first born, your son Êśâw: I have done as you have commanded me.

28. And Yitschâq was very greatly astonished, and said: Who is he that has hunted and caught and brought it to me, and I have eaten of all before you came, and have blessed him: And he shall be blessed, and all his seed forever.

29. And it came to pass when Êśâw heard the words of his father Yitschâq that he cried with an exceeding great and bitter cry, and said unto his father: Bless me, even me also, father.

30. And he said unto him: Your brother came with guile, and has taken away your blessing. And he said: Now I know why his name is named Yaăqôb: Behold, he has supplanted me these two times: He took away my birth right, and now he has taken away my blessing.

31. And he said: Have you not reserved a blessing for me, father? And Yitschâq answered and said unto Êśâw: Behold, I have made him your master, and all his brethren I have given to him for servants, and with plenty of corn and wine and oil I have strengthened him: And what now shall I do for you, my son?.

32. And Êśâw said to Yitschâq, his father: Do you have but one blessing, O father? Bless me, even me also, father:

33. And Êśâw lifted up his voice and wept. And Yitschâq answered and said unto him: Behold, far from the dew of the earth shall be your dwelling, and far from the dew of shâmayim from above.

34. And by your sword you will live, and you will serve your brother. And it shall come to pass when you become great, and do shake his yoke from off your neck, you shall sin a complete sin unto death, and your seed shall be rooted out from under shâmayim.

35. And Êśâw kept threatening Yaăqôb because of the blessing wherewith his father blessed him, and he said in his heart: May the days of mourning for my father now come, so that I may slay my brother Yaăqôb.

Ribqâh alarmed at Êśâw's threats prevails on Yitschâq to send Yaăqôb to Ăram Năhărayim, 1-12. Yitschâq comforts Ribqâh on the departure of Yaăqôb, 13-18. Yaăqôb's dream and vow at Bêythêl, 19-27. (Cf. Gen. xxviii.)

Chapter 27

1. And the words of Êśâw, her elder son, were told to Ribqâh in a dream, and Ribqâh sent and called Yaăqôb her younger son, and said unto him:

2. Behold Êśâw your brother will take vengeance on you so as to kill you.

3. Now, therefore, my son, obey my voice, and arise and you flee to Lâbân, my brother, to Chârân, and tarry with him a few days until your brother's anger turns away, and

he remove his anger from you, and forget all that you have done; then I will send and fetch you from thence.

4. And Yaăqôb said: I am not afraid; if he wishes to kill me, I will kill him.

5. But she said unto him: Do not let me be bereft of both my sons on one day.

6. And Yaăqôb said to Ribqâh his mother: Behold, you know that my father has become old, and does not see because his eyes are dull, and if I leave him it will be evil in his eyes, because I leave him and go away from you, and my father will be angry, and will curse me. I will not go; when he sends me, only then I will go.

7. And Ribqâh said to Yaăqôb: I will go in and speak to him, and he will send you away.

8. And Ribqâh went in and said to Yitschâq: I loathe my life because of the two daughters of Chêth, whom Êsâw has taken him as women; and if Yaăqôb take a woman from among the daughters of the land such as these, for what purpose do I further live, for the daughters of Kenaan are evil.

9. And Yitschâq called Yaăqôb and blessed him, and admonished him and said unto him:

10. Do not take you a woman of any of the daughters of Kenaan; arise and go to Ăram Naharayim, to the house of Bethûêl, your mother's father, and take you a woman from thence of the daughters of Lâbân, your mother's brother.

11. And Yahuah Shadday Êl bless you and increase and multiply you that you may become a company of nations, and give you the blessings of my father Abrâhâm, to you and to your seed after you, that you may inherit the land of your sojourning and all the land which Êlôhîym gave to Abrâhâm: Go, my son, in peace.

12. And Yitschâq sent Yaăqôb away, and he went to Ăram Naharayim, to Lâbân the son of Bethûêl the Ărâm (אֲרָם), the brother of Ribqâh, Yaăqôb's mother.

13. And it came to pass after Yaăqôb had arisen to go to Ăram Naharayim that the spirit of Ribqâh was grieved after her son, and she wept.

14. And Yitschâq said to Ribqâh: My sister, do not weep on account of Yaăqôb, my son; for he goes in peace, and in peace will he return.

15. Êlôhîym Elyôn Êl will preserve him from all evil, and will be with him; for he will not forsake him all his days;

16. For I know that his ways will be prospered in all things wherever he goes, until he return in peace to us, and we see him in peace.

17. Do not fear on his account, my sister, for he is on the upright path and he is a perfect man: And he is faithful and will not perish. Do not weep.

18. And Yitschâq comforted Ribqâh on account of her son Yaăqôb, and blessed him.

19. And Yaăqôb went from the Well of the Oath to go to Chârân on the first year of the second week in the forty fourth jubilee, and he came to Lûz on the mountains, that is, Bêythêl, on the beginning of the first month of this week, and he came to the place at even and turned from the way to the west of the road that night: And he slept there; for the sun had set.

20. And he took one of the stones of that place and laid it at his head under the tree, and he was journeying alone, and he slept.

21. And he dreamt that night, and behold a ladder set up on the earth, and the top of it reached to shâmayim, and behold, the

angels of Yahuah ascended and descended on it: and behold, Yahuah stood upon it.

22. And he spoke to Yaăqôb and said: I am Yahuah Êlôhîym of Abrâhâm, your father, and the Êlôhîym of Yitscḥâq; the land whereon you are sleeping, to you I will give it, and to your seed after you.

23. And your seed shall be as the dust of the earth, and you shall increase to the west and to the east, to the north and the south, and in you and in your seed shall all the families of the nations be blessed.

24. And behold, I will be with you, and will keep you whithersoever you go, and I will bring you again into this land in peace; for I will not leave you until I do everything that I told you of.

25. And Yaăqôb awoke from his sleep, and said, truly this place is the house of Yahuah, and I did not know it. And he was afraid and said: Dreadful is this place which is none other than the house of Êlôhîym, and this is the gate of shâmayim.

26. And Yaăqôb arose early in the morning, and took the stone which he had put under his head and set it up as a pillar for a sign, and he poured oil upon the top of it. And he called the name of that place Bêythêl; but the name of the place was Lûz at the first.

27. And Yaăqôb vowed a vow unto Yahuah, saying: If Yahuah will be with me, and will keep me in this way that I go, and give me bread to eat and raiment to put on, so that I come again to my father's house in peace, then shall Yahuah be my Êlôhîym, and this stone which I have set up as a pillar for a sign in this place, shall be Yahuah's house, and of all that you give me, I shall give the tenth to you, my Êlôhîym.

Chapter 28

1. And he went on his journey, and came to the land of the east, to Lâbân, the brother of Ribqâh, and he was with him, and served him for Râchêl his daughter one week.

2. And in the first year of the third week he said unto him: Give me my woman, for whom I have served you seven years; and Lâbân said unto Yaăqôb: I will give you your woman.

3. And Lâbân made a feast, and took Lêâh his elder daughter, and he gave her to Yaăqôb as a woman, and he gave Zilpâh his handmaid for a handmaid; and Yaăqôb did not know, for he thought that she was Râchêl.

4. And he went in unto her, and behold, she was Lêâh; and Yaăqôb was angry with Lâbân, and said unto him: Why have you dealt thus with me? Did not I serve you for Râchêl and not for Lêâh? Why you have wronged me?.

5. Take your daughter, and I will go; for you have done evil to me. For Yaăqôb loved Râchêl more than Lêâh; for Lêâh's eyes were weak, but her form was very handsome; but Râchêl had beautiful eyes and a beautiful and very handsome form.

6. And Lâbân said to Yaăqôb: It is not done so in our country, to give the younger before the elder. And it is not right to do this; for thus it is ordained and written in the shâmayim tablets, that no one should give his younger daughter before the elder; but the elder, one gives first and after her the younger and the man who does so, they set down guilt against him in shâmayim, and none is righteous that does this thing, for this deed is evil before Yahuah.

7. And you command the children of Yâshârêl that they do not this thing; let them neither

take nor give the younger before they have given the elder, for it is very wicked.

8. And Lâbân said to Yaăqôb: Let the seven days of the feast of this one pass by, and I shall give you Râchêl, that you may serve me another seven years, that you may pasture my sheep as you did in the former week.

9. And on the day when the seven days of the feast of Lêâh had passed, Lâbân gave Râchêl to Yaăqôb that he might serve him another seven years, and he gave to Râchêl Bilhâh, the sister of Zilpâh, as a handmaid.

10. And he served yet other seven years for Râchêl, for Lêâh had been given to him for nothing.

11. And Yahuah opened the womb of Lêâh, and she conceived and bare Yaăqôb a son, and he called his name Reûbên, on the fourteenth day of the ninth month, in the first year of the third week.

12. But the womb of Râchêl was closed, for Yahuah saw that Lêâh was hated and Râchêl loved.

13. And again Yaăqôb went in unto Lêâh, and she conceived, and bare Yaăqôb a second son, and he called his name Shimôn (בִּלְהָה), on the twenty first of the tenth month, and in the third year of this week.

14. And again Yaăqôb went in unto Lêâh, and she conceived, and bare him a third son, and he called his name Lêwîy (לֵוִי), in the beginning of the first month in the sixth year of this week.

15. And again Yaăqôb went in unto her, and she conceived, and bare him a fourth son, and he called his name Yahûdâh (יְהוּדָה), on the fifteenth of the third month, in the first year of the fourth week.

16. And on account of all this Râchêl envied Lêâh, for she did not bear, and she said to Yaăqôb: Give me children; and Yaăqôb said: I have withheld from you the fruits of your womb? I have forsaken you?

17. And when Râchêl saw that Lêâh had borne four sons to Yaăqôb, Reûbên and Shimôn and Lêwîy and Yahûdâh, she said unto him: Go in unto Bilhâh my handmaid, and she will conceive, and bear a son unto me. And she gave him Bilhâh her handmaid to woman.

18. And he went in unto her, and she conceived, and bare him a son, and he called his name Dân, on the ninth of the sixth month, in the sixth year of the third week.

19. And Yaăqôb went in again unto Bilhâh a second time, and she conceived, and bare Yaăqôb another son, and Râchêl called his name Naphtâlîy, on the fifth of the seventh month, in the second year of the fourth week.

20. And when Lêâh saw that she had become sterile and did not bear, she envied Râchêl, and she also he gave her handmaid Zilpâh to Yaăqôb to woman, and she conceived, and bare a son, and Lêâh called his name Gâd, on the twelfth of the eighth month, in the third year of the fourth week.

21. And he went in again unto her, and she conceived, and bare him a second son, and Lêâh called his name Âshêr, on the second of the eleventh month, in the fifth year of the fourth week.

22. And Yaăqôb went in unto Lêâh, and she conceived, and bare a son, and she called his name Yiśśâśkâr (יִשָּׂשכָר), on the fourth of the fifth month, in the fourth year of the fourth week, and she gave him to a nurse.

23. And Yaăqôb went in again unto her, and she conceived, and bare two children, a son and a daughter, and she called the name of the son Zebûlûn, and the name of the daughter Dîynâh, in the seventh of the seventh month, in the sixth year of the fourth week.

24. And Yahuah was gracious to Râchêl, and opened her womb, and she conceived, and bare a son, and she called his name Yôsêph (יוֹסֵף), on the beginning of the fourth month, in the sixth year in this fourth week.

25. And in the days when Yôsêph was born, Yaăqôb said to Lâbân: Give me my women and sons, and let me go to my father Yitschâq, and let me make me a house; for I have completed the years in which I have served you for your two daughters, and I will go to the house of my father.

26. And Lâbân said to Yaăqôb: Tarry with me for your wages, and pasture my flock for me again, and take your wages.

27. And they agreed with one another that he should give him as his wages those of the lambs and kids which were born black and spotted and white, these were to be his wages.

28. And all the sheep brought forth spotted and speckled and black, variously marked, and they brought forth again lambs like themselves, and all that were spotted were Yaăqôb's and those which were not were Lâbân's.

29. And Yaăqôb's possessions multiplied exceedingly, and he possessed oxen and sheep and asses and camels, and menservants and maidservants.

30. And Lâbân and his sons envied Yaăqôb, and Lâbân took back his sheep from him, and he observed him with evil intent.

Chapter 29

1. And it came to pass when Râchêl had borne Yôsêph that Lâbân went to shear his sheep; for they were distant from him a three days' journey.

2. And Yaăqôb saw that Lâbân was going to shear his sheep, and Yaăqôb called Lêâh and Râchêl, and spoke kindly unto them that they should come with him to the land of Kenaan.

3. For he told them how he had seen everything in a dream, even all that he had spoken unto him that he should return to his father's house, and they said: To every place whither you go we will go with you.

4. And Yaăqôb blessed the Êlôhîym of Yitschâq his father, and the Êlôhîym of Abrâhâm his father's father, and he arose and mounted his women and his children, and took all his possessions and crossed the river, and came to the land of Gilâd, and Yaăqôb hid his intention from Lâbân and did not tell him.

5. And in the seventh year of the fourth week Yaăqôb turned his face toward Gilâd in the first month, on the twenty first thereof. And Lâbân pursued after him and overtook Yaăqôb in the mountain of Gilâd in the third month, on the thirteenth thereof.

6. And Yahuah did not suffer him to injure Yaăqôb; for he appeared to him in a dream by night. And Lâbân spoke to Yaăqôb.

7. And on the fifteenth of those days Yaăqôb made a feast for Lâbân, and for all who came with him, and Yaăqôb swore to Lâbân that day, and Lâbân also to Yaăqôb, that neither should cross the mountain of Gilâd to the other with evil purpose.

8. And he made there a heap for a witness; wherefore the name of that place is called: Galyêd (גַּלְעֵד), after this heap.

9. But before they used to call the land of Gilâd the land of the Râphâ; for it was the land of the Râphâ, and the Râphâ were born there, nephîyl whose height was ten, nine, eight down to seven cubits.

10. And their habitation was from the land of the children of Ammôn to Mount

Chermôn, and the seats of their kingdom were Karnaim, Ashtârôth, and Edreîy, and Mîsûr, and Beôn.

11. And Yahuah destroyed them because of the evil of their deeds; for they were very malignant, and the Ĕmôrîy dwelt in their stead, wicked and sinful, and there is no people today which has wrought to the full all their sins, and they have no longer length of life on the earth.

12. And Yaăqôb sent away Lâbân, and he departed into Ăram Naharayim, the land of the East, and Yaăqôb returned to the land of Gilâd.

13. And he passed over the Yabbôq in the ninth month, on the eleventh thereof. And on that day Êśâw, his brother, came to him, and he was reconciled to him, and departed from him unto the land of Śêîyr, but Yaăqôb dwelt in tents.

14. And in the first year of the fifth week in this jubilee he crossed the Yardên, and dwelt beyond the Yardên, and he pastured his sheep from the sea of the heap unto Bêyth Sheân, and unto Dôthân and unto the forest of Aqrâb (עְקְרָב).

15. And he sent to his father Yitschâq of all his substance, clothing, and food, and meat, and drink, and milk, and butter, and cheese, and some dates of the valley.

16. And to his mother Ribqâh also four times a year, between the times of the months, between ploughing and reaping, and between autumn and the rain season and between winter and spring, to the tower of Abrâhâm.

17. For Yitschâq had returned from the Well of the Oath and gone up to the tower of his father Abrâhâm, and he dwelt there apart from his son Êśâw.

18. For in the days when Yaăqôb went to Ăram Naharayim, Êśâw took to himself a woman Machălath, the daughter of Yishmâêl, and he gathered together all the flocks of his father and his women, and went up and dwelt on Mount Śêîyr, and left Yitschâq his father at the Well of the Oath alone.

19. And Yitschâq went up from the Well of the Oath and dwelt in the tower of Abrâhâm his father on the mountains of Chebrôn,

20. And thither Yaăqôb sent all that he did send to his father and his mother from time to time, all they needed, and they blessed Yaăqôb with all their heart and with all their soul.

Chapter 30

1. And in the first year of the sixth week he went up to Shâlêm (שָׁלֵם), to the east of Shekem, in peace, in the fourth month.

2. And there they carried off Dîynâh, the daughter of Yaăqôb, into the house of Shekem, the son of Chămôr, the Chiwwîy, the prince of the land, and he lay with her and defiled her, and she was a little girl, a child of twelve years.

3. And he besought his father and her brothers that she might be given to him to woman. And Yaăqôb and his sons were wroth because of the men of Shekem; for they had defiled Dîynâh, their sister, and they spoke to them with evil intent and dealt deceitfully with them and beguiled them.

4. And Shimôn and Lêwîy came unexpectedly to Shekem and executed judgment on all the men of Shekem, and slew all the men whom they found in it, and did not leave not a single one remaining in it: They slew all in torments because they had dishonored their sister Dîynâh.

5. And thus let it not again be done from henceforth that a daughter of Yâshârêl

be defiled; for judgment is ordained in shâmayim against them that they should destroy with the sword all the men of the Shekem because they had wrought shame in Yâshârêl.

6. And Yahuah delivered them into the hands of the sons of Yaăqôb that they might exterminate them with the sword and execute judgment upon them, and that it might not thus be done again in Yâshârêl that a virgin of Yâshârêl should be defiled.

7. And if there is any man who wishes in Yâshârêl to give his daughter or his sister to any man who is of the seed of the Gentiles he shall surely die, and they shall stone him with stones; for he has wrought shame in Yâshârêl; and they shall burn the woman with fire, because she has dishonored the name of the house of her father, and she shall be rooted out of Yâshârêl.

8. And do not let an adulteress and no uncleanness be found in Yâshârêl throughout all the days of the generations of the earth; for Yâshârêl is qâdôsh unto Yahuah, and every man who has defiled it shall surely die: they shall stone him with stones.

9. For thus it has been ordained and written in the shâmayim tablets regarding all the seed of Yâshârêl: He who defiles it shall surely die, and he shall be stoned with stones.

10. And to this law there is no limit of days, and no remission, nor any atonement: but the man who has defiled his daughter shall be rooted out in the midst of all Yâshârêl, because he has given of his seed to Môlek, and wrought impiously so as to defile it.

11. And you do, Môsheh, command the children of Yâshârêl and exhort them not to give their daughters to the Gentiles, and not to take for their sons any of the daughters of the Gentiles, for this is abominable before Yahuah.

12. For this reason I have written for you in the words of the Law all the deeds of the Shekem, which they wrought against Dîynâh, and how the sons of Yaăqôb spoke, saying: We will not give our daughter to a man who is uncircumcised; for that were a reproach unto us.

13. And it is a reproach to Yâshârêl, to those who live, and to those that take the daughters of the Gentiles; for this is unclean and abominable to Yâshârêl.

14. And Yâshârêl will not be free from this uncleanness if it has a woman of the daughters of the Gentiles, or has given any of its daughters to a man who is of any of the Gentiles.

15. For there will be plague upon plague, and curse upon curse, and every judgment and plague and curse will come upon him: If he does this thing, or hides his eyes from those who commit uncleanness, or those who defile the sanctuary of Yahuah, or those who profane his qâdôsh name, then will the whole nation together be judged for all the uncleanness and profanation of this man.

16. And there will be no respect of persons and no consideration of persons and no receiving at his hands of fruits and offerings and burnt offerings and fat, nor the fragrance of sweet savor, so as to accept it: and so fare every man or woman in Yâshârêl who defiles the sanctuary.

17. For this reason I have commanded you, saying: Testify this testimony to Yâshârêl: see how the Shekem fared and their sons: how they were delivered into the hands of two sons of Yaăqôb, and they slew them under tortures, and it was reckoned unto them for righteousness, and it is written down to them for righteousness.

18. And the seed of Lêwîy was chosen for the Kehûnnâh (כְּהֻנָּה), and to be Lêwîy, that they might minister before Yahuah, as we, continually, and that Lêwîy and his sons may be blessed forever; for he was zealous to execute righteousness and judgment and vengeance on all those who arose against Yâshârêl.

19. And so they inscribe as a testimony in his favor on the shâmayim tablets blessing and righteousness before the Êlôhîym of all:

20. And we remember the righteousness which the man fulfilled during his life, at all periods of the year; until a thousand generations they will record it, and it will come to him and to his descendants after him, and he has been recorded on the shâmayim tablets as a friend and a righteous man.

21. All this account I have written for you, and have commanded you to say to the children of Yâshârêl, that they should not commit sin nor transgress the ordinances nor break the covenant which has been ordained for them, but that they should fulfil it and be recorded as friends.

22. But if they transgress and work uncleanness in every way, they will be recorded on the shâmayim tablets as adversaries, and they will be destroyed out of the book of life, and they will be recorded in the book of those who will be destroyed and with those who will be rooted out of the earth.

23. And on the day when the sons of Yaăqôb slew Shekem a writing was recorded in their favor in shâmayim that they had executed righteousness and uprightness and vengeance on the sinners, and it was written for a blessing.

24. And they brought Dîynâh, their sister, out of the house of Shekem, and they took captive everything that was in Shekem, their sheep and their oxen and their asses, and all their wealth, and all their flocks, and brought them all to Yaăqôb their father.

25. And he reproached them because they had put the city to the sword for he feared those who dwelt in the land, the Kenaanîy and the Perizzîy.

26. And the dread of Yahuah was upon all the cities which are around about Shekem, and they did not rise to pursue after the sons of Yaăqôb; for terror had fallen upon

Chapter 31

1. And on the beginning of the month Yaăqôb spoke to all the people of his house. saying: Purify yourselves and change your garments, and let us arise and go up to Bêythêl, where I vowed a vow to him on the day when I fled from the face of Êśâw my brother, because he has been with me and brought me into this land in peace, and put you away from the strange gods that are among you.

2. And they gave up the strange gods and that which was in their ears and which was on their necks and the idols which Râchêl stole from Lâbân her father she gave wholly to Yaăqôb. And he burnt and broke them to pieces and destroyed them, and hid them under an oak which is in the land of Shekem.

3. And he went up on the beginning of the seventh month to Bêythêl. And he built an altar at the place where he had slept, and he set up a pillar there, and he sent word to his father Yitschâq to come to him to his sacrifice, and to his mother Ribqâh.

4. And Yitschâq said: Let my son Yaăqôb come, and let me see him before I die.

5. And Yaăqôb went to his father Yitschâq and to his mother Ribqâh, to the house of his father Abrâhâm, and he took two of his sons

with him, Lêwîy and Yahûdâh, and he came to his father Yitschâq and to his mother Ribqâh.

6. And Ribqâh came forth from the tower to the front of it to kiss Yaăqôb and embrace him; for her spirit had revived when she heard: Behold Yaăqôb your son has come; and she kissed him.

7. And she saw his two sons, and she recognized them, and said unto him: Are these your sons, my son? And she embraced them and kissed them, and blessed them, saying: In you shall the seed of Abrâhâm become illustrious, and you shall prove a blessing on the earth.

8. And Yaăqôb went in to Yitschâq his father, to the chamber where he lay, and his two sons were with him, and he took the hand of his father, and stooping down he kissed him, and Yitschâq clung to the neck of Yaăqôb his son, and wept upon his neck.

9. And the darkness left the eyes of Yitschâq, and he saw the two sons of Yaăqôb, Lêwîy, and Yahûdâh, and he said: Are these your sons, my son? For they are like you.

10. And he said unto him that they were truly his sons: And you have truly seen that they are truly my sons.

11. And they came near to him, and he turned and kissed them and embraced them both together.

12. And the spirit of prophecy came down into his mouth, and he took Lêwîy by his right hand and Yahûdâh by his left.

13. And he turned to Lêwîy first, and began to bless him first, and said unto him: May the Êlôhîym of all, the very Yahuah of all the ages, bless you and your children throughout all the ages.

14. And may Yahuah give to you and to your seed greatness and great glory, and cause you and your seed, from among all flesh, to approach him to serve in his sanctuary as the angels of the presence and as the qâdôsh ones. Even as they, shall the seed of your sons be for glory and greatness and qôdesh, and he may make them great unto all the ages.

15. And they shall be judges and princes, and chiefs of all the seed of the sons of Yaăqôb; they shall speak the word of Yahuah in righteousness, and they shall judge all his judgments in righteousness. And they shall declare my ways to Yaăqôb and my paths to Yâshârêl. The blessing of Yahuah shall be given in their mouths to bless all the seed of the beloved.

16. Your mother has called your name Lêwîy, and justly has she called your name; you shall be joined to Yahuah and be the companion of all the sons of Yaăqôb; let his table be yours, and you do and your sons eat thereof; and may your table be full unto all generations, and your food do not fail unto all the ages.

17. And let all who hate you fall down before you, and let all your adversaries be rooted out and perish; and blessed be he that blesses you, and cursed be every nation that curses you.

18. And to Yahûdâh he said: May Yahuah give you strength and power to tread down all that hate you; a prince you shall be, you and one of your sons, over the sons of Yaăqôb; may your name and the name of your sons go forth and traverse every land and region. Then shall the Gentiles fear before your face, and all the nations shall quake and all the peoples shall quake.

19. In you shall be the help of Yaăqôb, and in you are found the salvation of Yâshârêl.

20. And when you sit on the throne of honor of your righteousness there shall be great

peace for all the seed of the sons of the beloved; blessed be he that blesses you, and all that hate you and afflict you and curse you shall be rooted out and destroyed from the earth and be accursed.

21. And turning he kissed him again and embraced him, and rejoiced greatly; for he had seen the sons of Yaăqôb his son in very truth.

22. And he went forth from between his feet and fell down and bowed down to him, and he blessed them and rested there with Yitschâq his father that night, and they eat and drank with joy.

23. And he made the two sons of Yaăqôb sleep, the one on his right hand and the other on his left, and it was counted to him for righteousness.

24. And Yaăqôb told his father everything during the night, how Yahuah had shown him great mercy, and how he had prospered him in all his ways, and protected him from all evil.

25. And Yitschâq blessed the Êlôhîym of his father Abrâhâm, who had not withdrawn his mercy and his righteousness from the sons of his servant Yitschâq.

26. And in the morning Yaăqôb told his father Yitschâq the vow which he had vowed to Yahuah, and the vision which he had seen, and that he had built an altar, and that everything was ready for the sacrifice to be made before Yahuah as he had vowed, and that he had come to set him on an ass.

27. And Yitschâq said unto Yaăqôb his son: I am not able to go with you; for I am old and not able to bear the way: Go, my son, in peace; for I am one hundred and sixty five years this day; I am no longer able to journey; set your mother on an ass and let her go with you.

28. And I know, my son, that you have come on my account, and may this day be blessed on which you have seen me alive, and I also have seen you, my son.

29. May you prosper and fulfil the vow which you have vowed; and do not put off your vow; for you shall be called to account as touching the vow; now therefore make haste to perform it, and may he be pleased who has made all things, to whom you have vowed the vow.

30. And he said to Ribqâh: Go with Yaăqôb your son; and Ribqâh went with Yaăqôb her son, and Debôrâh with her, and they came to Bêythêl.

31. And Yaăqôb remembered the prayer with which his father had blessed him and his two sons, Lêwîy and Yahûdâh, and he rejoiced and blessed the Êlôhîym of his fathers, Abrâhâm and Yitschâq.

32. And he said: Now I know that I have an eternal hope, and my sons also, before the Êlôhîym of all; and thus is it ordained concerning the two; and they record it as an eternal testimony unto them on the shâmayim tablets how Yitschâq blessed them.

Chapter 32

1. And he abode that night at Bêythêl, and Lêwîy dreamed that they had ordained and made him the Kôhên of Êlôhîym Elyôn Êl, him and his sons forever; and he awoke from his sleep and blessed Yahuah.

2. And Yaăqôb rose early in the morning, on the fourteenth of this month, and he gave a tithe of all that came with him, both of men and cattle, both of gold and every vessel and garment, yea, he gave tithes of all.

3. And in those days Râchêl became pregnant with her son Binyâmîyn. And Yaăqôb

counted his sons from him upwards and Lêwîy fell to the portion of Yahuah, and his father clothed him in the garments of the Kehûnnâh and filled his hands.

4. And on the fifteenth of this month, he brought to the altar fourteen oxen from among the cattle, and twenty eight rams, and forty nine sheep, and seven lambs, and twenty one kids of male goats as a burnt offering on the altar of sacrifice, well pleasing for a sweet savor before Êlôhîym.

5. This was his offering, in consequence of the vow which he had vowed that he would give a tenth, with their fruit offerings and their drink offerings.

6. And when the fire had consumed it, he burnt incense on the fire over the fire, and for a thank offering two oxen and four rams and four sheep, four male goats, and two sheep of a year old, and two kids of male goats; and thus he did daily for seven days.

7. And he and all his sons and his men were eating this with joy there during seven days and blessing and thanking Yahuah, who had delivered him out of all his tribulation and had given him his vow.

8. And he tithed all the clean animals, and made a burnt sacrifice, but the unclean animals he did not give to Lêwîy his son, and he gave him all the souls of the men.

9. And Lêwîy discharged the Kôhên office at Bêythêl before Yaăqôb his father in preference to his ten brothers, and he was a Kôhên there, and Yaăqôb gave his vow: thus he tithed again the tithe to Yahuah and sanctified it, and it became qâdôsh unto him.

10. And for this reason it is ordained on the shâmayim tablets as a law for the tithing again the tithe to eat before Yahuah from year to year, in the place where it is chosen that his name should dwell, and to this law there is no limit of days forever.

11. This ordinance is written that it may be fulfilled from year to year in eating the second tithe before Yahuah in the place where it has been chosen, and nothing shall remain over from it from this year to the year following.

12. For in its year shall the seed be eaten till the days of the gathering of the seed of the year, and the wine till the days of the wine, and the oil till the days of its season.

13. And all that is left thereof and becomes old, let it be regarded as polluted: Let it be burnt with fire, for it is unclean.

14. And thus let them eat it together in the sanctuary, and do not let them suffer it to become old.

15. And all the tithes of the oxen and sheep shall be qâdôsh unto Yahuah, and shall belong to his Kôhên, which they will eat before him from year to year; for thus is it ordained and engraved regarding the tithe on the shâmayim tablets.

16. And on the following night, on the twenty second day of this month, Yaăqôb resolved to build that place, and to surround the court with a wall, and to sanctify it and make it qâdôsh forever, for himself and his children after him.

17. And Yahuah appeared to him by night and blessed him and said unto him: Your name shall not be called Yaăqôb, but Yâshârêl shall they name your name.

18. And he said unto him again: I am Yahuah who created the shâmayim and the earth, and I will increase you and multiply you exceedingly, and kings shall come forth from you, and they shall judge everywhere

wherever the foot of the sons of men has trodden.

19. And I will give to your seed all the earth which is under shâmayim, and they shall judge all the nations according to their desires, and after that they shall get possession of the whole earth and inherit it forever.

20. And he finished speaking with him, and he went up from him. And Yaăqôb looked till he had ascended into shâmayim.

21. And he saw in a vision of the night, and behold an angel descended from shâmayim with seven tablets in his hands, and he gave them to Yaăqôb, and he read them and knew all that was written therein which would befall him and his sons throughout all the ages.

22. And he showed him all that was written on the tablets, and said unto him: Do not build this place, and do not make it an eternal sanctuary, and do not dwell here; for this is not the place. Go to the house of Abrâhâm your father and dwell with Yitschâq your father until the day of the death of your father.

23. For in Mitsrayim you shall die in peace, and in this land you shall be buried with honor in the sepulcher of your fathers, with Abrâhâm and Yitschâq.

24. Do not fear, for as you have seen and read it, thus shall it all be; and you do write down everything as you have seen and read.

25. And Yaăqôb said: Yahuah, how can I remember all that I have read and seen? And he said unto him: I will bring all things to your remembrance.

26. And he went up from him, and he awoke from his sleep, and he remembered everything which he had read and seen, and he wrote down all the words which he had read and seen.

27. And he celebrated there yet another day, and he sacrificed thereon according to all that he sacrificed on the former days, and called its name "Addition", for this day was added and the former days he called "The Feast".

28. And thus it was manifested that it should be, and it is written on the shâmayim tablets: wherefore it was revealed to him that he should celebrate it, and add it to the seven days of the feast.

29. And its name was called "Addition" because that it was recorded among the days of the feast days, according to the number of the days of the year.

30. And in the night, on the twenty third of this month, Debôrâh, Ribqâh's nurse died, and they buried her beneath the city under the oak of the river, and he called the name of this place, Allôn Bâkûth (אַלּוֹן בָּכוּת) and the oak: The oak of the mourning of Debôrâh.

31. And Ribqâh went and returned to her house to his father Yitschâq, and Yaăqôb sent by her hand rams and sheep and male goats that she should prepare a meal for his father such as he desired.

32. And he went after his mother till he came to the land of Kibrâh (כִּבְרָה), and he dwelt there.

33. And Râchêl bare a son in the night, and called his name Benônîy (בֶּן־אוֹנִי); for she suffered in giving him birth: but his father called his name Binyâmîyn, on the eleventh of the eighth month in the first of the sixth week of this jubilee.

34. And Râchêl died there and she was buried in the land of Ephrâth, the same is Bêyth

Lechem, and Yaăqôb built a pillar on the grave of Râchêl, on the road above her grave.

Chapter 33

1. And Yaăqôb went and dwelt to the south of Magdalâdrâêf. And he went to his father Yitschâq, he and Lêâh his woman, on the beginning of the tenth month.

2. And Reûbên saw Bilhâh, Râchêl's maid, the concubine of his father, bathing in water in a secret place, and he loved her.

3. And he hid himself at night, and he entered the house of Bilhâh at night, and he found her sleeping alone on a bed in her house.

4. And he lay with her, and she awoke and saw, and behold Reûbên was lying with her in the bed, and she uncovered the border of her covering and seized him, and cried out, and discovered that it was Reûbên.

5. And she was ashamed because of him, and released her hand from him, and he fled.

6. And she lamented because of this thing exceedingly, and did not tell it to anyone.

7. And when Yaăqôb returned and sought her, she said unto him: I am not clean for you, for I have been defiled as regards you; for Reûbên has defiled me, and has lain with me in the night, and I was asleep, and did not discover until he uncovered my skirt and slept with me.

8. And Yaăqôb was exceedingly wroth with Reûbên because he had lain with Bilhâh, because he had uncovered his father's skirt.

9. And Yaăqôb did not approach her again because Reûbên had defiled her. And as for any man who uncovers his father's skirt his deed is wicked exceedingly, for he is abominable before Yahuah.

10. For this reason it is written and ordained on the shâmayim tablets that a man should not lie with his father's woman, and should not uncover his father's skirt, for this is unclean: they shall surely die together, the man who lies with his father's woman and the woman also, for they have wrought uncleanness on the earth.

11. And there shall be nothing unclean before our Êlôhîym in the nation which he has chosen for himself as a possession.

12. And again, it is written a second time: Cursed be he who lies with the woman of his father, for he has uncovered his father's shame; and all the qâdôsh of Yahuah said: So be it; so be it.

13. And you do, Môsheh, command the children of Yâshârêl that they observe this word; for it entails a punishment of death; and it is unclean, and there is no atonement forever to atone for the man who has committed this, but he is to be put to death and slain, and stoned with stones, and rooted out from the midst of the people of our Êlôhîym.

14. For to no man who does so in Yâshârêl is it permitted to remain alive a single day on the earth, for he is abominable and unclean.

15. And do not let them say: To Reûbên was granted life and forgiveness after he had lain with his father's concubine, and to her also though she had a husband, and her husband Yaăqôb, his father, was still alive.

16. For until that time there had not been revealed the ordinance and judgment and law in its completeness for all, but in your days, it has been revealed, as a law of seasons and of days, and an everlasting law for the everlasting generations.

17. And for this law there is no consummation of days, and no atonement for it, but

they must both be rooted out in the midst of the nation: On the day whereon they committed it they shall slay them.

18. And you do, Môsheh, write it down for Yâshârêl that they may observe it, and do according to these words, and not commit a sin unto death; for Yahuah our Êlôhîym is judge, who respects not persons and accepts not gifts.

19. And tell them these words of the covenant, that they may hear and observe, and be on their guard with respect to them, and not be destroyed and rooted out of the land; for an uncleanness, and an abomination, and a contamination, and a pollution are all they who commit it on the earth before our Êlôhîym.

20. And there is no greater sin than the fornication which they commit on earth; for Yâshârêl is a qâdôsh nation unto Yahuah its Êlôhîym, and a nation of inheritance, and a Kôhên and royal nation and for his own possession; and there shall no such uncleanness appear in the midst of the qâdôsh nation.

21. And in the third year of this sixth week Yaăqôb and all his sons went and dwelt in the house of Abrâhâm, near Yitschâq his father and Ribqâh his mother.

22. And these were the names of the sons of Yaăqôb: the first born Reûbên, Shimôn, Lêwîy, Yahûdâh, Yiśśâśkâr, Zebûlûn, the sons of Lêâh; and the sons of Râchêl, Yôsêph and Binyâmîyn; and the sons of Bilhâh, Dân and Naphtali; and the sons of Zilpâh, Gâd and Âshêr; and Dîynâh, the daughter of Lêâh, the only daughter of Yaăqôb.

23. And they came and bowed themselves to Yitschâq and Ribqâh, and when they saw them they blessed Yaăqôb and all his sons, and Yitschâq rejoiced exceedingly, for he saw the sons of Yaăqôb, his younger son and he blessed them.

Chapter 34

1. And in the sixth year of this week of this forty fourth jubilee Yaăqôb sent his sons to pasture their sheep, and his servants with them to the pastures of Shekem.

2. And the seven kings of the Ĕmôrîy assembled themselves together against them, to slay them, hiding themselves under the trees, and to take their cattle as a prey.

3. And Yaăqôb and Lêwîy and Yahûdâh and Yôsêph were in the house with Yitschâq their father; for his spirit was sorrowful, and they could not leave him: And Binyâmîyn was the youngest, and for this reason remained with his father.

4. And there came the king of Tappûach (תַּפּוּחַ) and the king of Arêsâ, and the king of Sêragân, and the king of Shîylôh (שִׁילֹה), and the king of Gaash, and the king of Bêyth Chôrôn (בֵּית חוֹרוֹן), and the king of Maanishâkîr, and all those who dwell in these mountains and who dwell in the woods in the land of Kenaan.

5. And they announced this to Yaăqôb saying: Behold, the kings of the Ĕmôrîy have surrounded your sons, and plundered their herds.

6. And he arose from his house, he and his three sons and all the servants of his father, and his own servants, and he went against them with six thousand men, who carried swords.

7. And he slew them in the pastures of Shekem, and pursued those who fled, and he slew them with the edge of the sword, and he slew Arêsâ and Tappûach and Sêragân and Shîylôh and Maanishâkîr and Gaash, and he recovered his herds.

8. And he prevailed over them, and imposed tribute on them that they should pay him

tribute, five fruit products of their land, and he built Rôbêl and Timnath cheres (תִּמְנַת חֶרֶס).

9. And he returned in peace, and made peace with them, and they became his servants, until the day that he and his sons went down into Mitsrayim.

10. And in the seventh year of this week he sent Yôsêph to learn about the welfare of his brothers from his house to the land of Shekem, and he found them in the land of Dôthân.

11. And they dealt treacherously with him, and formed a plot against him to slay him, but changing their minds, they sold him to Yishmâêlîy merchants, and they brought him down into Mitsrayim, and they sold him to Pôṭîyphar, the eunuch of Parôh, the chief of the cooks, Kôhên of the city of Êlêw.

12. And the sons of Yaăqôb slaughtered a kid, and dipped the coat of Yôsêph in the blood, and sent it to Yaăqôb their father on the tenth of the seventh month.

13. And he mourned all that night, for they had brought it to him in the evening, and he became feverish with mourning for his death, and he said: An evil beast has devoured Yôsêph; and all the members of his house mourned with him that day, and they were grieving and mourning with him all that day.

14. And his sons and his daughter rose up to comfort him, but he refused to be comforted for his son.

15. And on that day Bilhâh heard that Yôsêph had perished, and she died mourning him, and she was living in Kibrâh, and Dîynâh also, his daughter, died after Yôsêph had perished.

16. And there came these three mournings upon Yâshârêl in one month. And they buried Bilhâh over against the tomb of Râchêl, and Dîynâh also his daughter, they buried there.

17. And he mourned for Yôsêph one year, and did not cease, for he said: Let me go down to the grave mourning for my son.

18. For this reason it is ordained for the children of Yâshârêl that they should afflict themselves on the tenth of the seventh month, on the day that the news which made him weep for Yôsêph came to Yaăqôb his father, that they should make atonement for themselves thereon with a young goat on the tenth of the seventh month, once a year, for their sins; for they had grieved the affection of their father regarding Yôsêph his son.

19. And this day has been ordained that they should grieve thereon for their sins, and for all their transgressions and for all their errors, so that they might cleanse themselves on that day once a year.

20. And after Yôsêph perished, the sons of Yaăqôb took unto themselves women. The name of Reûbên's woman is Âdâ; and the name of Shimôn's woman is Âdîbââ, a Kenaanîy; and the name of Lêwîy's woman is Mêlkâ, of the daughters of Ârâm, of the seed of the sons of Terach; and the name of Yahûdâh's woman, Bêtâsûêl, a Kenaanîy; and the name of Yiśśâśkâr's woman, Hêzâqâ: and the name of Zebûlûn's woman, Nîimâ; and the name of Dân's woman, Êglâ; and the name of Naphtali's woman, Râsûu, of Ărâm Nahărayim; and the name of Gâd's woman, Mâkâ; and the name of Âshêr's woman, Ĭyôa; and the name of Yôsêph's woman, Âsnath, the Mitsrîy; and the name of Binyâmîyn's woman, Iyasâkâ.

21. And Shimôn repented, and took a second woman from Ărâm Nahărayim as his brothers.

Chapter 35

1. And in the first year of the first week of the forty fifth jubilee Ribqâh called Yaăqôb, her son, and commanded him regarding his father and regarding his brother, that he should honor them all the days of his life.

2. And Yaăqôb said: I will do everything as you have commanded me; for this thing will be honor and greatness to me, and righteousness before Yahuah, that I should honor them.

3. And you too, mother, know from the time I was born until this day, all my deeds and all that is in my heart, that I always think good concerning all.

4. And how I should not do this thing which you have commanded me, that I should honor my father and my brother!

5. Tell me, mother, what perversity you have seen in me and I shall turn away from it, and mercy will be upon me.

6. And she said unto him: My son, I have not seen in you all my days any perverse but only upright deeds. And yet I will tell you the truth, my son: I shall die this year, and I shall not survive this year in my life; for I have seen in a dream the day of my death, that I should not live beyond a hundred and fifty five years: And behold I have completed all the days of my life which I am to live.

7. And Yaăqôb laughed at the words of his mother because his mother had said unto him that she should die; and she was sitting opposite to him in possession of her strength, and she was not infirm in her strength; for she went in and out and saw, and her teeth were strong, and no ailment had touched her all the days of her life.

8. And Yaăqôb said unto her: Blessed I am, mother, if my days approach the days of your life, and my strength remain with me thus as your strength: and you will not die, for you are jesting idly with me regarding your death.

9. And she went in to Yitschâq and said unto him: One petition I make unto you: Make Êśâw swear that he will not injure Yaăqôb, nor pursue him with enmity; for you know Êśâw's thoughts that they are perverse from his youth, and there is no goodness in him; for he desires after your death to kill him.

10. And you know all that he has done since the day Yaăqôb his brother went to Chârân until this day: How he has forsaken us with his whole heart, and has done evil to us; your flocks he has taken to himself, and carried off all your possessions from before your face.

11. And when we implored and besought him for what was our own, he did as a man who was taking pity on us.

12. And he is bitter against you because you did bless Yaăqôb your perfect and upright son; for there is no evil but only goodness in him, and since he came from Chârân unto this day he has not robbed us of aught, for he brings us everything in its season always, and rejoices with all his heart when we take at his hands and he blesses us, and has not parted from us since he came from Chârân until this day, and he remains with us continually at home honoring us.

13. And Yitschâq said unto her: I, too, know and see the deeds of Yaăqôb who is with us, how that with all his heart he honors us; but I loved Êśâw formerly more than Yaăqôb, because he was the firstborn; but now I love Yaăqôb more than Êśâw, for he has done manifold evil deeds, and there is no righteousness in him, for all his ways are unrighteousness and violence, and there is no righteousness around him.

14. And now my heart is troubled because of all his deeds, and neither he nor his seed is to be saved, for they are those who will be destroyed from the earth and who will be rooted out from under shâmayim, for he has forsaken the Êlôhîym of Abrâhâm and gone after his women and after their uncleanness and after their error, he and his children.

15. And you do bid me make him swear that he will not slay Yaăqôb his brother; even if he swear he will not abide by his oath, and he will not do good but evil only.

16. But if he desires to slay Yaăqôb, his brother, into Yaăqôb's hands will he be given, and he will not escape from his hands, for he will descend into his hands.

17. And you do not fear on account of Yaăqôb; for the guardian of Yaăqôb is great and powerful and honored, and praised more than the guardian of Êśâw.

18. And Ribqâh sent and called Êśâw and he came to her, and she said unto him: I have a petition, my son, to make unto you, and you do promise to do it, my son.

19. And he said: I will do everything that you say unto me, and I will not refuse your petition.

20. And she said unto him: I ask you that the day I die, you will take me in and bury me near Śârâh, your father's mother, and that you and Yaăqôb will love each other and that neither will desire evil against the other, but mutual love only, and so you will prosper, my sons, and be honored in the midst of the land, and no enemy will rejoice over you, and you will be a blessing and a mercy in the eyes of all those that love you.

21. And he said: I will do all that you have told me, and I shall bury you on the day you die near Śârâh, my father's mother, as you have desired that her bones may be near your bones.

22. And Yaăqôb, my brother, also, I shall love above all flesh; for I have not a brother in all the earth but him only: and this is no great merit for me if I love him; for he is my brother, and we were sown together in your body, and together we came forth from your womb, and if I do not love my brother, whom shall I love?

23. And I, myself, beg you to exhort Yaăqôb concerning me and concerning my sons, for I know that he will assuredly be king over me and my sons, for on the day my father blessed him he made him the higher and me the lower.

24. And I swear unto you that I shall love him, and not desire evil against him all the days of my life but good only.

25. And he swore unto her regarding all this matter. And she called Yaăqôb before the eyes of Êśâw, and gave him commandment according to the words which she had spoken to Êśâw.

26. And he said: I shall do your pleasure; believe me that no evil will proceed from me or from my sons against Êśâw, and I shall be first in naught save in love only.

27. And they ate and drank, she and her sons that night, and she died, three jubilees and one week and one year old, on that night, and her two sons, Êśâw and Yaăqôb, buried her in the double cave near Śârâh, their father's mother.

Chapter 36

1. And in the sixth year of this week Yitschâq called his two sons Êśâw and Yaăqôb, and they came to him, and he said unto them: My sons, I am going the way of my fathers, to the eternal house where my fathers are.

2. Wherefore bury me near Abrâhâm my father, in the double cave in the field of Ephrôn the Chittîy, where Abrâhâm purchased a sepulcher to bury in; in the sepulcher which I dug for myself, there bury me.

3. And I command you this, my sons, that you practice righteousness and uprightness on the earth, so that Yahuah may bring upon you all that Yahuah said that he would do to Abrâhâm and to his seed.

4. And love one another, my sons, your brothers as a man who loves his own soul, and let each seek in what he may benefit his brother, and act together on the earth; and let them love each other as their own souls.

5. And concerning the question of idols, I command and admonish you to reject them and hate them, and do not love them, for they are full of deception for those that worship them and for those that bow down to them.

6. You remember, my sons, Yahuah Êlôhîym of Abrâhâm your father, and how I too worshipped him and served him in righteousness and in joy, that he might multiply you and increase your seed as the stars of shâmayim in multitude, and establish you on the earth as the plant of righteousness which will not be rooted out unto all the generations forever.

7. And now I shall make you swear a great oath for there is no oath which is greater than it by the name glorious and honored and great and splendid and wonderful and mighty, which created the shâmayim and the earth and all things together, that you will fear him and worship him.

8. And that each will love his brother with affection and righteousness, and that neither will desire evil against his brother from henceforth forever all the days of your life so that you may prosper in all your deeds and not be destroyed.

9. And if either of you devises evil against his brother, know that from henceforth everyone that devises evil against his brother shall fall into his hand, and shall be rooted out of the land of the living, and his seed shall be destroyed from under shâmayim.

10. But on the day of turbulence and execration and indignation and anger, with flaming devouring fire as he burnt Sedôm, so likewise he will burn his land and his city and all that is his, and he shall be blotted out of the book of the discipline of the children of men, and not be recorded in the book of life, but in that which is appointed to destruction, and he shall depart into eternal execration; so that their condemnation may be always renewed in hate and in execration and in wrath and in torment and in indignation and in plagues and in disease forever.

11. I say and testify to you, my sons, according to the judgment which shall come upon the man who wishes to injure his brother.

12. And he divided all his possessions between the two on that day and he gave the larger portion to him that was the first born, and the tower and all that was about it, and all that Abrâhâm possessed at the Well of the Oath.

13. And he said: This larger portion I will give to the firstborn.

14. And Êśâw said, I have sold to Yaăqôb and given my birthright to Yaăqôb; to him let it be given, and I have not a single word to say regarding it, for it is his.

15. And Yitschâq said, may a blessing rest upon you, my sons, and upon your seed this day, for you have given me rest, and my heart is not pained concerning the

birthright, lest you should work wickedness on account of it.

16. May Êlôhîym Elyôn Êl bless the man that works righteousness, him and his seed forever.

17. And he ended commanding them and blessing them, and they ate and drank together before him, and he rejoiced because there was one mind between them, and they went forth from him and rested that day and slept.

18. And Yitschâq slept on his bed that day rejoicing; and he slept the eternal sleep, and died one hundred and eighty years old. He completed twenty five weeks and five years; and his two sons Êśâw and Yaăqôb buried him.

19. And Êśâw went to the land of Ĕdôm, to the mountains of Śêîyr, and dwelt there.

20. And Yaăqôb dwelt in the mountains of Chebrôn, in the tower of the land of the sojourning of his father Abrâhâm, and he worshipped Yahuah with all his heart and according to the visible commands according as he had divided the days of his generations.

21. And Lêâh his woman died in the fourth year of the second week of the forty fifth jubilee, and he buried her in the double cave near Ribqâh his mother to the left of the grave of Śârâh, his father's mother

22. And all her sons and his sons came to mourn over Lêâh his woman with him and to comfort him regarding her, for he was lamenting her for he loved her exceedingly after Râchêl her sister died;

23. For she was perfect and upright in all her ways and honored Yaăqôb, and all the days that she lived with him he did not hear from her mouth a harsh word, for she was gentle and peaceable and upright and honorable.

24. And he remembered all her deeds which she had done during her life and he lamented her exceedingly; for he loved her with all his heart and with all his soul.

Chapter 37

1. And on the day that Yitschâq the father of Yaăqôb and Êśâw died, the sons of Êśâw heard that Yitschâq had given the portion of the elder to his younger son Yaăqôb and they were very angry.

2. And they strove with their father, saying: Why has your father given Yaăqôb the portion of the elder and passed over you, although you are the elder and Yaăqôb the younger?

3. And he said unto them because I sold my birthright to Yaăqôb for a small mess of lentils, and on the day my father sent me to hunt and catch and bring him something that he should eat and bless me, he came with guile and brought my father food and drank, and my father blessed him and put me under his hand.

4. And now our father has caused us to swear, me and him, that we shall not mutually devise evil, either against his brother, and that we shall continue in love and in peace each with his brother and not make our ways corrupt.

5. And they said unto him, we shall not hearken unto you to make peace with him; for our strength is greater than his strength, and we are more powerful than he; we shall go against him and slay him, and destroy him and his sons. And if you will not go with us, we shall do hurt to you also.

6. And now hearken unto us: Let us send to Ărâm and Pelesheth (פְּלֶשֶׁת) and Môâb and Ammôn, and let us choose for ourselves chosen men who are ardent for battle, and let

us go against him and do battle with him, and let us exterminate him from the earth before he grows strong.

7. And their father said unto them: Do not go and do not make war with him lest you fall before him.

8. And they said unto him: This too, is exactly your mode of action from your youth until this day, and you are putting your neck under his yoke.

9. We shall not hearken to these words. And they sent to Ărâm, and to Hădôrâm (הֲדוֹרָם) to the friend of their father, and they hired along with them one thousand fighting men, chosen men of war.

10. And there came to them from Môâb and from the children of Ammôn, those who were hired, one thousand chosen men, and from Pelesheth, one thousand chosen men of war, and from Ĕdôm and from the Chôrîy (חֹרִי) one thousand chosen fighting men, and from the Kittîy mighty men of war.

11. And they said unto their father: Go forth with them and lead them, else we shall slay you.

12. And he was filled with wrath and indignation on seeing that his sons were forcing him to go before them to lead them against Yaăqôb his brother.

13. But afterward he remembered all the evil which lay hidden in his heart against Yaăqôb his brother; and he did not remember the oath which he had sworn to his father and to his mother that he would devise no evil all his days against Yaăqôb his brother.

14. And notwithstanding all this, Yaăqôb did not know that they were coming against him to battle, and he was mourning for Lêâh, his woman, until they approached very near to the tower with four thousand warriors and chosen men of war.

15. And the men of Chebrôn sent to him saying: Behold your brother has come against you, to fight you, with four thousand girt with the sword, and they carry shields and weapons; for they loved Yaăqôb more than Êśâw. So they told him; for Yaăqôb was a more liberal and merciful man than Êśâw.

16. But Yaăqôb would not believe until they came very near to the tower.

17. And he closed the gates of the tower; and he stood on the battlements and spoke to his brother Êśâw and said: Noble is the comfort wherewith you have come to comfort me for my woman who has died. Is this the oath that you did swear to your father and again to your mother before they died? You have broken the oath, and on the moment that you did swear to your father you were condemned.

18. And then Êśâw answered and said unto him: Neither the children of men nor the beasts of the earth have any oath of righteousness which in swearing they have sworn an oath valid forever; but every day they devise evil one against another, and how each may slay his adversary and foe.

19. And you do hate me and my children forever. And there is no observing the tie of brotherhood with you.

20. Hear these words which I declare unto you, if the boar can change its skin and make its bristles as soft as wool, or if it can cause horns to sprout forth on its head like the horns of a stag or of a sheep. Then I will observe the tie of brotherhood with you

and if the breasts separated themselves from their mother, for you have not been a brother to me.

21. And if the wolves make peace with the lambs so as not to devour or do them violence, and if their hearts are towards them for good, then there shall be peace in my heart towards you.

22. And if the lion becomes the friend of the ox and makes peace with him and if he is bound under one yoke with him and ploughs with him, then will I make peace with you.

23. And when the raven becomes white as the râzâ, then know that I have loved you and shall make peace with you. You shall be rooted out, and your sons shall be rooted out, and there shall be no peace for you.

24. And when Yaăqôb saw that he was so evilly disposed towards him with his heart, and with all his soul as to slay him, and that he had come springing like the wild boar which comes upon the spear that pierces and kills it, and does not recoil from it;

25. Then he spoke to his own and to his servants that they should attack him and all his companions.

Chapter 38

1. And after that Yahûdâh spoke to Yaăqôb, his father, and said unto him: Bend your bow, father, and send forth your arrows and cast down the adversary and slay the enemy; and may you have the power, for we shall not slay your brother, for he is such as you, and he is like you let us give him this honor.

2. Then Yaăqôb bent his bow and sent forth the arrow and struck Êśâw, his brother on his right breast and slew him.

3. And again he sent forth an arrow and struck Ădôrân the Ărammîy (אֲרַמִּי), on the left breast, and drove him backward and slew him.

4. And then went forth the sons of Yaăqôb, they and their servants, dividing themselves into companies on the four sides of the tower.

5. And Yahûdâh went forth in front, and Naphtali and Gâd with him and fifty servants with him on the south side of the tower, and they slew all they found before them, and not one individual of them escaped.

6. And Lêwîy and Dân and Âshêr went forth on the east side of the tower, and fifty men with them, and they slew the fighting men of Môâb and Ammôn.

7. And Reûbên and Yiśśâśkâr and Zebûlûn went forth on the north side of the tower, and fifty men with them, and they slew the fighting men of the Pelishtîy.

8. And Shimôn and Binyâmîyn and Chănôk, Reûbên's son, went forth on the west side of the tower, and fifty men with them, and they slew of Ĕdôm and of the Chôrîy four hundred men, stout warriors; and six hundred fled, and four of the sons of Êśâw fled with them, and left their father lying slain, as he had fallen on the hill which is in Hădôrâm.

9. And the sons of Yaăqôb pursued after them to the mountains of Śêîyr. And Yaăqôb buried his brother on the hill which is in Hădôrâm, and he returned to his house.

10. And the sons of Yaăqôb pressed hard upon the sons of Êśâw in the mountains of Śêîyr, and bowed their necks so that they became servants of the sons of Yaăqôb.

11. And they sent to their father to inquire whether they should make peace with them or slay them.

12. And Yaăqôb sent word to his sons that they should make peace, and they made peace with them, and placed the yoke of servitude upon them, so that they paid tribute to Yaăqôb and to his sons always.

13. And they continued to pay tribute to Yaăqôb until the day that he went down into Mitsrayim.

14. And the sons of Ĕdôm have not got quit of the yoke of servitude which the twelve sons of Yaăqôb had imposed on them until this day.

15. And these are the kings that reigned in Ĕdôm before there reigned any king over the children of Yâshârêl until this day in the land of Ĕdôm.

16. And Bela (בֶּלַע), the son of Beôr, reigned in Ĕdôm, and the name of his city was Dinhâbâh (דִּנְהָבָה).

17. And Bela died, and Yôbâb, the son of Zerach of Botsrâh (בָּצְרָה), reigned in his stead.

18. And Yôbâb died, and Chûshâm (חוּשָׁם), of the land of Têymân (תֵּימָן), reigned in his stead.

19. And Chûshâm died, and Hădad (הֲדַד), the son of Bedad (בְּדַד), who slew Midyân in the field of Môab, reigned in his stead, and the name of his city was Ăwîyth.

20. And Hădad died, and Śamlâh (שַׂמְלָה), from Maśrêqâh (מַשְׂרֵקָה), reigned in his stead.

21. And Śamlâh died, and Shâûl (שָׁאוּל) of Rechôbôth (רְחֹבוֹת) by the river, reigned in his stead.

22. And Shâûl died, and Baal Chânân (בַּעַל חָנָן), the son of Akbôr, reigned in his stead.

23. And Baal Chânân, the son of Akbôr died, and Hădar reigned in his stead, and the name of his woman was Mehêyṭabêl (מְהֵיטַבְאֵל), the daughter of Maṭrêd (מַטְרֵד), the daughter of Mêy zâhâb (מֵי זָהָב).

24. These are the kings who reigned in the land of Ĕdôm.

Chapter 39

1. And Yaăqôb dwelt in the land of his father's sojournings in the land of Kenaan. These are the generations of Yaăqôb.

2. And Yôsêph was seventeen years old when they took him down into the land of Mitsrayim, and Pôṭîyphar, an eunuch of Parôh, the chief cook bought him.

3. And he set Yôsêph over all his house and the blessing of Yahuah came upon the house of the Mitsrîy on account of Yôsêph, and Yahuah prospered him in all that he did.

4. And the Mitsrîy committed everything into the hands of Yôsêph; for he saw that Yahuah was with him, and that Yahuah prospered him in all that he did.

5. And Yôsêph's appearance was comely and very beautiful was his appearance, and his master's woman lifted up her eyes and saw Yôsêph, and she loved him and besought him to lie with her.

6. But he did not surrender his soul, and he remembered Yahuah and the words which Yaăqôb, his father, used to read from among the words of Abrâhâm, that no man should commit fornication with a woman who has a husband; that for him the punishment of death has been ordained in the shâmayim before Êlôhîym Elyôn Êl, and the sin will be recorded against him in the eternal books continually before Yahuah.

7. And Yôsêph remembered these words and refused to lie with her.

8. And she besought him for a year, but he refused and would not listen.

9. But she embraced him and held him fast in the house in order to force him to lie with her, and closed the doors of the house and held him fast; but he left his garment in her hands and broke through the door and fled without from her presence.

10. And the woman saw that he would not lie with her, and she calumniated him in the presence of his master, saying: Your Êber

servant, whom you love, sought to force me so that he might lie with me; and it came to pass when I lifted up my voice that he fled and left his garment in my hands when I held him, and he broke through the door.

11. And the Mitsrîy saw the garment of Yôsêph and the broken door, and heard the words of his woman, and cast Yôsêph into prison into the place where the prisoners were kept whom the king imprisoned.

12. And he was there in the prison; and Yahuah gave Yôsêph favor in the sight of the chief of the prison guards and compassion before him, for he saw that Yahuah was with him, and that Yahuah made all that he did to prosper.

13. And he committed all things into his hands, and the chief of the prison guards knew of nothing that was with him, for Yôsêph did everything, and Yahuah perfected it.

14. And he remained there two years. And in those days Parôh, king of Mitsrayim was wroth against his two eunuchs, against the chief butler, and against the chief baker, and he put them in ward in the house of the chief cook, in the prison where Yôsêph was kept.

15. And the chief of the prison guards appointed Yôsêph to serve them; and he served before them.

16. And they both dreamed a dream, the chief butler and the chief baker, and they told it to Yôsêph.

17. And as he interpreted to them so it befell them, and Parôh restored the chief butler to his office and the chief baker he slew, as Yôsêph had interpreted to them.

18. But the chief butler forgot Yôsêph in the prison, although he had informed him what would befall him, and did not remember to inform Parôh how Yôsêph had told him, for he forgot.

Chapter 40

1. And in those days Parôh dreamed two dreams in one night concerning a famine which was to be in all the land, and he awoke from his sleep and called all the interpreters of dreams that were in Mitsrayim, and magicians, and told them his two dreams, and they were not able to declare them.

2. And then the chief butler remembered Yôsêph and spoke of him to the king, and he brought him forth from the prison, and he told his two dreams before him.

3. And he said before Parôh that his two dreams were one, and he said unto him: Seven years shall come in which there shall be plenty over all the land of Mitsrayim, and after that seven years of famine, such a famine as has not been in all the land.

4. And now let Parôh appoint overseers in all the land of Mitsrayim, and let them store up food in every city throughout the days of the years of plenty, and there will be food for the seven years of famine, and the land will not perish through the famine, for it will be very severe.

5. And Yahuah gave Yôsêph favor and mercy in the eyes of Parôh, and Parôh said unto his servants. We shall not find such a wise and discreet man as this man, for the spirit of Yahuah is with him.

6. And he appointed him the second in all his kingdom and gave him authority over all Mitsrayim, and caused him to ride in the second chariot of Parôh.

7. And he clothed him with byssus garments, and he put a gold chain upon his neck, and a herald proclaimed before him "Êl, Êl wa

Âbîyr" and placed a ring on his hand and made him ruler over all his house, and magnified him, and said unto him. Only on the throne shall I be greater than you.

8. And Yôsêph ruled over all the land of Mitsrayim, and all the princes of Parôh, and all his servants, and all who did the king's business loved him, for he walked in uprightness, for he was without pride and arrogance, and he had no respect of persons, and did not accept gifts, but he judged in uprightness all the people of the land.

9. And the land of Mitsrayim was at peace before Parôh because of Yôsêph, for Yahuah was with him, and gave him favor and mercy for all his generations before all those who knew him and those who heard concerning him, and Parôh's kingdom was well ordered, and there was no adversary and no evil person therein.

10. And the king called Yôsêph's name Tsâphnath Panêach (צָפְנַתפַּעְנֵחַ), and gave Yôsêph to woman the daughter of Pôṭîy phera (פּוֹטִי פֶרַע), the daughter of the Kôhên of Ôn (אוֹן), the chief cook.

11. And on the day that Yôsêph stood before Parôh he was thirty years old, when he stood before Parôh.

12. And in that year Yitschâq died. And it came to pass as Yôsêph had said in the interpretation of his two dreams, according as he had said it, there were seven years of plenty over all the land of Mitsrayim, and the land of Mitsrayim abundantly produced, one measure producing eighteen hundred measures.

13. And Yôsêph gathered food into every city until they were full of corn until they could no longer count and measure it for its multitude.

Chapter 41

1. And in the forty fifth jubilee, in the second week, and in the second year, Yahûdâh took for his first born Êr, a woman from the daughters of Ărâm, named Tâmâr.

2. But he hated, and did not lie with her, because his mother was of the daughters of Kenaan, and he wished to take him a woman of the kinsfolk of his mother, but Yahûdâh, his father, would not permit him.

3. And this Êr, the first born of Yahûdâh, was wicked, and Yahuah slew him.

4. And Yahûdâh said unto Ônân, his brother: Go in unto your brother's woman and perform the duty of a husband's brother unto her, and raise up seed unto your brother.

5. And Ônân knew that the seed would not be his, but his brother's only, and he went into the house of his brother's woman, and spilt the seed on the ground, and he was wicked in the eyes of Yahuah, and he slew him.

6. And Yahûdâh said unto Tâmâr, his daughter in law: Remain in your father's house as a widow till Shêlâh my son be grown up, and I shall give you to him to woman.

7. And he grew up; but Bêdsûêl, the woman of Yahûdâh, did not permit her son Shêlâh to marry. And Bêdsûêl, the woman of Yahûdâh, died in the fifth year of this week.

8. And in the sixth year Yahûdâh went up to shear his sheep at Timnâh. And they told Tâmâr: Behold your father in law goes up to Timnâh to shear his sheep.

9. And she put off her widow's clothes, and put on a veil, and adorned herself, and sat in the gate adjoining the way to Timnâh.

10. And as Yahûdâh was going along he found her, and thought her to be a harlot,

and he said unto her: Let me come in unto you; and she said unto him: Come in, and he went in.

11. And she said unto him: Give me my hire; and he said unto her: I have nothing in my hand save my ring that is on my finger, and my necklace, and my staff which is in my hand.

12. And she said unto him: Give them to me until you do send me my hire, and he said unto her: I will send unto you a kid of male goats; and he gave them to her, and he went in unto her, and she conceived by him.

13. And Yahûdâh went unto his sheep, and she went to her father's house.

14. And Yahûdâh sent a kid of male goats by the hand of his shepherd, an Ădûllâmîy, and he did not find her; and he asked the people of the place, saying: Where is the harlot who was here? And they said unto him: There is no harlot here with us.

15. And he returned and informed him, and said unto him that he had not found her: I asked the people of the place, and they said unto me: There is no harlot here.

16. And he said: Let her keep them lest we become a cause of derision. And when she had completed three months, it was manifest that she was with child, and they told Yahûdâh, saying: Behold Tâmâr, your daughter in law, is with child by whoredom.

17. And Yahûdâh went to the house of her father, and said unto her father and her brothers: Bring her forth, and let them burn her, for she has wrought uncleanness in Yâshârêl.

18. And it came to pass when they brought her forth to burn her that she sent to her father in law the ring and the necklace, and the staff, saying: Discern whose are these, for by him am I with child.

19. And Yahûdâh acknowledged, and said: Tâmâr is more righteous than I am.

20. And therefore do not let them burn her and for that reason she was not given to Shêlâh, and he did not approach her again.

21. And after that she bare two sons, Perets and Zerach, in the seventh year of this second week.

22. And thereupon the seven years of fruitfulness were accomplished, of which Yôsêph spoke to Parôh.

23. And Yahûdâh acknowledged that the deed which he had done was evil, for he had lain with his daughter in law, and he esteemed it hateful in his eyes, and he acknowledged that he had transgressed and gone astray, for he had uncovered the skirt of his son, and he began to lament and to supplicate before Yahuah because of his transgression.

24. And we told him in a dream that it was forgiven him because he supplicated earnestly, and lamented, and did not commit it again.

25. And he received forgiveness because he turned from his sin and from his ignorance, for he transgressed greatly before our Êlôhîym; and every one that acts thus, everyone who lies with his mother in law, let them burn him with fire that he may burn therein, for there is uncleanness and pollution upon them, with fire let them burn them.

26. And you do command the children of Yâshârêl that there be no uncleanness among them, for everyone who lies with his daughter in law or with his mother in law has wrought uncleanness; with fire let them burn the man who has lain with her, and likewise the woman, and he will turn away wrath and punishment from Yâshârêl.

27. And unto Yahûdâh we said that his two sons had not lain with her, and for this reason his seed was established for a second generation, and would not be rooted out.

28. For in singleness of eye he had gone and sought for punishment, namely, according to the judgment of Abrâhâm, which he had commanded his sons, Yahûdâh had sought to burn her with fire.

Chapter 42

1. And in the first year of the third week of the forty fifth jubilee the famine began to come into the land, and the rain refused to be given to the earth, for none whatever fell.

2. And the earth grew barren, but in the land of Mitsrayim there was food, for Yôsêph had gathered the seed of the land in the seven years of plenty and had preserved it.

3. And the Mitsrîy came to Yôsêph that he might give them food, and he opened the store houses where the grain of the first year was, and he sold it to the people of the land for gold.

4. Now the famine was very sore in the land of Kenaan, and Yaăqôb heard that there was food in Mitsrayim, and he sent his ten sons that they should procure food for him in Mitsrayim; but Binyâmîyn he did not send, and the ten sons of Yaăqôb arrived in Mitsrayim among those that went there.

5. And Yôsêph recognized them, but they did not recognize him, and he spoke unto them and questioned them, and he said unto them: Are you not spies and have you not come to explore the approaches of the land? And he put them in ward.

6. And after that he set them free again, and detained Shimôn alone and sent off his nine brothers.

7. And he filled their sacks with corn, and he put their gold in their sacks, and they did not know.

8. And he commanded them to bring their younger brother, for they had told him their father was living and their younger brother.

9. And they went up from the land of Mitsrayim and they came to the land of Kenaan; and they told their father all that had befallen them, and how the master of the country had spoken roughly to them, and had seized Shimôn till they should bring Binyâmîyn.

10. And Yaăqôb said: You have bereaved me of my children! Yôsêph is not and Shimôn also is not, and you will take Binyâmîyn away. On me has your wickedness come.

11. And he said: My son will not go down with you lest per chance he fall sick; for their mother gave birth to two sons, and one has perished, and this one also you will take from me. If per chance he took a fever on the road, you would bring down my old age with sorrow unto death.

12. For he saw that their money had been returned to every man in his sack, and for this reason he feared to send him.

13. And the famine increased and became sore in the land of Kenaan, and in all lands save in the land of Mitsrayim, for many of the children of the Mitsrîy had stored up their seed for food from the time when they saw Yôsêph gathering seed together and putting it in storehouses and preserving it for the years of famine.

14. And the people of Mitsrayim fed themselves thereon during the first year of their famine.

15. But when Yâshârêl saw that the famine was very sore in the land, and that there

was no deliverance, he said unto his sons: Go again, and procure food for us that we do not die.

16. And they said: We shall not go; unless our youngest brother go with us, we shall not go.

17. And Yâshârêl saw that if he did not send him with them, they should all perish because of the famine,

18. And Reûbên said: Give him into my hand, and if I do not bring him back to you, slay my two sons instead of his soul.

19. And he said unto him: He shall not go with you. And Yahûdâh came near and said: Send him with me, and if I do not bring him back to you, let me bear the blame before you all the days of my life.

20. And he sent him with them in the second year of this week on the first day of the month, and they came to the land of Mitsrayim with all those who went, and they had presents in their hands, stacte and almonds and terebinth nuts and pure honey.

21. And they went and stood before Yôsêph, and he saw Binyâmîyn his brother, and he knew him, and said unto them: Is this your youngest brother? And they said unto him: It is he. And he said "Yahuah be gracious to you, my son"

22. And he sent him into his house and he brought forth Shimôn unto them and he made a feast for them, and they presented to him the gift which they had brought in their hands.

23. And they ate before him and he gave them all a portion, but the portion of Binyâmîyn was seven times larger than that of any of theirs.

24. And they ate and drank and arose and remained with their asses.

25. And Yôsêph devised a plan whereby he might learn their thoughts as to whether thoughts of peace prevailed among them, and he said to the steward who was over his house: Fill all their sacks with food, and return their money unto them into their vessels, and my cup, the silver cup out of which I drink, put it in the sack of the youngest, and send them away.

Chapter 43

1. And he did as Yôsêph had told him, and filled all their sacks for them with food and put their money in their sacks, and put the cup in Binyâmîyn's sack.

2. And early in the morning they departed, and it came to pass that, when they had gone from thence, Yôsêph said unto the steward of his house: Pursue them, run and seize them, saying: For good you have requited me with evil; you have stolen from me the silver cup out of which my master drinks. And bring back to me their youngest brother, and fetch him quickly before I go forth to my seat of judgment.

3. And he ran after them and said unto them according to these words.

4. And they said unto him: Êlôhîym forbid that your servants should do this thing, and steal from the house of your master any utensil, and the money also which we found in our sacks the first time, we your servants brought back from the land of Kenaan.

5. How then should we steal any utensil? Behold here we are and our sacks search, and wherever you find the cup in the sack of any man among us, let him be slain, and we and our asses will serve your master.

6. And he said unto them: Not so, the man with whom I find, him only I shall take as a servant, and you shall return in peace unto your house.

7. And as he was searching in their vessels, beginning with the eldest and ending with the youngest, it was found in Binyâmîyn's sack.

8. And they rent their garments, and laded their asses, and returned to the city and came to the house of Yôsêph, and they all bowed themselves on their faces to the ground before him.

9. And Yôsêph said unto them: You have done evil. And they said: What shall we say and how shall we defend ourselves? Our master has discovered the transgression of his servants; behold we are the servants of our master, and our asses also.

10. And Yôsêph said unto them: I too fear Yahuah; as for you, you go to your homes and let your brother be my servant, for you have done evil. You do not know that a man delights in his cup as I with this cup? And yet you have stolen it from me.

11. And Yahûdâh said: O my master, let your servant, I pray you, speak a word in my master's ear: Two brothers did your servant's mother bear to our father: One went away and was lost, and has not been found, and he alone is left of his mother, and your servant our father loves him, and his life also is bound up with the life of this lad.

12. And it will come to pass, when we go to your servant our father, and the lad is not with us, that he will die, and we shall bring down our father with sorrow unto death.

13. Now rather let me, your servant, abide instead of the boy as a bondsman unto my master, and let the lad go with his brethren, for I became surety for him at the hand of your servant our father, and if I do not bring him back, your servant will hear the blame to our father forever.

14. And Yôsêph saw that they were all accordant in goodness one with another, and he could not refrain himself, and he told them that he was Yôsêph.

15. And he conversed with them in the Êber tongue and fell on their neck and wept.

16. But did not know him not and they began to weep. And he said unto them: Do not weep not over me, but hasten and bring my father to me; and you see that it is my mouth that speaks and the eyes of my brother Binyâmîyn see.

17. For behold this is the second year of the famine, and there are still five years without harvest or fruit of trees or ploughing.

18. Come down quickly you and your households, so that you do not perish through the famine, and do not be grieved for your possessions, for Yahuah sent me before you to set things in order that many people might live.

19. And tell my father that I am still alive, and you, behold, you see that Yahuah has made me as a father to Parôh, and ruler over his house and over all the land of Mitsrayim.

20. And tell my father of all my glory, and all the riches and glory that Yahuah has given me.

21. And by the command of the mouth of Parôh he gave them chariots and provisions for the way, and he gave them all many colored raiment and silver.

22. And to their father he sent raiment and silver and ten asses which carried corn, and he sent them away.

23. And they went up and told their father that Yôsêph was alive, and was measuring out corn to all the nations of the earth, and that he was ruler over all the land of Mitsrayim.

24. And their father did not believe it, for he was beside himself in his mind; but when he saw the wagons which Yôsêph had sent, the life of his spirit revived, and he said: It is

enough for me if Yôsêph lives; I will go down and see him before I die.

Chapter 44

1. And Yâshârêl took his journey from Chârân from his house on the beginning of the third month, and he went on the way of the Well of the Oath, and he offered a sacrifice to the Êlôhîym of his father Yitschâq on the seventh of this month.

2. And Yaăqôb remembered the dream that he had seen at Bêythêl, and he feared to go down into Mitsrayim.

3. And while he was thinking of sending word to Yôsêph to come to him, and that he would not go down, he remained there seven days, if per chance he could see a vision as to whether he should remain or go down.

4. And he celebrated the harvest festival of the first fruits with old grain, for in all the land of Kenaan there was not a handful of seed in the land, for the famine was over all the beasts and cattle and birds, and also over man.

5. And on the sixteenth Yahuah appeared unto him, and said unto him: Yaăqôb, Yaăqôb; and he said: Here I am. And he said unto him: I am the Êlôhîym of your fathers, the Êlôhîym of Abrâhâm and Yitschâq; do not fear to go down into Mitsrayim, for I will make there of you a great nation I will go down with you, and I will bring you up again, and in this land you shall be buried, and Yôsêph shall put his hands upon your eyes.

6. Do not fear; go down into Mitsrayim.

7. And his sons rose up, and his sons' sons, and they placed their father and their possessions upon wagons.

8. And Yâshârêl rose up from the Well of the Oath on the sixteenth of this third month, and he went to the land of Mitsrayim.

9. And Yâshârêl sent Yahûdâh before him to his son Yôsêph to examine the land of Gôshen, for Yôsêph had told his brothers that they should come and dwell there that they might be near him.

10. And this was the goodliest land in the land of Mitsrayim, and near to him, for all of them and also for the cattle.

11. And these are the names of the sons of Yaăqôb who went into Mitsrayim with Yaăqôb their father.

12. Reûbên, the first born of Yâshârêl; and these are the names of his sons Chănôk, and Pallû, and Chetsrôn and karmîy - five.

13. Shimôn and his sons; and these are the names of his sons: Yamûêl, and Yâmîyn, and Ôhad, and Yâkîyn, and Tsôchar, and Shâûl, the son of the Tsephath (צְפַת) woman - seven.

14. Lêwîy and his sons; and these are the names of his sons: Gêreshôn, and Qehâth, and Merârîy - four.

15. Yahûdâh and his sons; and these are the names of his sons: Shêlâh, and Perets, and Zerach - four.

16. Yiśśâśkâr and his sons; and these are the names of his sons: Tôlâ, and Pûah, and Yôb (יוֹב), and Shimrôn - five.

17. Zebûlûn and his sons; and these are the names of his sons: Sered, and Êylôn, and Yachleêl - four.

18. And these are the sons of Yaăqôb and their sons whom Lêâh bore to Yaăqôb in Ărâm Nahărayim, six, and their one sister, Dîynâh and all the souls of the sons of Lêâh, and their sons, who went with Yaăqôb their father into Mitsrayim, were twenty nine, and Yaăqôb their father being with them, they were thirty.

19. And the sons of Zilpâh, Lêâh's handmaid, the woman of Yaăqôb, who bore unto Yaăqôb Gâd and Âshêr (אָשֵׁר).

20. And these are the names of their sons who went with him into Mitsrayim. The sons of Gâd: Tsiphyôn, and Chaggîy, and Shûnîy, and Etsbôn, and Êrîy, and Arêlîy, and Ărôdîy - eight.

21. And the sons of Âshêr: Yimnâh, and Yishwâh, and Yishwîy, and Berîyâh, and Śerach, their one sister - six.

22. All the souls were fourteen, and all those of Lêâh were forty four.

23. And the sons of Râchêl, the woman of Yaăqôb: Yôsêph and Binyâmîyn.

24. And there were born to Yôsêph in Mitsrayim before his father came into Mitsrayim, those whom Âsnath, daughter of Pôṭîyphar Kôhên of Ôn bare unto him, Menashsheh, and Ephrayim – three.

25. And the sons of Binyâmîyn: Bela and Beker and Ashbêl, Gêrâ, and Naămân, and Êchîy, and Rôsh, and Mûppîym, and Chûppîym, and Ard - eleven.

26. And all the souls of Râchêl were fourteen.

27. And the sons of Bilhâh, the handmaid of Râchêl, the woman of Yaăqôb, whom she bare to Yaăqôb, were Dân and Naphtali.

28. And these are the names of their sons who went with them into Mitsrayim. And the sons of Dân were Chûshîym, and Sâmôn, and Âsûdî and Ĭyaka, and Shelômôh - six.

29. And they died the year in which they entered into Mitsrayim, and there was left to Dân Chûshîym alone.

30. And these are the names of the sons of Naphtali Yachtseêl, and Gûnîy and Yêtser, and Shillêm, and Ĭw.

31. And Ĭw, who was born after the years of famine, died in Mitsrayim.

32. And all the souls of Râchêl were twenty six.

33. And all the souls of Yaăqôb which went into Mitsrayim were seventy souls. These are his children and his children's children, in all seventy, but five died in Mitsrayim before Yôsêph, and had no children.

34. And in the land of Kenaan two sons of Yahûdâh died, Êr and Ônân, and they had no children, and the children of Yâshârêl buried those who perished, and they were reckoned among the seventy Gentile nations.

Chapter 45

1. And Yâshârêl went into the country of Mitsrayim, into the land of Gôshen, on the beginning of the fourth month, in the second year of the third week of the forty fifth jubilee.

2. And Yôsêph went to meet his father Yaăqôb, to the land of Gôshen, and he fell on his father's neck and wept.

3. And Yâshârêl said unto Yôsêph: Now let me die since I have seen you, and now may Yahuah Êlôhîym of Yâshârêl be blessed. The Êlôhîym of Abrâhâm and the Êlôhîym of Yitscĥâq who has not withheld his mercy and his grace from his servant Yaăqôb.

4. It is enough for me that I have seen your face while I am yet alive; yea, true is the vision which I saw at Bêythêl. Blessed be Yahuah my Êlôhîym forever and ever, and blessed be his name.

5. And Yôsêph and his brothers ate bread before their father and drank wine, and Yaăqôb rejoiced with exceeding great joy because he saw Yôsêph eating with his brothers and drinking before him, and he blessed the Bârâ of all things who had preserved him, and had preserved for him his twelve sons.

6. And Yôsêph had given to his father and to his brothers as a gift the right of dwelling

in the land of Gôshen and in Ramesês and all the region round about, which he ruled over before Parôh. And Yâshârêl and his sons dwelt in the land of Gôshen, the best part of the land of Mitsrayim and Yâshârêl was one hundred and thirty years old when he came into Mitsrayim.

7. And Yôsêph nourished his father and his brethren and also their possessions with bread as much as sufficed them for the seven years of the famine.

8. And the land of Mitsrayim suffered because of the famine, and Yôsêph acquired all the land of Mitsrayim for Parôh in return for food, and he got possession of the people and their cattle and everything for Parôh.

9. And the years of the famine were accomplished, and Yôsêph gave to the people in the land seed and food that they might sow the land in the eighth year, for the river had overflowed all the land of Mitsrayim.

10. For in the seven years of the famine it had not overflowed and had irrigated only a few places on the banks of the river, but now it overflowed and the Mitsrîy sowed the land, and it bore much corn that year.

11. And this was the first year of the fourth week of the forty fifth jubilee.

12. And Yôsêph took of the corn of the harvest the fifth part for the king and left four parts for them for food and for seed, and Yôsêph made it an ordinance for the land of Mitsrayim until this day.

13. And Yâshârêl lived in the land of Mitsrayim seventeen years, and all the days which he lived were three jubilees, one hundred and forty seven years, and he died in the fourth year of the fifth week of the forty fifth jubilee.

14. And Yâshârêl blessed his sons before he died and told them everything that would befall them in the land of Mitsrayim; and he made known to them what would come upon them in the last days, and blessed them and gave to Yôsêph two portions in the land.

15. And he slept with his fathers, and he was buried in the double cave in the land of Kenaan, near Abrâhâm his father in the grave which he dug for himself in the double cave in the land of Chebrôn.

16. And he gave all his books and the books of his fathers to Lêwîy his son that he might preserve them and renew them for his children until this day.

Chapter 46

1. And it came to pass that after Yaăqôb died the children of Yâshârêl multiplied in the land of Mitsrayim, and they became a great nation, and they were of one accord in heart, so that brother loved brother and every man helped his brother, and they increased abundantly and multiplied exceedingly, ten weeks of years, all the days of the life of Yôsêph.

2. And there was no adversary nor any evil all the days of the life of Yôsêph which he lived after his father Yaăqôb, for all the Mitsrîy honored the children of Yâshârêl all the days of the life of Yôsêph.

3. And Yôsêph died being a hundred and ten years old; seventeen years he lived in the land of Kenaan, and ten years he was a servant, and three years in prison, and eighty years he was under the king, ruling all the land of Mitsrayim.

4. And he died and all his brethren and all that generation.

5. And he commanded the children of Yâshârêl before he died that they should carry his bones with them when they went forth from the land of Mitsrayim.

6. And he made them swear regarding his bones, for he knew that the Mitsrîy would not again bring forth and bury him in the land of Kenaan, for Mâkâmârôn, king of Kenaan, while dwelling in the land of Ashshûr (אַשּׁוּר), fought in the valley with the king of Mitsrayim and slew him there, and pursued after the Mitsrîy to the gates of Êrmôn.

7. But he was not able to enter, for another, a new king, had become king of Mitsrayim, and he was stronger than he, and he returned to the land of Kenaan, and the gates of Mitsrayim were closed, and none went out and none came into Mitsrayim.

8. And Yôsêph died in the forty sixth jubilee, in the sixth week, in the second year, and they buried him in the land of Mitsrayim, and all his brethren died after him.

9. And the king of Mitsrayim went forth to war with the king of Kenaan in the forty seventh jubilee, in the second week in the second year, and the children of Yâshârêl brought forth all the bones of the children of Yaăqôb save the bones of Yôsêph, and they buried them in the field in the double cave in the mountain.

10. And the most of them returned to Mitsrayim, but a few of them remained in the mountains of Chebrôn, and Amrâm your father remained with them.

11. And the king of Kenaan was victorious over the king of Mitsrayim, and he closed the gates of Mitsrayim.

12. And he devised an evil device against the children of Yâshârêl of afflicting them and he said unto the people of Mitsrayim: Behold the people of the children of Yâshârêl have increased and multiplied more than we.

13. Come and let us deal wisely with them before they become too many, and let us afflict them with slavery before war come upon us and before they too fight against us; else they will join themselves unto our enemies and get them up out of our land, for their hearts and faces are towards the land of Kenaan.

14. And he set over them taskmasters to afflict them with slavery; and they built strong cities for Parôh, Pithôm, and Ramesê and they built all the walls and all the fortifications which had fallen in the cities of Mitsrayim.

15. And they made them serve with rigor, and the more they dealt evilly with them, the more they increased and multiplied.

16. And the people of Mitsrayim abominated the children of Yâshârêl

Chapter 47

1. And in the seventh week, in the seventh year, in the forty seventh jubilee, your father went forth from the land of Kenaan, and you were born in the fourth week, in the sixth year thereof, in the forty eighth jubilee; this was the time of tribulation on the children of Yâshârêl.

2. And Parôh, king of Mitsrayim, issued a command regarding them that they should cast all their male children which were born into the river.

3. And they cast them in for seven months until the day that you were born.

4. And your mother hid you for three months, and they told regarding her. And she made an ark for you, and covered it with pitch and asphalt, and placed it in the flags on the bank of the river, and she placed you in it seven days, and your mother came by night and suckled you, and by day Miryâm, your sister, guarded you from the birds.

5. And in those days Tharmuth, the daughter of Parôh, came to bathe in the river, and she heard thy voice crying, and she told her maidens to bring you forth, and they brought you unto her.

6. And she took you out of the ark, and she had compassion on you.

7. And your sister said unto her: Shall I go and call unto you one of the Êber women to nurse and suckle this babe for you?

8. And she said unto her: Go. And she went and called your mother Yôkebed, and she he gave her wages, and she nursed you.

9. And afterwards, when you were grown up, they brought you unto the daughter of Parôh, and you did become her son, and Amrâm your father taught you writing, and after you had completed three weeks they brought you into the royal court.

10. And you were three weeks of years at court until the time when you did go forth from the royal court and did see a Mitsrîy smiting your friend who was of the children of Yâshârêl, and you did slay him and hide him in the sand.

11. And on the second day you did find two of the children of Yâshârêl striving together, and you did say to him who was doing the wrong: Why do you smite your brother?

12. And he was angry and indignant, and said: Who made you a prince and a judge over us? Do you think to kill me as you killed the Mitsrîy yesterday? And you did fear and fled on account of these words.

Chapter 48

1. And in the sixth year of the third week of the forty ninth jubilee you did depart and dwelt in the land of Midyân, five weeks and one year. And you did return into Mitsrayim in the second week in the second year in the fiftieth jubilee.

2. And you yourself know what he spoke unto you on Mount Sîynay, and what prince Mastêmâ desired to do with you when you were returning into Mitsrayim on the way when you did meet him at the lodging place.

3. Did he not with all his power seek to slay you and deliver the Mitsrîy out of your hand when he saw that you were sent to execute judgment and vengeance on the Mitsrîy?

4. And I delivered you out of his hand, and you did perform the signs and wonders which you were sent to perform in Mitsrayim against Parôh, and against all his house, and against his servants and his people.

5. And Yahuah executed a great vengeance on them for Yâshârêl's sake, and smote them through the plagues of blood and frogs, lice and dog flies, and malignant boils breaking forth in blains; and their cattle by death; and by hail stones, thereby he destroyed everything that grew for them; and by locusts which devoured the residue which had been left by the hail, and by darkness; and by the death of the first born of men and animals, and on all their idols Yahuah took vengeance and burned them with fire.

6. And everything was sent through your hand, that you should declare these things before they were done, and you did speak with the king of Mitsrayim before all his servants and before his people.

7. And everything took place according to your words; ten great and terrible judgments came on the land of Mitsrayim that you might execute vengeance on it for Yâshârêl.

8. And Yahuah did everything for Yâshârêl's sake, and according to his covenant, which he had ordained with Abrâhâm that he

would take vengeance on them as they had brought them by force into bondage.

9. And the prince Mastêmâ stood up against you, and sought to cast you into the hands of Parôh, and he helped the Mitsrîy sorcerers, and they stood up and wrought before you.

10. The evils indeed we permitted them to work, but the remedies we did not allow to be wrought by their hands.

11. And Yahuah smote them with malignant ulcers, and they were not able to stand, for we destroyed them so that they could not perform a single sign.

12. And notwithstanding all these signs and wonders the prince Mastêmâ was not put to shame because he took courage and cried to the Mitsrîy to pursue after you with all the powers of the Mitsrîy, with their chariots, and with their horses, and with all the hosts of the peoples of Mitsrayim.

13. And I stood between the Mitsrîy and Yâshârêl, and we delivered Yâshârêl out of his hand, and out of the hand of his people, and Yahuah brought them through the midst of the sea as if it were dry land.

14. And all the peoples whom he brought to pursue after Yâshârêl, Yahuah our Êlôhîym cast them into the midst of the sea, into the depths of the abyss beneath the children of Yâshârêl, even as the people of Mitsrayim had cast their children into the river, he took vengeance on 1,000,000 of them, and one thousand strong and energetic men were destroyed on account of one suckling of the children of your people which they had thrown into the river.

15. And on the fourteenth day and on the fifteenth and on the sixteenth and on the seventeenth and on the eighteenth the prince Mastêmâ was bound and imprisoned behind the children of Yâshârêl that he might not accuse them.

16. And on the nineteenth we let them loose that they might help the Mitsrîy and pursue the children of Yâshârêl.

17. And he hardened their hearts and made them stubborn, and the device was devised by Yahuah our Êlôhîym that he might smite the Mitsrîy and cast them into the sea.

18. And on the fourteenth we bound him that he might not accuse the children of Yâshârêl on the day when they asked the Mitsrîy for vessels and garments, vessels of silver, and vessels of gold, and vessels of bronze, in order to despoil the Mitsrîy in return for the bondage in which they had forced them to serve.

19. And we did not lead forth the children of Yâshârêl from Mitsrayim empty handed.

Chapter 49

1. Remember the commandment which Yahuah commanded you concerning the Pesach (פֶּסַח), that you should celebrate it in its season on the fourteenth of the first month, that you should kill it before it is evening, and that they should eat it by night on the evening of the fourteenth before the time of the rising of the sun.

2. For on this night, the beginning of the festival and the beginning of the joy, you were eating the Pesach in Mitsrayim, when all the powers of Mastêmâ had been let loose to slay all the first born in the land of Mitsrayim, from the first born of Parôh to the first born of the captive maidservant in the mill, and to the cattle.

3. And this is the sign which Yahuah gave them: Into every house on the lintels of which they saw the blood of a lamb of the first year,

into that house they should not enter to slay, but should pass by it, that all those should be saved that were in the house because the sign of the blood was on its lintels.

4. And the powers of Yahuah did everything according as Yahuah commanded them, and they passed by all the children of Yâshârêl, and the plague did not come upon them to destroy from among them any soul either of cattle, or man, or dog.

5. And the plague was very grievous in Mitsrayim, and there was no house in Mitsrayim where there was not one dead, and weeping and lamentation.

6. And all Yâshârêl was eating the flesh of the paschal lamb, and drinking the wine, and was lauding, and blessing, and giving thanks to Yahuah Êlôhîym of their fathers, and was ready to go forth from under the yoke of Mitsrayim, and from the evil bondage.

7. And you remember this day all the days of your life, and observe it from year to year all the days of your life, once a year, on its day, according to all the law thereof, and do not adjourn it from day today, or from month to month.

8. For it is an eternal ordinance, and engraved on the shâmayim tablets regarding all the children of Yâshârêl that they should observe it every year on its day once a year, throughout all their generations; and there is no limit of days, for this is ordained forever.

9. And the man who is free from uncleanness, and does not come to observe it on occasion of its day, so as to bring an acceptable offering before Yahuah, and to eat and to drink before Yahuah on the day of its festival, that man who is clean and close at hand shall be cut off: Because he did not offer the offering of Yahuah in its appointed season, he shall take the guilt upon himself.

10. Let the children of Yâshârêl come and observe the Pesach on the day of its fixed time, on the fourteenth day of the first month, between the evenings, from the third part of the day to the third part of the night, for two portions of the day are given to the light, and a third part to the evening.

11. This is that which Yahuah commanded you that you should observe it between the evenings.

12. And it is not permissible to slay it during any period of the light, but during the period bordering on the evening, and let them eat it at the time of the evening, until the third part of the night, and whatever is left over of all its flesh from the third part of the night and onwards, let them burn it with fire.

13. And they shall not cook it with water, nor shall they eat it raw, but roast on the fire: They shall eat it with diligence, its head with the inwards thereof and its feet they shall roast with fire, and not break any bone thereof; for of the children of Yâshârêl no bone shall be crushed.

14. For this reason Yahuah commanded the children of Yâshârêl to observe the Pesach on the day of its fixed time, and they shall not break a bone thereof; for it is a festival day, and a day commanded, and there may be no passing over from day today, and month to month, but on the day of its festival let it be observed.

15. And you do command the children of Yâshârêl to observe the Pesach throughout their days, every year, once a year on the day of its fixed time, and it shall come for a memorial well pleasing before Yahuah, and no plague shall come upon them to slay or to smite in that year in which they celebrate the Pesach in its season in every respect according to his command.

16. And they shall not eat it outside the sanctuary of Yahuah, but before the sanctuary of Yahuah, and all the people of the congregation of Yâshârêl shall celebrate it in its appointed season.

17. And every man who has come upon its day shall eat it in the sanctuary of your Êlôhîym before Yahuah from twenty years old and upward; for thus is it written and ordained that they should eat it in the sanctuary of Yahuah.

18. And when the children of Yâshârêl come into the land which they are to possess, into the land of Kenaan, and set up the tabernacle of Yahuah in the midst of the land in one of their tribes until the sanctuary of Yahuah has been built in the land, let them come and celebrate the Pesach in the midst of the tabernacle of Yahuah, and let them slay it before Yahuah from year to year.

19. And in the days when the house has been built in the name of Yahuah in the land of their inheritance, they shall go there and slay the Pesach in the evening, at sunset, at the third part of the day.

20. And they shall offer its blood on the threshold of the altar, and shall place its fat on the fire which is upon the altar, and they shall eat its flesh roasted with fire in the court of the house which has been sanctified in the name of Yahuah.

21. And they may not celebrate the Pesach in their cities, nor in any place save before the tabernacle of Yahuah, or before his house where his name has dwelt. And they shall not go astray from Yahuah.

22. And you do, Môsheh, command the children of Yâshârêl to observe the ordinances of the Pesach, as it was commanded unto you; you declare unto them every year and the day of its days, and the festival of Unleavened Bread, that they should eat unleavened bread seven days, and that they should observe its festival, and that they bring an offering every day during those seven days of joy before Yahuah on the altar of your Êlôhîym.

23. For you celebrated this festival with haste when you went forth from Mitsrayim till you entered into the wilderness of Shûr; for on the shore of the sea you completed it.

Chapter 50

1. And after this law I made known to you the days of the Shabbâth in the desert of Sîynay, which is between Êylim and Sîynay.

2. And I told you of the Shabbâth of the land on Mount Sîynay, and I told you of the jubilee years in the Shabbâth of years: But the year thereof I have not told you till you enter the land which you are to possess.

3. And the land also shall keep its Shabbâth while they dwell upon it, and they shall know the jubilee year.

4. Wherefore I have ordained for you the year weeks and the years and the jubilees: There are forty nine jubilees from the days of Âdâm until this day, and one week and two years: And there are yet forty years distant for learning the commandments of Yahuah, until they pass over into the land of Kenaan, crossing the Yardên to the west.

5. And the jubilees shall pass by, until Yâshârêl is cleansed from all guilt of fornication, and uncleanness, and pollution, and sin, and error, and dwells with confidence in all the land, and there shall be no more an adversary or any evil one, and the land shall be clean from that time forevermore.

6. And behold the commandment regarding the Shabbâth. I have written them down for you and all the judgments of its laws.

7. Six days you shall labor, but on the seventh day is the Shabbâth of Yahuah your Êlôhîym. In it you shall do no manner of work, you and your sons, and your men servants and your maidservants, and all your cattle and the sojourner also who is with you.

8. And the man that does any work on it shall die: Whoever desecrates that day, whoever lies with his woman, or whoever says he will do something on it, that he will set out on a journey thereon in regard to any buying or selling: And whoever draws water thereon which he had not prepared for himself on the sixth day, and whoever takes up any burden to carry it out of his tent or out of his house shall die.

9. You shall do no work whatever on the Shabbâth day save what you have prepared for yourselves on the sixth day, so as to eat, and drink, and rest, and keep Shabbâth from all work on that day, and to bless Yahuah your Êlôhîym, who has given you a day of festival and a qâdôsh day: And a day of the qâdôsh kingdom for all Yâshârêl is this day among their days forever.

10. For great is the honor which Yahuah has given to Yâshârêl that they should eat and drink and be satisfied on this festival day, and rest thereon from all labor which belongs to the labor of the children of men save burning lebônâh and bringing offerings and sacrifices before Yahuah for days and for Shabbâth.

11. This work alone shall be done on the Shabbâth days in the sanctuary of Yahuah your Êlôhîym; that they may atone for Yâshârêl with sacrifice continually from day today for a memorial well pleasing before Yahuah, and that he may receive them always from day today according as you have been commanded.

12. And every man who does any work thereon, or goes a journey, or tills his farm, whether in his house or any other place, and whoever lights a fire, or rides on any beast, or travels by ship on the sea, and whoever strikes or kills anything, or slaughters a beast or a bird, or whoever catches an animal or a bird or a fish, or whoever fasts or makes war on the Shabbâth:

13. The man who does any of these things on the Shabbâth shall die, so that the children of Yâshârêl shall observe the Shabbâth according to the commandments regarding the Shabbâth of the land, as it is written in the tablets, which he gave into my hands that I should write out for you the laws of the seasons, and the seasons according to the division of their days.

Book of Sirach & Bible Parallels (Dabar Yahuah Scriptures Study Guide)

This study guide highlights parallels between the Book of Sirach (Ecclesiasticus / Ben Sira) and other books of the Bible. The Book of Sirach, part of the wisdom tradition, draws heavily from Proverbs, Psalms, and Ecclesiastes, while also anticipating teachings found in the New Testament. This table lists key passages in Sirach that are either quoted, echoed, or thematically similar to canonical scriptures.

Comparison Table: Sirach & The Traditional Bible

Sirach Passage	Biblical Parallels	Theme / Connection
Sirach 1:1	Prov 2:6	All wisdom comes from Yahuah.
Sirach 1:12–13	Prov 1:7; Prov 9:10	Fear of Yahuah is the foundation of wisdom.
Sirach 2:1–5	Jas 1:2–4; 1 Pet 4:12	Endurance in trials proves faith.
Sirach 3:3–7	Exod 20:12; Eph 6:1–3	Honor father and mother brings blessing.
Sirach 5:7	Prov 27:1; Heb 3:15	Warning against delaying repentance.
Sirach 7:10	Luke 18:1; Matt 6:2–4	Persistence in prayer; almsgiving emphasized.
Sirach 10:12–13	Prov 16:18; Jas 4:6	Pride leads to downfall.
Sirach 11:18–19	Luke 12:16–21	Rich fool parable connection.
Sirach 15:11–20	Deut 30:19; Jas 1:13	Free will and human responsibility for sin.
Sirach 17:1–14	Gen 2–3; Deut 30:15–19	Creation, command, and moral choice.
Sirach 18:30–31	Prov 25:28; Gal 5:16	Self-control against desires.
Sirach 21:2	Prov 4:14–15; Rom 6:12	Sin compared to a deadly serpent.
Sirach 28:2	Matt 6:14–15; Mark 11:25	Forgive others to be forgiven.
Sirach 34:16	Ps 34:7; Ps 46:1–2	Those who fear Yahuah have hope and safety.
Sirach 35:12–13	Deut 10:17–18; Acts 10:34	Yahuah shows no partiality.
Sirach 37:16	Prov 15:22; Luke 14:28	Counsel before action.
Sirach 40:17	Tobit 4:7–9; Matt 6:19–21	Almsgiving is heavenly treasure.
Sirach 44–50	Heb 11	Praises patriarchs and heroes of faith.
Sirach 51:1–12	Ps 18; Ps 103	Psalm-like hymn of thanksgiving.

Summary of Key Parallels

1. Wisdom Foundations – Sirach echoes Proverbs, Job, Psalms, and Ecclesiastes.

2. Moral Exhortations – Strong parallels with New Testament teachings (Matthew, James, Paul).

3. Practical Piety – Persistence in prayer, charity, forgiveness, and humility.

4. Historical Praise – Chapters 44–50 recall Yasharel's heroes, much like Hebrews 11.

5. Theological Anchors – Fear of Yahuah, rejection of sin, free will, and divine justice.

Bên Sirâ (בן סירא) Son of Sirach

Prologue

Wisdom of Yahusha, the Son of Sirâ

1. Since many great and important things have been passed down to us through the Law and the Nâbîy,

2. And by others who have followed in their footsteps,

3. For which things Yâshârêl ought to be praised for learning and wisdom and not only must the readers become skilled themselves, but also be able to help those outside the community, both through speech and writing,

4. My grandfather Yahusha, having devoted himself deeply to the reading of the law, the Nâbîy, and the other books of our ancestors, and having gained sound understanding from them, was also moved to write something concerning learning and wisdom,

5. With the intent that those who desire to learn and are devoted to these matters might benefit even more in living according to the law.

6. Therefore, I ask you to read it with kindness and attention, and to forgive us if we seem to fall short in the wording, though we have worked hard to interpret it.

7. For the same ideas expressed in Êber, when translated into another language, do not always carry the same power,

8. And not only with this book, but also with the law itself, the Nâbîy, and the rest of the writings, there is a noticeable difference when they are spoken in their original language.

9. In the thirty eighth year, when I came to Mitsrayim during the reign of Euergetes and spent some time there, I found a book of great learning.

10. Therefore, I considered it very necessary to apply effort and diligence in translating it, using great care and skill during that time, to complete the book and present it for those who, living in a foreign land, are eager to learn and have already been trained in conduct to live according to the law.

Chapter 1

1. All wisdom comes from Yahuah, and is with him forever.

2. Who can number the sand of the sea, and the drops of rain, and the days of eternity?

3. Who can find out the height of shâmayim, and the breadth of the earth, and the deep, and wisdom?

4. Wisdom has been created before all things, and the understanding of prudence from everlasting.

5. The word of Êlôhîym Elyôn Êl is the fountain of wisdom; and her ways are everlasting commandments.

6. To whom has the root of wisdom been revealed? Or who has known her wise counsels?

7. Unto whom has the knowledge of wisdom been made manifest? And who has understood her great experience?

8. There is one wise and greatly to be feared, Yahuah sitting upon his throne.

9. He created her, and saw her, and numbered her, and poured her out upon all his works.

10. She is with all flesh according to his gift, and he has given her to them that love him.

11. The fear of Yahuah is honor, and glory, and gladness, and a crown of rejoicing.

12. The fear of Yahuah makes a merry heart, and gives joy, and gladness, and a long life.

13. Whoso fears Yahuah, it shall go well with him at the last, and he shall find favor in the day of his death.

14. To fear Yahuah is the beginning of wisdom: And it was created with the faithful in the womb.

15. She has built an everlasting foundation with men, and she shall continue with their seed.

16. To fear Yahuah is fullness of wisdom, and fills men with her fruits.

17. She fills all their house with things desirable, and the garners with her increase.

18. The fear of Yahuah is a crown of wisdom, making peace and perfect health to flourish; both which are the gifts of Êlôhîym: And it enlarges their rejoicing that love him.

19 Wisdom rains down skill and knowledge of understanding standing, and exalts them to honor that hold her fast.

20. The root of wisdom is to fear Yahuah, and the branches thereof are long life.

21. The fear of Yahuah drives away sins: And where it is present, it turns away wrath.

22. A furious man cannot be justified; for the sway of his fury shall be his destruction.

23. A patient man will tear for a time, and afterward joy shall spring up unto him.

24. He will hide his words for a time, and the lips of many shall declare his wisdom.

25. The parables of knowledge are in the treasures of wisdom: but godliness is an abomination to a sinner.

26. If you desire wisdom, keep the commandments, and Yahuah shall give her unto you.

27. For the fear of Yahuah is wisdom and instruction: And faith and meekness are his delight.

28. Do not distrust the fear of Yahuah when you are poor: And do not come unto him with a double heart.

29. Do not be a hypocrite in the sight of men, and take good heed what you speak.

30. Do not do not exalt, lest you fall, and bring dishonor upon your soul, and so Êlôhîym discovers your secrets, and cast you down in the midst of the congregation, because you did not come in truth to the fear of Yahuah, but your heart is full of deceit.

Chapter 2

1. My son, if you come to serve Yahuah, prepare your soul for temptation.

2. Set your heart right, and constantly endure, and do not make haste in time of trouble.

3. Cleave unto him, and do not depart away, that you may be increased at your last end.

4. Whatsoever is brought upon you take cheerfully, and be patient when you are changed to a low estate.

5. For gold is tried in the fire, and acceptable men in the furnace of adversity.

6. Believe in him, and he will help you; order your way right, and trust in him.

7. You that fear Yahuah, wait for his mercy; and do not go aside, lest you fall.

8. You that fear Yahuah, believe him; and your reward shall not fail.

9. You that fear Yahuah, hope for good, and for everlasting joy and mercy.

10. Look at the generations of old, and see; did ever any trust in Yahuah, and was confounded? Or did any abide in his fear, and was forsaken? Or whom did he ever despise, that called upon him?

11. For Yahuah is full of compassion and mercy, longsuffering, and very pitiful, and forgives sins, and saves in time of affliction.

12. Woe be to fearful hearts, and faint hands, and the sinner that goes two ways!

13. Woe unto him that is fainthearted! For he does not believe; therefore he shall not be defended.

14. Woe unto you that have lost patience! And what will you do when Yahuah shall visit you?

15. They that fear Yahuah will not disobey his word; and they that love him will keep his ways.

16. They that fear Yahuah will seek that which is well, pleasing unto him; and they that love him shall be filled with the law.

17. They that fear Yahuah will prepare their hearts, and humble their souls in his sight,

18. Saying, we will fall into the hands of Yahuah, and not into the hands of men: For as his majesty is, so is his mercy.

Chapter 3

1. Hear me your father, O children, and do thereafter, that you may be safe.

2. For Yahuah has given the father honor over the children, and has confirmed the authority of the mother over the sons.

3. Whoso honors his father makes an atonement for his sins:

4. And he that honors his mother is as one that lays up treasure.

5. Whoso honors his father shall have joy of his own children; and when he makes his prayer, he shall be heard.

6. He that honors his father shall have a long life; and he that is obedient unto Yahuah shall be a comfort to his mother.

7. He that fears Yahuah will honor his father, and will do service unto his parents, as to his masters.

8. Honor your father and mother both in word and deed that a blessing may come upon you from them.

9. For the blessing of the father establishes the houses of children; but the curse of the mother roots out foundations.

10. Do not glory in the dishonor of your father; for your father's dishonor is no glory unto you.

11. For the glory of a man is from the honor of his father; and a mother in dishonor is a reproach to the children.

12. My son, help your father in his age, and do not grieve him as long as he lives.

13. And if his understanding fail, have patience with him; and do not despise him when you are in your full strength.

14. For the relieving of your father shall not be forgotten: And instead of sins it shall be added to build you up.

15. In the day of your affliction it shall be remembered; your sins also shall melt away, as the ice in the fair warm weather.

16. He that forsakes his father is as a blasphemer; and he that angers his mother is cursed: of Êlôhîym.

17. My son, go on with your business in meekness; so you shall be beloved of him that is approved.

18. The greater you are, the more humble yourself, and you shall find favor before Yahuah.

19. Many are in high place, and of renown: But mysteries are revealed unto the meek.

20. For the power of Yahuah is great, and he is honored of the lowly.

21. Do not seek out things that are too hard for you, neither search the things that are above your strength.

22. But what is commanded you, think thereupon with reverence, for it is not needful for you to see with your eyes the things that are in secret.

23. Do not be curious in unnecessary matters: For more things are showed unto you than men understand.

24. For many are deceived by their own vain opinion; and an evil suspicion has overthrown their judgment.

25. Without eyes you shall want light: Do not profess the knowledge therefore that you do not have.

26. A stubborn heart shall fare evil at the last; and he that loves danger shall perish therein.

27. An obstinate heart shall be laden with sorrows; and the wicked man shall heap sin upon sin.

28. In the punishment of the proud there is no remedy; for the plant of wickedness has taken root in him.

29. The heart of the prudent will understand a parable; and an attentive ear is the desire of a wise man.

30. Water will quench a flaming fire; and alms makes an atonement for sins.

31. And he that requites good turns is mindful of that which may come hereafter; and when he falls, he shall find a stay.

Chapter 4

1. My son, do not defraud the poor of his living, and do not make the needy eyes to wait long.

2. Do not make a hungry soul sorrowful; neither provoke a man in his distress.

3. Do not add more trouble to a heart that is vexed; and do not defer to give to him that is in need.

4. Do not reject the supplication of the afflicted; neither turn away your face from a poor man.

5. Do not turn away your eye from the needy, and give him none occasion to curse you:

6. For if he curse you in the bitterness of his soul, his prayer shall be heard of him that made him.

7. Get yourself the love of the congregation, and bow your head to a great man.

8. Do not let it grieve you to bow down your ear to the poor, and give him a friendly answer with meekness.

9. Deliver him that suffers wrong from the hand of the oppressor; and do not be faint-hearted when you sit in judgment.

10. Be as a father unto the fatherless, and instead of a husband unto their mother: So you shall be as the son of Elyôn Êl, and he shall love you more than your mother does.

11. Wisdom exalts her children, and lays hold of them that seek her.

12. He that loves her loves life; and they that seek to her early shall be filled with joy.

13. He that holds her fast shall inherit glory; and wherever she enters, Yahuah will bless.

14. They that serve her shall minister to the Qâdôsh Êl: And them that love her Yahuah does love.

15. Whoso gives ear unto her shall judge the nations: And he that attends unto her shall dwell securely.

16. If a man commit himself unto her, he shall inherit her; and his generation shall hold her in possession.

17. For at the first she will walk with him by crooked ways, and bring fear and dread upon him, and torment him with her discipline, until she may trust his soul, and try him by her laws.

18. Then she will return the straightway unto him, and comfort him, and show him her secrets.

19. But if he goes wrong, she will forsake him, and give him over to his own ruin.

20. Observe the opportunity, and beware of evil; and do not be ashamed when it concerns your soul.

21. For there is a shame that brings sin; and there is a shame which is glory and grace.

22. Do not accept no person against your soul, and do not let the reverence of any man cause you to fall.

23. And do not refrain to speak, when there is occasion to do good, and do not hide your wisdom in her beauty.

24. For by speech wisdom shall be known: And learning by the word of the tongue.

25. In no wise speak against the truth; but be abashed of the error of your ignorance.

26. Do not be ashamed to confess your sins; and do not force the course of the river.

27. Do not make yourself an underling to a foolish man; neither accept the person of the mighty.

28. Strive for the truth unto death, and Yahuah shall fight for you.

29. Do not be hasty in your tongue, and in your deeds slack and remiss.

30. Do not be as a lion in your house, nor frantic among your servants.

31. Do not let your hand be stretched out to receive, and shut when you should repay.

Chapter 5

1. Do not set your heart upon your goods; and do not say, I have enough for my life.

2. Do not follow your own mind and your strength, to walk in the ways of your heart:

3. And do not say, who shall control me for my works? For Yahuah will surely revenge your pride.

4. Do not say, I have sinned, and what harm has happened unto me? For Yahuah is long-suffering, he will in no wise let you go.

5. Concerning propitiation, do not be without fear to add sin unto sin:

6. And do not say his mercy is great; he will be pacified for the multitude of my sins: For mercy and wrath come from him, and his indignation rests upon sinners.

7. Make no tarrying to turn to Yahuah, and do not put off from day today: For suddenly shall the wrath of Yahuah come forth, and in your security you shall be destroyed, and perish in the day of vengeance.

8. Do not set your heart upon goods unjustly gotten, for they shall not profit you in the day of calamity.

9. Do not move with every wind, and do not go into every way: For so does the sinner that has a double tongue.

10. Be steadfast in your understanding; and let your word be the same.

11. Be swift to hear; and let your life be sincere; and with patience give answer.

12. If you have understanding, answer your neighbor; if not, lay your hand upon your mouth.

13. Honor and shame is in talk: And the tongue of man is his fall.

14. Do not be called a whisperer, and do not lie in wait with your tongue: For a foul shame is upon the thief, and an evil condemnation upon the double tongue.

15. Do not be ignorant of anything in a great matter or a small.

Chapter 6

1. Instead of a friend do not become an enemy; for thereby you shall inherit an ill name, shame, and reproach: Even so shall a sinner that has a double tongue.

2. Do not extol yourself in the counsel of your own heart; that your soul do not be torn in pieces as a bull straying alone.

3. You shall eat up your leaves, and lose your fruit, and leave yourself as a dry tree.

4. A wicked soul shall destroy him that has it, and shall make him to be laughed to scorn of his enemies.

5. Sweet language will multiply friends: And a fair speaking tongue will increase kind greetings.

6. Be in peace with many: Nevertheless have but one counsellor of a thousand.

7. If you would get a friend, prove him first and do not be hasty to credit him.

8. For some man is a friend for his own occasion, and will not abide in the day of your trouble.

9. And there is a friend, who being turned to enmity, and strife will discover your reproach.

10. Again, some friend is a companion at the table, and will not continue in the day of your affliction.

11. But in your prosperity he will be as yourself, and will be bold over your servants.

12. If you are brought low, he will be against you, and will hide himself from your face.

13. Separate yourself from your enemies, and take heed of your friends.

14. A faithful friend is a strong defense: And he that has found such an one has found a treasure.

15. Nothing does countervail a faithful friend, and his excellency is invaluable.

16. A faithful friend is the remedy of life; and they that fear Yahuah shall find him.

17. Whoso fears Yahuah shall direct his friendship right: For as he is, so shall his neighbor be also.

18. My son, gather instruction from your youth up: So you shall find wisdom till your old age.

19. Come unto her as one that plows and sows, and wait for her good fruits: For you shall not toil much in laboring about her, but you shall eat of her fruits right soon.

20. She is very unpleasant to the unlearned: He that is without understanding will not remain with her.

21. She will lie upon him as a mighty stone of trial; and he will cast her from him ere it be long.

22. For wisdom is according to her name, and she is not manifested unto many.

23. Give ear, my son, receive my advice, and do not refuse my counsel,

24. And put your feet into her fetters, and your neck into her chain.

25. Bow down your shoulder, and bear her, and do not be grieved with her bonds.

26. Come unto her with your whole heart, and keep her ways with all your power.

27. Search, and seek, and she shall be made known unto you: And when you have got hold of her, do not let her go.

28. For at the last you shall find her rest, and that shall be turned to your joy.

29. Then shall her fetters be a strong defense for you, and her chains a robe of glory.

30. For there is a golden ornament upon her, and her bands are purple lace.

31. You shall put her on as a robe of honor, and shall put her about you as a crown of joy.

32. My son, if you will, you shall be taught: And if you will apply your mind, you shall be prudent.

33. If you love to hear, you shall receive understanding: And if you bow your ear, you shall be wise,

34. Stand in the multitude of the elders; and cleave unto him that is wise.

35. Be willing to hear every godly discourse; and do not let the parables of understanding escape you.

36. And if you see a man of understanding, get you betimes unto him, and let your foot wear the steps of his door.

37. Let your mind be upon the ordinances of Yahuah and meditate continually in his commandments: He shall establish your heart, and give you wisdom at your own desire.

Chapter 7

1. Do no evil, so shall no harm come unto you.

2. Depart from the unjust, and iniquity shall turn away from you.

3. My son, do not sow upon the furrows of unrighteousness, and you shall not reap them sevenfold.

4. Do not seek of Yahuah preeminence, neither of the king the seat of honor.

5. Do not justify yourself before Yahuah; and do not boast of your wisdom before the king.

6. Do not seek to be judge, not being able to take away iniquity; lest at any time you fear the person of the mighty, a stumbling block in the way of your uprightness.

7. Do not offend against the multitude of a city, and then you shall not cast yourself down among the people.

8. Do not bind one sin upon another; for in one you shall not be unpunished.

9. Do not say, Êlôhîym will look upon the multitude of my offerings, and when I offer to Êlôhîym Elyôn Êl, he will accept it.

10. Do not be fainthearted when you make your prayer, and do not neglect to give alms.

11. Laugh no man to scorn in the bitterness of his soul: For there is one which humbles and exalts.

12. Do not devise a lie against your brother; neither do the like to your friend.

13. Do not use to make any manner of lie: For the custom thereof is not good.

14. Do not use many words in a multitude of elders, and do not make much babbling when you pray.

15. Do not hate laborious work, neither husbandry, which Elyôn Êl has ordained.

16. Do not number yourself among the multitude of sinners, but remember that wrath will not tarry long.

17. Humble yourself greatly: For the vengeance of the ungodly is fire and worms.

18. Do not change a friend for any good by no means; neither a faithful brother for the gold of Ôphîyr.

19. Do not forgo a wise and good woman: For her grace is above gold.

20. Whereas your servant works truly, do not entreat him evil, nor the hireling that bestows himself wholly for you.

21. Let your soul love a good servant, and do not defraud him of liberty.

22. Do you have cattle? Have an eye to them: And if they are for your profit, keep them with you.

23. Do you have you children? Instruct them, and bow down their neck from their youth.

24. Do you have you daughters? Have a care of their body, and do not show yourself cheerful toward them.

25. Marry your daughter, and so you shall have performed a weighty matter: But give her to a man of understanding.

26. Do you have you a wife after your mind? Do not forsake her: But do not give yourself over to a light woman.

27. Honor your father with your whole heart, and do not forget the sorrows of your mother.

28. Remember that you were begotten of them; and how can you recompense them the things that they have done for you?

29. Fear Yahuah with all your soul, and reverence his Kôhên.

30. Love him that made you with all your strength, and do not forsake his ministers.

31. Fear Yahuah, and honor the Kôhên; and give him his portion, as it is commanded you; the first fruits, and the trespass offering, and the gift of the shoulders, and the sacrifice of sanctification, and the first fruits of the holy things.

32. And stretch your hand unto the poor, that your blessing may be perfected.

33. A gift has grace in the sight of every man living; and for the dead do not detain it.

34. Do not fail to be with them that weep, and mourn with them that mourn.

35. Do not be slow to visit the sick: For that shall make you to be beloved.

36. Whatsoever you take in hand, remember the end, and you shall never do amiss.

Chapter 8

1. Do not strive with a mighty man lest you fall into his hands.

2. Do not be at variance with a rich man, lest he overweigh you: For gold has destroyed many, and perverted the hearts of kings.

3. Do not strive with a man that is full of tongue, and does not heap wood upon his fire.

4. Do not jest with a rude man, lest your ancestors be disgraced.

5. Do not reproach a man that turns from sin, but remember that we are all worthy of punishment.

6. Do not dishonor a man in his old age: For even some of us wax old.

7. Do no to rejoice over your greatest enemy being dead, but remember that we die all.

8. Do not despise the discourse of the wise, but acquaint yourself with their proverbs: For of them you shall learn instruction, and how to serve great men with ease.

9. Do not miss the discourse of the elders: For they also learned of their fathers, and of them you shall learn understanding, and to give answer as need requires.

10. Do not kindle the coals of a sinner, lest you be burnt with the flame of his fire.

11. Do not rise up in anger at the presence of an injurious person, lest he lie in wait to entrap you in your words.

12. Do not lend unto him that is mightier than yourself; for if you lend him, count it but lost.

13. Do not be surety above your power: For if you are surety, take care to pay it.

14. Do not go to law with a judge; for they will judge for him according to his honor.

15. Do not travel by the way with a bold fellow, lest he becomes grievous unto you: For he will do according to his own will, and you shall perish with him through his folly.

16. Do not strive with an angry man, and do not go with him into a solitary place: For blood is as nothing in his sight, and where there is no help, he will overthrow you.

17. Do not consult with a fool; for he cannot keep counsel.

18. Do no secret thing before a stranger; for you do not know what he will bring forth.

19. Do not open your heart to every man, lest he requite you with a shrewd turn.

Chapter 9

1. Do not be jealous over the woman of your bosom, and do not teach her an evil lesson against yourself.

2. Do not give your soul unto a woman to set her foot upon your substance.

3. Do not meet with a harlot, lest you fall into her snares.

4. Do not use much the company of a woman that is a singer, lest you be taken with her attempts.

5. Do not gaze on a maid that you do not fall by those things that are precious in her.

6. Do not give your soul unto harlots, that you do not lose your inheritance.

7. Do not look round about you in the streets of the city, neither wander you in the solitary place thereof.

8. Turn away your eye from a beautiful woman, and do not look upon another's beauty; for many have been deceived by the beauty of a woman; for herewith love is kindled as a fire.

9. Do not sit at all with another man's woman, nor sit down with her in your arms, and do not spend your money with her at the wine; lest your heart incline unto her, and so through your desire you fall into destruction.

10. Do not forsake an old friend; for the new is not comparable to him: A new friend is as new wine; when it is old, you shall drink it with pleasure.

11. Do not envy the glory of a sinner: For you do not know what shall be his end.

12. Do not delight in the thing that the ungodly have pleasure in; but remember

they shall not go unpunished unto their grave.

13. Keep you far from the man that has power to kill; so you shall not doubt the fear of death: And if you come unto him, make no fault, lest he take away your life presently: Remember that you go in the midst of snares, and that you walk upon the battlements of the city.

14. As near as you can, guess at your neighbor, and consult with the wise.

15. Let your talk be with the wise, and all your communication in the law of Elyôn Êl.

16. And let just men eat and drink with you; and let your glorying be in the fear of Yahuah.

17. For the hand of the artificer the work shall be commended: And the wise ruler of the people for his speech.

18. A man of an ill tongue is dangerous in his city; and he that is rash in his talk shall be hated.

Chapter 10

1. A wise judge will instruct his people; and the government of a prudent man is well ordered.

2. As the judge of the people is himself, so are his officers; and what manner of man the ruler of the city is, such are all they that dwell therein.

3. An unwise king destroys his people; but through the prudence of them which are in authority the city shall be inhabited.

4. The power of the earth is in the hand of Yahuah, and in due time he will set over it one that is profitable.

5. In the hand of Êlôhîym is the prosperity of man: And upon the person of the scribe shall he lay his honor.

6. Do not bear hatred to your neighbor for every wrong; and do nothing at all by injurious practices.

7. Pride is hateful before Êlôhîym and man: And by both does one commit iniquity.

8. Because of unrighteous dealings, injuries, and riches got by deceit, the kingdom is translated from one people to another.

9. Why is earth and ashes proud? There is not a more wicked thing than a covetous man: For such an one sets his own soul to sale; because while he lives he casts away his bowels.

10. The physician cuts off a long disease; and he that is today a king tomorrow shall die.

11. For when a man is dead, he shall inherit creeping things, beasts, and worms.

12. The beginning of pride is when one departs from Êlôhîym, and his heart is turned away from his Bârâ.

13. For pride is the beginning of sin, and he that has it shall pour out abomination: And therefore Yahuah brought upon them strange calamities, and overthrew them utterly.

14. Yahuah has cast down the thrones of proud princes, and set up the meek in their stead.

15. Yahuah has plucked up the roots of the proud nations, and planted the lowly in their place.

16. Yahuah overthrew countries of the heathen, and destroyed them to the foundations of the earth.

17. He took some of them away, and destroyed them, and has made their memorial to cease from the earth.

18. Pride was not made for men, nor furious anger for them that are born of a woman.

19. They that fear Yahuah are a sure seed, and they that love him an honorable plant: They that do not regard the law are a dishonorable seed; they that transgress the commandments are a deceivable seed.

20. Among brethren he that is chief is honorable; so are they that fear Yahuah in his eyes.

21. The fear of Yahuah goes before the obtaining of authority: But roughness and pride is the losing thereof.

22. Whether he be rich, noble, or poor, their glory is the fear of Yahuah.

23. It is not meet to despise the poor man that has understanding; neither is it convenient to magnify a sinful man.

24. Great men, and judges, and potentates, shall be honored; yet is there none of them greater than he that fears Yahuah.

25. Unto the servant that is wise shall they that are free do service: And he that has knowledge will not grudge when he is reformed.

26. Do not be over wise in doing your business; and do not boast yourself in the time of your distress.

27. Better is he that labors, and abounds in all things, than he that boasts himself, and wants bread.

28. My son, glorify your soul in meekness, and give it honor according to the dignity thereof.

29. Who will justify him that sins against his own soul? And who will honor him that dishonors his own life?

30. The poor man is honored for his skill, and the rich man is honored for his riches.

31. He that is honored in poverty, how much more in riches? And he that is dishonorable in riches, how much more in poverty?

Chapter 11

1. Wisdom lifts up the head of him that is of low degree, and makes him to sit among great men.

2. Do not commend a man for his beauty; neither abhor a man for his outward appearance.

3. The bee is little among such as fly; but her fruit is the chief of sweet things.

4. Do not boast of your clothing and raiment, and do not exalt yourself in the day of honor: For the works of Yahuah are wonderful, and his works among men are hidden.

5. Many kings have sat down upon the ground; and one that was never thought of has worn the crown.

6. Many mighty men have been greatly disgraced; and the honorable delivered into other men's hands.

7. Do not blame before you have examined the truth: Understand first, and then rebuke.

8. Do not answer before you have heard the cause: Neither interrupt men in the midst of their talk.

9. Do not strive in a matter that do not concern you; and do not sit in judgment with sinners.

10. My son, do not meddle with many matters: For if you meddle much, you shall not be innocent; and if you follow after, you shall not obtain, neither shall you escape by fleeing.

11. There is one that labors, and takes pains, and makes haste, and is so much the more behind.

12. Again, there is another that is slow, and has need of help, wanting ability, and full of poverty; yet the eye of Yahuah looked upon him for good, and set him up from his low estate,

13. And lifted up his head from misery; so that many that saw it marveled at him.

14. Prosperity and adversity, life and death, poverty and riches, come of Yahuah.

15. Wisdom, knowledge, and understanding of the law, are of Yahuah: Love, and the way of good works, are from him.

16. Error and darkness had their beginning together with sinners: And evil shall wax old with them that glory therein.

17. The gift of Yahuah remains with the godly, and his favor brings prosperity for ever.

18. There is that waxes rich by his wariness and pinching, and this is the portion of his reward:

19. Whereas he says, I have found rest, and now will eat continually of my goods; and yet he does not know what time shall come upon him, and that he must leave those things to others, and die.

20. Be steadfast in your covenant, and be conversant therein, and wax old in your work.

21. Do not marvel at the works of sinners; but trust in Yahuah, and abide in your labor: For it is an easy thing in the sight of Yahuah on the sudden to make a poor man rich.

22. The blessing of Yahuah is in the reward of the godly, and suddenly he makes his blessing flourish.

23. Do not say, what profit is there of my service? And what good things shall I have hereafter?

24. Again, do not say, I have enough, and possess many things, and what evil shall I have hereafter?

25. In the day of prosperity there is a forgetfulness of affliction: And in the day of affliction there is no more remembrance of prosperity.

26. For it is an easy thing unto Yahuah in the day of death to reward a man according to his ways.

27. The affliction of an hour makes a man forget pleasure: And in his end his deeds shall be discovered.

28. Judge none blessed before his death: For a man shall be known in his children.

29. Do not bring every man into your house: For the deceitful man has many trains.

30. Like as a partridge taken and kept in a cage, so is the heart of the proud; and like as a spy, he watches for your fall:

31. For he lies in wait, and turns good into evil, and in things worthy praise will lay blame upon you.

32. Of a spark of fire a heap of coals is kindled: And a sinful man lays wait for blood.

33. Take heed of a mischievous man, for he works wickedness; lest he bring upon you a perpetual blot.

34. Receive a stranger into your house, and he will disturb you, and turn you out of your own.

Chapter 12

1. When you will do good know to whom you do it; so you shall be thanked for your benefits.

2. Do good to the godly man, and you shall find a recompense; and if not from him, yet from Elyôn Êl.

3. There can no good come to him that is always occupied in evil, nor to him that gives no alms.

4. Give to the godly man, and do not help a sinner.

5. Do well unto him that is lowly, but do not give to the ungodly: Hold back your bread, and do not give it unto him, lest he overmaster you thereby: For else you shall receive twice as much evil for all the good you shall have done unto him.

6. For Elyôn Êl hates sinners, and will repay vengeance unto the ungodly, and keeps them against the mighty day of their punishment.

7. Give unto the good, and do not help the sinner.

8. A friend cannot be known in prosperity: And an enemy cannot be hidden in adversity.

9. In the prosperity of a man enemies will be grieved: But in his adversity even a friend will depart.

10. Never trust your enemy: For like as iron rusts, so is his wickedness.

11. Though he humble himself, and go crouching, yet take good heed and beware of him, and you shall be unto him as if you had wiped a looking glass, and you shall know that his rust has not been altogether wiped away.

12. Do not set him by you, lest, when he has overthrown you, he stand up in your place; neither let him sit at your right hand, lest he seek to take your seat, and you at the last remember my words, and be pricked therewith.

13. Who will pity a charmer that is bitten with a serpent, or any such as come nigh wild beasts?

14. So one that goes to a sinner, and is defiled with him in his sins, who will pity?.

15. For a while he will abide with you, but if you arraign to fall, he will not tarry.

16. An enemy speaks sweetly with his lips, but in his heart he imagines how to throw you into a pit: He will weep with his eyes, but if he finds opportunity, he will not be satisfied with blood.

17. If adversity come upon you, you shall find him there first; and though he pretend to help you, yet shall he undermine you.

18. He will shake his head, and clap his hands, and whisper much, and change his countenance.

Chapter 13

1. He that touches pitch shall be defiled therewith; and he that has fellowship with a proud man shall be like unto him.

2. Do not burden yourself above your power while you live; and have no fellowship with one that is mightier and richer than yourself: For how agree the kettle and the earthen pot together? For if the one is smitten against the other, it shall be broken.

3. The rich man has done wrong, and yet he threatens withal: The poor is wronged, and he must entreat also.

4. If you are for his profit, he will use you: But if you have nothing, he will forsake you.

5. If you have any thing, he will live with you: Yea, he will make you bare, and will not be sorry for it.

6. If he have need of you, he will deceive you, and smile upon you, and put you in hope; he will speak you fair, and say, what do you want?

7. And he will shame you by his meats, until he have drawn you dry twice or thrice, and at the last he will laugh you to scorn afterward, when he sees you, he will forsake you, and shake his head at you.

8. Beware that you do not be deceived and brought down in your jollity.

9. If you are invited of a mighty man, withdraw yourself, and so much the more will he invite you.

10. Do not press you upon him, lest you be put back; stand not far off, lest you be forgotten.

11. Do not affect to be made equal unto him in talk, and do not believe his many words: For with much communication will he tempt you, and smiling upon you will get out your secrets:

12. But cruelly he will lay up your words, and will not spare to do you hurt, and to put you in prison.

13. Observe, and take good heed, for you walk in peril of your overthrowing: When you hear these things, awake in your sleep.

14. Love Yahuah all your life, and call upon him for your salvation.

15. Every beast loves his like, and every man loves his neighbor.

16. All flesh consorts according to kind, and a man will cleave to his like.

17. What fellowship has the wolf with the lamb? So the sinner with the godly.

18. What agreement is there between the hyena and a dog? And what peace between the rich and the poor?

19. As the wild ass is the lion's prey in the wilderness: So the rich eat up the poor.

20. As the proud hate humility: So does the rich abhor the poor.

21. A rich man beginning to fall is held up of his friends: But a poor man being down is thrust away by his friends.

22. When a rich man is fallen, he has many helpers: He speaks things not to be spoken, and yet men justify him: The poor man slipped, and yet they rebuked him too; he spoke wisely, and could have no place.

23. When a rich man speaks, every man holds his tongue, and, look, what he says, they extol it to the clouds: But if the poor man speak, they say, what fellow is this? And if he stumble, they will help to overthrow him.

24. Riches are good unto him that has no sin, and poverty is evil in the mouth of the ungodly.

25. The heart of a man changes his countenance, whether it is for good or evil: And a merry heart makes a cheerful countenance.

26. A cheerful countenance is a token of a heart that is in prosperity; and the finding out of parables is a wearisome labor of the mind.

Chapter 14

1. Blessed is the man that has not slipped with his mouth, and is not pricked with the multitude of sins.

2. Blessed is he whose conscience has not condemned him, and who is not fallen from his hope in Yahuah.

3. Riches are not comely for a niggard: And what should an envious man do with money?

4. He that gathers by defrauding his own soul gathers for others that shall spend his goods riotously.

5. He that is evil to himself, to whom will he be good? He shall not take pleasure in his goods.

6. There is none worse than he that envies himself; and this is a recompense of his wickedness.

7. And if he does good, he does it unwillingly; and at the last he will declare his wickedness.

8. The envious man has a wicked eye; he turns away his face, and despises men.

9. A covetous man's eye is not satisfied with his portion; and the iniquity of the wicked dries up his soul.

10. A wicked eye envies his bread, and he is a niggard at his table.

11. My son, according to your ability do good to yourself, and give Yahuah his due offering.

12. Remember that death will not be long in coming, and that the covenant of the grave is not showed unto you.

13. Do good unto your friend before you die, and according to your ability stretch out your hand and give to him.

14. Do not defraud yourself of the good day, and do not let the part of a good desire overpass you.

15. You shall not leave your travails unto another? And your labors to be divided by lot?

16. Give, and take, and sanctify your soul; for there is no seeking of delicacies in the grave.

17. All flesh waxes old as a garment: For the covenant from the beginning is, you shall die the death.

18. As of the green leaves on a thick tree, some fall, and some grow; so is the generation of flesh and blood, one comes to an end, and another is born.

19. Every work rots and consumes away, and the worker thereof shall go withal.

20. Blessed is the man that does meditate good things in wisdom, and that reasons of holy things by his understanding.

21. He that considers her ways in his heart shall also have understanding in her secrets.

22. Go after her as one that traces, and lie in wait in her ways.

23. He that pries in at her windows shall also hearken at her doors.

24. He that does lodge near her house shall also fasten a pin in her walls.

25. He shall pitch his tent nigh unto her, and shall lodge in a lodging where good things are.

26. He shall set his children under her shelter, and shall lodge under her branches.

27. By her he shall be covered from heat, and in her glory he shall dwell.

Chapter 15

1. He that fears Yahuah will do good, and he that has the knowledge of the law shall obtain her.

2. And as a mother she shall meet him, and receive him as a woman married of a virgin.

3. With the bread of understanding she shall feed him, and give him the water of wisdom to drink.

4. He shall be stayed upon her, and shall not be moved; and shall rely upon her, and shall not be confounded.

5. She shall exalt him above his neighbors, and in the midst of the congregation she shall open his mouth.

6. He shall find joy and a crown of gladness, and she shall cause him to inherit an everlasting name.

7. But foolish men shall not attain unto her, and sinners shall not see her.

8. For she is far from pride, and men that are liars cannot remember her.

9. Praise is not seemly in the mouth of a sinner, for it was not sent him of Yahuah.

10. For praise shall be uttered in wisdom, and Yahuah will prosper it.

11. Do not say you, it is through Yahuah that I fell away: For you ought not to do the things that he hates.

12. Do not say you, he has caused me to err: For he has no need of the sinful man.

13. Yahuah hates all abomination; and they that fear Êlôhîym do not love it.

14. He himself made man from the beginning, and left him in the hand of his counsel;

15. If you will, to keep the commandments, and to perform acceptable faithfulness.

16. He has set fire and water before you: Stretch forth your hand unto whether you will.

17. Before man is life and death; and whether he likes shall be given him.

18. For the wisdom of Yahuah is great, and he is mighty in power, and beholds all things:

19. And his eyes are upon them that fear him, and he knows every work of man.

20. He has commanded no man to do wickedly, neither he has given no man license to sin.

Chapter 16

1. Do not desire a multitude of unprofitable children, neither delight in ungodly sons.

2. Though they multiply, do not rejoice in them, except the fear of Yahuah be with them.

3. Do not trust you in their life, neither respect their multitude: For one that is just is better than a thousand; and better it is to die without children, than to have them that are ungodly.

4. For by one that has understanding shall the city be replenished: But the kindred of the wicked shall speedily become desolate.

5. Many such things I have seen with my eyes, and my ear he hazard greater things than these.

6. In the congregation of the ungodly shall a fire be kindled; and in a rebellious nation wrath is set on fire.

7. He was not pacified toward the old Nephîyl, who fell away in the strength of their foolishness.

8. Neither he spared the place where Lôt sojourned, but abhorred them for their pride.

9. He did not pity the people of perdition, who were taken away in their sins:

10. Nor the six hundred thousand footmen, who were gathered together in the hardness of their hearts.

11. And if there be one stiff-necked among the people, it is marvel if he escape unpunished: For mercy and wrath are with him; he is mighty to forgive, and to pour out displeasure.

12. As his mercy is great, so is his correction also: He judges a man according to his works

13. The sinner shall not escape with his spoils: And the patience of the godly shall not be frustrate.

14. Make way for every work of mercy: For every man shall find according to his works.

15. Yahuah hardened Parôh, that he should not know him, that his powerful works might be known to the world.

16. His mercy is manifest to every creature; and he has separated his light from the darkness with an adamant.

17. Do not say you, I will hide myself from Yahuah: Shall any remember me from above? I shall not be remembered among so many people: For what is my soul among such an infinite number of creatures?

18. Behold, the shâmayim, and the shâmayim of shâmayim, the deep, and the earth, and all that therein is, shall be moved when he shall visit.

19. The mountains also and foundations of the earth be shaken with trembling, when Yahuah looks upon them.

20. No heart can think upon these things worthily: And who is able to conceive his ways?

21. It is a tempest which no man can see: For the most part of his works are hid.

22. Who can declare the works of his justice? Or who can endure them? For his covenant is afar off, and the trial of all things is in the end.

23. He that wants understanding will think upon vain things: And a foolish man erring imagines follies.

24. My son, hearken unto me, and learn knowledge, and mark my words with your heart.

25. I will show forth doctrine in weight, and declare his knowledge exactly.

26. The works of Yahuah are done in judgment from the beginning: And from the time he made them he disposed the parts thereof.

27. He garnished his works for ever, and in his hand are the chief of them unto all generations: They neither labor, nor are weary, nor cease from their works.

28. None of them hinders another, and they shall never disobey his word.

29. After this Yahuah looked upon the earth, and filled it with his blessings.

30. With all manner of living things he has covered the face thereof; and they shall return into it again.

Chapter 17

1. Yahuah created man of the earth, and turned him into it again.

2. He gave them few days, and a short time, and power also over the things therein.

3. He endued them with strength by themselves, and made them according to his image,

4. And put the fear of man upon all flesh, and gave him dominion over beasts and fowls.

5. They received the use of the five operations of Yahuah, and in the sixth place he imparted them understanding, and in the seventh speech, an interpreter of the cogitations thereof.

6. Counsel, and a tongue, and eyes, ears, and a heart, he gave them to understand.

7. Withal he filled them with the knowledge of understanding, and showed them good and evil.

8. He set his eye upon their hearts, that he might show them the greatness of his works.

9. He gave them to glory in his marvelous acts forever, that they might declare his works with understanding.

10. And the elect shall praise his qâdôsh name.

11. Beside this he gave them knowledge, and the law of life for a heritage.

12. He made an everlasting covenant with them, and showed them his judgments.

13. Their eyes saw the majesty of his glory, and their ears heard his glorious voice.

14. And he said unto them, beware of all unrighteousness; and he gave every man commandment concerning his neighbor.

15. Their ways are ever before him, and shall not be hid from his eyes.

16. Every man from his youth is given to evil; neither could they make to themselves fleshy hearts for stone.

17. For in the division of the nations of the whole earth he set a ruler over every people; but Yâshârêl is Yahuah's portion:

18. Whom, being his firstborn, he nourishes with discipline, and giving him the light of his love does not forsake him.

19. Therefore all their works are as the sun before him, and his eyes are continually upon their ways.

20. None of their unrighteous deeds are hid from him, but all their sins are before Yahuah.

21. But Yahuah being gracious and knowing his workmanship, neither left nor forsook them, but spared them.

22. The alms of a man is as a signet with him, and he will keep the good deeds of man as the apple of the eye, and give repentance to his sons and daughters.

23. Afterwards he will rise up and reward them, and render their recompense upon their heads.

24. But unto them that repent, he granted them return, and comforted those that failed in patience.

25. Return unto Yahuah, and forsake your sins, make your prayer before his face, and offend less.

26. Turn again to Elyôn Êl, and turn away from iniquity: For he will lead you out of darkness into the light of health, and you hate abomination vehemently.

27. Who shall praise Elyôn Êl in the grave, instead of them which live and give thanks?

28. Thanksgiving perishes from the dead, as from one that is not: The living and sound in heart shall praise Yahuah.

29. How great is the loving-kindness of Yahuah our Êlôhîym, and his compassion unto such as turn unto him in qôdesh!

30. For all things cannot be in men, because the Bên Âdâm is not immortal.

31. What is brighter than the sun? Yet the light thereof fails; and flesh and blood will imagine evil.

32. He views the power of the height of shâmayim; and all men are but earth and ashes.

Chapter 18

1 He that lives forever has created all things in general.

2. Yahuah only is righteous, and there is none other but he,

3. Who governs the world with the palm of his hand, and all things obey his will: For he is the Melek of all, by his power dividing holy things among them from profane.

4. To whom he has given power to declare his works? And who shall find out his noble acts?

5. Who shall number the strength of his majesty? And who shall also tell out his mercies?

6. As for the wondrous works of Yahuah, there may nothing be taken from them, neither may anything be put unto them, neither can the ground of them be found out.

7. When a man has done, then he begins; and when he leaves off, then he shall be doubtful.

8. What is man, and whereto serves he? What is his good, and what is his evil?

9. The number of a man's days at the most are a hundred years.

10. As a drop of water unto the sea, and a gravel stone in comparison of the sand; so are a thousand years to the days of eternity.

11. Therefore is Êlôhîym patient with them, and pours forth his mercy upon them.

12. He saw and perceived their end to be evil; therefore he multiplied his compassion.

13. The mercy of man is toward his neighbor; but the mercy of Yahuah is upon all flesh: He reproves, and nurtures, and teaches and brings again, as a shepherd his flock.

14. He has mercy on them that receive discipline, and that diligently seek after his judgments.

15. My son, do not blemish your good deeds, neither use uncomfortable words when you give anything.

16. Shall not the dew assuage the heat? So is a word better than a gift.

17. Lo, is not a word better than a gift? But both are with a gracious man.

18. A fool will upbraid churlishly, and a gift of the envious consumes the eyes.

19. Learn before you speak, and user remedies or ever you be sick.

20. Before judgment examine yourself, and in the day of visitation you shall find mercy.

21. Humble yourself before you be sick, and in the time of sins show repentance.

22. Let anything hinder you to pay your vow in due time, and do not defer until death to be justified.

23. Before you pray, prepare yourself; and do not be as one that tempts Yahuah.

24. Think upon the wrath that shall be at the end, and the time of vengeance, when he shall turn away his face.

25. When you have enough, remember the time of hunger: And when you are rich, think upon poverty and need.

26. From the morning until the evening the time is changed, and all things are soon done before Yahuah.

27. A wise man will fear in everything, and in the day of sinning he will beware of offence: But a fool will not observe time.

28. Every man of understanding knows wisdom, and will give praise unto him that found her.

29. They that were of understanding in sayings became also wise themselves, and poured forth exquisite parables.

30. Do not go after your lusts, but refrain yourself from your appetites.

31. If you give your soul the desires that please her, she will make you a laughing-stock to your enemies that malign you.

32. Do not take pleasure in much good cheer, neither be tied to the expense thereof.

33. Do not be made a beggar by banqueting upon borrowing, when you nothing in your purse: For you shall lie in wait for your own life, and be talked on.

Chapter 19

1. A laboring man that is given to drunkenness shall not be rich: And he that contemns small things shall fall by little and little.

2. Wine and women will make men of understanding to fall away: And he that cleaves to harlots will become impudent.

3. Moths and worms shall have him to heritage, and a bold man shall be taken away.

4. He that is hasty to give credit is light-minded; and he that sins shall offend against his own soul.

5. Whoso takes pleasure in wickedness shall be condemned: But he that resists pleasures crowns his life.

6. He that can rule his tongue shall live without strife; and he that hates babbling shall have less evil.

7. Do not rehearse unto another that which is told unto you, and you shall fare never the worse.

8. Whether it be to friend or foe, do not talk of other men's lives; and if you can without offence, do not reveal them.

9. For he heard and observed you, and when time comes he will hate you.

10. If you have heard a word, let it die with you; and be bold, it will not burst you.

11. A fool travails with a word, as a woman in labor of a child.

12. As an arrow that sticks in a man's thigh, so is a word within a fool's belly.

13. Admonish a friend, it may be he has not done it: And if he have done it, that he does it no more.

14. Admonish your friend, it may be he has not said it: And if he has, that he does not speak it again.

15. Admonish a friend: For many times it is a slander, and do not believe every tale.

16. There is one that slips in his speech, but not from his heart; and who is he that has not offended with his tongue?

17. Admonish your neighbor before you threaten him; and not being angry, give place to the law of Elyôn Êl.

18. The fear of Yahuah is the first step to be accepted of him, and wisdom obtains his love.

19. The knowledge of the commandments of Yahuah is the doctrine of life: And they that do things that please him shall receive the fruit of the tree of immortality.

20. The fear of Yahuah is all wisdom; and in all wisdom is the performance of the law, and the knowledge of his omnipotence.

21. If a servant say to his master, I will not do as it pleases you; though afterward he does it, he angers him that nourishes him.

22. The knowledge of wickedness is not wisdom, neither at any time the counsel of sinners prudence.

23. There is a wickedness, and the same an abomination; and there is a fool wanting in wisdom.

24. He that has small understanding, and fears Êlôhîym, is better than one that has much wisdom, and transgresses the law of Elyôn Êl.

25. There is an exquisite subtlety, and the same is unjust; and there is one that turns aside to make judgment appear; and there is a wise man that justifies in judgment.

26. There is a wicked man that hangs down his head sadly; but inwardly he is full of deceit,

27. Casting down his countenance, and making as if he did not heard: Where he is not known, he will do you a mischief before you be aware.

28. And if for want of power he be hindered from sinning, yet when he finds opportunity he will do evil.

29. A man may be known by his look, and one that has understanding by his countenance, when you meet him.

30. A man's attire, and excessive laughter, and gait, show what he is.

Chapter 20

1. There is a reproof that is not comely: again, some man holds his tongue, and he is wise.

2. It is much better to reprove, than to be angry secretly: And he that confesses his fault shall be preserved from hurt.

3. How good is it, when you are reproved, to show repentance! For so you shall escape willful sin.

4. As is the lust of an eunuch to deflower a virgin; so is he that executes judgment with violence.

5. There is one that keeps silence, and is found wise: And another by much babbling becomes hateful.

6. Some man holds his tongue, because he has not to answer: And some keeps silence, knowing his time.

7. A wise man will hold his tongue till he sees opportunity: But a babbler and a fool will regard no time.

8. He that uses many words shall be abhorred; and he that takes to himself authority therein shall be hated.

9. There is a sinner that has good success in evil things; and there is a gain that turns to loss.

10. There is a gift that shall not profit you; and there is a gift whose recompense is double.

11. There is an abasement because of glory; and there is that lifts up his head from a low estate.

12. There is that buys much for a little, and repays it sevenfold.

13. A wise man by his words makes him beloved: But the graces of fools shall be poured out.

14. The gift of a fool shall do you no good when you I have it; neither yet of the envious for his necessity: For he looks to receive many things for one.

15. He gives little, and upbraids much; he opens his mouth like a crier; today he lends, and tomorrow he will ask it again: Such an one is to be hated of Êlôhîym and man.

16. The fool says, I have no friends, I have no thank for all my good deeds, and they that eat my bread speak evil of me.

17. How oft, and of how many shall he be laughed to scorn? For he does not know right what it is to have; and it is all one unto him as if he had it not.

18. To slip upon a pavement is better than to slip with the tongue: So the fall of the wicked shall come speedily.

19. An unseasonable tale will always be in the mouth of the unwise.

20. A wise sentence shall be rejected when it comes out of a fool's mouth; for he will not speak it in due season.

21. There is that is hindered from sinning through want: And when he takes rest, he shall not be troubled.

22. There is that destroys his own soul through bashfulness, and by accepting of persons overthrows himself.

23. There is that for bashfulness promises to his friend, and makes him his enemy for nothing.

24. A lie is a foul blot in a man, yet it is continually in the mouth of the untaught.

25. A thief is better than a man that is accustomed to lie: But they both shall have destruction to heritage.

26. The disposition of a liar is dishonorable, and his shame is ever with him.

27. A wise man shall promote himself to honor with his words: And he that has understanding will please great men.

28. He that tills his land shall increase his heap: And he that pleases great men shall get pardon for iniquity.

29. Presents and gifts blind the eyes of the wise, and stop up his mouth that he cannot reprove.

30. Wisdom that is hid, and treasure that is hoarded up, what profit is in them both?

31. Better is he that hides his folly than a man that hides his wisdom.

32. Necessary patience in seeking Yahuah is better than he that leads his life without a guide.

Chapter 21

1. My son, have you sinned? Do so no more, but ask pardon for your former sins.

2. Flee from sin as from the face of a serpent: For if you come too near it, it will bite you: The teeth thereof are as the teeth of a lion, slaying the souls of men.

3. All iniquity is as a two edged sword, the wounds whereof cannot be healed.

4. To terrify and do wrong will waste riches: Thus the house of proud men shall be made desolate.

5. A prayer out of a poor man's mouth reaches to the ears of Êlôhîym, and his judgment comes speedily.

6. He that hates to be reproved is in the way of sinners: But he that fears Yahuah will repent from his heart.

7. An eloquent man is known far and near; but a man of understanding knows when he slips.

8. He that builds his house with other men's money is like one that gathers himself stones for the tomb of his burial.

9. The congregation of the wicked is like tow wrapped together: And the end of them is a flame of fire to destroy them.

10. The way of sinners is made plain with stones, but at the end thereof is the pit of sheôl.

11. He that keeps the law of Yahuah gets the understanding thereof: And the perfection of the fear of Yahuah is wisdom.

12. He that is not wise will not be taught: But there is a wisdom which multiplies bitterness.

13. The knowledge of a wise man shall abound like a flood: And his counsel is like a pure fountain of life.

14. The inner parts of a fool are like a broken vessel, and he will hold no knowledge as long as he lives.

15. If a skilful man hear a wise word, he will commend it, and add unto it: But as soon as one of no understanding hears it, it displeases him, and he casts it behind his back.

16. The talking of a fool is like a burden in the way: But grace shall be found in the lips of the wise.

17. They enquire at the mouth of the wise man in the congregation, and they shall ponder his words in their heart.

18. As is a house that is destroyed, so is wisdom to a fool: And the knowledge of the unwise is as talk without sense.

19. Doctrine unto fools is as fetters on the feet, and like manacles on the right hand.

20. A fool lifts up his voice with laughter; but a wise man does scarce smile a little.

21. Learning is unto a wise man as an ornament of gold, and like a bracelet upon his right arm.

22. A foolish man's foot is soon in his neighbor's house: But a man of experience is ashamed of him.

23. A fool will peep in at the door into the house: But he that is well nurtured will stand without.

24. It is the rudeness of a man to hearken at the door: But a wise man will be grieved with the disgrace.

25. The lips of talkers will be telling such things as do not pertain unto them: But the words of such as have understanding are weighed in the balance.

26. The heart of fools is in their mouth: But the mouth of the wise is in their heart.

27. When the ungodly curses the adversary, he curses his own soul.

28. A whisperer defiles his own soul, and is hated wherever he dwells.

Chapter 22

1. A slothful man is compared to a filthy stone, and everyone will hiss him out to his disgrace.

2. A slothful man is compared to the filth of a dunghill: Every man that takes it up will shake his hand.

3. An evil nurtured man is the dishonor of his father that begat him: And a foolish daughter is born to his loss.

4. A wise daughter shall be the heir of her husband: But she that lives dishonestly is her father's heaviness.

5. She that is bold dishonors both her father and her husband, but they both shall despise her.

6. A tale out of season is as music in mourning: But stripes and correction of wisdom are never out of time.

7. Whoso teaches a fool is as one that glues a potsherd together, and as he that wakes one from a sound sleep.

8. He that tells a tale to a fool speaks to one in a slumber: When he has told his tale, he will say, what is the matter?

9. If children live honestly, and have wherewithal, they shall cover the baseness of their parents.

10. But children, being haughty, through disdain and want of nurture do stain the nobility of their kindred.

11. Weep for the dead, for he has lost the light: And weep for the fool, for he wants understanding: Make little weeping for the dead, for he is at rest: But the life of the fool is worse than death.

12. Seven days do men mourn for him that is dead; but for a fool and an ungodly man all the days of his life.

13. Do not talk much with a fool, and do not go to him that has no understanding: Beware of him, lest you have trouble, and you shall never be defiled with his fooleries: Depart from him, and you shall find rest, and never be disquieted with madness.

14. What is heavier than lead? And what is the name thereof, but a fool?

15. Sand, and salt, and a mass of iron, is easier to bear, than a man without understanding.

16. As timber girt and bound together in a building cannot be loosed with shaking: So the heart that is established by advised counsel shall fear at no time.

17. A heart settled upon a thought of understanding is as a fair plastering on the wall of a gallery.

18. Pales set on a high place will never stand against the wind: So a fearful heart in the imagination of a fool cannot stand against any fear.

19. He that pricks the eye will make tears to fall: And he that pricks the heart makes it to show her knowledge.

20. Whoso casts a stone at the birds frays them away: And he that upbraids his friend breaks friendship.

21. Though you drew a sword at your friend, yet do not despair: For there may be a returning to favor.

22. If you have opened your mouth against your friend, do not fear; for there may be a reconciliation: Except for upbraiding, or pride, or disclosing of secrets, or a treacherous wound: For these things every friend will depart.

23. Be faithful to your neighbor in his poverty, that you may rejoice in his prosperity: Abide steadfast unto him in the time of his trouble, that you may be heir with him in his heritage: For a mean estate is not always to be contemned: Nor the rich that is foolish to be had in admiration.

24. As the vapor and smoke of a furnace goes before the fire; so reviling before blood.

25. I will not be ashamed to defend a friend; neither will I hide myself from him.

26. And if any evil happen unto me by him, every one that hears it will beware of him.

27. Who shall set a watch before my mouth, and a seal of wisdom upon my lips, that I do not fall suddenly by them, and that my tongue do not destroy me?

Chapter 23

1. Yahuah, father and governor of all my whole life, do not leave me to their counsels, and do not let me fall by them.

2. Who will set scourges over my thoughts, and the discipline of wisdom over my heart? That they do not spare me for my ignorance, and it does not pass by my sins:

3. Lest my ignorance increase, and my sins abound to my destruction, and I fall before my adversaries, and my enemy rejoice over me, whose hope is far from your mercy.

4. O Yahuah, father and Êlôhîym of my life, do not give me a proud look, but turn away from your servants always a haughty mind.

5. Turn away from me vain hopes and concupiscence, and you shall hold him up that is desirous always to serve you.

6. Do not let the greediness of the belly nor lust of the flesh take hold of me; and do not give over me your servant into an impudent mind.

7. Hear, O you children, the discipline of the mouth: He that keeps it shall never be taken in his lips.

8. The sinner shall be left in his foolishness: Both the evil speaker and the proud shall fall thereby.

9. Do not accustom your mouth to swearing; neither use yourself to the naming of the Qâdôsh Êl.

10. For as a servant that is continually beaten shall not be without a blue mark: So he that swears and names Êlôhîym continually shall not be faultless.

11. A man that uses much swearing shall be filled with iniquity, and the plague shall never depart from his house: If he shall offend, his sin shall be upon him: And if he does not acknowledge his sin, he makes a double offence: And if he swears in vain, he shall not be innocent, but his house shall be full of calamities.

12. There is a word that is clothed about with death: Êlôhîym grant that it does not be found in the heritage of Yaăqôb; for all such things shall be far from the godly, and they shall not wallow in their sins.

13. Do not use your mouth to intemperate swearing, for therein is the word of sin.

14. Remember your father and your mother, when you sit among great men. Do not be forgetful before them, and so you by your custom become a fool, and wish that you had not been born, and curse the day of your nativity.

15. The man that is accustomed to opprobrious words will never be reformed all the days of his life.

16. Two sorts of men multiply sin, and the third will bring wrath: A hot mind is as a burning fire, it will never be quenched till it is consumed: A fornicator in the body of his flesh will never cease till he has kindled a fire.

17. All bread is sweet to a whoremonger, he will not leave off till he die.

18. A man that breaks wedlock, saying thus in his heart, who sees me? I am compassed about with darkness, the walls cover me, and nobody sees me; what do I need to fear? Elyôn Êl will not remember my sins:

19. Such a man only fears the eyes of men, and does not know that the eyes of Yahuah are ten thousand times brighter than the sun, beholding all the ways of men, and considering the most secret parts.

20. He knew all things were ever they were created; so also after they were perfected he looked upon them all.

21. This man shall be punished in the streets of the city, and where he does not suspect he shall be taken.

22. Thus shall it go also with the woman that leaves her husband, and brings in an heir by another.

23. For first, she has disobeyed the law of Elyôn Êl; and secondly, she has trespassed against her own husband; and thirdly, she has played the whore in adultery, and brought children by another man.

24. She shall be brought out into the congregation, and inquisition shall be made of her children.

25. Her children shall not take root, and her branches shall bring forth no fruit.

26. She shall leave her memory to be cursed, and her reproach shall not be blotted out.

27. And they that remain shall know that there is nothing better than the fear of Yahuah, and that there is nothing sweeter than to take heed unto the commandments of Yahuah.

28. It is great glory to follow Yahuah, and to be received of him is long life.

Chapter 24

1. Wisdom shall praise herself, and shall glory in the midst of her people.

2. In the congregation of Elyôn Êl she shall open her mouth, and triumph before his power.

3. I came out of the mouth of Elyôn Êl, and covered the earth as a cloud.

4. I dwelt in high places, and my throne is in a cloudy pillar.

5. I alone compassed the circuit of shâmayim, and walked in the bottom of the deep.

6. In the waves of the sea and in all the earth, and in every people and nation, I got a possession.

7. With all these I sought rest: And in whose inheritance shall I abide?

8. So the Bârâ of all things gave me a commandment, and he that made me caused my tabernacle to rest, and said: Let your dwelling be in Yaăqôb, and your inheritance in Yâshârêl.

9. He created me from the beginning before the world, and I shall never fail.

10. In the holy tabernacle I served before him; and so was I established in Tsîyôn.

11. Likewise in the beloved city he gave me rest, and in Yarûshâlaim was my power.

12. And I took root in an honorable people, even in the portion of Yahuah's inheritance.

13. I was exalted like a cedar in Lebânôn, and as a cypress tree upon the mountains of Chermôn.

14. I was exalted like a palm tree in Êyn gedîy, and as a rose plant in Yerîychô, as a fair olive tree in a pleasant field, and grew up as a plane tree by the water.

15. I gave a sweet smell like cinnamon and aspalathus, and I yielded a pleasant odor like the best myrrh, as galbanum, and onyx, and sweet storax, and as the fume of lebônâh in the tabernacle.

16. As the turpentine tree I stretched out my branches, and my branches are the branches of honor and grace.

17. As the vine I brought forth pleasant savor, and my flowers are the fruit of honor and riches.

18. I am the mother of fair love, and fear, and knowledge, and holy hope: I therefore, being eternal, am given to all my children which are named of him.

19. Come unto me, all you that be desirous of me, and fill yourselves with my fruits.

20. For my memorial is sweeter than honey, and my inheritance than the honeycomb.

21. They that eat me shall yet be hungry, and they that drink me shall yet be thirsty.

22. He that obeys me shall never be confounded, and they that work by me shall not do amiss.

23. All these things are the book of the covenant of Êlôhîym Elyôn Êl, even the law which Môsheh commanded for a heritage unto the congregations of Yaăqôb.

24. Do not faint to be strong in Yahuah; that he may confirm you, cleave unto him: For Yahuah Shadday Êl is Êlôhîym alone, and beside him there is no other Yâsha (יֵשַׁע).

25. He fills all things with his wisdom, as Pîyshôn (פִּישׁוֹן) and as Chiddeqel in the time of the new fruits.

26. He makes the understanding to abound like Perâth (פְּרָת), and as Yardên (יַרְדֵּן) in the time of the harvest.

27. He makes the doctrine of knowledge appear as the light, and as Gîychôn (גִּיחוֹן) in the time of vintage.

28. The first man did not know her perfectly: No more shall the last find her out.

29. For her thoughts are more than the sea, and her counsels profounder than the great deep.

30. I also came out as a brook from a river, and as a conduit into a Garden.

31. I said, I will water my best Garden, and will water abundantly my Garden bed: And, lo, my brook became a river, and my river became a sea.

32. I will yet make doctrine to shine as the morning, and will send forth her light afar off.

33. I will yet pour out doctrine as prophecy, and leave it to all ages forever.

34. Behold that I have not labored for myself only, but for all them that seek wisdom.

Chapter 25

1. In three things I was beautified, and stood up beautiful both before Êlôhîym and men: The unity of brethren, the love of neighbors, a man and a woman that agree together.

2. Three sorts of men my soul hates, and I am greatly offended at their life: A poor man that is proud, a rich man that is a liar, and an old adulterer that dotes.

3. If you have gathered nothing in your youth, how can you find anything in your age?

4. O how comely a thing is judgment for gray hairs, and for ancient men to know counsel!

5. O how comely is the wisdom of old men, and understanding and counsel to men of honor.

6. Much experience is the crown of old men, and the fear of Êlôhîym is their glory.

7. There be nine things which I have judged in my heart to be happy, and the tenth I will utter with my tongue: A man that has joy of his children; and he that lives to see the fall of his enemy:

8. Well is him that dwells with a woman of understanding, and that has not slipped with his tongue, and that has not served a man more unworthy than himself:

9. Well is him that has found prudence, and he that speaks in the ears of them that will hear:

10. O how great is he that finds wisdom! Yet is there none above him that fears Yahuah.

11. But the love of Yahuah passes all things for illumination: He that holds it, whereto shall he be likened?

12. The fear of Yahuah is the beginning of his love: And faith is the beginning of cleaving unto him.

13. Give me any plague, but the plague of the heart: And any wickedness, but the wickedness of a woman:

14. And any affliction, but the affliction from them that hate me: And any revenge, but the revenge of enemies.

15. There is no head above the head of a serpent; and there is no wrath above the wrath of an enemy.

16. I had rather dwell with a lion and a dragon, than to keep house with a wicked woman.

17. The wickedness of a woman changes her face, and darkens her countenance like sackcloth.

18. Her husband shall sit among his neighbors; and when he hears it shall sigh bitterly.

19. All wickedness is but little to the wickedness of a woman: Let the portion of a sinner fall upon her.

20. As the climbing up a sandy way is to the feet of the aged, so is a woman full of words to a quiet man.

21. Do not stumble at the beauty of a woman, and do not desire her for pleasure.

22. A woman, if she maintain her husband, is full of anger, impudence, and much reproach.

23. A wicked woman abates the courage, makes a heavy countenance and a wounded heart: A woman that will not comfort her husband in distress makes weak hands and feeble knees.

24. Of the woman came the beginning of sin, and through her we all die.

25. Give the water no passage; neither a wicked woman liberty to gad abroad.

26. If she does not go as you would have her, cut her off from your flesh, and give her a bill of divorce, and let her go.

Chapter 26

1. Blessed is the man that has a virtuous woman, for the number of his days shall be double.

2. A virtuous woman rejoices her husband, and he shall fulfil the years of his life in peace.

3. A good woman is a good portion, which shall be given in the portion of them that fear Yahuah.

4. Whether a man be rich or poor, if he has a good heart toward Yahuah, he shall at all times rejoice with a cheerful countenance.

5. There are three things that my heart fears; and for the fourth I was sore afraid: The slander of a city, the gathering together of an unruly multitude, and a false accusation: All these are worse than death.

6. But a grief of heart and sorrow is a woman that is jealous over another woman, and a scourge of the tongue which communicates with all.

7. An evil wife is a yoke shaken to and fro: He that has hold of her is as though he held a scorpion.

8. A drunken woman and a gadder abroad causes great anger, and she will not cover her own shame.

9. The whoredom of a woman may be known in her haughty looks and eyelids.

10. If your daughter is shameless, keep her in strictly, lest she abuses herself through overmuch liberty.

11. Watch over an impudent eye: And do not marvel if she trespass against you.

12. She will open her mouth, as a thirsty traveler when he has found a fountain, and drink of every water near her: By every hedge she will sit down, and open her quiver against every arrow.

13. The grace of a woman delights her husband, and her discretion will fatten his bones.

14. A silent and loving woman is a gift of Yahuah; and there is nothing so much worth as a mind well instructed.

15. A shamefaced and faithful woman is a double grace, and her continent mind cannot be valued.

16. As the sun when it arises in the high shâmayim; so is the beauty of a good wife in the ordering of her house.

17. As the clear light is upon the holy candlestick; so is the beauty of the face in ripe age.

18. As the golden pillars are upon the sockets of silver; so are the fair feet with a constant heart.

19. My son, keep the flower of your age sound; and do not give your strength to strangers.

20. When you have gotten a fruitful possession through all the field, sow it with your own seed, trusting in the goodness of your stock.

21. So your race which you leave shall be magnified, having the confidence of their good descent.

22. A harlot shall be accounted as spittle; but a married woman is a tower against death to her husband.

23. A wicked woman is given as a portion to a wicked man: But a godly woman is given to him that fears Yahuah.

24. A dishonest woman contemns shame: But an honest woman will reverence her husband.

25. A shameless woman shall be counted as a dog; but she that is shamefaced will fear Yahuah.

26. A woman that honors her husband shall be judged wise of all; but she that dishonors him in her pride shall be counted ungodly of all.

27. A loud crying woman and a scold shall be sought out to drive away the enemies.

28. There are two things that grieve my heart; and the third makes me angry: A man of war that suffers poverty; and men of understanding that are not set by; and one that returns from righteousness to sin; Yahuah prepares such an one for the sword.

29. A merchant shall hardly keep himself from doing wrong; and a huckster shall not be freed from sin.

Chapter 27

1. Many have sinned for a small matter; and he that seeks for abundance will turn his eyes away.

2. As a nail sticks fast between the joining of the stones; so does sin stick close between buying and selling.

3. Unless a man hold himself diligently in the fear of Yahuah, his house shall soon be overthrown.

4. As when one sifts with a sieve, the refuse remains; so the filth of man in his talk.

5. The furnace proves the potter's vessels; so the trial of man is in his reasoning.

6. The fruit declares if the tree have been dressed; so is the utterance of a conceit in the heart of man.

7. Praise no man before you hear him speak; for this is the trial of men.

8. If you follow righteousness, you shall obtain her, and put her on, as a glorious long robe.

9. The birds will resort unto their like; so will truth return unto them that practice in her.

10. As the lion lies in wait for the prey; so sin for them that work iniquity.

11. The discourse of a godly man is always with wisdom; but a fool changes as the moon.

12. If you are among the indiscreet, observe the time; but be continually among men of understanding.

13. The discourse of fools is irksome, and their sport is the wantonness of sin.

14. The talk of him that swears much makes the hair stand upright; and their brawls make one stop his ears.

15. The strife of the proud is blood shedding, and their reviling are grievous to the ear.

16. Whoso discovers secrets loses his credit; and shall never find friend to his mind.

17. Love your friend, and be faithful unto him: But if you betray his secrets, follow no more after him.

18. For as a man has destroyed his enemy; so have you lost the love of your neighbor.

19. As one that lets a bird go out of his hand, so have you let your neighbor go, and shall not get him again.

20. Follow after him no more, for he is too far off; he is as a roe escaped out of the snare.

21. As for a wound, it may be bound up; and after reviling there may be reconcilement: But he that betrays secrets is without hope.

22. He that winks with the eyes works evil: And he that knows him will depart from him.

23. When you are present, he will speak sweetly, and will admire your words: But at the last he will twist his mouth, and slander your sayings.

24. I have hated many things, but nothing like him; for Yahuah will hate him.

25. Whoso casts a stone on high casts it on his own head; and a deceitful stroke shall make wounds.

26. Whoso digs a pit shall fall therein: And he that sets a trap shall be taken therein.

27. He that works mischief, it shall fall upon him, and he shall not know whence it comes.

28. Mockery and reproach are from the proud; but vengeance, as a lion, shall lie in wait for them.

29. They that rejoice at the fall of the righteous shall be taken in the snare; and anguish shall consume them before they die.

30. Malice and wrath, even these are abominations; and the sinful man shall have them both.

Chapter 28

1. The vengeful shall find vengeance from Yahuah, and he will surely keep his sins in remembrance.

2. Forgive your neighbor the hurt that he has done unto you, so shall your sins also be forgiven when you pray.

3. One man bears hatred against another, and does he seek pardon from Yahuah?

4. He shows no mercy to a man, which is like himself: And does he ask forgiveness of his own sins?

5. If he that is but flesh nourish hatred, who will entreat for pardon of his sins?

6. Remember your end, and let enmity cease; remember corruption and death, and abide in the commandments.

7. Remember the commandments, and bear no malice to your neighbor: Remember the covenant of Elyôn Êl, and wink at ignorance.

8. Abstain from strife, and you shall diminish your sins: For a furious man will kindle strife,

9. A sinful man disquiets friends, and makes debate among them that are at peace.

10. As the matter of the fire is, so it burns: And as a man's strength is, so is his wrath; and according to his riches his anger rises; and the stronger they are which contend, the more they will be inflamed.

11. A hasty contention kindles a fire: And a hasty fighting sheds blood.

12. If you blow the spark, it shall burn: If you spit upon it, it shall be quenched: And both these come out of your mouth.

13. Curse the whisperer and double tongued: For such have destroyed many that were at peace.

14. A backbiting tongue has disquieted many, and driven them from nation to nation: Strong cities have it pulled down, and overthrown the houses of great men.

15. A backbiting tongue has cast out virtuous women, and deprived them of their labors.

16. Whoso hearkens unto it shall never find rest, and never dwell quietly.

17. The stroke of the whip makes marks in the flesh: But the stroke of the tongue breaks the bones.

18. Many have fallen by the edge of the sword: But not so many as have fallen by the tongue.

19. Well is he that is defended through the venom thereof; who has not drawn the yoke thereof, nor has been bound in her bands.

20. For the yoke thereof is a yoke of iron, and the bands thereof are bands of brass.

21. The death thereof is an evil death, the grave were better than it.

22. It shall not have rule over them that fear Êlôhîym, neither shall they be burned with the flame thereof.

23. Such as forsake Yahuah shall fall into it; and it shall burn in them, and not be quenched; it shall be sent upon them as a lion, and devour them as a leopard.

24. Look that you hedge your possession about with thorns, and bind up your silver and gold,

25. And weigh your words in a balance, and make a door and bar for your mouth.

26. Beware you do not slide by it, lest you fall before him that lies in wait.

Chapter 29

1. He that is merciful will lend unto his neighbor; and he that strengthens his hand keeps the commandments.

2. Lend to your neighbor in time of his need, and pay you your neighbor again in due season.

3. Keep your word, and deal faithfully with him, and you shall always find the thing that is necessary for you.

4. Many, when a thing was lent them, reckoned it to be found, and put them to trouble that helped them.

5. Till he has received, he will kiss a man's hand; and for his neighbor's money he will speak submissively: But when he should repay, he will prolong the time, and return words of grief, and complain of the time.

6. If he prevail, he shall hardly receive the half, and he will count as if he had found it: If not, he has deprived him of his money, and he has gotten him an enemy without cause: He pays him with cursing and railings; and for honor he will pay him disgrace.

7. Many therefore have refused to lend for other men's ill dealing, fearing to be defrauded.

8. Yet have you patience with a man in poor estate, and do not delay to show him mercy.

9. Help the poor for the commandment's sake, and do not turn him away because of his poverty.

10. Lose your money for your brother and your friend, and do not let it rust under a stone to be lost.

11. Lay up your treasure according to the commandments of Elyôn Êl, and it shall bring you more profit than gold.

12. Shut up alms in your storehouses: And it shall deliver you from all affliction.

13. It shall fight for you against your enemies better than a mighty shield and strong spear.

14. An honest man is surety for his neighbor: But he that is impudent will forsake him.

15. Do not forget the friendship of your surety, for he has given his life for you.

16. A sinner will overthrow the good estate of his surety:

17. And he that is of an unthankful mind will leave him in danger that delivered him.

18. Suretiship has undone many of good estate, and shaken them as a wave of the sea: Mighty men have it driven from their houses, so that they wandered among strange nations.

19. A wicked man transgressing the commandments of Yahuah shall fall into suretiship: And he that undertakes and follows other men's business for gain shall fall into suits.

20. Help your neighbor according to your power, and beware that you yourself do not fall into the same.

21. The chief thing for life is water, and bread, and clothing, and a house to cover shame.

22. Better is the life of a poor man in a mean cottage, than delicate fare in another man's house.

23. Be it little or much, hold you contented, that you do not hear the reproach of your house.

24. For it is a miserable life to go from house to house: For where you are a stranger, you do not dare open your mouth.

25. You shall entertain, and feast, and have no thanks: Moreover you shall hear bitter words:

26. Come, you stranger, and furnish a table, and feed me of that you have ready.

27. Give place, you stranger, to an honorable man; my brother comes to be lodged, and I have need of my house.

28. These things are grievous to a man of understanding; the upbraiding of houseroom, and reproaching of the lender.

Chapter 30

1. He that loves his son causes him oft to feel the rod, that he may have joy of him in the end.

2. He that chastises his son shall have joy in him, and shall rejoice of him among his acquaintance.

3. He that teaches his son grieves the enemy: And before his friends he shall rejoice of him.

4. Though his father die, yet he is as though he was not dead: For he has left one behind him that is like himself.

5. While he lived, he saw and rejoiced in him: And when he died, he was not sorrowful.

6. He left behind him an avenger against his enemies, and one that shall requite kindness to his friends.

7. He that makes too much of his son shall bind up his wounds; and his bowels will be troubled at every cry.

8. A horse not broken becomes headstrong: And a child left to himself will be wilful.

9. Coddle your child, and he shall make you afraid: Play with him, and he will bring you to heaviness.

10. Do not laugh with him, lest you have sorrow with him, and lest you gnash your teeth in the end.

11. Give him no liberty in his youth, and do not wink at his follies.

12. Bow down his neck while he is young, and beat him on the sides while he is a child, lest he wax stubborn, and be disobedient unto you, and so bring sorrow to your heart.

13. Chastise your son, and hold him to labor, lest his lewd behavior be an offence unto you.

14. Better is the poor, being sound and strong of constitution, than a rich man that is afflicted in his body.

15. Health and good estate of body are above all gold, and a strong body above infinite wealth.

16. There is no riches above a sound body, and no joy above the joy of the heart.

17. Death is better than a bitter life or continual sickness.

18. Delicates poured upon a mouth shut up are as messes of meat set upon a grave.

19. What good does the offering unto an idol? For neither can it eat nor smell: So is he that is persecuted of Yahuah.

20. He sees with his eyes and groans, as an eunuch that embraces a virgin and sighs.

21. Do not give over your mind to heaviness, and do not afflict yourself in your own counsel.

22. The gladness of the heart is the life of man, and the joyfulness of a man prolongs his days.

23. Love your own soul, and comfort your heart, remove sorrow far from you: For sorrow has killed many, and there is no profit therein.

24. Envy and wrath shorten the life, and carefulness brings age before the time.

25. A cheerful and good heart will have a care of his meat and diet.

Chapter 31

1. Watching for riches consumes the flesh, and the care thereof drives away sleep.

2. Watching care will not let a man slumber, as a sore disease breaks sleep,

3. The rich has great labor in gathering riches together; and when he rests, he is filled with his delicates.

4. The poor labors in his poor estate; and when he leaves off, he is still needy.

5. He that loves gold shall not be justified, and he that follows corruption shall have enough thereof.

6. Gold has been the ruin of many, and their destruction was present.

7. It is a stumbling block unto them that sacrifice unto it, and every fool shall be taken therewith.

8. Blessed is the rich that is found without blemish, and has not gone after gold.

9. Who is he? And we will call him blessed: For wonderful things he has done among his people.

10. Who has been tried thereby, and found perfect? Then let him glory. Who might offend, and has not offended? Or done evil, and has not done it?

11. His goods shall be established, and the congregation shall declare his alms.

12. If you sit at a bountiful table, do not be greedy upon it, and do not say, there is much meat on it.

13. Remember that a wicked eye is an evil thing: And what is created more wicked than an eye? Therefore it weeps upon every occasion.

14. Do not stretch your hand whithersoever it looks, and do not thrust it with him into the dish.

15. Do not judge your neighbor by yourself: And be discreet in every point.

16. Eat as it becomes a man, those things which are set before you; and devour note, lest you be hated.

17. Leave off first for manners' sake; and do not be insatiable, lest you offend.

18. When you sit among many, do not reach your hand out first of all.

19. A very little is sufficient for a man well nurtured, and he does not fetch not his wind short upon his bed.

20. Sound sleep comes of moderate eating: He rises early, and his wits are with him: But the pain of watching, and choler, and pangs of the belly, are with an insatiable man.

21. And if you have been forced to eat, arise, go forth, vomit, and you shall have rest.

22. My son, hear me, and do not despise me, and at the last you shall find as I told you: In all your works be quick, so shall there no sickness come unto you.

23. Whoso is liberal of his meat, men shall speak well of him; and the report of his good housekeeping will be believed.

24. But against him that is a niggard of his meat the whole city shall murmur; and the testimonies of his niggardness shall not be doubted of.

25. Do not show your valiantness in wine; for wine has destroyed many.

26. The furnace proves the edge by dipping: So does wine the hearts of the proud by drunkenness.

27. Wine is as good as life to a man, if it be drunk moderately: What life is then to a man that is without wine? For it was made to make men glad.

28. Wine measurably drunk and in season brings gladness of the heart, and cheerfulness of the mind:

29. But wine drunken with excess makes bitterness of the mind, with brawling and quarrelling.

30. Drunkenness increases the rage of a fool till he offend: It diminishes strength, and makes wounds.

31. Do not rebuke your neighbor at the wine, and do not despise him in his mirth: Give him no despiteful words, and do not press upon him with urging him to drink.

Chapter 32

1. If you are made the master of a feast, do not lift yourself up, but be among them as one of the rest; take diligent care for them, and so sit down.

2. And when you have done all your office, take your place, that you may be merry with them, and receive a crown for your well ordering of the feast.

3. Speak, you that are the elder, for it becomes you, but with sound judgment; and do not hinder music.

4. Do not pour out words where there is a musician, and do not show forth wisdom out of time.

5. A concert of music in a banquet of wine is as a signet of carbuncle set in gold.

6. As a signet of an emerald set in a work of gold, so is the melody of music with pleasant wine.

7. Speak, young man, if there is need of you: And yet scarcely when you are twice asked.

8. Let your speech be short, comprehending much in few words; be as one that knows and yet holds his tongue.

9. If you are among great men, do not make yourself equal with them; and when ancient men are in place, do not use many words.

10. Before the thunder goes lightning; and before a shamefaced man shall go favor.

11. Rise up betimes, and do not be the last; but get you home without delay.

12. There take your pastime, and do what you will: But do not sin by proud speech.

13. And for these things bless him that made you, and has replenished you with his good things.

14. Whoso fears Yahuah will receive his discipline; and they that seek him early shall find favor.

15. He that seeks the law shall be filled therewith: But the hypocrite will be offended thereat.

16. They that fear Yahuah shall find judgment, and shall kindle justice as a light.

17. A sinful man will not be reproved, but finds an excuse according to his will.

18. A man of counsel will be considerate; but a strange and proud man is not daunted with fear, even when of himself he has done without counsel.

19. Do nothing without advice; and when you have once done, do not repent.

20. Do not go in a way wherein you may fall, and do not stumble among the stones.

21. Do not be confident in a plain way.

22. And beware of your own children.

23. In every good work trust your own soul; for this is the keeping of the commandments.

24. He that believes in Yahuah takes heed to the commandment; and he that trusts in him shall fare never the worse.

Chapter 33

1. There shall no evil happen unto him that fears Yahuah; but in temptation even again he will deliver him.

2. A wise man does not hates the law; but he that is a hypocrite therein is as a ship in a storm.

3. A man of understanding trusts in the law; and the law is faithful unto him, as an oracle.

4. Prepare what to say, and so you shall be heard: And bind up instruction, and then make answer.

5. The heart of the foolish is like a cartwheel; and his thoughts are like a rolling axel tree.

6. A stallion horse is as a mocking friend, he neighs under every one that sits upon him.

7. Why does one day excel another, when as all the light of every day in the year is of the sun?

8. By the knowledge of Yahuah they were distinguished: And he altered seasons and feasts.

9. Some of them he has made high days, and hallowed them, and some of them he has made ordinary days.

10. And all men are from the ground, and Âdâm was created of earth:

11. In much knowledge Yahuah has divided them, and made their ways diverse.

12. Some of them he has blessed and exalted and some of them he sanctified, and set near himself: But some of them he has cursed and brought low, and turned out of their places.

13. As the clay is in the potter's hand, to fashion it at his pleasure: So man is in the hand of him that made him, to render to them as likes him best.

14. Good is set against evil, and life against death: So is the godly against the sinner, and the sinner against the godly.

15. So look upon all the works of Elyôn Êl; and there are two and two, one against another.

16. I awaked up last of all, as one that gathers after the grape gatherers: By the blessing of Yahuah I profited, and tread my winepress like a gatherer of grapes.

17. Consider that I did not labor for myself only, but for all them that seek learning.

18. Hear me, O you great men of the people, and hearken with your ears, you rulers of the congregation.

19. Do not give your son and woman, your brother and friend, power over you while you live, and do not give your goods to another: Lest it repent you, and you entreat for the same again.

20. As long as you live and have breath in you, do not give yourself over to any.

21. For better it is that your children should seek to you, than that you should stand to their courtesy.

22. In all your works keep to yourself the preeminence; do not leave a stain in your honor.

23. At the time when you shall end your days, and finish your life, distribute your inheritance.

24. Fodder, a wand, and burdens, are for the ass; and bread, correction, and work, for a servant.

25. If you set your servant to labor, you shall find rest: But if you let him go idle, he shall seek liberty.

26. A yoke and a collar do bow the neck: So are tortures and torments for an evil servant.

27. Send him to labor, that he is not idle; for idleness teaches much evil.

28. Set him to work, as is fit for him: If he is not obedient, put on more heavy fetters.

29. But do not be excessive toward any; and without discretion do nothing.

30. If you have a servant, let him be unto you as yourself, because you have bought him with a price.

31. If you have a servant, entreat him as a brother: For you have need of him, as of your own soul: If you entreat him evil, and he run from you, which way will you go to seek him?

Chapter 34

1. The hopes of a man void of understanding are vain and false: And dreams lift up fools.

2. Whoso regards dreams is like him that catches at a shadow, and follows after the wind.

3. The vision of dreams is the resemblance of one thing to another, even as the likeness of a face to a face.

4. Of an unclean thing what can be cleansed? And from that thing which is false what truth can come?

5. Divinations, and soothsaying, and dreams, are vain: And the heart fancies, as a woman's heart in travail.

6. If they are not sent from Elyôn Êl in your visitation, do not set your heart upon them.

7. For dreams have deceived many, and they have failed that put their trust in them.

8. The law shall be found perfect without lies: And wisdom is perfection to a faithful mouth.

9. A man that has travelled knows many things; and he that has much experience will declare wisdom.

10. He that has no experience knows little: But he that has travelled is full of prudence.

11. When I travelled, I saw many things; and I understand more than I can express.

12. I was often times in danger of death: Yet I was delivered because of these things.

13. The spirit of those that fear Yahuah shall live; for their hope is in him that saves them.

14. Whoso fears Yahuah shall not fear nor be afraid; for he is his hope.

15. Blessed is the soul of him that fears Yahuah: To whom does he look? And who is his strength?

16. For the eyes of Yahuah are upon them that love him, he is their mighty protection and strong stay, a defense from heat, and a cover from the sun at noon, a preservation from stumbling, and a help from falling.

17. He raises up the soul, and lightens the eyes: He gives health, life, and blessing.

18. He that sacrifices of a thing wrongfully gotten, his offering is ridiculous; and the gifts of unjust men are not accepted.

19. Elyôn Êl is not pleased with the offerings of the wicked; neither is he pacified for sin by the multitude of sacrifices.

20. Whoso brings an offering of the goods of the poor does as one that kills the son before his father's eyes.

21. The bread of the needy is their life: He that defrauds him thereof is a man of blood.

22. He that takes away his neighbor's living slays him; and he that defrauds the laborer of his hire is a blood shedder.

23. When one builds, and another pulls down, what profit have they then but labor?

24. When one prays, and another curses, whose voice will Yahuah hear?

25. He that washes himself after the touching of a dead body, if he touch it again, what avails his washing?

26. So is it with a man that fasts for his sins, and goes again, and does the same: Who will hear his prayer? Or what does his humbling profit him?

Chapter 35

1. He that keeps the law brings offerings enough: He that takes heed to the commandment offers a peace offering.

2. He that requires a good turn offers fine flour; and he that gives alms sacrifices praise.

3. To depart from wickedness is a thing pleasing to Yahuah; and to forsake unrighteousness is a propitiation.

4. You shall not appear empty before Yahuah.

5. For all these things are to be done because of the commandment.

6. The offering of the righteous makes the altar fat, and the sweet savor thereof is before Elyôn Êl.

7. The sacrifice of a just man is acceptable and the memorial thereof shall never be forgotten.

8. Give Yahuah his honor with a good eye, and do not diminish the first fruits of your hands.

9. In all your gifts show a cheerful countenance, and dedicate your tithes with gladness.

10. Give unto Elyôn Êl according as he has enriched you; and as you have gotten, give with a cheerful eye.

11. For Yahuah recompenses, and will give you seven times as much.

12. Do not think to corrupt with gifts; for such he will not receive: And do not trust to unrighteous sacrifices; for Yahuah is judge, and with him is no respect of persons.

13. He will not accept any person against a poor man, but will hear the prayer of the oppressed.

14. He will not despise the supplication of the fatherless; nor the widow, when she pours out her complaint.

15. Do not the tears run down the widow's cheeks? And is not her cry against him that causes them to fall?

16. He that serves Yahuah shall be accepted with favor, and his prayer shall reach unto the clouds.

17. The prayer of the humble pierces the clouds: And till it comes nigh, he will not be comforted; and will not depart, till Elyôn Êl shall behold to judge righteously, and execute judgment.

18. For Yahuah will not be slack, neither will Shadday Êl be patient toward them, till he have smitten in sunder the loins of the unmerciful, and repaid vengeance to the heathen; till he have taken away the multitude of the proud, and broken the scepter of the unrighteous;

19. Till he has rendered to every man according to his deeds, and to the works of men according to their devices; till he has judged the cause of his people, and made them to rejoice in his mercy.

20. Mercy is seasonable in the time of affliction, as clouds of rain in the time of drought.

Chapter 36

1. Have mercy upon us, O Yahuah Êlôhîym of all, and behold us:

2. And send your fear upon all the nations that do not seek after you.

3. Lift up your hand against the strange nations, and let them see your power.

4. As you were sanctified in us before them: So be you magnified among them before us.

5. And let them know you, as we have known you, that there is no Êlôhîym but only you, O Êlôhîym.

6. Show new signs, and make other strange wonders: Glorify your hand and your right arm, that they may set forth your wondrous works.

7. Raise up indignation, and pour out wrath: Take away the adversary, and destroy the enemy.

8. Make the time short, remember the covenant, and let them declare your wonderful works.

9. Let him that escapes be consumed by the rage of the fire; and let them perish that oppress the people.

10. Smite in sunder the heads of the rulers of the heathen that say: There is none other but we.

11. Gather all the tribes of Yaăqôb together, and inherit you them, as from the beginning.

12. O Yahuah, have mercy upon the people that is called by your name, and upon Yâshârêl, whom you have named your firstborn.

13. O be merciful unto Yarûshâlaim, your qâdôsh city, the place of your rest.

14. Fill Tsîyôn with your unspeakable oracles, and your people with your glory:

15. Give testimony unto those that you have possessed from the beginning, and raise up Nâbîy that have been in your name.

16. Reward them that wait for you, and let your Nâbîy be found faithful.

17. O Yahuah, hear the prayer of your servants, according to the blessing of Ahărôn over your people, that all they which dwell upon the earth may know that you are Yahuah, Ôlâm Êl.

18. The belly devours all meats, yet is one meat better than another.

19. As the palate tastes divers kinds of venison: So does a heart of understanding false speeches.

20. A froward heart causes heaviness: but a man of experience will recompense him.

21. A woman will receive every man, yet is one daughter better than another.

22. The beauty of a woman cheers the countenance, and a man loves nothing better.

23. If there is kindness, meekness, and comfort, in her tongue, then is not her husband like other men.

24. He that gets a wife begins a possession, a help like unto himself, and a pillar of rest.

25. Where no hedge is, there the possession is spoiled: And he that has no woman will wander up and down mourning.

26. Who will trust a thief well appointed, that skips from city to city? So who will believe a man that has no house, and lodges wherever the night takes him?

Chapter 37

1 Every friend says, I am his friend also: But there is a friend, which is only a friend in name.

2. Is it not a grief unto death, when a companion and friend is turned to an enemy?

3. O wicked imagination, whence came you in to cover the earth with deceit?

4. There is a companion, which rejoices in the prosperity of a friend, but in the time of trouble will be against him.

5. There is a companion, which helps his friend for the belly, and takes up the buckler against the enemy.

6. Do not forget your friend in your mind, and do not be unmindful of him in your riches.

7. Every counsellor extols counsel; but there is some that counsels for himself.

8. Beware of a counsellor, and know before what need he has; for he will counsel for himself; lest he cast the lot upon you,

9. And say unto you, your way is good: And afterward he stand on the other side, to see what shall befall you.

10. Do not consult with one that suspects you: And hide your counsel from such as envy you.

11. Neither consult with a woman touching her of whom she is jealous; neither with a coward in matters of war; nor with a merchant concerning exchange; nor with a buyer of selling; nor with an envious man of thankfulness; nor with an unmerciful man touching kindness; nor with the slothful for any work; nor with a hireling for a year of finishing work; nor with an idle servant of much business: Do not hearken unto these in any matter of counsel.

12. But be continually with an oddly man, whom you know to keep the commandments of Yahuah, whose, mind is according to your mind, and will sorrow with you, if you shall miscarry.

13. And let the counsel of your own heart stand: For there is no man more faithful unto you than it.

14. For a man's mind is sometime wont to tell him more than seven watchmen, that sit above in a high tower.

15. And above all this pray to Elyôn Êl, that he will direct your way in truth.

16. Let reason go before every enterprise, and counsel before every action.

17. The countenance is a sign of changing of the heart.

18. Four manner of things appear: Good and evil, life and death: But the tongue rules over them continually.

19. There is one that is wise and teaches many, and yet is unprofitable to himself.

20. There is one that shows wisdom in words, and is hated: He shall be destitute of all food.

21. For grace is not given, him from Yahuah, because he is deprived of all wisdom.

22. Another is wise to himself; and the fruits of understanding are commendable in his mouth.

23. A wise man instructs his people; and the fruits of his understanding do not fail.

24. A wise man shall be filled with blessing; and all they that see him shall count him happy.

25. The days of the life of man may be numbered: But the days of Yâshârêl are innumerable.

26. A wise man shall inherit glory among his people, and his name shall be perpetual.

27. My son, prove your soul in your life, and see what is evil for it, and do not give that unto it.

28. For all things are not profitable for all men, neither has every soul pleasure in everything.

29. Do not be insatiable in any dainty thing, nor too greedy upon meats:

30. For excess of meats brings sickness, and surfeiting will turn into choler.

31. By surfeiting have many perished; but he that takes heed prolongs his life.

Chapter 38

1. Honor a physician with the honor due unto him for the uses which you may have of him: For Yahuah has created him.

2. For of Elyôn Êl comes healing, and he shall receive honor of the king.

3. The skill of the physician shall lift up his head: And in the sight of great men he shall be in admiration.

4. Yahuah has created remedies out of the earth; and he that is wise will not abhor them.

5. Was not the water made sweet with wood, that the virtue thereof might be known?

6. And he has given men skill, that he might be honored in his marvelous works.

7. With such does he heal men, and takes away their pains.

8. Of such does the apothecary make a confection; and of his works there is no end; and from him is peace over all the earth,

9. My son, in your sickness do not be negligent: But pray unto Yahuah, and he will make you whole.

10. Leave off from sin, and order your hands right, and cleanse your heart from all wickedness.

11. Give a sweet savor, and a memorial of fine flour; and make a fat offering, as a dead man.

12. Then give place to the physician, for Yahuah has created him: Do not let him go from you, for you have need of him.

13. There is a time when in their hands there is good success.

14 For they shall also pray unto Yahuah, that he would prosper that, which they give for ease and remedy to prolong life.

15. He that sins before his Âśâh (עָשָׂה), let him fall into the hand of the physician.

16. My son, let tears fall down over the dead, and begin to lament, as if you had suffered great harm yourself; and then cover his body according to the custom, and do not neglect his burial.

17. Weep bitterly, and make great moan, and use lamentation, as he is worthy, and that a day or two, lest you are evil spoken of: And then comfort yourself for your heaviness.

18. For of heaviness comes death, and the heaviness of the heart breaks strength.

19. In affliction also sorrow remains: And the life of the poor is the curse of the heart.

20. Take no heaviness to heart: Drive it away, and remember the last end.

21. Do not forget it, for there is no turning again: You shall not do him good, but hurt yourself.

22. Remember my judgment: For yours also shall be so; yesterday for me, and today for you.

23. When the dead is at rest, let his remembrance rest; and be comforted for him, when his spirit is departed from him.

24. The wisdom of a learned man comes by opportunity of leisure: And he that has little business shall become wise.

25. How can he get wisdom that holds the plough, and that glories in the goad, that drives oxen, and is occupied in their labors, and whose talk is of bullocks?

26. He gives his mind to make furrows; and is diligent to give the cattle fodder.

27. So every carpenter and work master, that labors night and day: And they that cut and grave seals, and are diligent to make great variety, and give themselves to counterfeit imagery, and watch to finish a work:

28. The smith also sitting by the anvil, and considering the iron work, the vapor of the fire wastes his flesh, and he fights with the heat of the furnace: The noise of the hammer and the anvil is ever in his ears, and his eyes look still upon the pattern of the thing that he makes; he sets his mind to finish his work, and watches to polish it perfectly:

29. So does the potter sitting at his work, and turning the wheel about with his feet, who is always carefully set at his work, and makes all his work by number;

30. He fashions the clay with his arm, and bows down his strength before his feet; he applies himself to lead it over; and he is diligent to make clean the furnace:

31. All these trust to their hands: And everyone is wise in his work.

32. Without these cannot a city be inhabited: And they shall not dwell where they will, nor go up and down:

33. They shall not be sought for in public counsel, nor sit high in the congregation: They shall not sit on the judges' seat, nor understand the sentence of judgment: They cannot declare justice and judgment; and they shall not be found where parables are spoken.

34. But they will maintain the state of the world, and all their desire is in the work of their craft.

Chapter 39

1. But he that gives his mind to the law of Elyôn Êl, and is occupied in the meditation thereof, will seek out the wisdom of all the ancient, and be occupied in prophecies.

2. He will keep the sayings of the renowned men: And where subtle parables are, he will be there also.

3. He will seek out the secrets of grave sentences, and be conversant in dark parables.

4. He shall serve among great men, and appear before princes: He will travel through strange countries; for he has tried the good and the evil among men.

5. He will give his heart to resort early to Yahuah that made him, and will pray before Elyôn Êl, and will open his mouth in prayer, and make supplication for his sins.

6. When the great Yahuah will, he shall be filled with the spirit of understanding: He shall pour out wise sentences, and give thanks unto Yahuah in his prayer.

7. He shall direct his counsel and knowledge, and in his secrets he shall meditate.

8. He shall show forth that which he has learned, and shall glory in the law of the covenant of Yahuah.

9. Many shall commend his understanding; and so long as the world endures, it shall not be blotted out; his memorial shall not depart away, and his name shall live from generation to generation.

10. Nations shall show forth his wisdom, and the congregation shall declare his praise.

11. If he dies, he shall leave a greater name than a thousand: And if he lives, he shall increase it.

12. Yet I have more to say, which I have thought upon; for I am filled as the moon at the full.

13. Hearken unto me, you qâdôsh children, and bud forth as a rose growing by the brook of the field:

14. And give you a sweet savor as lebônâh, and flourish as a lily, send forth a smell, and sing a song of praise, bless Yahuah in all his works.

15. Magnify his name, and show forth his praise with the songs of your lips, and with harps, and in praising him you shall say after this manner:

16. All the works of Yahuah are exceeding good, and whatsoever he commands shall be accomplished in due season.

17. And none may say, what is this? Wherefore is that? For at time convenient they shall all be sought out: At his commandment the waters stood as a heap, and at the words of his mouth the receptacles of waters.

18. At his commandment is done whatsoever pleases him; and none can hinder, when he will save.

19. The works of all flesh are before him, and nothing can be hid from his eyes.

20. He sees from everlasting to everlasting; and there is nothing wonderful before him.

21. A man does not need to say, what is this? Wherefore is that? For he has made all things for their uses.

22. His blessing covered the dry land as a river, and watered it as a flood.

23. As he has turned the waters into saltiness: So shall the heathen inherit his wrath.

24. As his ways are plain unto the holy; so are they stumbling blocks unto the wicked.

25. For the good are good things created from the beginning: So evil things for sinners.

26. The principal things for the whole use of man's life are water, fire, iron, and salt, flour of wheat, honey, milk, and the blood of the grape, and oil, and clothing.

27. All these things are for good to the godly: So to the sinners they are turned into evil.

28. There are spirits that are created for vengeance, which in their fury lay on sore strokes; in the time of destruction they pour out their force, and appease the wrath of him that made them.

29. Fire, and hail, and famine, and death, all these were created for vengeance;

30. Teeth of wild beasts, and scorpions, serpents, and the sword punishing the wicked to destruction.

31. They shall rejoice in his commandment, and they shall be ready upon earth, when need is; and when their time is come, they shall not transgress his word.

32. Therefore from the beginning I was resolved, and thought upon these things, and have left them in writing.

33. All the works of Yahuah are good: And he will give every needful thing in due season.

34. So that a man cannot say, this is worse than that: For in time they shall all be well approved.

35. And therefore praise you Yahuah with the whole heart and mouth, and bless the name of Yahuah.

Chapter 40

1. Great travail is created for every man, and a heavy yoke is upon the sons of Âdâm, from the day that they go out of their mother's womb, till the day that they return to the mother of all things.

2. Their imagination of things to come, and the day of death, trouble their thoughts, and cause fear of heart;

3. From him that sits on a throne of glory, unto him that is humbled in earth and ashes;

4. From him that wears purple and a crown, unto him that is clothed with a linen frock.

5. Wrath, and envy, trouble, and unquietness, fear of death, and anger, and strife, and in the time of rest upon his bed his night sleep, do change his knowledge.

6. A little or nothing is his rest, and afterward he is in his sleep, as in a day of keeping watch, troubled in the vision of his heart, as if he were escaped out of a battle.

7. When all is safe, he awakes, and marvels that the fear was nothing.

8. Such things happen unto all flesh, both man and beast, and that is sevenfold more upon sinners.

9. Death, and bloodshed, strife, and sword, calamities, famine, tribulation, and the scourge;

10. These things are created for the wicked, and for their sakes came the flood.

11. All things that are of the earth shall turn to the earth again: And that which is of the waters does return into the sea.

12. All bribery and injustice shall be blotted out: But true dealing shall endure forever.

13. The goods of the unjust shall be dried up like a river, and shall vanish with noise, like a great thunder in rain.

14. While he opens his hand he shall rejoice: So shall transgressors come to nothing.

15. The children of the ungodly shall not bring forth many branches: But are as unclean roots upon a hard rock.

16. The weed growing upon every water and bank of a river shall be pulled up before all grass.

17. Bountifulness is as a most fruitful Garden, and mercifulness endures forever.

18. To labor, and to be content with that a man has, is a sweet life: But he that finds a treasure is above them both.

19. Children and the building of a city continue a man's name: But a blameless woman is counted above them both.

20. Wine and music rejoice the heart: But the love of wisdom is above them both.

21. The pipe and the psaltery make sweet melody: But a pleasant tongue is above them both.

22. Your eye desires favor and beauty: But more than both corn while it is green.

23. A friend and companion never meet amiss: But above both is a woman with her husband.

24. Brethren and help are against time of trouble: But alms shall deliver more than them both.

25. Gold and silver make the foot stand sure: But counsel is esteemed above them both.

26. Riches and strength lift up the heart: But the fear of Yahuah is above them both: There is no want in the fear of Yahuah, and it does not need to seek help.

27. The fear of Yahuah is a fruitful Garden, and covers him above all glory.

28. My son, do not lead a beggar's life; for better it is to die than to beg.

29. The life of him that depends on another man's table is not to be counted for a life; for he pollutes himself with other men's meat: But a wise man well nurtured will beware thereof.

30. Begging is sweet in the mouth of the shameless: But in his belly there shall burn a fire.

Chapter 41

1. O death, how bitter is the remembrance of you to a man that lives at rest in his possessions, unto the man that has nothing to vex him, and that has prosperity in all things: Yea, unto him that is yet able to receive meat!

2. O death, acceptable is your sentence unto the needy, and unto him whose strength fails that is now in the last age, and is vexed with all things, and to him that despairs, and has lost patience!

3. Do not fear the sentence of death, remember them that have been before you, and that come after; for this is the sentence of Yahuah over all flesh.

4. And why are you against the pleasure of Elyôn Êl? There is no inquisition in the grave, whether you have lived ten, or a hundred, or a thousand years.

5. The children of sinners are abominable children, and they that are conversant in the dwelling of the ungodly.

6. The inheritance of sinners' children shall perish, and their posterity shall have a perpetual reproach.

7. The children will complain of an ungodly father, because they shall be reproached for his sake.

8. Woe be unto you, ungodly men, which have forsaken the law of Êlôhîym Elyôn Êl! For if you increase, it shall be to your destruction:

9. And if you are born, you shall be born to a curse: And if you dies, a curse shall be your portion.

10. All that are of the earth shall turn to earth again: So the ungodly shall go from a curse to destruction.

11. The mourning of men is about their bodies: But an ill name of sinners shall be blotted out.

12. Have regard to your name; for that shall continue with you above a thousand great treasures of gold.

13. A good life has but few days: But a good name endures forever.

14. My children, keep discipline in peace: For wisdom that is hid, and a treasure that is not seen, what profit is in them both?

15. A man that hides his foolishness is better than a man that hides his wisdom.

16. Therefore be shamefaced according to my word: For it is not good to retain all shamefacedness; neither is it altogether approved in everything.

17. Be ashamed of whoredom before father and mother: And of a lie before a prince and a mighty man;

18. Of an offence before a judge and ruler; of iniquity before a congregation and people; of unjust dealing before your partner and friend;

19. And of theft in regard of the place where you sojourn, and in regard of the truth of Êlôhîym and his covenant; and to lean with your elbow upon the meat; and of scorning to give and take;

20. And of silence before them that salute you; and to look upon a harlot;

21. And to turn away your face from your kinsman; or to take away a portion or a gift; or to gaze upon another man's woman.

22. Or to be over busy with his maid, and do not come not her bed; or of upbraiding speeches before friends; and after you have given, do not upbraid;

23. Or of iterating and speaking again that which you have heard; and of revealing of secrets.

24. So you shall be truly shamefaced and find favor before all men.

Chapter 42

1. Of these things do not be you ashamed, and accept no person to sin thereby:

2. Of the law of Elyôn Êl, and his covenant; and of judgment to justify the ungodly;

3. Of reckoning with your partners and travelers; or of the gift of the heritage of friends;

4. Of exactness of balance and weights; or of getting much or little;

5. And of merchants' indifferent selling; of much correction of children; and to make the side of an evil servant to bleed.

6. Sure keeping is good, where an evil woman is; and shut up, where many hands are.

7. Deliver all things in number and weight; and put all in writing that you give out, or receive in.

8. Do not be ashamed to inform the unwise and foolish, and the extreme aged that

contends with those that are young: Thus you shall be truly learned, and approved of all men living.

9. The father wakes for the daughter, when no man knows; and the care for her takes away sleep: When she is young, lest she pass away the flower of her age; and being married, lest she should be hated:

10. In her virginity, lest she should be defiled and gotten with child in her father's house; and having an husband, lest she should misbehave herself; and when she is married, lest she should be barren.

11. Keep a sure watch over a shameless daughter, lest she make you a laughingstock to your enemies, and a byword in the city, and a reproach among the people, and make you ashamed before the multitude.

12. Do not behold every body's beauty, and do not sit in the midst of women.

13. For from garments comes a moth, and from women wickedness.

14. Better is the churlishness of a man than a courteous woman, a woman, I say, which brings shame and reproach.

15. I will now remember the works of Yahuah, and declare the things that I have seen: In the words of Yahuah are his works.

16. The sun that gives light looks upon all things, and the work thereof is full of the glory of Yahuah.

17. Yahuah has not given power to the qôdesh to declare all his marvelous works, which Yahuah Shadday Êl firmly settled, that whatsoever is might be established for his glory.

18. He seeks out the deep, and the heart, and considers their crafty devices: For Yahuah knows all that may be known, and he beholds the signs of the world.

19. He declares the things that are past, and for to come, and reveals the steps of hidden things.

20. No thought escapes him, neither any word is hidden from him.

21. He has garnished the excellent works of his wisdom, and he is from everlasting to everlasting: Unto him may nothing be added, neither can he be diminished, nor he has no need of any counsellor.

22. Oh how desirable are all his works! And that a man may see even to a spark.

23. All these things live and remain forever for all uses, and they are all obedient.

24. All things are double one against another: And he has made nothing imperfect.

25. One thing establishes the good or another: And who shall be filled with beholding his glory?

Chapter 43

1. The pride of the height, the clear firmament, the beauty of shâmayim, with his glorious show;

2. The sun when it appears, declaring at his rising a marvelous instrument, the work of Elyôn Êl:

3. At noon it parches the country, and who can abide the burning heat thereof?

4. A man blowing a furnace is in works of heat, but the sun burns the mountains three times more; breathing out fiery vapors, and sending forth bright beams, it dims the eyes.

5. Great is Yahuah that made it; and at his commandment runs hastily.

6. He made it also to serve in the season for a declaration of times, and a sign of the world.

7. From the moon is the sign of some feasts, a light that decreases in her perfection.

8. The month is called after her name, increasing wonderfully in her changing, being an instrument of the armies above, shining in the firmament of shâmayim;

9. The beauty of shâmayim, the glory of the stars, an ornament giving light in the highest places of Yahuah.

10. At the commandment of the Qâdôsh Êl they will stand in their order, and never faint in their watches.

11. Look upon the rainbow, and praise him that made it; very beautiful it is in the brightness thereof.

12. It compasses the shâmayim about with a glorious circle, and the hands of Elyôn Êl have bended it.

13. By his commandment he makes the snow to fall a place, and sends swiftly the lightning of his judgment.

14. Through this the treasures are opened: And clouds fly forth as fowls.

15. By his great power he makes the clouds firm, and the hailstones are broken small.

16. At his sight the mountains are shaken, and at his will the south wind blows.

17. The noise of the thunder makes the earth to tremble: So does the northern storm and the whirlwind: As birds flying he scatters the snow, and the falling down thereof is as the lighting of grasshoppers:

18. The eye marvels at the beauty of the whiteness thereof, and the heart is astonished at the raining of it.

19. The hoarfrost also as salt he pours on the earth, and being congealed, it lies on the top of sharp stakes.

20. When the cold north wind blows, and the water is congealed into ice, it abides upon every gathering together of water, and clothes the water as with a breastplate.

21. It devours the mountains, and burns the wilderness, and consumes the grass as fire.

22. A present remedy of all is a mist coming speedily, a dew coming after heat refreshes.

23. By his counsel he appeases the deep, and plants islands therein.

24. They that sail on the sea tell of the danger thereof; and when we hear it with our ears, we marvel thereat.

25. For therein be strange and wondrous works, variety of all kinds of beasts and whales created.

26. By him the end of them has prosperous success, and by his word all things consist.

27. We may speak much, and yet come short: Wherefore in sum, he is all.

28. How shall we be able to magnify him? For he is great above all his works.

29. Yahuah is terrible and very great, and marvelous is his power.

30. When you glorify Yahuah, exalt him as much as you can; for even yet will he far exceed: And when you exalt him, put forth all your strength, and do not be weary; for you can never go far enough.

31. Who has seen him that he might tell us? And who can magnify him as he is?

32. There are yet hid greater things than these be, for we have seen but a few of his works.

33. For Yahuah has made all things; and to the godly he has given wisdom.

Chapter 44

1. Let us now praise famous men, and our fathers that begat us.

2. Yahuah has wrought great glory by them through his great power from the beginning.

3. Such as did bear rule in their kingdoms, men renowned for their power, giving counsel by their understanding, and declaring prophecies:

4. Leaders of the people by their counsels, and by their knowledge of learning meet for the people, wise and eloquent are their instructions:

5. Such as found out musical tunes, and recited verses in writing:

6. Rich men furnished with ability, living peaceably in their habitations:

7. All these were honored in their generations, and were the glory of their times.

8. There are of them that have left a name behind them, that their praises might be reported.

9. And some there be, which have no memorial; who are perished, as though they had never been; and are become as though they had never been born; and their children after them.

10. But these were merciful men, whose righteousness has not been forgotten.

11. With their seed shall continually remain a good inheritance, and their children are within the covenant.

12. Their seed stands fast, and their children for their sakes.

13. Their seed shall remain forever, and their glory shall not be blotted out.

14. Their bodies are buried in peace; but their name lives for evermore.

15. The people will tell of their wisdom, and the congregation will show forth their praise.

16. Chănôk pleased Yahuah, and was translated, being an example of repentance to all generations.

17. Nôach was found perfect and righteous; in the time of wrath he was taken in exchange for the world; therefore was he left as a remnant unto the earth, when the flood came.

18. An everlasting covenant was made with him, that all flesh should perish no more by the flood.

19. Abrâhâm was a great father of many people: In glory was there none like unto him;

20. Who kept the law of Elyôn Êl, and was in covenant with him: He established the covenant in his flesh; and when he was proved, he was found faithful.

21. Therefore he assured him by an oath, that he would bless the nations in his seed, and that he would multiply him as the dust of the earth, and exalt his seed as the stars, and cause them to inherit from sea to sea, and from the river unto the utmost part of the land.

22. With Yitschâq did he establish likewise for Abrâhâm his father's sake the blessing of all men, and the covenant, and made it rest upon the head of Yaăqôb. He acknowledged him in his blessing, and gave him a heritage, and divided his portions; among the twelve tribes did he part them.

Chapter 45

1. And he brought out of him a merciful man, which found favor in the sight of all flesh, even Môsheh, beloved of Êlôhîym and men, whose memorial is blessed.

2. He made him like to the glorious qôdesh, and magnified him, so that his enemies stood in fear of him.

3. By his words he caused the wonders to cease, and he made him glorious in the sight of kings, and gave him a commandment for his people, and showed him part of his glory.

4. He sanctified him in his faithfulness and meekness, and chose him out of all men.

5. He made him to hear his voice, and brought him into the dark cloud, and gave him commandments before his face, even the law of life and knowledge, that he might teach Yaăqôb his covenants, and Yâshârêl his judgments.

6. He exalted Ahărôn, a qâdôsh man like unto him, even his brother, of the tribe of Lêwîy.

7. An everlasting covenant he made with him and gave him the kehûnnâh among the people; he beautified him with comely ornaments, and clothed him with a robe of glory.

8. He put upon him perfect glory; and strengthened him with rich garments, with breeches, with a long robe, and the êphôd.

9. And he compassed him with pomegranates, and with many golden bells round about, that as he went there might be a sound, and a noise made that might be heard in the temple, for a memorial to the children of his people;

10. With an holy garment, with gold, and blue silk, and purple, the work of the embroiderer, with a breastplate of judgment, and with Ûrîym and Tûmmîym;

11. With twisted scarlet, the work of the cunning workman, with precious stones graven like seals, and set in gold, the work of the jeweler, with a writing engraved for a memorial, after the number of the tribes of Yâshârêl.

12. He set a crown of gold upon the mitre, wherein was engraved qôdesh, an ornament of honor, a costly work, the desires of the eyes, goodly and beautiful.

13. Before him there were none such, neither did ever any stranger put them on, but only his children and his children's children perpetually.

14. Their sacrifices shall be wholly consumed every day twice continually.

15. Môsheh consecrated him, and anointed him with holy oil: This was appointed unto him by an everlasting covenant, and to his seed, so long as the shâmayim should remain, that they should minister unto him, and execute the office of the kehûnnâh, and bless the people in his name.

16. He chose him out of all men living to offer sacrifices to Yahuah, incense, and a sweet savor, for a memorial, to make reconciliation for his people.

17. He gave unto him his commandments, and authority in the statutes of judgments, that he should teach Yaăqôb the testimonies, and inform Yâshârêl in his laws.

18. Strangers conspired together against him, and maligned him in the wilderness, even the men that were of Dâthân's and Ăbîyrâm's side, and the congregation of Qôrach (קֹרַח), with fury and wrath.

19. This Yahuah saw, and it displeased him, and in his wrathful indignation were they consumed: He did wonders upon them, to consume them with the fiery flame.

20. But he made Ahărôn more honorable, and gave him a heritage, and divided unto him

the first fruits of the increase; especially he prepared bread in abundance:

21. For they eat of the sacrifices of Yahuah, which he gave unto him and his seed.

22. Howbeit in the land of the people he had no inheritance, neither had he had any portion among the people: For Yahuah himself is his portion and inheritance.

23. The third in glory is Pîynechâs (פִּינְחָס) the son of Elâzâr, because he had zeal in the fear of Yahuah, and stood up with good courage of heart: When the people were turned back, and made reconciliation for Yâshârêl.

24. Therefore was there a covenant of peace made with him, that he should be the chief of the sanctuary and of his people, and that he and his posterity should have the dignity of the Kehûnnâh forever:

25. According to the covenant made with Dâwid son of Yishay (יִשַׁי), of the tribe of Yahûdâh (יהודה), that the inheritance of the king should be to his posterity alone: So the inheritance of Ahărôn should also be unto his seed.

26. Êlôhîym give you wisdom in your heart to judge his people in righteousness, that their good things do not be abolished, and that their glory may endure forever.

Chapter 46

1. Yahusha the son a Nûn was valiant in the wars, and was the successor of Môsheh in prophecies, who according to his name was made great for the saving of the elect of Êlôhîym, and taking vengeance of the enemies that rose up against them, that he might set Yâshârêl in their inheritance.

2. How great glory he got, when he did lift up his hands, and stretched out his sword against the cities!

3. Who before him so stood to it? For Yahuah himself brought his enemies unto him.

4. Did not the sun go back by his means? And was not one day as long as two?

5. He called upon Yahuah Elyôn Êl, when the enemies pressed upon him on every side; and Yahuah Gibbôr Êl heard him.

6. And with hailstones of mighty power he made the battle to fall violently upon the nations, and in the descent of Bêyth Chôrôn he destroyed them that resisted, that the nations might know all their strength, because he fought in the sight of Yahuah, and he followed Gibbôr Êl.

7. In the time of Môsheh also he did a work of mercy, he and Kâlêb the son of Yaphûnneh, in that they withstood the congregation, and withheld the people from sin, and appeased the wicked murmuring.

8. And of six hundred thousand people on foot, they two were preserved to bring them in to the heritage, even unto the land that flows with milk and honey.

9. Yahuah gave strength also unto Kâlêb, which remained with him unto his old age: So that he entered upon the high places of the land, and his seed obtained it for a heritage:

10. That all the children of Yâshârêl might see that it is good to follow Yahuah.

11. And concerning the judges, everyone by name, whose heart did not go a whoring, nor departed from Yahuah, let their memory be blessed.

12. Let their bones flourish out of their place, and let the name of them that were honored be continued upon their children.

13. Shemûêl, the Nâbîy of Yahuah, beloved of his Yahuah, established a kingdom, and anointed princes over his people.

14. By the law of Yahuah he judged the congregation, and Yahuah had respect unto Yaăqôb.

15. By his faithfulness he was found a true Nâbîy, and by his word he was known to be faithful in vision.

16. He called upon the mighty Yahuah, when his enemies pressed upon him on every side, when he offered the sucking lamb.

17. And Yahuah thundered from shâmayim, and with a great noise made his voice to be heard.

18. And he destroyed the rulers of the Tsôr (צֹר), and all the princes of the Pelishtîy.

19. And before his long sleep he made protestations in the sight of Yahuah and his anointed, I have not taken any man's goods, so much as a shoe: And no man did accuse him.

20. And upon his death he prophesied, and showed the king his end, and lifted up his testimony from the earth in prophecy, to blot out the wickedness of the people.

Chapter 47

1. And after him rose up Nâthân to prophesy in the time of Dâwid.

2. As is the fat taken away from the peace offering, so was Dâwid chosen out of the children of Yâshârêl.

3. He played with lions as with kids, and with bears as with lambs.

4. Did he not slew a Nephîyl, when he was yet but young? And did he not take away reproach from the people, when he lifted up his hand with the stone in the sling, and beat down the boasting of Golyath?

5. For he called upon Yahuah Elyôn Êl; and he gave him strength in his right hand to slay that mighty warrior, and set up the horn of his people.

6. So the people honored him with ten thousands, and praised him in the blessings of Yahuah, in that he gave him a crown of glory.

7. For he destroyed the enemies on every side, and brought to nothing the Pelishtîy his adversaries, and broke their horn in sunder unto this day.

8. In all his works he praised the Qâdôsh Elyôn Êl with words of glory; with his whole heart he sang songs, and loved him that made him.

9. He set singers also before the altar, that by their voices they might make sweet melody, and daily sing praises in their songs.

10. He beautified their feasts, and set in order the solemn times until the end, that they might praise his holy name, and that the temple might sound from morning.

11. Yahuah took away his sins, and exalted his horn forever: He gave him a covenant of kings, and a throne of glory in Yâshârêl.

12. After him rose up a wise son, and for his sake he dwelt at large.

13. Shelômôh reigned in a peaceable time, and was honored; for Êlôhîym made all quiet round about him, that he might build a house in his name, and prepare his sanctuary for ever.

14. How wise were you in your youth and, as a flood, filled with understanding!

15. Your soul covered the whole earth, and you filled it with dark parables.

16. Your name went far unto the islands; and for your peace you were beloved.

17. The countries marveled at you for your songs, and proverbs, and parables, and interpretations.

18. By the name of Yahuah Êlôhîym, which is called Yahuah Êlôhîym of Yâshârêl, you did gather gold as tin and did multiply silver as lead.

19. You did bow your loins unto women, and by your body you were brought into subjection.

20. You did stain your honor, and pollute your seed: So that you brought wrath upon thy children, and were grieved for your folly.

21. So the kingdom was divided, and out of Ephrayim ruled a rebellious kingdom.

22. But Yahuah will never leave off his mercy, neither shall any of his works perish, neither will he abolish the posterity of his elect, and the seed of him that loves him he will not take away: Wherefore he gave a remnant unto Yaăqôb, and out of him a root unto Dâwid.

23. Thus rested Shelômôh with his fathers, and of his seed he left behind him Rechabâm, even the foolishness of the people, and one that had no understanding, who turned away the people through his counsel. There was also Yârobâm the son of Nebât, who caused Yâshârêl to sin, and showed Ephrayim the way of sin:

24. And their sins were multiplied exceedingly, that they were driven out of the land.

25. For they sought out all wickedness, till the vengeance came upon them.

Chapter 48

1. Then stood up Êlîyâhû the Nâbîy as fire, and his word burned like a lamp.

2. He brought a sore famine upon them, and by his zeal he diminished their number.

3. By the word of Yahuah he shut up the shâmayim, and also three times brought down fire.

4. O Êlîyâhû, how were you honored in your wondrous deeds! And who may glory like unto you!

5. Who did raise up a dead man from death, and his soul from the place of the dead, by the word of Elyôn Êl:

6. Who brought kings to destruction, and honorable men from their bed:

7. Who heard the rebuke of Yahuah in Sîynay, and in Chôrêb the judgment of vengeance:

8. Who anointed kings to take revenge, and Nâbîy to succeed after him:

9. Who was taken up in a whirlwind of fire, and in a chariot of fiery horses:

10. Who was ordained for reproofs in their times, to pacify the wrath of Yahuah's judgment, before it broke forth into fury, and to turn the heart of the father unto the son, and to restore the tribes of Yaăqôb.

11. Blessed are they that saw you, and slept in love; for we shall surely live.

12. Êlîyâhû it was, who was covered with a whirlwind: and Ĕlîysheba was filled with his spirit: While he lived, he was not moved with the presence of any prince, neither could any bring him into subjection.

13. No word could overcome him; and after his death his body prophesied.

14. He did wonders in his life, and at his death were his works marvelous.

15. For all this the people did not repent, neither they departed from their sins, till they were spoiled and carried out of their land, and were scattered through all the earth: Yet there remained a small people, and a ruler in the house of Dâwid:

16. Of whom some did that which was pleasing to Êlôhîym, and some multiplied sins.

17. Chizqîyâhu fortified his city, and brought in water into the midst thereof: He dug the hard rock with iron, and made wells for waters.

18. In his time Sanchêrîyb came up, and sent Rabshâqêh, and lifted up his hand against Tsîyôn, and boasted proudly.

19. Then trembled their hearts and hands, and they were in pain, as women in travail.

20. But they called upon Yahuah which is merciful, and stretched out their hands toward him: And immediately the Qâdôsh Êl heard them out of shâmayim, and delivered them by the ministry of Yashayâhû.

21. He smote the host of the Ashshûr, and his angel destroyed them.

22. For Chizqîyâhu had done the thing that pleased Yahuah, and was strong in the ways of Dâwid his father, as Yashayâhû the Nâbîy, who was great and faithful in his vision, had commanded him.

23. In his time the sun went backward, and he lengthened the king's life.

24. He saw by an excellent spirit what should come to pass at the last, and he comforted them that mourned in Tsîyôn.

25. He showed what should come to pass forever, and secret things or ever they came.

Chapter 49

1 The remembrance of Yôshîyâhû is like the composition of the perfume that is made by the art of the apothecary: It is sweet as honey in all mouths, and as music at a banquet of wine.

2. He behaved himself uprightly in the conversion of the people, and took away the abominations of iniquity.

3. He directed his heart unto Yahuah, and in the time of the ungodly he established the worship of Êlôhîym.

4. All, except Dâwid and Chizqîyâhu and Yôshîyâhû, were defective: For they forsook the law of Elyôn Êl, even the kings of Yahûdâh failed.

5. Therefore he gave their power unto others, and their glory to a strange nation.

6. They burnt the chosen city of the sanctuary, and made the streets desolate, according to the prophecy of Yirmeyâhû.

7. For they entreated him evil, who nevertheless was a Nâbîy, sanctified in his mother's womb, that he might root out, and afflict, and destroy; and that he might build up also, and plant.

8. It was Yachezqêl who saw the glorious vision, which was showed him upon the chariot of the Kerûb.

9. For he made mention of the enemies under the figure of the rain, and directed them that went right.

10. And of the twelve Nâbîy let the memorial be blessed, and let their bones flourish again out of their place: For they comforted Yaăqôb, and delivered them by assured hope.

11. How shall we magnify Zerûbbâbel? Even he was as a signet on the right hand:

12. So was Yahusha the son of Yahôtsâdâq: Who in their time built the house, and set up a holy temple to Yahuah, which was prepared for everlasting glory.

13. And among the elect was Nechemyâh, whose renown is great, who raised up for us the walls that were fallen, and set up the gates and the bars, and raised up our ruins again.

14. But upon the earth was no man created like Chănôk; for he was taken from the earth.

15. Neither was there a young man born like Yôsêph, a governor of his brethren, a stay of the people, whose bones were regarded of Yahuah.

16. Shêm and Shêth were in great honor among men, and so was Âdâm above every living thing in creation.

Chapter 50

1 Shimôn the high Kôhên, the son of Ôniâs, who in his life repaired the house again, and in his days fortified the temple:

2. And by him was built from the foundation the double height, the high fortress of the wall about the temple:

3. In his days the cistern to receive water, being in compass as the sea, was covered with plates of brass:

4. He took care of the temple that it should not fall, and fortified the city against besieging:

5. How was he honored in the midst of the people in his coming out of the sanctuary!

6. He was as the morning star in the midst of a cloud, and as the moon at the full:

7. As the sun shining upon the temple of Elyôn Êl, and as the rainbow giving light in the bright clouds:

8. And as the flower of roses in the spring of the year, as lilies by the rivers of waters, and as the branches of the lebônâh tree in the time of summer:

9. As fire and incense in the censer, and as a vessel of beaten gold set with all manner of precious stones:

10. And as a fair olive tree budding forth fruit, and as a cypress tree which grows up to the clouds.

11. When he put on the robe of honor, and was clothed with the perfection of glory, when he went up to the holy altar, he made the garment of qôdesh honorable.

12. When he took the portions out of the Kôhên's hands, he himself stood by the hearth of the altar, compassed about, as a young cedar in Lebânôn; and as palm trees compassed they him round about.

13. So were all the sons of Ahărôn in their glory, and the offerings of Yahuah in their hands, before all the congregation of Yâshârêl.

14. And finishing the service at the altar, that he might adorn the offering of Elyôn Shadday Êl,

15. He stretched out his hand to the cup, and poured of the blood of the grape, he poured out at the foot of the altar a sweet smelling savor unto Elyôn Êl Melek of all.

16. Then shouted the sons of Ahărôn, and sounded the silver trumpets, and made a great noise to be heard, for a remembrance before Elyôn Êl.

17. Then all the people together hasted, and fell down to the earth upon their faces to worship their Yahuah Êlôhîym Shadday, Elyôn Êl.

18. The singers also sang praises with their voices, with great variety of sounds was there made sweet melody.

19. And the people besought Yahuah, Elyôn Êl, by prayer before him that is merciful, till the solemnity of Yahuah was ended, and they had finished his service.

20. Then he went down, and lifted up his hands over the whole congregation of the children of Yâshârêl, to give the blessing of Yahuah with his lips, and to rejoice in his name.

21. And they bowed themselves down to worship the second time, that they might receive a blessing from Elyôn Êl.

22. Now therefore bless you the Êlôhîym of all, which only does wondrous things everywhere, which exalts our days from the womb, and deals with us according to his mercy.

23. He grant us joyfulness of heart, and that peace may be in our days in Yâshârêl forever:

24. That he would confirm his mercy with us, and deliver us at his time!

25. There are two manner of nations which my heart abhors, and the third is no nation:

26. They that sit upon the mountain of Shômerôn, and they that dwell among the Pelishtîy, and that foolish people that dwell in Shekem.

27. Yahusha the son of Sirâ of Yarûshâlaim has written in this book the instruction of understanding and knowledge, who out of his heart poured forth wisdom.

28. Blessed is he that shall be exercised in these things; and he that lays them up in his heart shall become wise.

29. For if he does them, he shall be strong to all things: For the light of Yahuah leads him, who gives wisdom to the godly. Blessed be the name of Yahuah forever. Âmên, Âmên.

Chapter 51

1. A prayer of Yahusha the son of Sirâ. I will thank you, O Yahuah and Melek, and praise you, O Êlôhîym my Yâsha: I do give praise unto your name.

2. For you are my defender and helper, and has preserved my body from destruction, and from the snare of the slanderous tongue, and from the lips that forge lies, and has been my helper against my adversaries:

3. And have delivered me, according to the multitude of they mercies and greatness of your name, from the teeth of them that were ready to devour me, and out of the hands of such as sought after my life, and from the manifold afflictions which I had;

4. From the choking of fire on every side, and from the midst of the fire which I did not kindle;

5. From the depth of the belly of sheôl, from an unclean tongue, and from lying words.

6. By an accusation to the king from an unrighteous tongue my soul drew near even unto death, my life was near to the sheôl beneath.

7. They compassed me on every side, and there was no man to help me: I looked for the succor of men, but there was none.

8. Then I thought upon your mercy, O Yahuah, and upon your acts of old, how you deliver such as wait for you, and save them out of the hands of the enemies.

9. Then I lifted up my supplications from the earth, and prayed for deliverance from death.

10. I called upon Yahuah, the father of my master, that he would not leave me in the days of my trouble, and in the time of the proud, when there was no help.

11. I will praise your name continually, and will sing praises with thanksgiving; and so my prayer was heard:

12. For you saved me from destruction, and delivered me from the evil time: Therefore I will give thanks, and praise you, and bless your name, O Yahuah.

13. When I was yet young, or ever I went abroad, I desired wisdom openly in my prayer.

14. I prayed for her before the temple, and will seek her out even to the end.

15. Even from the flower till the grape was ripe has my heart delighted in her: My foot went the right way, from my youth up I sought after her.

16. I bowed down my ear a little, and received her, and got much learning.

17. I profited therein, therefore I will ascribe glory unto him that gives me wisdom.

18. For I purposed to do after her, and earnestly I followed that which is good; so I shall not be confounded.

19. My soul has wrestled with her, and in my doings I was exact: I stretched forth my hands to the shâmayim above, and bewailed my ignorance of her.

20. I directed my soul unto her, and I found her in pureness: I have had my heart joined with her from the beginning, therefore I shall I be forsaken.

21. My heart was troubled in seeking her: Therefore I have gotten a good possession.

22. Yahuah has given me a tongue for my reward, and I will praise him therewith.

23. Draw near unto me, you unlearned, and dwell in the house of learning.

24. Wherefore are you slow, and what do you say to these things, seeing your souls are very thirsty?

25. I opened my mouth, and said, buy her for yourselves without money.

26. Put your neck under the yoke, and let your soul receive instruction: She is hard at hand to find.

27. Behold with your eyes, how that I have but little labor, and have gotten unto me much rest.

28. Get learning with a great sum of money, and get much gold by her.

29. Let your soul rejoice in his mercy, and do not be ashamed of his praise.

30. Work your work betimes, and in his time he will give you your reward.

Wisdom of Shelômôh & Traditional Bible Parallels

(Dabar Yahuah Scriptures Study Guide)

Introduction

The **Wisdom of Shelômôh**, part of the apocryphal/deuterocanonical writings, bridges Old Testament wisdom literature with New Testament theology. It emphasizes immortality, divine wisdom, righteousness vs. wickedness, idolatry, and the Word (Logos) of Elohiym. Many passages strongly influenced New Testament writers, especially Paul, John, and the author of Hebrews.

Comparison Table: Wisdom of Shelômôh vs. The Bible

Wisdom of Shelômôh Passage	Biblical Parallels	Theme / Connection
Wis 1:13–14 – "Yahuah did not make death, neither does He delight in the destruction of the living."	Gen 1:31; Ezek 18:32; 1 Cor 15:26	**Êlôhîym** created life, not death; death is an enemy.
Wis 2:23–24 – "Elohiym created man to be immortal… but by the envy of the devil death entered the world."	Gen 2–3; Rom 5:12; 1 Cor 15:21	Adam, sin, and death linked to the devil's envy.
Wis 3:1–4 – "The souls of the righteous are in the hand of Yahuah… immortality is their hope."	Ps 116:15; John 10:28; Rev 14:13	Security of the righteous in Êlôhîym, hope of eternal life.
Wis 4:7–9 – "The righteous man, though he die early, shall be at rest… old age is understanding."	Isa 57:1–2; Prov 16:31	True measure of life is wisdom, not length of years.
Wis 5:1–5 – The righteous vindicated before the ungodly at judgment.	Matt 25:31–46; Rev 20:12	Final judgment, righteous vs. wicked.
Wis 6:12–20 – Wisdom is radiant and leads to incorruption and friendship with Êlôhîym.	Prov 8; Jas 1:5; 1 Cor 1:30	Wisdom personified, gift from above.
Wis 7:22–30 – Wisdom is the breath of Êlôhîym's power, pure influence, reflection of eternal light.	Prov 8:22–31; Heb 1:3; John 1:1–4	Wisdom as divine reflection, foreshadowing the Logos.
Wis 8:7 – Wisdom teaches temperance, prudence, justice, and fortitude.	Prov 1:3; Gal 5:22–23	Virtues & fruits of wisdom.
Wis 9:1–18 – Shelômôh's prayer for wisdom.	1 Kgs 3:5–12; Jas 1:5	Asking Êlôhîym for wisdom with humility.
Wis 11:20–21 – Êlôhîym created the world with measure, number, and weight.	Isa 40:12; Job 28:25; Ps 104	Orderly creation.
Wis 13:1–5 – Creation reveals the Creator; those who fail to recognize Him are without excuse.	Ps 19:1; Rom 1:19–20	Natural revelation of Êlôhîym through creation.
Wis 14:12–21 – Idolatry originates from man's vain inventions.	Isa 44:9–20; Rom 1:22–23	Idolatry as human corruption.

Wisdom of Shelômôh Passage	Biblical Parallels	Theme / Connection
Wis 16:12 – "It was not herb nor ointment that healed them, but Your word, O Yahuah."	Exod 15:26; Ps 107:20	Êlôhîym's word as true healer.
Wis 18:14–16 – The Word of Yahuah leapt down from heaven, as a warrior of judgment.	Isa 55:11; John 1:14; Rev 19:11–13	The Word personified, foreshadowing Messiah.
Wis 19:18–21 – Creation obeys Êlôhîym's command, changing nature for His people's salvation.	Exod 14; Josh 10:12–14	Creation serves redemption.

Summary of Key Parallels

1. Creation & Death – Êlôhîym created humanity for immortality; death entered through sin and the devil's envy.

2. The Righteous & Immortality – Assurance of eternal life and vindication of the righteous at judgment.

3. Wisdom Personified – Echoes Proverbs 8; anticipates John 1 and Hebrews 1's portrayal of the Logos.

4. Natural Revelation – Creation itself testifies to Êlôhîym's power, leaving man without excuse (Psalms, Romans).

5. Idolatry Condemned – Like Isaiah and Paul, idolatry is traced to human corruption and folly.

6. The Word of Êlôhîym – Messiah prefigured as the Word (Logos), active in creation, salvation, and judgment.

Chokmâh (חָכְמָה) Shelômôh (שְׁלֹמֹה) - Wisdom of Solomon

Chapter 1

1. Love righteousness, you that are judges of the earth: Think of Yahuah with a good heart, and in simplicity of heart seek him.

2. For he will be found of them that do not tempt him; and shows himself unto such as do not distrust him.

3. For froward thoughts separate from Êlôhîym: And his power, when it is tried, reproves the unwise.

4. For into a malicious soul wisdom shall not enter; nor dwell in the body that is subject unto sin.

5. For the qâdôsh spirit of discipline will flee deceit, and remove from thoughts that are without understanding, and will not abide when unrighteousness comes in.

6. For wisdom is a loving spirit; and will not acquit a blasphemer of his words: For Êlôhîym is witness of his reins, and a true beholder of his heart, and a hearer of his tongue.

7. For the spirit of Yahuah fills the world: And that which contains all things has knowledge of the voice.

8. Therefore he that speaks unrighteous things cannot be hid: Neither shall vengeance, when it punishes, pass by him.

9. For inquisition shall be made into the counsels of the ungodly: And the sound of his words shall come unto Yahuah for the manifestation of his wicked deeds.

10. For the ear of jealousy hears all things: And the noise of murmurings is not hid.

11. Therefore beware of murmuring, which is unprofitable; and refrain your tongue from backbiting: For there is no word so secret, that shall go for nothing: And the mouth that slander slays the soul.

12. Do not seek death in the error of your life: And do not pull upon yourselves destruction with the works of your hands.

13. For Êlôhîym did not make death: Neither he has pleasure in the destruction of the living.

14. For he created all things, that they might have their being: And the generations of the world were healthful; and there is no poison of destruction in them, nor the kingdom of death upon the earth:

15. For righteousness is immortal:

16. But ungodly men with their works and words called it to them: For when they thought to I have it their friend, they consumed to nothing, and made a covenant with it, because they are worthy to take part with it.

Chapter 2

1. For the ungodly said, reasoning with themselves, but not right, our life is short and tedious, and in the death of a man there is no remedy: Neither was there any man known to have returned from the grave.

2. For we are born at all adventure: And we shall be hereafter as though we had never been: For the breath in our nostrils is as smoke, and a little spark in the moving of our heart:

3. Which being extinguished, our body shall be turned into ashes, and our spirit shall vanish as the soft air,

4. And our name shall be forgotten in time, and no man shall have our works in remembrance, and our life shall pass away as the trace of a cloud, and shall be dispersed as a mist, that is driven away with the beams of the sun, and overcome with the heat thereof.

5. For our time is a very shadow that passes away; and after our end there is no returning: For it is fast sealed, so that no man comes again.

6. Come on therefore, let us enjoy the good things that are present: And let us speedily use the creatures like as in youth.

7. Let us fill ourselves with costly wine and ointments: And let no flower of the spring pass by us:

8. Let us crown ourselves with rosebuds, before they are withered:

9. Let none of us go without his part of our voluptuousness: Let us leave tokens of our joyfulness in every place: For this is our portion, and our lot is this.

10. Let us oppress the poor righteous man, let us not spare the widow, nor reverence the ancient gray hairs of the aged.

11. Let our strength be the law of justice: For that which is feeble is found to be nothing worth.

12. Therefore let us lie in wait for the righteous; because he is not for our turn, and he is clean contrary to our doings: He upbraids us with our offending the law, and objects to our infamy the transgressing of our education.

13. He professes to have the knowledge of Êlôhîym: And he calls himself the child of Yahuah.

14. He was made to reprove our thoughts.

15. He is grievous unto us even to behold: For his life is not like other men's, his ways are of another fashion.

16. We are esteemed of him as counterfeits: He abstains from our ways as from filthiness: He pronounces the end of the just to be blessed, and makes his boast that Êlôhîym is his father.

17. Let us see if his words are true: And let us prove what shall happen in the end of him.

18. For if the just man is the son of Êlôhîym, he will help him, and deliver him from the hand of his enemies.

19. Let us examine him with despitefulness and torture, that we may know his meekness, and prove his patience.

20. Let us condemn him with a shameful death: For by his own saying he shall be respected.

21. Such things they did imagine, and were deceived: For their own wickedness has blinded them.

22. As for the mysteries of Êlôhîym, they did not know them: Neither they hoped for the wages of righteousness, nor discerned a reward for blameless souls.

23. For Êlôhîym created man to be immortal, and made him to be an image of his own eternity.

24. Nevertheless through envy of the devil came death into the world: And they that do hold of his side do find it.

Chapter 3

1. But the souls of the righteous are in the hand of Êlôhîym, and there shall no torment touch them.

2. In the sight of the unwise they seemed to die: And their departure is taken for misery,

3. And their going from us to be utter destruction: But they are in peace.

4. For though they are punished in the sight of men, yet is their hope full of immortality.

5. And having been a little chastised, they shall be greatly rewarded: For Êlôhîym proved them, and found them worthy for himself.

6. As gold in the furnace he has tried them, and received them as a burnt offering.

7. And in the time of their visitation they shall shine, and run to and fro like sparks among the stubble.

8. They shall judge the nations, and have dominion over the people, and their Yahuah shall reign forever.

9. They that put their trust in him shall understand the truth: And such as are faithful in love shall abide with him: For grace and mercy is to his qôdesh, and he has care for his elect.

10. But the ungodly shall be punished according to their own imaginations, which have neglected the righteous, and forsaken Yahuah.

11. For whoso despises wisdom and nurture, he is miserable, and their hope is vain, their labors unfruitful, and their works unprofitable:

12. Their women are foolish, and their children wicked:

13. Their offspring is cursed. Wherefore blessed is the barren that is undefiled, which has not known the sinful bed: She shall have fruit in the visitation of souls.

14. And blessed is the eunuch, which with his hands has wrought no iniquity, nor imagined wicked things against Êlôhîym: For unto him shall be given the special gift of faith, and an inheritance in the temple of Yahuah more acceptable to his mind.

15. For glorious is the fruit of good labors: And the root of wisdom shall never fall away.

16. As for the children of adulterers, they shall not come to their perfection, and the seed of an unrighteous bed shall be rooted out.

17. For though they live long, yet shall they be nothing regarded: And their last age shall be without honor.

18. Or, if they die quickly, they have no hope, neither comfort in the day of trial.

19. For horrible is the end of the unrighteous generation.

Chapter 4

1. Better it is to have no children, and to have virtue: For the memorial thereof is immortal: Because it is known with Êlôhîym, and with men.

2. When it is present, men take example at it; and when it is gone, they desire it: It wears a crown, and triumphs forever, having gotten the victory, striving for undefiled rewards.

3. But the multiplying brood of the ungodly shall not thrive, nor take deep rooting from bastard slips, nor lay any fast foundation.

4. For though they flourish in branches for a time; yet standing do not last, they shall be shaken with the wind, and through the force of winds they shall be rooted out.

5. The imperfect branches shall be broken off, their fruit unprofitable, not ripe to eat, yea, meet for nothing.

6. For children begotten of unlawful beds are witnesses of wickedness against their parents in their trial.

7. But though the righteous are prevented with death, yet he shall be in rest.

8. For honorable age is not that which stands in length of time, nor that is measured by number of years.

9. But wisdom is the gray hair unto men, and an unspotted life is old age.

10. He pleased Êlôhîym, and was beloved of him: So that living among sinners he was translated.

11. Yea speedily was he taken away, lest that wickedness should alter his understanding, or deceit beguile his soul.

12. For the bewitching of naughtiness does obscure things that are honest; and the wandering of concupiscence does undermine the simple mind.

13. He, being made perfect in a short time, fulfilled a long time:

14. For his soul pleased Yahuah: Therefore he hasted to take him away from among the wicked.

15. This the people saw, and did not understand it, neither laid they up this in their minds, that his grace and mercy is with his qôdesh, and that he has respect unto his chosen.

16. Thus the righteous that is dead shall condemn the ungodly which are living; and youth that is soon perfected the many years and old age of the unrighteous.

17. For they shall see the end of the wise, and shall not understand what Êlôhîym in his counsel has decreed of him, and to what end Yahuah has set him in safety.

18. They shall see him, and despise him; but Êlôhîym shall laugh them to scorn: And they shall hereafter be a vile carcass, and a reproach among the dead forevermore.

19. For he shall rend them, and cast them down headlong, that they shall be speechless; and he shall shake them from the foundation; and they shall be utterly laid waste, and be in sorrow; and their memorial shall perish.

20. And when they cast up the accounts of their sins, they shall come with fear: And their own iniquities shall convince them to their face.

Chapter 5

1. Then shall the righteous man stand in great boldness before the face of such as have afflicted him, and made no account of his labors.

2. When they see it, they shall be troubled with terrible fear, and shall be amazed at the strangeness of his salvation, so far beyond all that they looked for.

3. And they repenting and groaning for anguish of spirit shall say within themselves, this was he, whom we had sometimes in derision, and a proverb of reproach:

4. We fools accounted his life madness, and his end to be without honor:

5. How is he numbered among the children of Êlôhîym, and his lot is among the qôdesh!

6. Therefore have we erred from the way of truth, and the light of righteousness has not shined unto us, and the sun of righteousness did not rise upon us.

7. We wearied ourselves in the way of wickedness and destruction: Yea, we have gone through deserts, where there lay no way: But as for the way of Yahuah, we have not known it.

8. What has pride profited us? Or what good has riches with our vaunting brought us?

9. All those things are passed away like a shadow, and as a post that hasted by;

10. And as a ship that passes over the waves of the water, which when it is gone by, the trace thereof cannot be found, neither the pathway of the keel in the waves;

11. Or as when a bird has flown through the air, there is no token of her way to be found, but the light air being beaten with the stroke of her wings and parted with the violent noise and motion of them, is passed through, and therein afterwards no sign where she went is to be found;

12. Or like as when an arrow is shot at a mark, it parts the air, which immediately comes together again, so that a man cannot know where it went through:

13. Even so we in like manner, as soon as we were born, began to draw to our end, and had no sign of virtue to show; but were consumed in our own wickedness.

14. For the hope of the ungodly is like dust that is blown away with the wind; like a thin froth that is driven away with the storm; like as the smoke which is dispersed here and there with a tempest, and passes away as the remembrance of a guest that tarries but a day.

15. But the righteous live forevermore; their reward also is with Yahuah, and the care of them is with Elyôn Êl.

16. Therefore shall they receive a glorious kingdom, and a beautiful crown from Yahuah's hand: For with his right hand shall he cover them, and with his arm shall he protect them.

17. He shall take to him his jealousy for complete armor, and make the creature his weapon for the revenge of his enemies.

18. He shall put on righteousness as a breastplate, and true judgment instead of a helmet.

19. He shall take qôdesh for an invincible shield.

20. His severe wrath shall he sharpen for a sword, and the world shall fight with him against the unwise.

21. Then shall the right aiming thunderbolts go abroad; and from the clouds, as from a well drawn bow, shall they fly to the mark.

22. And hailstones full of wrath shall be cast as out of a stone bow, and the water of the sea shall rage against them, and the floods shall cruelly drown them.

23. Yea, a mighty wind shall stand up against them, and like a storm shall blow them away: Thus iniquity shall lay waste the whole earth, and ill dealing shall overthrow the thrones of the mighty.

Chapter 6

1. Hear therefore, O you kings, and understand; learn, you that are judges of the ends of the earth.

2. Give ear, you that rule the people, and glory in the multitude of nations.

3. For power is given you of Yahuah, and sovereignty from Elyôn Êl, who shall try your works, and search out your counsels.

4. Because, being ministers of his kingdom, you have not judged right, nor kept the law, nor walked after the counsel of Êlôhîym;

5. Horribly and speedily shall he come upon you: For a sharp judgment shall be to them that are in high places.

6. For mercy will soon pardon the meanest: But mighty men shall be mightily tormented.

7. For he which is Yahuah over all shall fear no man's person, neither shall he stand in

awe of any man's greatness: For he has made the small and great, and cares for all alike.

8. But a sore trial shall come upon the mighty.

9. Unto you therefore, O kings, I do speak, that you may learn wisdom, and not fall away.

10. For they that keep holiness qôdesh shall be justified qâdôsh: And they that have learned such things shall find what to answer.

11. Wherefore set your affection upon my words; desire them, and y shall be instructed.

12. Wisdom is glorious, and never fades away: Yea, she is easily seen of them that love her, and found of such as seek her.

13. She prevents them that desire her, in making herself first known unto them.

14. Whoso seeks her early shall have no great travail: For he shall find her sitting at his doors.

15. To think therefore upon her is perfection of wisdom: And whoso watches for her shall quickly be without care.

16. For she goes about seeking such as are worthy of her, shows herself favorably unto them in the ways, and meets them in every thought.

17. For the very true beginning of her is the desire of discipline; and the care of discipline is love;

18. And love is the keeping of her laws; and the giving heed unto her laws is the assurance of incorruption;

19. And incorruption makes us near unto Êlôhîym:

20. Therefore the desire of wisdom brings to a kingdom.

21. If your delight is then in thrones and scepters, O you kings of the people, honor wisdom, that you may reign forevermore.

22. As for wisdom, what she is, and how she came up, I will tell you, and will not hide mysteries from you: But will seek her out from the beginning of her nativity, and bring the knowledge of her into light, and will not pass over the truth.

23. Neither I will go with consuming envy; for such a man shall have no fellowship with wisdom.

24. But the multitude of the wise is the welfare of the world: And a wise king is the upholding of the people.

25. Receive therefore instruction through my words, and it shall do you good.

Chapter 7

1. I myself also am a mortal man, like to all, and the offspring of him that was first made of the earth,

2. And in my mother's womb was fashioned to be flesh in the time of ten months, being compacted in blood, of the seed of man, and the pleasure that came with sleep.

3. And when I was born, I drew in the common air, and fell upon the earth, which is of like nature, and the first voice which I uttered was crying, as all others do.

4. I was nursed in swaddling clothes, and that with cares.

5. For there is no king that had any other beginning of birth.

6. For all men have one entrance into life, and the like going out.

7. Wherefore I prayed, and understanding was given me: I called upon Êlôhîym, and the spirit of wisdom came to me.

8. I preferred her before scepters and thrones, and esteemed riches nothing in comparison of her.

9. I did not compare unto her any precious stone neither, because all gold in respect of her is as a little sand, and silver shall be counted as clay before her.

10. I loved her above health and beauty, and chose to have her instead of light: For the light that comes from her never goes out.

11. All good things together came to me with her, and innumerable riches in her hands.

12. And I rejoiced in them all, because wisdom goes before them: And I did not know that she was the mother of them.

13. I learned diligently, and do communicate her liberally: I do not hide her riches.

14. For she is a treasure unto men that never fails: Which they that use become the friends of Êlôhîym, being commended for the gifts that come from learning.

15. Êlôhîym has granted me to speak as I would, and to conceive as is meet for the things that are given me: Because it is he that leads unto wisdom, and directs the wise.

16. For in his hand are both we and our words; all wisdom also, and knowledge of workmanship.

17. For he has given me certain knowledge of the things that are, namely, to know how the world was made, and the operation of the elements:

18. The beginning, ending, and midst of the times: The alterations of the turning of the sun, and the change of seasons:

19. The circuits of years, and the positions of stars:

20. The natures of living creatures, and the furies of wild beasts: The violence of winds, and the reasoning of men: The diversities of plants and the virtues of roots:

21. And all such things as are either secret or manifest, them I know.

22. For wisdom, which is the worker of all things, taught me: For in her is an understanding spirit holy, one only, manifold, subtle, lively, clear, undefiled, plain, not subject to hurt, loving the thing that is good quick, which cannot be let, ready to do good,

23. Kind to man, steadfast, sure, free from care, having all power, overseeing all things, and going through all understanding, pure, and most subtle, spirits.

24. For wisdom is more moving than any motion: She passes and goes through all things because of her pureness.

25. For she is the breath of the power of Êlôhîym, and a pure influence flowing from the glory of Shadday Êl: Therefore can no defiled thing fall into her.

26. For she is the brightness of the everlasting light, the unspotted mirror of the power of Êlôhîym, and the image of his goodness.

27. And being but one, she can do all things: And remaining in herself, she makes all things new: And in all ages entering into qâdôsh souls, she makes them friends of Êlôhîym, and Nâbîy.

28. For Êlôhîym loves none but him that dwells with wisdom.

29. For she is more beautiful than the sun, and above all the order of stars: Being compared with the light, she is found before it.

30. For after this comes night: But vice shall not prevail against wisdom.

Chapter 8

1. Wisdom reaches from one end to another mightily: And sweetly does she order all things.

2. I loved her, and sought her out from my youth, I desired to make her my spouse, and I was a lover of her beauty.

3. In that she is conversant with Êlôhîym, she magnifies her nobility: Yea, Yahuah of all things himself loved her.

4. For she is privy to the mysteries of the knowledge of Êlôhîym, and a lover of his works.

5. If riches is a possession to be desired in this life; what is richer than wisdom that works all things?

6. And if prudence work; who of all that are is a more cunning workman than she?

7. And if a man love righteousness her labors are virtues: For she teaches temperance and prudence, justice and fortitude: Which are such things, as men can have nothing more profitable in their life.

8. If a man desire much experience, she knows things of old, and conjectures right what is to come: She knows the subtleties of speeches, and can expound dark sentences: She foresees signs and wonders, and the events of seasons and times.

9. Therefore I purposed to take her to me to live with me, knowing that she would is a counsellor of good things, and a comfort in cares and grief.

10. For her sake I shall have estimation among the multitude, and honor with the elders, though I am young.

11. I shall be found of a quick conceit in judgment, and shall be admired in the sight of great men.

12. When I hold my tongue, they shall bide my leisure, and when I speak, they shall give good ear unto me: If I talk much, they shall lay their hands upon their mouth.

13. Moreover by the means of her I shall obtain immortality, and leave behind me an everlasting memorial to them that come after me.

14. I shall set the people in order, and the nations shall be subject unto me.

15. Horrible tyrants shall be afraid, when they do but hear of me; I shall be found good among the multitude, and valiant in war.

16. After I am come into my house, I will repose myself with her: For her conversation has no bitterness; and to live with her has no sorrow, but mirth and joy.

17. Now when I considered these things in myself, and pondered them in my heart, how that to be allied unto wisdom is immortality;

18. And great pleasure it is to have her friendship; and in the works of her hands are infinite riches; and in the exercise of conference with her, prudence; and in talking with her, a good report; I went about seeking how to take her to me.

19. For I was a witty child, and had a good spirit.

20. Yea rather, being good, I came into a body undefiled.

21. Nevertheless, when I perceived that I could not otherwise obtain her, except Êlôhîym gave her to me; and that was a point of wisdom also to know whose gift she was; I prayed unto Yahuah, and besought him, and with my whole heart I said,

Chapter 9

1. O Êlôhîym of my fathers, and Yahuah of mercy, who has made all things with your word,

2. And ordained man through your wisdom, that he should have dominion over the creatures which you have made,

3. And order the world according to equity and righteousness, and execute judgment with an upright heart:

4. Give me wisdom that sits by your throne; and do not reject me from among your children:

5. For I your servant and son of your handmaid am a feeble person, and of a short time, and too young for the understanding of judgment and laws.

6. For though a man is never so perfect among the children of men, yet if your wisdom is not with him, he shall be nothing regarded.

7. You have chosen me to be a king of your people, and a judge of your sons and daughters:

8. You have commanded me to build a temple upon your qâdôsh mount, and an altar in the city wherein you dwell, a resemblance of the qâdôsh tabernacle, which you have prepared from the beginning.

9. And wisdom was with you: Which knows your works, and was present when you made the world, and knew what was acceptable in your sight, and right in your commandments.

10. O send her out of your qâdôsh shâmayim, and from the throne of your glory, that being present she may labor with me, that I may know what is pleasing unto you.

11. For she knows and understands all things, and she shall lead me soberly in my doings, and preserve me in her power.

12. So shall my works be acceptable, and then I shall judge your people righteously, and be worthy to sit in my father's seat.

13. For what man is he that can know the counsel of Êlôhîym? Or who can think what the will of Yahuah is?

14. For the thoughts of mortal men are miserable, and our devices are but uncertain.

15. For the corruptible body presses down the soul, and the earthy tabernacle weighs down the mind that muses upon many things.

16. And hardly do we guess right at things that are upon earth, and with labor do we find the things that are before us: But the things that are in shâmayim who has searched out?

17. And your counsel who has known, except you give wisdom, and send your qâdôsh spirit from above?

18. For so the ways of them which lived on the earth were reformed, and men were taught the things that are pleasing unto you, and were saved through wisdom.

Chapter 10

1. She preserved the first formed father of the world, that was created alone, and brought him out of his fall,

2. And gave him power to rule all things.

3. But when the unrighteous went away from her in his anger, he perished also in the fury wherewith he murdered his brother.

4. For whose cause the earth being drowned with the flood, wisdom again preserved it, and directed the course of the righteous in a piece of wood of small value.

5. Moreover, the nations in their wicked conspiracy being confounded, she found out the righteous, and preserved him blameless unto Êlôhîym, and kept him strong against his tender compassion toward his son.

6. When the ungodly perished, she delivered the righteous man, who fled from the fire which fell down upon the five cities.

7. Of whose wickedness even to this day the waste land that smokes is a testimony, and plants bearing fruit that never come to ripeness: And a standing pillar of salt is a monument of an unbelieving soul.

8. For not regarding wisdom, they got not only this hurt that they did not know the things which were good; but also left behind them to the world a memorial of their foolishness: So that in the things wherein they offended they could not so much as is hid.

9. But wisdom delivered from pain those that attended upon her.

10. When the righteous fled from his brother's wrath she guided him in right paths, showed him the kingdom of Êlôhîym, and gave him knowledge of qâdôsh things, made him rich in his travels, and multiplied the fruit of his labors.

11. In the covetousness of such as oppressed him she stood by him, and made him rich.

12. She defended him from his enemies, and kept him safe from those that lay in wait, and in a sore conflict she gave him the victory; that he might know that goodness is stronger than all.

13. When the righteous was sold, she did not forsake him, but delivered him from sin: She went down with him into the pit,

14. And did not leave him in bonds, till she brought him the scepter of the kingdom, and power against those that oppressed him: As for them that had accused him, she showed them to be liars, and gave him perpetual glory.

15. She delivered the righteous people and blameless seed from the nation that oppressed them.

16. She entered into the soul of the servant of Yahuah, and withstood dreadful kings in wonders and signs;

17. Rendered to the righteous a reward of their labors, guided them in a marvelous way, and was unto them for a cover by day, and a light of stars in the night season;

18. Brought them through the Red sea, and led them through much water:

19. But she drowned their enemies, and cast them up out of the bottom of the deep.

20. Therefore the righteous spoiled the ungodly, and praised your qâdôsh name, O Yahuah, and magnified with one accord your hand that fought for them.

21. For wisdom opened the mouth of the dumb, and made the tongues of them that cannot speak eloquent.

Chapter 11

1. She prospered their works in the hand of the qâdôsh Nâbîy.

2. They went through the wilderness that was not inhabited, and pitched tents in places where there lay no way.

3. They stood against their enemies, and were avenged of their adversaries.

4. When they were thirsty, they called upon you, and water was given them out of the flinty rock, and their thirst was quenched out of the hard stone.

5. For by what things their enemies were punished, by the same they in their need were benefited.

6. For instead of a perpetual running river troubled with foul blood,

7. For a manifest reproof of that commandment, whereby the infants were slain, you

gave unto them abundance of water by a means which they did not hope for:

8. Declaring by that thirst then how you had punished their adversaries.

9. For when they were tried although but in mercy chastised, they knew how the ungodly were judged in wrath and tormented, thirsting in another manner than the just.

10. For these you did admonish and try, as a father: But the other, as a severe king, you did condemn and punish.

11. Whether they were absent or present, they were vexed alike.

12. For a double grief came upon them, and a groaning for the remembrance of things past.

13. For when they heard by their own punishments the other to be benefited, they had some feeling of Yahuah.

14. For whom they respected with scorn, when he was long before thrown out at the casting forth of the infants, him in the end, when they saw what came to pass, they admired.

15. But for the foolish devices of their wickedness, wherewith being deceived they worshipped serpents void of reason, and vile beasts, you did send a multitude of unreasonable beasts upon them for vengeance;

16. That they might know, that wherewithal a man sins, by the same also shall he be punished.

17. For your almighty hand, that made the world of matter without form, wanted not means to send among them a multitude of bears or fierce lions,

18. Or unknown wild beasts, full of rage, newly created, breathing out either a fiery vapor, or filthy scents of scattered smoke, or shooting horrible sparkles out of their eyes:

19. Whereof not only the harm might dispatch them at once, but also the terrible sight utterly destroy them.

20. Yea, and without these might they have fallen down with one blast, being persecuted of vengeance, and scattered abroad through the breath of your power: But you have ordered all things in measure and number and weight.

21. For you can show your great strength at all times when you will; and who may withstand the power of your arm?

22. For the whole world before you is as a little grain of the balance, yea, as a drop of the morning dew that falls down upon the earth.

23. But you have mercy upon all; for you can do all things, and wink at the sins of men, because they should amend.

24. For you love all the things that are, and abhor nothing which you have made: For never would you have made any thing, if you had hated it.

25. And how could any thing have endured, if it had not been your will? Or been preserved, if not called by you?

26. But you spare all: For they are your, O Yahuah, you lover of souls.

Chapter 12

1. For your incorruptible spirit is in all things.

2. Therefore you chasten them by little and little that offend, and warn them by putting them in remembrance wherein they have offended, that leaving their wickedness they may believe on you, O Yahuah.

3. For it was your will to destroy by the hands of our fathers both those old inhabitants of your qâdôsh land,

4. Whom you hated for doing most odious works of witchcrafts, and wicked sacrifices;

5. And also those merciless murderers of children, and devourers of man's flesh, and the feasts of blood,

6. With their Kôhên out of the midst of their idolatrous crew, and the parents, that killed with their own hands souls destitute of help:

7. That the land, which you esteemed above all other, might receive a worthy colony of Êlôhîym's children.

8. Nevertheless even those you spared as men, and did send wasps, forerunners of your host, to destroy them by little and little.

9. Not that you were unable to bring the ungodly under the hand of the righteous in battle, or to destroy them at once with cruel beasts, or with one rough word:

10. But executing your judgments upon them by little and little, you gave them place of repentance, not being ignorant that they were a naughty generation, and that their malice was bred in them, and that their cogitation would never be changed.

11. For it was a cursed seed from the beginning; neither did you for fear of any man give them pardon for those things wherein they sinned.

12. For who shall say, what you have done? Or who shall withstand your judgment? Or who shall accuse you for the nations that perish, whom you made? Or who shall come to stand against you, to be revenged for the unrighteous men?

13. For neither is there any Êlôhîym but you that cares for all, to whom you might show that your judgment is not wrong.

14. Neither shall king or tyrant be able to set his face against you for any whom you have punished.

15. For so much then as you are righteous yourself, you ordered all things righteously: Thinking it not agreeable with your power to condemn him that has not deserved to be punished.

16. For your power is the beginning of righteousness, and because you are Yahuah of all, it makes you to be gracious unto all.

17. For when men will not believe that you are of a full power, you show your strength, and among them that know it you make their boldness manifest.

18. But you, mastering your power, judge with equity, and order us with great favor: For you may use power when you will.

19. But by such works you have taught your people that the just man should be merciful, and have made your children to be of a good hope that you give repentance for sins.

20. For if you did punish the enemies of your children, and the condemned to death, with such deliberation, giving them time and place, whereby they might be delivered from their malice:

21. With how great circumspection did you judge your own sons, unto whose fathers you have sworn, and made covenants of good promises?

22. Therefore, whereas you do chasten us, you scourge our enemies a thousand times more, to the intent that, when we judge, we should carefully think of your goodness,

and when we ourselves are judged, we should look for mercy.

23. Wherefore, whereas men have lived dissolutely and unrighteously, you have tormented them with their own abominations.

24. For they went astray very far in the ways of error, and held them for gods, which even among the beasts of their enemies were despised, being deceived, as children of no understanding.

25. Therefore unto them, as to children without the use of reason, you did send a judgment to mock them.

26. But they that would not be reformed by that correction, wherein he dallied with them, shall feel a judgment worthy of Êlôhîym.

27. For, look, for what things they grudged, when they were punished, that is, for them whom they thought to be gods; now being punished in them, when they saw it, they acknowledged him to be the true Êlôhîym, whom before they denied to know: And therefore came extreme damnation upon them.

Chapter 13

1. Surely vain are all men by nature, who are ignorant of Êlôhîym, and could not out of the good things that are seen know him that is: Neither by considering the works did they acknowledge the work master;

2. But deemed either fire, or wind, or the swift air, or the circle of the stars, or the violent water, or the lights of shâmayim, to be the gods which govern the world.

3. With whose beauty if they being delighted took them to be gods; let them know how much better Yahuah of them is: For the first author of beauty has created them.

4. But if they were astonished at their power and virtue, let them understand by them, how much mightier he is that made them.

5. For by the greatness and beauty of the creatures proportionally the maker of them is seen.

6. But yet for this they are the less to be blamed: For they peradventure err, seeking Êlôhîym, and desirous to find him.

7. For being conversant in his works they search him diligently, and believe their sight: Because the things are beautiful that are seen.

8. Howbeit neither are they to be pardoned.

9. For if they were able to know so much, that they could aim at the world; how did they not sooner find out Yahuah thereof?

10. But miserable are they, and in dead things is their hope, who call them gods, which are the works of men's hands, gold and silver, to show art in, and resemblances of beasts, or a stone good for nothing, the work of an ancient hand.

11. Now a carpenter that fells timber, after he has sawn down a tree meet for the purpose, and taken off all the bark skilfully round about, and has wrought it handsomely, and made a vessel thereof fit for the service of man's life;

12. And after spending the refuse of his work to dress his meat, has filled himself;

13. And taking the very refuse among those which served to no use, being a crooked piece of wood, and full of knots, has carved it diligently, when he had nothing else to do, and formed it by the skill of his understanding, and fashioned it to the image of a man;

14. Or made it like some vile beast, laying it over with vermilion, and with paint coloring it red, and covering every spot therein;

15. And when he had made a convenient room for it, set it in a wall, and made it fast with iron:

16. For he provided for it that it might not fall, knowing that it was unable to help itself; for it is an image, and has need of help:

17. Then he makes prayer for his goods, for his woman and children, and is not ashamed to speak to that which has no life.

18. For health he calls upon that which is weak: For life prays to that which is dead; for aid humbly beseeches that which has least means to help: And for a good journey he asks of that which cannot set a foot forward:

19. And for gaining and getting, and for good success of his hands, asks ability to do of him that is most unable to do anything.

Chapter 14

1. Again, one preparing himself to sail, and about to pass through the raging waves, calls upon a piece of wood more rotten than the vessel that carries him.

2. For verily desire of gain devised that, and the workman built it by his skill.

3. But your providence, O father, governs it: For you have made a way in the sea, and a safe path in the waves;

4. Showing that you can save from all danger: Yea, though a man went to sea without art.

5. Nevertheless you would not that the works of your wisdom should be idle, and therefore do men commit their lives to a small piece of wood, and passing the rough sea in a weak vessel are saved.

6. For in the old time also, when the proud nephîyl perished, the hope of the world governed by your hand escaped in a weak vessel, and left to all ages a seed of generation.

7. For blessed is the wood whereby righteousness comes.

8. But that which is made with hands is cursed, as well it, as he that made it: He, because he made it; and it, because, being corruptible, it was called Êlôhîym.

9. For the ungodly and his ungodliness are both alike hateful unto Êlôhîym.

10. For that which is made shall be punished together with him that made it.

11. Therefore even upon the idols of the Gentiles shall there be a visitation: Because in the creature of Êlôhîym they are become an abomination, and stumbling blocks to the souls of men, and a snare to the feet of the unwise.

12. For the devising of idols was the beginning of spiritual fornication, and the invention of them the corruption of life.

13. For neither were they from the beginning, neither shall they be forever.

14. For by the vain glory of men they entered into the world, and therefore shall they come shortly to an end.

15. For a father afflicted with untimely mourning, when he has made an image of his child soon taken away, now honored him as a god, which was then a dead man, and delivered to those that were under him ceremonies and sacrifices.

16. Thus in process of time an ungodly custom grown strong was kept as a law, and graven images were worshipped by the commandments of kings.

17. Whom men could not honor in presence, because they dwelt far off, they took the counterfeit of his visage from far, and made an express image of a king whom they honored, to the end that by this their

forwardness they might flatter him that was absent, as if he were present.

18. Also the singular diligence of the artificer did help to set forward the ignorant to more superstition.

19. For he, peradventure willing to please one in authority, forced all his skill to make the resemblance of the best fashion.

20. And so the multitude, allured by the grace of the work, took him now for a god, which a little before was but honored.

21. And this was an occasion to deceive the world: For men, serving either calamity or tyranny, did ascribe unto stones and stocks the incommunicable name.

22. Moreover this was not enough for them that they erred in the knowledge of Êlôhîym; but whereas they lived in the great war of ignorance, those so great plagues they called peace.

23. For while they slew their children in sacrifices, or used secret ceremonies, or made reveling of strange rites;

24. They kept neither lives nor marriages any longer undefiled: But either one slew another traitorously, or grieved him by adultery.

25. So that there reigned in all men without exception blood, manslaughter, theft, and dissimulation, corruption, unfaithfulness, tumults, perjury,

26. Disquieting of good men, forgetfulness of good turns, defiling of souls, changing of kind, disorder in marriages, adultery, and shameless uncleanness.

27. For the worshipping of idols not to be named is the beginning, the cause, and the end, of all evil.

28. For either they are mad when they are merry, or prophesy lies, or live unjustly, or else lightly forswear themselves.

29. For insomuch as their trust is in idols, which have no life; though they swear falsely, yet they do not look to be hurt.

30. Howbeit for both causes shall they be justly punished: Both because they did not think well of Êlôhîym, giving heed unto idols, and also unjustly swore in deceit, despising qôdesh.

31. For it is not the power of them by whom they swear: But it is the just vengeance of sinners, that punishes always the offence of the ungodly.

Chapter 15

1. But you, O Êlôhîym, are gracious and true, longsuffering, and in mercy ordering all things,

2. For if we sin, we are yours, knowing your power: But we will not sin, knowing that we are counted your.

3. For to know you is perfect righteousness: Yea, to know your power is the root of immortality.

4. For neither did the mischievous invention of men deceive us, nor an image spotted with divers colors, the painter's fruitless labor;

5. The sight whereof entices fools to lust after it, and so they desire the form of a dead image, that has no breath.

6. Both they that make them, they that desire them, and they that worship them, are lovers of evil things, and are worthy to have such things to trust upon.

7. For the potter, tempering soft earth, fashions every vessel with much labor for our

service: Yea, of the same clay he makes both the vessels that serve for clean uses, and likewise also all such as serve to the contrary: But what is the use of either sort, the potter himself is the judge.

8. And employing his labors lewdly, he makes a vain god of the same clay, even he which a little before was made of earth himself, and within a little while after returns to the same, out when his life which was lent him shall be demanded.

9. Notwithstanding his care is, not that he shall have much labor, nor that his life is short: But strives to excel goldsmiths and silversmiths, and endeavors to do like the workers in brass, and counts it his glory to make counterfeit things.

10. His heart is ashes, his hope is viler than earth, and his life of less value than clay:

11. Forasmuch as did not know his Âśâh, and him that inspired into him an active soul, and breathed in a living spirit.

12. But they counted our life a pastime, and our time here a market for gain: for, say they, we must be getting every way, though it be by evil means.

13. For this man, that of earthly matter makes brittle vessels and graven images, knows himself to offend above all others.

14. And all the enemies of your people, that hold them in subjection, are most foolish, and are more miserable than very babes.

15. For they counted all the idols of the heathen to be gods: Which neither have the use of eyes to see, nor noses to draw breath, nor ears to hear, nor fingers of hands to handle; and as for their feet, they are slow to go.

16. For man made them, and he that borrowed his own spirit fashioned them: But no man can make a god like unto himself.

17. For being mortal, he works a dead thing with wicked hands: For he himself is better than the things which he worships: whereas he lived once, but they never.

18. Yea, they worshipped those beasts also that are most hateful: For being compared together, some are worse than others.

19. Neither are they beautiful, so much as to be desired in respect of beasts: But they went without the praise of Êlôhîym and his blessing.

Chapter 16

1. Therefore by the like were they punished worthily, and by the multitude of beasts tormented.

2. Instead of which punishment, dealing graciously with your own people, you prepared for them meat of a strange taste, even quails to stir up their appetite:

3. To the end that they, desiring food, might for the ugly sight of the beasts sent among them loathe even that, which they must needs desire; but these, suffering penury for a short space, might be made partakers of a strange taste.

4. For it was requisite that upon them exercising tyranny should come penury, which they could not avoid: But to these it should only be showed how their enemies were tormented.

5. For when the horrible fierceness of beasts came upon these, and they perished with the stings of crooked serpents, your wrath did not endure forever:

6. But they were troubled for a small season, that they might be admonished, having a sign of salvation, to put them in remembrance of the commandment of your law.

7. For he that turned himself toward it was not saved by the thing that he saw, but by you, that are the Yâsha of all.

8. And in this you made your enemies confess, that it is you who deliver from all evil:

9. For them the biting of grasshoppers and flies killed, neither was there found any remedy for their life: For they were worthy to be punished by such.

10. But your sons not the very teeth of venomous dragons overcame: For your mercy was ever by them, and healed them.

11. For they were pricked, that they should remember your words; and were quickly saved, that not falling into deep forgetfulness, they might be continually mindful of your goodness.

12. For it was neither herb, nor mollifying plaster, that restored them to health: But your word, O Yahuah, which heals all things.

13. For you have power of life and death: You lead to the gates of sheôl, and bring up again.

14. A man indeed kills through his malice: And the spirit, when it is gone forth, does not return; neither the soul received comes again.

15. But it is not possible to escape your hand.

16. For the ungodly, that denied to know you, were scourged by the strength of your arm: With strange rains, hails, and showers, were they persecuted, that they could not avoid, and through fire were they consumed.

17. For, which is most to be wondered at, the fire had more force in the water, that quenches all things: For the world fights for the righteous.

18. For some time the flame was mitigated, that it might not burn up the beasts that were sent against the ungodly; but themselves might see and perceive that they were persecuted with the judgment of Êlôhîym.

19. And at another time it burns even in the midst of water above the power of fire, that it might destroy the fruits of an unjust land.

20. Instead whereof you fed your own people with angels' food, and did send them from shâmayim bread prepared without their labor, able to content every man's delight, and agreeing to every taste.

21. For your sustenance declared your sweetness unto your children, and serving to the appetite of the eater, tempered itself to every man's liking.

22. But snow and ice endured the fire, and did not melt, that they might know that fire burning in the hail, and sparkling in the rain, did destroy the fruits of the enemies.

23. But this again did even forget his own strength, that the righteous might be nourished.

24. For the creature that serves you, who are the maker increases his strength against the unrighteous for their punishment, and abates his strength for the benefit of such as put their trust in you.

25. Therefore even then was it altered into all fashions, and was obedient to your grace, that nourishes all things, according to the desire of them that had need:

26. That your children, O Yahuah, whom you love, might know, that it is not the growing of fruits that nourishes man: But that it is your word, which preserves them that put their trust in you.

27. For that which was not destroyed of the fire, being warmed with a little sunbeam, soon melted away:

28. That it might be known, that we must prevent the sun to give you thanks, and at the dayspring pray unto you.

29. For the hope of the unthankful shall melt away as the winter's hoar frost, and shall run away as unprofitable water.

Chapter 17

1. For great are your judgments, and cannot be expressed: Therefore unnurtured souls have erred.

2. For when unrighteous men thought to oppress the qâdôsh nation; they being shut up in their houses, the prisoners of darkness, and fettered with the bonds of a long night, lay there exiled from the eternal providence.

3. For while they supposed to lie hid in their secret sins, they were scattered under a dark veil of forgetfulness, being horribly astonished, and troubled with strange apparitions.

4. For neither might the corner that held them keep them from fear: But noises as of waters falling down sounded about them, and sad visions appeared unto them with heavy countenances.

5. No power of the fire might give them light: Neither could the bright flames of the stars endure to lighten that horrible night.

6. Only there appeared unto them a fire kindled of itself, very dreadful: For being much terrified, they thought the things which they saw to be worse than the sight they did not see.

7. As for the illusions of art magic, they were put down, and their vaunting in wisdom was reproved with disgrace.

8. For they, that promised to drive away terrors and troubles from a sick soul, were sick themselves of fear, worthy to be laughed at.

9. For though no terrible thing did fear them; yet being scared with beasts that passed by, and hissing of serpents,

10. They died for fear, denying that they saw the air, which could of no side be avoided.

11. For wickedness, condemned by her own witness, is very timorous, and being pressed with conscience, always forecasts grievous things.

12. For fear is nothing else but a betraying of the succors which reason offers.

13. And the expectation from within, being less, counts the ignorance more than the cause which brings the torment.

14. But they sleeping the same sleep that night, which was indeed intolerable, and which came upon them out of the bottoms of inevitable sheôl,

15. Were partly vexed with monstrous apparitions, and partly fainted, their heart failing them: For a sudden fear, and not looked for, came upon them.

16. So then whosoever there fell down was straightly kept, shut up in a prison without iron bars,

17. For whether he were husbandman, or shepherd, or a laborer in the field, he was overtaken, and endured that necessity, which could not be avoided: For they were all bound with one chain of darkness.

18. Whether it were a whistling wind, or a melodious noise of birds among the spreading branches, or a pleasing fall of water running violently,

19. Or a terrible sound of stones cast down, or a running that could not be seen of skipping beasts, or a roaring voice of most savage wild beasts, or a rebounding echo from the hollow mountains; these things made them to swoon for fear.

20. For the whole world shined with clear light, and none were hindered in their labor:

21. Over them only was spread a heavy night, an image of that darkness which should afterward receive them: But yet were they unto themselves more grievous than the darkness.

Chapter 18

1. Nevertheless your qôdesh had a very great light, whose voice they hearing, and not seeing their shape, because they also had not suffered the same things, they counted them happy.

2. But for that they did not hurt them now, of whom they had been wronged before, they thanked them, and besought them pardon for that they had been enemies.

3. Instead whereof you gave them a burning pillar of fire, both to be a guide of the unknown journey, and a harmless sun to entertain them honorably.

4. For they were worthy to be deprived of light and imprisoned in darkness, who had kept your sons shut up, by whom the uncorrupt light of the law was to be given unto the world.

5. And when they had determined to slay the babes of the qôdesh, one child being cast forth, and saved, to reprove them, you took away the multitude of their children, and destroyed them altogether in a mighty water.

6. Of that night were our fathers certified afore, that assuredly knowing unto what oaths they had given credence, they might afterwards be of good cheer.

7. So of your people was accepted both the salvation of the righteous, and destruction of the enemies.

8. For wherewith you did punish our adversaries, by the same you did glorify us, whom you had called.

9. For the righteous children of good men did sacrifice secretly, and with one consent made a qâdôsh law, that the qôdesh should be like partakers of the same good and evil, the fathers now singing out the songs of praise.

10. But on the other side there sounded an ill according cry of the enemies, and a lamentable noise was carried abroad for children that were bewailed.

11. The master and the servant were punished after one manner; and like as the king, so suffered the common person.

12. So they all together had innumerable dead with one kind of death; neither were the living sufficient to bury them: For in one moment the noblest offspring of them was destroyed.

13. For whereas they would not believe anything because of the enchantments; upon the destruction of the firstborn, they acknowledged this people to be the sons of Êlôhîym.

14. For while all things were in quiet silence, and that night was in the midst of her swift course,

15. Your almighty word leaped down from shâmayim out of your royal throne, as a fierce man of war into the midst of a land of destruction,

16. And brought your unfeigned commandment as a sharp sword, and standing up filled all things with death; and it touched the shâmayim, but it stood upon the earth.

17. Then suddenly visions of horrible dreams troubled them sore, and terrors came upon them unlooked for.

18. And one thrown here, and another there, half dead, showed the cause of his death.

19. For the dreams that troubled them did foreshow this, lest they should perish, and not know why they were afflicted.

20. Yea, the tasting of death touched the righteous also, and there was a destruction of the multitude in the wilderness: But the wrath di not endure long.

21. For then the blameless man made haste, and stood forth to defend them; and bringing the shield of his proper ministry, even prayer, and the propitiation of incense, set himself against the wrath, and so brought the calamity to an end, declaring that he was your servant.

22. So he overcame the destroyer, not with strength of body, nor did force of arms, but with a word subdue him that punished, alleging the oaths and covenants made with the fathers.

23. For when the dead were now fallen down by heaps one upon another, standing between, he stayed the wrath, and parted the way to the living.

24. For in the long garment was the whole world, and in the four rows of the stones was the glory of the fathers graven, and your majesty upon the diadem of his head.

25. Unto these the destroyer gave place, and was afraid of them: For it was enough that they only tasted of the wrath.

Chapter 19

1. As for the ungodly, wrath came upon them without mercy unto the end: For he knew before what they would do;

2. How that having given them leave to depart, and sent them hastily away, they would repent and pursue them.

3. For while they were yet mourning and making lamentation at the graves of the dead, they added another foolish device, and pursued them as fugitives, whom they had entreated to be gone.

4. For the destiny, whereof they were worthy, drew them unto this end, and made them forget the things that had already happened, that they might fulfil the punishment which was wanting to their torments:

5. And that your people might pass a wonderful way: But they might find a strange death.

6. For the whole creature in his proper kind was fashioned again anew, serving the peculiar commandments that were given unto them, that your children might be kept without hurt:

7. As namely, a cloud shadowing the camp; and where water stood before, dry land appeared; and out of the Red sea away without impediment; and out of the violent stream a green field:

8. Where through all the people went that were defended with your hand, seeing your marvelous strange wonders.

9. For they went at large like horses, and leaped like lambs, praising you, O Yahuah, who had delivered them.

10. For they were yet mindful of the things that were done while they sojourned in the strange land, how the ground brought forth flies instead of cattle, and how the river cast up a multitude of frogs instead of fishes.

11. But afterwards they saw a new generation of fowls, when, being led with their appetite, they asked delicate meats.

12. For quails came up unto them from the sea for their contentment.

13. And punishments came upon the sinners not without former signs by the force of thunders: For they suffered justly according to their own wickedness, insomuch as they used a harder and hateful behavior toward strangers.

14. For the Sedôm did not receive those, whom they knew not when they came: But these brought friends into bondage that had well deserved of them.

15. And not only so, but peradventure some respect shall be had of those, because they used strangers not friendly:

16. But these very grievously afflicted them, whom they had received with feastings, and were already made partakers of the same laws with them.

17. Therefore even with blindness were these stricken, as those were at the doors of the righteous man: When, being compassed about with horrible great darkness, every one sought the passage of his own doors.

18. For the elements were changed in themselves by a kind of harmony, like as in a psaltery notes change the name of the tune, and yet are always sounds; which may well be perceived by the sight of the things that have been done.

19. For earthly things were turned into watery, and the things, that before swam in the water, now went upon the ground.

20. The fire had power in the water, forgetting his own virtue: And the water forgot his own quenching nature.

21. On the other side, the flames did not waste the flesh of the corruptible living things, though they walked therein; neither melted they the icy kind of shâmayim meat that was of nature apt to melt.

22. For in all things, O Yahuah, you did magnify your people, and glorify them, neither you did lightly regard them: But did assist them in every time and place.

1 Ezrâ (Esdras) & The Traditional Bible Parallels

(Dabar Yahuah Scriptures Study Guide)

Introduction

1 Ezrâ is part of the apocryphal/deuterocanonical writings. It closely parallels the canonical Ezra and Nehemiah narratives but includes additional material such as the **"Three Guardsmen" debate**, which is not found in traditional canonical texts. This book clarifies events of the Babylonian exile, the return to Jerusalem, and the rebuilding of the temple, providing insights into Yahûdîy wisdom, leadership, and Êlôhîym's providence.

Comparison Table: 1 Ezrâ vs. The Bible

1 Ezrâ Passage	Biblical Parallels	Theme / Connection
1 Ezrâ 1:1–2 – "All Yasharel went into exile for seventy years."	2 Chr 36:21; Jer 25:11; Dan 9:2	Babylonian exile period.
1 Ezrâ 2:1–68 – Genealogies of returnees.	Ezra 2; Neh 7	Listing of families returning from exile.
1 Ezrâ 3:1–4 – Zerubbabel leads rebuilding of the altar.	Ezra 3:1–6	Reestablishment of temple worship.
1 Ezrâ 3:9–4:24 – Opposition from adversaries trying to halt rebuilding.	Ezra 4	Opposition from surrounding peoples; similar narrative.
1 Ezrâ 5:1–17 – Prophet Haggai encourages Zerubbabel.	Hag 1:1–15	Êlôhîym's word through prophets to motivate rebuilding.
1 Ezrâ 7:1–52 – "Three Guardsmen" debate over what is strongest: Wine, the King, Women.	Sirach 25:14–15; Prov 31	Wisdom and moral discussion; not in canonical Ezra/Nehemiah.
1 Ezrâ 8:1–68 – Ezra reads the Law before the people.	Neh 8; Deut 31:9–13	Public reading of Torah, covenant renewal.
1 Ezrâ 9:1–15 – Intermarriage with foreign women addressed.	Ezra 9–10	Social and religious reform among returning exiles.
1 Ezrâ 10:1–44 – Purification of Yasharel through separation from foreigners.	Ezra 10:1–44	Obedience to Torah, national and religious identity restored.
1 Ezrâ 12:1–20 – Leadership and governance established under Ezra.	Neh 8–9	Ensuring spiritual and civil order post-exile.

Summary of Key Parallels

1. Exile & Return – Confirms Babylonian exile period and return under Cyrus' decree.

2. Temple Rebuilding – Zerubbabel, Yêshûa, and the leaders reestablish worship.

3. Prophetic Encouragement – Haggai and Zechariah's roles emphasized.

4. Wisdom Literature – "Three Guardsmen" debate illustrates moral reasoning, absent in canonical Ezra.

5. Law & Covenant Renewal – Reading of Torah and reforms to restore Yasharel's spiritual identity.

6. Opposition & Perseverance – Highlights Êlôhîym's providence and the challenges in rebuilding community and temple.

1 Ezrâ (עֶזְרָא) - 1 Esdras

Chapter 1

1. And Yôshîyâhû held the feast of the Pesach in Yarûshâlaim unto his Yahuah, and offered the Pesach the fourteenth day of the first month;

2. Having set the Kôhên according to their daily courses, being arrayed in long garments, in the temple of Yahuah.

3. And he spoke unto the Lêwîy, the qâdôsh ministers of Yâshârêl that they should hallow themselves unto Yahuah, to set the qâdôsh ark of Yahuah in the house that king Shelômôh the son of Dâwid had built:

4. And said, you shall no more bear the ark upon your shoulders: Now therefore serve Yahuah your Êlôhîym, and minister unto his people Yâshârêl, and prepare you after your families and kindreds,

5. According as Dâwid the king of Yâshârêl prescribed, and according to the magnificence of Shelômôh his son: And standing in the temple according to the several dignity of the families of you the Lêwîy, who minister in the presence of your brethren the children of Yâshârêl,

6. Offer the Pesach in order, and make ready the sacrifices for your brethren, and keep the Pesach according to the commandment of Yahuah, which was given unto Môsheh.

7. And unto the people that was found there Yôshîyâhû gave thirty thousand lambs and kids, and three thousand calves: These things were given of the king's allowance, according as he promised, to the people, to the Kôhên, and to the Lêwîy.

8. And Chilqîyâhû (חִלְקִיָּהוּ), Zekaryâhû (זְכַרְיָה), and Yachîyêl (יְחִיאֵל), the governors of the temple, gave to the Kôhên for the Pesach two thousand and six hundred sheep, and three hundred calves.

9. And Yakonyâhû (יְכָנְיָהוּ), and Shemayâhû (שְׁמַעְיָהוּ), and Nethanêl (נְתַנְאֵל) his brother, and Chăshabyâhû (חֲשַׁבְיָהוּ), and Ochiel, and Yôrâm, captains over thousands, gave to the Lêwîy for the Pesach five thousand sheep, and seven hundred calves.

10. And when these things were done, the Kôhên and Lêwîy, having the unleavened bread, stood in very comely order according to the kindreds,

11. And according to the several dignities of the fathers, before the people, to offer to Yahuah, as it is written in the book of Môsheh: And thus they did in the morning.

12. And they roasted the Pesach with fire, as appertains: As for the sacrifices, they sod them in brass pots and pans with a good savor,

13. And set them before all the people: And afterward they prepared for themselves, and for the Kôhên their brethren, the sons of Ahărôn.

14. For the Kôhên offered the fat until night: And the Lêwîy prepared for themselves, and the Kôhên their brethren, the sons of Ahărôn.

15. The qâdôsh singers also, the sons of Âsâph, were in their order, according to the appointment of Dâwid, to wit, Âsâph, Zekaryâhû, and Yadûthûn (יְדוּתוּן), who was of the king's retinue.

16. Moreover the porters were at every gate; it was not lawful for any to go from his ordinary service: For their brethren the Lêwîy prepared for them.

17. Thus were the things that belonged to the sacrifices of Yahuah accomplished in that day, that they might hold the Pesach,

18. And offer sacrifices upon the altar of Yahuah, according to the commandment of king Yôshîyâhû.

19. So the children of Yâshârêl which were present held the Pesach at that time, and the feast of Unleavened Bread seven days.

20. And such a Pesach was not kept in Yâshârêl since the time of the Nâbîy Shemûêl.

21. Yea, all the kings of Yâshârêl did not hold such a Pesach as Yôshîyâhû, and the Kôhên, and the Lêwîy, and the Yahûdîy (יְהוּדִי), held with all Yâshârêl that were found dwelling at Yarûshâlaim.

22. In the eighteenth year of the reign of Yôshîyâhû was this Pesach kept.

23. And the works of Yôshîyâhû were upright before his Yahuah with a heart full of godliness.

24. As for the things that came to pass in his time, they were written in former times, concerning those that sinned, and did wickedly against Yahuah above all people and kingdoms, and how they grieved him exceedingly, so that the words of Yahuah rose up against Yâshârêl.

25. Now after all these acts of Yôshîyâhû it came to pass, that Parôh the king of Mitsrayim came to raise war at Karkemîysh (כַּרְכְּמִישׁ) upon Perâth: And Yôshîyâhû went out against him.

26. But the king of Mitsrayim sent to him, saying, what I have to do with you, O king of Yahûdâh (יְהוּדָה)?

27. I am not sent out from Yahuah Êlôhîym against you; for my war is upon Perâth: And now Yahuah is with me, yea, Yahuah is with me hasting me forward: Depart from me, and do not be against Yahuah.

28. Howbeit Yôshîyâhû did not turn back his chariot from him, but undertook to fight with him, not regarding the words of the Nâbîy Yirmeyâhû (יִרְמְיָהוּ) spoken by the mouth of Yahuah:

29. But joined battle with him in the plain of Megiddôn, and the princes came against king Yôshîyâhû.

30. Then the king said unto his servants, carry me away out of the battle; for I am very weak. And immediately his servants took him away out of the battle.

31. Then he got up upon his second chariot; and being brought back to Yarûshâlaim died, and was buried in his father's sepulcher.

32. And in all Yahûdâh they mourned for Yôshîyâhû, yea, Yirmeyâhû the Nâbîy lamented for Yôshîyâhû, and the chief men with the women made lamentation for him unto this day: And this was given out for an ordinance to be done continually in all the nation of Yâshârêl.

33. These things are written in the book of the stories of the kings of Yahûdâh, and every one of the acts that Yôshîyâhû did, and his glory, and his understanding in the law of Yahuah, and the things that he had done before, and the things now recited, are reported in the book of the kings of Yâshârêl and Yahûdâh.

34. And the people took Yahôâchâz the son of Yôshîyâhû, and made him king instead of Yôshîyâhû his father, when he was twenty and three years old.

35. And he reigned in Yahûdâh and in Yarûshâlaim three months: And then the

king of Mitsrayim deposed him from reigning in Yarûshâlaim.

36. And he set a tax upon the land of a hundred talents of silver and one talent of gold.

37. The king of Mitsrayim also made king Yahôyâqîym (יְהוֹיָקִים) his brother king of Yahûdâh and Yarûshâlaim.

38. And he bound Yahôyâqîym and the nobles: But Zarius his brother he apprehended, and brought him out of Mitsrayim.

39. Five and twenty years old was Yahôyâqîym when he was made king in the land of Yahûdâh and Yarûshâlaim; and he did evil before Yahuah.

40. Wherefore against him Nebûkkadnetstsar (נְבוּכַדְנֶצַּר) the king of Bâbel came up, and bound him with a chain of brass, and carried him into Bâbel.

41. Nebûkkadnetstsar also took of the qâdôsh vessels of Yahuah, and carried them away, and set them in his own temple at Bâbel.

42. But those things that are recorded of him, and of his uncleanness and impiety, are written in the chronicles of the kings.

43. And Yahôyâqîym his son reigned in his stead: He was made king being eighteen years old;

44. And reigned but three months and ten days in Yarûshâlaim; and did evil before Yahuah.

45. So after a year Nebûkkadnetstsar sent and caused him to be brought into Bâbel with the qâdôsh vessels of Yahuah;

46. And made Tsidqîyâhû king of Yahûdâh and Yarûshâlaim, when he was one and twenty years old; and he reigned eleven years:

47. And he did evil also in the sight of Yahuah, and did not care for the words that were spoken unto him by the Nâbîy Yirmeyâhû from the mouth of Yahuah.

48. And after that king Nebûkkadnetstsar had made him to swear by the name of Yahuah, he forswore himself, and rebelled; and hardening his neck, his heart, he transgressed the laws of Yahuah Êlôhîym of Yâshârêl.

49. The governors also of the people and of the Kôhên did many things against the laws, and passed all the pollutions of all nations, and defiled the temple of Yahuah, which was sanctified in Yarûshâlaim.

50. Nevertheless the Êlôhîym of their fathers sent by his messenger to call them back, because he spared them and his tabernacle also.

51. But they had his messengers in derision; and, look, when Yahuah spoke unto them, they made a sport of his Nâbîy:

52. So far forth, that he, being wroth with his people for their great ungodliness, commanded the kings of the Kaśdîy to come up against them;

53. Who slew their young men with the sword, yea, even within the compass of their qâdôsh temple, and spared neither young man nor maid, old man nor child, among them; for he delivered all into their hands.

54. And they took all the qâdôsh vessels of Yahuah, both great and small, with the vessels of the ark of Êlôhîym, and the king's treasures, and carried them away into Bâbel.

55. As for the house of Yahuah, they burnt it, and broke down the walls of Yarûshâlaim, and set fire upon her towers:

56. And as for her glorious things, they never ceased till they had consumed and brought them all to nothing: And the people that

were not slain with the sword he carried unto Bâbel:

57. Who became servants to him and his children, till the Pâras (פָּרַס) reigned, to fulfil the word of Yahuah spoken by the mouth of Yirmeyâhû:

58. Until the land had enjoyed her Shabbâth, the whole time of her desolation she shall rest, until the full term of seventy years.

Chapter 2

1. In the first year of Kôresh (כּוֹרֶשׁ) king of the Pâras, that the word of Yahuah might be accomplished, that he had promised by the mouth of Yirmeyâhû;

2. Yahuah raised up the spirit of Kôresh the king of the Pâras, and he made proclamation through all his kingdom, and also by writing,

3. Saying, thus says Kôresh king of the Pâras; Yahuah of Yâshârêl, Yahuah Elyôn Êl, has made me king of the whole world,

4. And commanded me to build him a house at Yarûshâlaim in Yahûdâh.

5. If therefore there are any of you that are of his people, let Yahuah, even his Yahuah, be with him, and let him go up to Yarûshâlaim that is in Yahûdâh, and build the house of Yahuah of Yâshârêl: For he is Yahuah that dwells in Yarûshâlaim.

6. Whosoever then dwell in the places about, let them help him, those, I say, that are his neighbors, with gold, and with silver,

7. With gifts, with horses, and with cattle, and other things, which have been set forth by vow, for the temple of Yahuah at Yarûshâlaim.

8. Then the chief of the families of Yahûdâh and of the tribe of Binyâmîyn stood up; the Kôhên also, and the Lêwîy, and all they whose mind Yahuah had moved to go up, and to build a house for Yahuah at Yarûshâlaim,

9. And they that dwelt round about them, and helped them in all things with silver and gold, with horses and cattle, and with very many free gifts of a great number whose minds were stirred up thereto.

10. King Kôresh also brought forth the qâdôsh vessels, which Nebûkkadnetstsar had carried away from Yarûshâlaim, and had set up in his temple of idols.

11. Now when Kôresh king of the Pâras had brought them forth, he delivered them to Mithredâth (מִתְרְדָת) his treasurer:

12. And by him they were delivered to Shêshbatstsar (שֵׁשְׁבַּצַּר) the governor of Yahûdâh.

13. And this was the number of them; a thousand golden cups, and a thousand of silver, censers of silver twenty nine, vials of gold thirty, and of silver two thousand four hundred and ten, and a thousand other vessels.

14. So all the vessels of gold and of silver, which were carried away, were five thousand four hundred threescore and nine.

15. These were brought back by Shêshbatstsar, together with them of the captivity, from Bâbel to Yarûshâlaim.

16. But in the time of Artachshashtâ (אַרְתַּחְשַׁשְׁתָּא) king of the Pâras, Bishlâm (בִּשְׁלָם), and Mithredâth, and Tâbêl, and Rechûm (רְחוּם), and Beeltethmus, and Shimsay (שִׁמְשַׁי) the secretary, with others that were in commission with them, dwelling in Shômerôn (שֹׁמְרוֹן) and other places, wrote unto him against them that dwelt in Yahûdâh and Yarûshâlaim these letters following;

17. To king Artachshashtâ our master, your servants, Rechûm the storywriter, and Shimsay the scribe, and the rest of their council, and the judges that are in Ărâm and Phoenicia.

18. Be it now known to the master king, that the Yahûdîy that are up from you to us, being come into Yarûshâlaim, that rebellious and wicked city, do build the marketplaces, and repair the walls of it and do lay the foundation of the temple.

19. Now if this city and the walls thereof be made up again, they will not only refuse to give tribute, but also rebel against kings.

20. And forasmuch as the things pertaining to the temple are now in hand, we think it does not meet to neglect such a matter,

21. But to speak unto our Yahuah the king, to the intent that, if it is your pleasure it may be sought out in the books of your fathers:

22. And you shall find in the chronicles what is written concerning these things, and shall understand that that city was rebellious, troubling both kings and cities:

23. And that the Yahûdîy were rebellious, and raised always wars therein; for which cause even this city was made desolate.

24. Wherefore now we do declare unto you, O Yahuah the king, that if this city is built again, and the walls thereof set up a new, you shall from henceforth have no passage into Ărâm and Phoenicia.

25. Then the king wrote back again to Rechûm the storywriter, to Beeltethmus, to Shimsay the scribe, and to the rest that were in commission, and dwellers in Shômerôn and Ărâm (אֲרָם) and Phoenicia, after this manner;

26. I have read the epistle which you have sent unto me: Therefore I commanded to make diligent search, and it has been found that that city was from the beginning practicing against kings;

27. And the men therein were given to rebellion and war: And that mighty kings and fierce were in Yarûshâlaim, who reigned and exacted tributes in Ărâm and Phoenicia.

28. Now therefore I have commanded to hinder those men from building the city, and heed to be taken that there be no more done in it;

29. And that those wicked workers proceed no further to the annoyance of kings,

30. Then king Artachshashtâ his letters being read, Rechûm, and Shimsay the scribe, and the rest that were in commission with them, removing in haste toward Yarûshâlaim with a troop of horsemen and a multitude of people in battle array, began to hinder the builders; and the building of the temple in Yarûshâlaim ceased until the second year of the reign of Dâreyâwêsh (דְּרְיָוֶשׁ) king of the Pâras.

Chapter 3

1. Now when Dâreyâwêsh reigned, he made a great feast unto all his subjects, and unto all his household, and unto all the princes of Mâday and Pâras,

2. And to all the governors and captains and lieutenants that were under him, from Yahûdâh unto Kûsh (כּוּשׁ), of a hundred twenty and seven provinces.

3. And when they had eaten and drunken, and being satisfied were gone home, then Dâreyâwêsh the king went into his bedchamber, and slept, and soon after awoke.

4. Then three young men that were of the guard that kept the king's body, spoke one to another;

5. Let every one of us speak a sentence: He that shall overcome, and whose sentence shall seem wiser than the others, unto him shall the king Dâreyâwêsh give great gifts, and great things in token of victory:

6. As, to be clothed in purple, to drink in gold, and to sleep upon gold, and a chariot with bridles of gold, and an head tire of fine linen, and a chain about his neck:

7. And he shall sit next to Dâreyâwêsh because of his wisdom, and shall be called Dâreyâwêsh his cousin.

8. And then everyone wrote his sentence, sealed it, and laid it under king Dâreyâwêsh his pillow;

9. And said that, when the king is risen, some will give him the writings; and of whose side the king and the three princes of Pâras shall judge that his sentence is the wisest, to him shall the victory be given, as was appointed.

10. The first wrote: Wine is the strongest.

11. The second wrote: The king is strongest.

12: The third wrote: Women are strongest: But above all things truth bears away the victory.

13. Now when the king was risen up, they took their writings, and delivered them unto him, and so he read them:

14. And sending forth he called all the princes of Pâras and Mâday, and the governors, and the captains, and the lieutenants, and the chief officers;

15. And he sat down in the royal seat of judgment; and the writings were read before them.

16. And he said: Call the young men, and they shall declare their own sentences. So they were called, and came in.

17. And he said unto them: Declare unto us your mind concerning the writings. Then the first began, who had spoken of the strength of wine;

18. And he said thus, O you men, how exceeding strong is wine! It causes all men to err that drink it:

19. It makes the mind of the king and of the fatherless child to be all one; of the bondman and of the freeman, of the poor man and of the rich:

20. It turns also every thought into jollity and mirth, so that a man remembers neither sorrow nor debt:

21. And it makes every heart rich, so that a man remembers neither king nor governor; and it makes to speak all things by talents:

22. And when they are in their cups, they forget their love both to friends and brethren, and a little after draw out swords:

23. But when they are from the wine, they do not remember what they have done.

24. O you men, is not wine the strongest, that enforces to do thus? And when he had so spoken, he held his peace.

Chapter 4

1. Then the second that had spoken of the strength of the king, began to say,

2. O you men, do not men excel in strength that bear rule over sea and land and all things in them?

3. But yet the king is mightier: For he is master of all these things, and has dominion over them; and whatsoever he commands them they do.

4. If he bid them make war the one against the other, they do it: If he sends them out

against the enemies, they go, and break down mountains walls and towers.

5. They slay and are slain, and do not transgress the king's commandment: If they get the victory, they bring all to the king, as well the spoil, as all things else.

6. Likewise for those that are no soldiers, and do not have to do with wars, but use farming, when they have reaped again that which they had sown, they bring it to the king, and compel one another to pay tribute unto the king.

7. And yet he is but one man: If he commands to kill, they kill; if he commands to spare, they spare;

8. If he commands to smite, they smite; if he commands to make desolate, they make desolate; if he commands to build, they build;

9. If he commands to cut down, they cut down; if he commands to plant, they plant.

10. So all his people and his armies obey him: Furthermore he lies down, he eats and drinks, and takes his rest:

11. And these keep watch round about him, neither may any one depart, and do his own business, neither disobey they him in anything.

12. O you men, how should not the king be mightiest, when in such sort he is obeyed? And he held his tongue.

13. Then the third, who had spoken of women, and of the truth, (this was Zerûbbâbel) began to speak.

14. O you men, it is not the great king, nor the multitude of men, neither is it wine, that excels; who is it then that rules them, or has dominion over them? Are they not women?

15. Women have borne the king and all the people that bear rule by sea and land.

16. Even of them came they: And they nourished them up that planted the vineyards, from whence the wine comes.

17. These also make garments for men; these bring glory unto men; and without women men cannot be.

18. Yea, and if men have gathered together gold and silver, or any other goodly thing, do they not love a woman which is comely in favor and beauty?

19. And letting all those things go, do they not gape, and even with open mouth fix their eyes fast on her; and have not all men more desire unto her than unto silver or gold, or any goodly thing whatsoever?

20. A man leaves his own father that brought him up, and his own country, and cleaves unto his woman.

21. He does not stick to spend his life with his woman. And remembers neither father, nor mother, nor country.

22. By this also you must know that women have dominion over you: Do you not labor and toil, and give and bring all to the woman?

23. Yea, a man takes his sword, and goes his way to rob and to steal, to sail upon the sea and upon rivers;

24. And looks upon a lion, and goes in the darkness; and when he has stolen, spoiled, and robbed, he brings it to his love.

25. Wherefore a man loves his woman better than father or mother.

26. Yea, many there are that have run out of their wits for women, and become servants for their sakes.

27. Many also have perished, have erred, and sinned, for women.

28. And now do you not believe me? Is not the king great in his power? Do not all regions fear to touch him?

29. Yet did I see him and Apame the king's concubine, the daughter of the admirable Bartacus, sitting at the right hand of the king,

30. And taking the crown from the king's head, and setting it upon her own head; she also struck the king with her left hand.

31. And yet for all this the king gaped and gazed upon her with open mouth: If she laughed upon him, he laughed also: But if she took any displeasure at him, the king was fain to flatter, that she might be reconciled to him again.

32. O you men, how can it be but women should be strong, seeing they do thus?

33. Then the king and the princes looked one upon another: So he began to speak of the truth.

34. O you men, are not women strong? Great is the earth, high is the shâmayim, swift is the sun in his course, for he compasses the shâmayim round about, and fetches his course again to his own place in one day.

35. Is he not great that makes these things? Therefore great is the truth, and stronger than all things.

36. All the earth cries upon the truth, and the shâmayim blesses it: All works shake and tremble at it, and with it is no unrighteous thing.

37. Wine is wicked, the king is wicked, women are wicked, all the children of men are wicked, and such are all their wicked works; and there is no truth in them; in their unrighteousness also they shall perish.

38. As for the truth, it endures, and is always strong; it lives and conquers forevermore.

39. With her there is no accepting of persons or rewards; but she does the things that are just, and refrains from all unjust and wicked things; and all men do well like of her works.

40. Neither in her judgment is any unrighteousness; and she is the strength, kingdom, power, and majesty, of all ages. Blessed be the Êl Ĕmûnâh (אֱמוּנָה).

41. And with that he held his peace. And all the people then shouted, and said: Great is truth, and mighty above all things.

42. Then the king said unto him, ask what you will more than is appointed in the writing, and we will give it you, because you are found wisest; and you shall sit next me, and shall be called my cousin.

43. Then he said unto the king: Remember your vow, which you have vowed to build Yarûshâlaim, in the day when you came to your kingdom,

44. And to send away all the vessels that were taken away out of Yarûshâlaim, which Kôresh set apart, when he vowed to destroy Bâbel, and to send them again thither.

45. You also have vowed to build up the temple, which the Ĕdômîy burned when Yahûdâh was made desolate by the Kaśdîy.

46. And now, O master the king, this is that which I require, and which I desire of you, and this is the princely liberality proceeding from yourself: I desire therefore that you make good the vow, the performance whereof with your own mouth you have vowed to the King of shâmayim.

47. Then Dâreyâwêsh the king stood up, and kissed him, and wrote letters for him unto all the treasurers and lieutenants and captains and governors, that they should safely convey on their way both him, and all those that go up with him to build Yarûshâlaim.

48. He wrote letters also unto the lieutenants that were in Ărâm and Phoenicia, and unto them in Lebânôn, that they should bring cedar wood from Lebânôn unto Yarûshâlaim, and that they should build the city with him.

49. Moreover he wrote for all the Yahûdîy that went out of his realm up into Yahûdâh, concerning their freedom that no officer, no ruler, no lieutenant, nor treasurer, should forcibly enter into their doors;

50. And that all the country which they hold should be free without tribute; and that the Ĕdômîy should give over the villages of the Yahûdîy which then they held:

51. Yea, that there should be yearly given twenty talents to the building of the temple, until the time that it were built;

52. And other ten talents yearly, to maintain the burnt offerings upon the altar every day, as they had a commandment to offer seventeen:

53. And that all they that went from Bâbel to build the city should have free liberty, as well they as their posterity, and all the Kôhên that went away.

54. He wrote also concerning the charges, and the Kôhên' vestments wherein they minister;

55. And likewise for the charges of the Lêwîy, to be given them until the day that the house were finished, and Yarûshâlaim built up.

56. And he commanded to give to all that kept the city pensions and wages.

57. He sent away also all the vessels from Bâbel, that Kôresh had set apart; and all that Kôresh had given in commandment, the same he charged also to be done, and sent unto Yarûshâlaim.

58. Now when this young man was gone forth, he lifted up his face to shâmayim toward Yarûshâlaim, and praised the Melek of shâmayim,

59. And said: From you comes victory, from you comes wisdom, and yours is the glory, and I am your servant.

60. Blessed are you, who have given me wisdom: For to you I give thanks, O Yahuah of our fathers.

61. And so he took the letters, and went out, and came unto Bâbel, and told it all his brethren.

62. And they praised the Êlôhîym of their fathers, because he had given them freedom and liberty.

63. To go up, and to build Yarûshâlaim, and the temple which is called by his name: And they feasted with instruments of music and gladness seven days.

Chapter 5

1. After this were the principal men of the families chosen according to their tribes, to go up with their women and sons and daughters, with their menservants and maidservants, and their cattle.

2. And Dâreyâwêsh sent with them a thousand horsemen, till they had brought them back to Yarûshâlaim safely, and with musical instruments tambourines and flutes.

3. And all their brethren played, and he made them go up together with them.

4. And these are the names of the men which went up, according to their families among their tribes, after their several heads.

5. The Kôhên, the sons of Pîynechâs (פִּינְחָס) the son of Ahărôn: Yahusha the son of Yahôtsâdâq (יְהוֹצָדְק), the son of Śerâyâhû (שְׂרָיָהוּ), and Yahôyâqîym the son of

Yahôtsâdâq, the son of Shealtîyêl (שְׁאַלְתִּיאֵל), of the house of Dâwid, out of the kindred of Perets, of the tribe of Yahûdâh;

6. Who spoke wise sentences before Dâreyâwêsh the king of Pâras in the second year of his reign, in the month Nîysân, which is the first month.

7. And these are they of Yahûdâh that came up from the captivity, where they dwelt as strangers, whom Nebûkkadnetstsar the king of Bâbel had carried away unto Bâbel.

8. And they returned unto Yarûshâlaim, and to the other parts of Yahûdâh, every man to his own city, who came with Zerûbbâbel, with Yahusha, Nechemyâh, and Zekaryâhû, and Resaiah, Eneneus, Mordekay. Beelsarus, Aspharasus, Reelius, Roimus, and Baănâ, their guides.

9. The number of them of the nation, and their governors, sons of Parôsh (פַּרְעֹשׁ), two thousand a hundred seventy and two; the sons of Shephaṭyâhû (שְׁפַטְיָהוּ), four hundred seventy and two:

10. The sons of Ârach (אָרַח), seven hundred fifty and six:

11. The sons of Pachath Môâb, two thousand eight hundred and twelve:

12. The sons of Êylâm, a thousand two hundred fifty and four: The sons of Zattû, nine hundred forty and five: The sons of Chorbe, seven hundred and five: the sons of Bânîy, six hundred forty and eight:

13. The sons of Bêbay, six hundred twenty and three: The sons of Azgâd, three thousand two hundred twenty and two:

14. The sons of Ădônîyqâm, six hundred sixty and seven: The sons of Bigway, two thousand sixty and six: The sons of Âdîyn, four hundred fifty and four:

15. The sons of Âṭêr, ninety and two: The sons of Kilan and Azetas threescore and seven: The sons of Azzûr, four hundred thirty and two:

16. The sons of Chănanyâhû (חֲנַנְיָהוּ), a hundred and one: The sons of Arôm, thirty two: And the sons of Bêtsay, three hundred twenty and three: The sons of Chârîyph, a hundred and twelve:

17. The sons of Meterus, three thousand and five: The sons of Bêyth lechem, a hundred twenty and three:

18. They of Neṭôphâh, fifty and five: They of Ănâthôth, a hundred fifty and eight: They of Bêyth Azmâweth (בֵּית עַזְמָוֶת), forty and two:

19. They of Qiryath Yaârîym (קִרְיַת יְעָרִים), twenty and five: They of Kephîyrâh and Beêrôth, seven hundred forty and three: They of Pyra, seven hundred:

20. They of Chadiasans and Ammidians, four hundred twenty and two: They of Râmâh and Geba, six hundred twenty and one:

21. They of Mikmâs, a hundred twenty and two: They of Betolius, fifty and two: The sons of Nephis, a hundred fifty and six:

22. The sons of Lôd (לֹד) Châdîyd (חָדִיד) and Ônô, seven hundred twenty and five: The sons of Yarîychô (יְרִיחוֹ), two hundred forty and five:

23. The sons of Senââh, three thousand three hundred and thirty.

24. The Kôhên: The sons of Yadayâh (יְדַעְיָה), the son of Yahusha among the sons of Sanasib, nine hundred seventy and two: The sons of Immêr, a thousand fifty and two:

25. The sons of Pashchûr (פַּשְׁחוּר), a thousand forty and seven: The sons of Carme, a thousand and seventeen.

26. The Lêwîy: The sons of Yahusha, and Qadmîy'l (קַדְמִיאֵל), and Bannas, and Hôdawyâh, seventy and four.

27. The qâdôsh singers: The sons of Âsâph, a hundred twenty and eight.

28. The porters: The sons of Shallûm, the sons of Âṭêr, the sons of Talmôn, the sons of Aqqûb, the sons of Chăṭîyṭâ (חֲטִיטָא), the sons of Shôbay, in all a hundred thirty and nine.

29. The servants of the temple: The sons of Êśâw, the sons of Chăśûphâ, the sons of Tabbâôth, the sons of Qêyrôs, the sons of Tsîychâ, the sons of Pâdôn, the sons of Lebânâ, the sons of Chăgâbâ,

30. The sons of Aqqûb, the sons of Ûthay, the sons of Ketab, the sons of Chăgâbâ, the sons of Śalmay, the sons of Chânân, the sons of Cathua, the sons of Giddêl,

31. The sons of Reâyâh, the sons of Retsîyn, the sons of Neqôdâ, the sons of Chaseba, the sons of Gazzâm, the sons of Ûzzâ, the sons of Pâsêach, the sons of Hazrah, the sons of Besay, the sons of Asna, the sons of Meûnîy, the sons of Nephûshsîym, the sons of Baqbûq, the sons of Chăqûphâ, the sons of Charchûr, the sons of Pharakim, the sons of Batslûth.

32. The sons of Mechîydâ, the sons of Charshâ, the sons of Sîyserâ, the sons of Barqôs, the sons of Serar, the sons of Temach, the sons of Netsîyach, the sons of Chăṭîyphâ.

33. The sons of the servants of Shelômôh: The sons of Azaphiot, the sons of Perîydâ, the sons of Yaălâ, the sons of Darqôn, the sons of Yâshârêl, the sons of Sapheth,

34. The sons of Agia, the sons of Pôkereth Tsebâyîym, the sons of Sarothie, the sons of Masiah, the sons of Gar, the sons of Addus, the sons of Suba, the sons of Apherra, the sons of Barodis, the sons of Sabat, the sons of Allom.

35. All the ministers of the temple, and the sons of the servants of Shelômôh, were three hundred seventy and two.

36. These came up from Têl melach and Têl charshâ, Kerûb leading them, and Addôn and Immêr;

37. Neither could they show their families, nor their stock, how they were of Yâshârêl: The sons of Delâyâhû, the son of Ṭôbîyâhû, the sons of Neqôdâ, six hundred fifty and two.

38. And of the Kôhên that usurped the office of the Kehûnnâh, and were not found: The sons of Chăbâyâh, the sons of Qôts, the sons of Yaddus, who married Agia one of the daughters of Barzillay, and was named after his name.

39. And when the description of the kindred of these men was sought in the register, and was not found, they were removed from executing the office of the Kehûnnâh:

40. For unto them said Nechemyâh and Attharias, that they should not be partakers of the qâdôsh things, till there arose up a high Kôhên clothed with doctrine and truth.

41. So of Yâshârêl, from them of twelve years old and upward, they were all in number forty thousand, beside menservants and women servants two thousand three hundred and sixty.

42. Their menservants and handmaids were seven thousand three hundred forty and seven: The singing men and singing women, two hundred forty and five:

43. Four hundred thirty and five camels, seven thousand thirty and six horses, two hundred forty and five mules, five thousand five hundred twenty and five beasts used to the yoke.

44. And certain of the chief of their families, when they came to the temple of Êlôhîym that is in Yarûshâlaim, vowed to set up the house again in his own place according to their ability,

45. And to give into the qâdôsh treasury of the works a thousand pounds of gold, five thousand of silver, and a hundred Kôhên vestments.

46. And so dwelt the Kôhên and the Lêwîy and the people in Yarûshâlaim, and in the country, the singers also and the porters; and all Yâshârêl in their villages.

47. But when the seventh month was at hand, and when the children of Yâshârêl were every man in his own place, they came all together with one consent into the open place of the first gate which is toward the east.

48. Then Yahusha the son of Yahôtsâdâq stood up, and his brethren the Kôhên and Zerûbbâbel the son of Shealtîyêl, and his brethren, and made ready the altar of the Êlôhîym of Yâshârêl,

49. To offer burnt sacrifices upon it, according as it is expressly commanded in the book of Môsheh the man of Êlôhîym.

50. And there were gathered unto them out of the other nations of the land, and they erected the altar upon his own place, because all the nations of the land were at enmity with them, and oppressed them; and they offered sacrifices according to the time, and burnt offerings to Yahuah both morning and evening.

51. Also they held the feast of tabernacles, as it is commanded in the law, and offered sacrifices daily, as was meet:

52. And after that, the continual offerings, and the sacrifice of the Shabbâth, and of the new months, and of all qâdôsh feasts.

53. And all they that had made any vow to Êlôhîym began to offer sacrifices to Êlôhîym from the first day of the seventh month, although the temple of Yahuah was not yet built.

54. And they gave unto the masons and carpenters money, meat, and drink, with cheerfulness.

55. Unto them of Tsîydôn also and Tsôr (צֹר) they gave cares, that they should bring cedar trees from Lebânôn, which should be brought by floats to the haven of Yâphô (יָפוֹ), according as it was commanded them by Kôresh king of the Pâras.

56. And in the second year and second month after his coming to the temple of Êlôhîym at Yarûshâlaim began Zerûbbâbel the son of Shealtîyêl, and Yahusha the son of Yahôtsâdâq, and their brethren, and the Kôhên, and the Lêwîy, and all they that were come unto Yarûshâlaim out of the captivity:

57. And they laid the foundation of the house of Êlôhîym in the first day of the second month, in the second year after they were come to Yahûdâh and Yarûshâlaim.

58. And they appointed the Lêwîy from twenty years old over the works of Yahuah. Then Yahusha stood up, and his sons and brethren, and Qadmîyl his brother, and the sons of Chênâdâd, with the sons of Yoda the son of Iliadun, with their sons and brethren, all Lêwîy, with one accord setters forward of the business, laboring to advance the works in the house of Êlôhîym. So the workmen built the temple of Yahuah.

59. And the Kôhên stood arrayed in their vestments with musical instruments and trumpets; and the Lêwîy the sons of Âsâph had cymbals,

60. Singing songs of thanksgiving, and praising Yahuah, according as Dâwid the king of Yâshârêl had ordained.

61. And they sung with loud voices songs to the praise of Yahuah, because his mercy and glory is forever in all Yâshârêl.

62. And all the people sounded trumpets, and shouted with a loud voice, singing songs of thanksgiving unto Yahuah for the rearing up of the house of Yahuah.

63. Also of the Kôhên and Lêwîy, and of the chief of their families, the ancients who had seen the former house came to the building of this with weeping and great crying.

64. But many with trumpets and joy shouted with loud voice,

65. Insomuch that the trumpets might not be heard for the weeping of the people: Yet the multitude sounded marvelously, so that it was heard afar off.

66. Wherefore when the enemies of the tribe of Yahûdâh and Binyâmîyn heard it, they came to know what that noise of trumpets should mean.

67. And they perceived that they that were of the captivity did build the temple unto Yahuah Êlôhîym of Yâshârêl.

68. So they went to Zerûbbâbel and Yahusha, and to the chief of the families, and said unto them, we will build together with you.

69. For we likewise, as you, do obey your Yahuah, and do sacrifice unto him from the days of Êsar-chaddôn (אֵסַר־חַדֹּן) the king of the Ashshûr, who brought us hither.

70. Then Zerûbbâbel and Yahusha and the chief of the families of Yâshârêl said unto them: It is not for us and you to build together a house unto Yahuah our Êlôhîym.

71. We ourselves alone will build unto Yahuah of Yâshârêl, according as Kôresh the king of the Pâras has commanded us.

72. But the heathen of the land lying heavy upon the inhabitants of Yahûdâh, and holding them strait, hindered their building;

73. And by their secret plots, and popular persuasions and commotions, they hindered the finishing of the building all the time that king Kôresh lived: So they were hindered from building for the space of two years, until the reign of Dâreyâwêsh.

Chapter 6

1. Now in the second year of the reign of Dâreyâwêsh Chaggay and Zekaryâhû the son of Iddô, the Nâbîy, prophesied unto the Yahûdîy in Yahûdâh and Yarûshâlaim in the name of Yahuah Êlôhîym of Yâshârêl, which was upon them.

2. Then Zerûbbâbel stood up the son of Shealtîyêl, and Yahusha the son of Yahôtsâdâq, and began to build the house of Yahuah at Yarûshâlaim, the Nâbîy of Yahuah being with them, and helping them.

3. At the same time came unto them Tattenay (תַּתְּנַי) the governor of Ărâm and Phoenicia, with Shethar bôzenay (שְׁתַר בּוֹזְנַי) and his companions, and said unto them,

4. By whose appointment do you build this house and this roof, and perform all the other things? And who are the workmen that perform these things?

5. Nevertheless the elders of the Yahûdîy obtained favor, because Yahuah had visited the captivity;

6. And they were not hindered from building, until such time as signification was given unto Dâreyâwêsh concerning them, and an answer received.

7. The copy of the letters which Tattenay, governor of Ărâm and Phoenicia, and Shethar

bôzenay, with their companions, rulers in Ărâm and Phoenicia, wrote and sent unto Dâreyâwêsh: To king Dâreyâwêsh, greeting:

8. Let all things be known unto our Yahuah the king, that being come into the country of Yahûdâh, and entered into the city of Yarûshâlaim we found in the city of Yarûshâlaim the ancients of the Yahûdîy that were of the captivity,

9. Building a house unto Yahuah, great and new, of hewn and costly stones, and the timber already laid upon the walls.

10. And those works are done with great speed, and the work goes on prosperously in their hands, and with all glory and diligence it is made.

11. Then we asked these elders, saying, by whose commandment do you build this house, and lay the foundations of these works?

12. Therefore to the intent that we might give knowledge unto you by writing, we demanded of them who were the chief doers, and we required of them the names in writing of their principal men.

13. So they gave us this answer, we are the servants of Yahuah which made shâmayim and earth.

14. And as for this house, it was built many years ago by a king of Yâshârêl great and strong, and was finished.

15. But when our fathers provoked Êlôhîym unto wrath, and sinned against Yahuah of Yâshârêl which is in shâmayim, he gave them over into the power of Nebûkkadnetstsar king of Bâbel, of the Kaśdîy;

16. Who pulled down the house, and burned it, and carried away the people captives unto Bâbel.

17. But in the first year that king Kôresh reigned over the country of Bâbel Kôresh the king wrote to build up this house.

18. And the qâdôsh vessels of gold and of silver, that Nebûkkadnetstsar had carried away out of the house at Yarûshâlaim, and had set them in his own temple those Kôresh the king brought forth again out of the temple at Bâbel, and they were delivered to Zerûbbâbel and to Shêshbatstsar the ruler,

19. With commandment that he should carry away the same vessels, and put them in the temple at Yarûshâlaim; and that the temple of Yahuah should be built in his place.

20. Then the same Shêshbatstsar, being come hither, laid the foundations of the house of Yahuah at Yarûshâlaim; and from that time to this being still a building, it is not yet fully ended.

21. Now therefore, if it seem good unto the king, let search be made among the records of king Kôresh:

22. And if it is found that the building of the house of Yahuah at Yarûshâlaim has been done with the consent of king Kôresh, and if our master the king is so minded, let him signify unto us thereof.

23. Then king Dâreyâwêsh commanded to seek among the records at Bâbel: And so at Ecbatana (אַחְמְתָא) the palace, which is in the country of Mâday, there was found a roll wherein these things were recorded.

24. In the first year of the reign of Kôresh, king Kôresh commanded that the house of Yahuah at Yarûshâlaim should be built again, where they do sacrifice with continual fire:

25. Whose height shall be sixty cubits and the breadth sixty cubits, with three rows of hewn stones, and one row of new wood of

that country; and the expenses thereof to be given out of the house of king Kôresh:

26. And that the qâdôsh vessels of the house of Yahuah, both of gold and silver, that Nebûkkadnetstsar took out of the house at Yarûshâlaim, and brought to Bâbel, should be restored to the house at Yarûshâlaim, and be set in the place where they were before.

27. And also he commanded that Tattenay the governor of Ărâm and Phoenicia, and Shethar bôzenay, and their companions, and those which were appointed rulers in Ărâm and Phoenicia, should be careful not to meddle with the place, but suffer Zerûbbâbel, the servant of Yahuah, and governor of Yahûdâh, and the elders of the Yahûdîy, to build the house of Yahuah in that place.

28. I have commanded also to have it built up whole again; and that they look diligently to help those that are of the captivity of the Yahûdîy, till the house of Yahuah is finished:

29. And out of the tribute of Ărâm and Phoenicia a portion carefully to be given these men for the sacrifices of Yahuah, that is, to Zerûbbâbel the governor, for bullocks, and rams, and lambs;

30. And also corn, salt, wine, and oil, and that continually every year without further question, according as the Kôhên that be in Yarûshâlaim shall signify to be daily spent:

31. That offerings may be made to Êlôhîym Elyôn Êl for the king and for his children, and that they may pray for their lives.

32. And he commanded that whosoever should transgress, yea, or make light of anything afore spoken or written, out of his own house should a tree be taken, and he thereon be hanged, and all his goods seized for the king.

33. Yahuah therefore, whose name is there called upon, utterly destroy every king and nation, that stretches out his hand to hinder or damage that house of Yahuah in Yarûshâlaim.

34. I Dâreyâwêsh the king have ordained that according unto these things it'd be done with diligence.

Chapter 7

1. Then Tattenay the governor of Ărâm and Phoenicia, and Shethar bôzenay, with their companions following the commandments of king Dâreyâwêsh,

2. Did very carefully oversee the qâdôsh works, assisting the ancients of the Yahûdîy and governors of the temple.

3. And so the qâdôsh works prospered, when Chaggay and Zekaryâhû the Nâbîy prophesied.

4. And they finished these things by the commandment of Yahuah Êlôhîym of Yâshârêl, and with the consent of Kôresh, Dâreyâwêsh, and Artachshashtâ, kings of Pâras.

5. And thus was the qâdôsh house finished in the three and twentieth day of the month Ădâr, in the sixth year of Dâreyâwêsh king of the Pâras.

6. And the children of Yâshârêl, the Kôhên, and the Lêwîy, and others that were of the captivity, that were added unto them, did according to the things written in the book of Môsheh.

7. And to the dedication of the temple of Yahuah they offered a hundred bullocks two hundred rams, four hundred lambs;

8. And twelve goats for the sin of all Yâshârêl, according to the number of the chief of the tribes of Yâshârêl.

9. The Kôhên also and the Lêwîy stood arrayed in their vestments, according to

their kindreds, in the service of Yahuah Êlôhîym of Yâshârêl, according to the book of Môsheh: And the porters at every gate.

10. And the children of Yâshârêl that were of the captivity held the Pesach the fourteenth day of the first month, after that the Kôhên and the Lêwîy were sanctified.

11. They that were of the captivity were not all sanctified together: But the Lêwîy were all sanctified together.

12. And so they offered the Pesach for all them of the captivity, and for their brethren the Kôhên, and for themselves.

13. And the children of Yâshârêl that came out of the captivity did eat, even all they that had separated themselves from the abominations of the people of the land, and sought Yahuah.

14. And they kept the feast of Matstsâh (מַצָּה) seven days, making merry before Yahuah,

15. For that he had turned the counsel of the king of Ashshûr toward them, to strengthen their hands in the works of Yahuah Êlôhîym of Yâshârêl.

Chapter 8

1. And after these things, when Artachshashtâ the king of the Pâras reigned came Ezrâ (עֶזְרָא) the son of Śerâyâhû, the son of Ăzaryâhû (עֲזַרְיָהוּ), the son of Chilqîyâhû (חִלְקִיָּהוּ), the son of Shallûm,

2. The son of Tsâdôq (צָדוֹק), the son of Ăchîytûb (אֲחִיטוּב), the son of Ămaryâhû, the son of Ăzaryâhû (עֲזַרְיָהוּ), the son of Merâyôth (מְרָיוֹת), the son of Zerachyâh, the son of Ûzzîy, the son of Bûqqîy, the son of Ăbîyshûa, the son of Pîynechâs, the son of Elâzâr, the son of Ahărôn the chief Kôhên.

3. This Ezrâ went up from Bâbel, as a scribe, being very ready in the law of Môsheh that was given by the Êlôhîym of Yâshârêl.

4. And the king did him honor: For he found grace in his sight in all his requests.

5. There went up with him also certain of the children of Yâshârêl, of the Kôhên of the Lêwîy, of the qâdôsh singers, porters, and ministers of the temple, unto Yarûshâlaim,

6. In the seventh year of the reign of Artachshashtâ, in the fifth month, this was the king's seventh year; for they went from Bâbel in the first day of the first month, and came to Yarûshâlaim, according to the prosperous journey which Yahuah gave them.

7. For Ezrâ had very great skill, so that he omitted nothing of the law and commandments of Yahuah, but taught all Yâshârêl the ordinances and judgments.

8. Now the copy of the commission, which was written from Artachshashtâ the king, and came to Ezrâ the Kôhên and reader of the law of Yahuah, is this that follows;

9. King Artachshashtâ unto Ezrâ the Kôhên and reader of the law of Yahuah sends greeting:

10. Having determined to deal graciously, I have given order that such of the nation of the Yahûdîy, and of the Kôhên and Lêwîy being within our realm, as are willing and desirous should go with you unto Yarûshâlaim.

11. As many therefore as have a mind thereunto, let them depart with you, as it has seemed good both to me and my seven friends the counsellors;

12. That they may look unto the affairs of Yahûdâh and Yarûshâlaim, agreeably to that which is in the law of Yahuah;

13. And carry the gifts unto Yahuah of Yâshârêl to Yarûshâlaim, which I and my friends have vowed, and all the gold and

silver that in the country of Bâbel can be found, to Yahuah in Yarûshâlaim,

14. With that also which is given of the people for the temple of Yahuah their Êlôhîym at Yarûshâlaim: And that silver and gold may be collected for bullocks, rams, and lambs, and things thereunto appertaining;

15. To the end that they may offer sacrifices unto Yahuah upon the altar of Yahuah their Êlôhîym, which is in Yarûshâlaim.

16. And whatsoever you and your brethren will do with the silver and gold that do, according to the will of your Êlôhîym.

17. And the qâdôsh vessels of Yahuah, which are given you for the use of the temple of your Êlôhîym, which is in Yarûshâlaim, you shall set before your Êlôhîym in Yarûshâlaim.

18. And whatsoever thing else you shall remember for the use of the temple of your Êlôhîym, you shall give it out of the king's treasury.

19. And I king Artachshashtâ have also commanded the keepers of the treasures in Ărâm and Phoenicia, that whatsoever Ezrâ the Kôhên and the reader of the law of Êlôhîym Elyôn Êl shall send for, they should give it him with speed,

20. To the sum of a hundred talents of silver, likewise also of wheat even to a hundred cores, and a hundred pieces of wine, and other things in abundance.

21. Let all things be performed after the law of Êlôhîym diligently unto Êlôhîym Elyôn Êl, that wrath does not come upon the kingdom of the king and his sons.

22. I command you also, that you require no tax, nor any other imposition, of any of the Kôhên, or Lêwîy, or qâdôsh singers, or porters, or ministers of the temple, or of any that have doings in this temple, and that no man have authority to impose any thing upon them.

23. And you, Ezrâ, according to the wisdom of Êlôhîym ordain judges and justices that they may judge in all Ărâm and Phoenicia all those that know the law of your Êlôhîym; and those that do not know it you shall teach.

24. And whosoever shall transgress the law of your Êlôhîym, and of the king, shall be punished diligently, whether it is by death, or other punishment, by penalty of money, or by imprisonment.

25. Then Ezrâ the scribe said: Blessed is the only Yahuah Êlôhîym of my fathers, who has put these things into the heart of the king, to glorify his house that is in Yarûshâlaim:

26. And has honored me in the sight of the king, and his counsellors, and all his friends and nobles.

27. Therefore I was encouraged by the help of Yahuah my Êlôhîym, and gathered together men of Yâshârêl to go up with me.

28. And these are the chief according to their families and several dignities that went up with me from Bâbel in the reign of king Artachshashtâ:

29. Of the sons of Pîynechâs, Gêreshôn: Of the sons of îythâmâr, Dânîyêl (דָּנִיֵּאל): Of the sons of Dâwid, Chaṭṭûsh (חַטּוּשׁ) the son of Shekanyâhû (שְׁכַנְיָהוּ):

30. Of the sons of Parôsh, Zekaryâhû; and with him were counted a hundred and fifty men:

31. Of the sons of Pachath Môâb, Elyehôêynay (אֶלְיְהוֹעֵינַי), the son of Zerachyâh (זְרַחְיָה), and with him two hundred men:

32. Of the sons of Zattû, Shekanyâhû the son of Yachăzîyêl (יַחֲזִיאֵל), and with him three hundred men: Of the sons of Âdîynn, Ebed the son of Yahônâthân (יְהוֹנָתָן), and with him two hundred and fifty men:

33. Of the sons of Êylâm, Yôshîyâhû son of Gotholias, and with him seventy men:

34. Of the sons of Shephaṭyâhû, Zebadyâhû son of Mîykâêl, and with him threescore and ten men:

35. Of the sons of Yôâb, Ôbadyâhû son of Yachîyêl, and with him two hundred and twelve men:

36. Of the sons of Bânîy, Shelômîyth (שְׁלֹמִית) son of Yôsiphyâh, and with him a hundred and threescore men:

37. Of the sons of Bêbay, Zekaryâhû son of Bêbay, and with him twenty and eight men:

38. Of the sons of Azgâd, Yôchânân (יוֹחָנָן) son of Qâṭân, and with him a hundred and ten men:

39. Of the sons of Ădônîyqâm the last, and these are the names of them, Êlîypheleṭ, Yaîyêl (יְעִיאֵל), and Shemayâhû, and with them seventy men:

40. Of the sons of Bigway, Ûthay the son of Zabbûd (זַבּוּד), and with him seventy men.

41. And these I gathered together to the river called Ahăwâ (אַהֲוָא), where we pitched our tents three days: And then I surveyed them.

42. But when I had found there none of the Kôhên and Lêwîy,

43. Then I sent unto Ĕlîyezer, and Iduel, and Maasman,

44. And Elnâthân, and Shemayâhû (שְׁמַעְיָהוּ), and Yârîyb, and Nâthân, Elnâthân, Zekaryâhû, and Meshûllâm (מְשֻׁלָּם), principal men and learned.

45. And I bade them that they should go unto Iddô the captain, who was in the place of the treasury:

46. And commanded them that they should speak unto Iddô, and to his brethren, and to the treasurers in that place, to send us such men as might execute the Kôhên's office in the house of Yahuah.

47. And by the mighty hand of our Yahuah they brought unto us skilful men of the sons of Machlîy the son of Lêwîy, the son of Yâshârêl, Shêrêbyâh, and his sons, and his brethren, who were eighteen.

48. And Chăshabyâhû, and Annus and Yashayâhû (יְשַׁעְיָהוּ) his brother, of the sons of Chănanyâhû, and their sons, were twenty men.

49. And of the servants of the temple whom Dâwid had ordained, and the principal men for the service of the Lêwîy to wit, the servants of the temple two hundred and twenty, the catalogue of whose names were showed.

50. And there I vowed a fast unto the young men before our Yahuah, to desire of him a prosperous journey both for us and them that were with us, for our children, and for the cattle:

51. For I was ashamed to ask the king footmen, and horsemen, and conduct for safeguard against our adversaries.

52. For we had said unto the king, that the power of Yahuah our Êlôhîym should be with them that seek him, to support them in all ways.

53. And again we besought our Yahuah as touching these things, and found him favorable unto us.

54. Then I separated twelve of the chief of the Kôhên, Shêrêbyâh, and Chăshabyâhû, and ten men of their brethren with them:

55. And I weighed them the gold, and the silver, and the qâdôsh vessels of the house of our Yahuah, which the king, and his council, and the princes, and all Yâshârêl, had given.

56. And when I had weighed it, I delivered unto them six hundred and fifty talents of silver, and silver vessels of a hundred talents, and a hundred talents of gold,

57. And twenty golden vessels, and twelve vessels of brass, even of fine brass, glittering like gold.

58. And I said unto them: Both you are qâdôsh unto Yahuah, and the vessels are qâdôsh, and the gold and the silver is a vow unto Yahuah, Yahuah of our fathers.

59. Watch you, and keep them till you deliver them to the chief of the Kôhên and Lêwîy, and to the principal men of the families of Yâshârêl, in Yarûshâlaim, into the chambers of the house of our Êlôhîym.

60. So the Kôhên and the Lêwîy, who had received the silver and the gold and the vessels, brought them unto Yarûshâlaim, into the temple of Yahuah.

61. And from the river Ahăwâ we departed the twelfth day of the first month, and came to Yarûshâlaim by the mighty hand of our Yahuah, which was with us: And from the beginning of our journey Yahuah delivered us from every enemy, and so we came to Yarûshâlaim.

62. And when we had been there three days, the gold and silver that was weighed was delivered in the house of our Yahuah on the fourth day unto Merêmôth the Kôhên the son of Ûrîyâhû (אוּרִיָהוּ).

63. And with him was Elâzâr the son of Pîynechâs, and with them were Yôzâbâd the son of Yashûa (יֵשׁוּעַ) and Nôadyâh the son of Binnûy, Lêwîy: All was delivered them by number and weight.

64. And all the weight of them was written up the same hour.

65. Moreover they that were come out of the captivity offered sacrifice unto Yahuah Êlôhîym of Yâshârêl, even twelve bullocks for all Yâshârêl, fourscore and sixteen rams,

66. Threescore and twelve lambs, goats for a peace offering, twelve; all of them a sacrifice to Yahuah.

67. And they delivered the king's commandments unto the king's stewards and to the governors of Ărâm and Phoenicia; and they honored the people and the temple of Êlôhîym.

68. Now when these things were done, the rulers came unto me, and said,

69. The nation of Yâshârêl, the princes, the Kôhên and Lêwîy, have not put away from them the strange people of the land, nor the pollutions of the Gentiles to wit, of the Kenaanîy, Chittîy, Perizzîy (פְּרִזִּי), Yabûsîy (יְבוּסִי), and the Môâbîy, Mitsrîy, and Ědômîy.

70. For both they and their sons have married with their daughters, and the qâdôsh seed is mixed with the strange people of the land; and from the beginning of this matter the rulers and the great men have been partakers of this iniquity.

71. And as soon as I had heard these things, I rent my clothes, and the qâdôsh garment, and pulled off the hair from off my head and beard, and sat me down sad and very heavy.

72. So all they that were then moved at the word of Yahuah Êlôhîym of Yâshârêl assembled unto me, while I mourned for the iniquity: But I sat still full of heaviness until the evening sacrifice.

73. Then rising up from the fast with my clothes and the qâdôsh garment rent, and bowing my knees, and stretching forth my hands unto Yahuah,

74. I said, O Yahuah, I am confounded and ashamed before your face;

75. For our sins are multiplied above our heads, and our ignorance have reached up unto shâmayim.

76. Forever since the time of our fathers we have been and are in great sin, even unto this day.

77. And for our sins and our fathers' we with our brethren and our kings and our Kôhên were given up unto the kings of the earth, to the sword, and to captivity, and for a prey with shame, unto this day.

78. And now in some measure has mercy been showed unto us from you, O Yahuah, that there should be left us a root and a name in the place of your sanctuary;

79. And to discover unto us a light in the house of Yahuah our Êlôhîym, and to give us food in the time of our servitude.

80. Yea, when we were in bondage, we were not forsaken of our Yahuah; but he made us gracious before the kings of Pâras, so that they gave us food;

81. Yea, and honored the temple of our Yahuah, and raised up the desolate Tsîyôn, that they have given us a sure abiding in Yahûdâh and Yarûshâlaim.

82. And now, O Yahuah, what shall we say, having these things? For we have transgressed your commandments, which you gave by the hand of your servants the Nâbîy, saying,

83. That the land, which you enter into to possess as a heritage, is a land polluted with the pollutions of the strangers of the land, and they have filled it with their uncleanness.

84. Therefore now you shall not join your daughters unto their sons, neither shall you take their daughters unto your sons.

85. Moreover you shall never seek to have peace with them, that you may be strong, and eat the good things of the land, and that you may leave the inheritance of the land unto your children forevermore.

86. And all that is befallen is done unto us for our wicked works and great sins; for you, O Yahuah, did make our sins light,

87. And did give unto us such a root: But we have turned back again to transgress your law, and to mingle ourselves with the uncleanness of the nations of the land.

88. Might you not be angry with us to destroy us, till you had left us neither root, seed, nor name?

89. O Yahuah of Yâshârêl, you are true: For we are left a root this day.

90. Behold, now are we before you in our iniquities, for we cannot stand any longer because of these things before you.

91. And as Ezrâ in his prayer made his confession, weeping, and lying flat upon the ground before the temple, there gathered unto him from Yarûshâlaim a very great multitude of men and women and children: For there was great weeping among the multitude.

92. Then Shekanyâhû the son of Yachîyêl, one of the sons of Yâshârêl, called out, and said, O Ezrâ, we have sinned against Yahuah Êlôhîym, we have married strange women of the nations of the land, and now is all Yâshârêl aloft.

93. Let us make an oath to Yahuah, that we will put away all our women, which we have taken of the heathen, with their children,

94. Like as you have decreed, and as many as do obey the law of Yahuah.

95. Arise and put in execution: For to you does this matter appertain, and we will be with you: Do valiantly.

96. So Ezrâ arose, and took an oath of the chief of the Kôhên and Lêwîy of all Yâshârêl to do after these things; and so they swore.

Chapter 9

1. Then Ezrâ rising from the court of the temple went to the chamber of Yahôchânân (יְהוֹחָנָן) the son of Elyâshîyb,

2. And remained there, and did eat no meat nor drink water, mourning for the great iniquities of the multitude.

3. And there was a proclamation in all Yahûdâh and Yarûshâlaim to all them that were of the captivity, that they should be gathered together at Yarûshâlaim:

4. And that whosoever did not meet there within two or three days according as the elders that bare rule appointed, their cattle should be seized to the use of the temple, and himself cast out from them that were of the captivity.

5. And in three days were all they of the tribe of Yahûdâh and Binyâmîyn gathered together at Yarûshâlaim the twentieth day of the ninth month.

6. And all the multitude sat trembling in the broad court of the temple because of the present foul weather.

7. So Ezrâ arose up, and said unto them, you have transgressed the law in marrying strange women, thereby to increase the sins of Yâshârêl.

8. And now by confessing give glory unto Yahuah Êlôhîym of our fathers,

9. And do his will, and separate yourselves from the heathen of the land, and from the strange women.

10. Then the whole multitude cried, and said with a loud voice, like as you have spoken, so will we do.

11. But forasmuch as the people are many, and it is foul weather, so that we cannot stand without, and this is not a work of a day or two, seeing our sin in these things is spread far:

12. Therefore let the rulers of the multitude stay, and let all them of our habitations that have strange women come at the time appointed,

13. And with them the rulers and judges of every place, till we turn away the wrath of Yahuah from us for this matter.

14. Then Yahônâthân the son of Ăśâhêl and Yachzeyâh the son of Tiqwâh (תִּקְוָה) accordingly took this matter upon them: And Meshûllâm and Lêwîy and Shabbethay helped them.

15. And they that were of the captivity did according to all these things.

16. And Ezrâ the Kôhên chose unto him the principal men of their families, all by name: And in the first day of the tenth month they sat together to examine the matter.

17. So their cause that held strange women was brought to an end in the first day of the first month.

18. And of the Kôhên that were come together, and had strange women, there were found:

19. Of the sons of Yahusha the son of Yahôtsâdâq, and his brethren; Maăśêyâhû and Ĕlîyezer, and Yârîyb and Gedalyâhû (גְּדַלְיָהוּ).

20. And they gave their hands to put away their women and to offer rams to make reconcilement for their errors.

21. And of the sons of Immêr; Chănânîy, and Zebadyâhû, and Chârim, and Shemayâhû, and Yachîyêl, and Ûzzîyâhû.

22. And of the sons of Pashchûr; Elyehôêynay, Maăśêyâhu, Yishmâêl, and Nethanêl, and Yôzâbâd and Elâśâh.

23. And of the Lêwîy; Yôzâbâd, and Shimîy, and Qêlâyâh, who was called Kelitah, and Pethachyâh, and Yahûdâh, and Yônâh.

24. Of the qâdôsh singers; Elyâshîyb, Zakkûr.

25. Of the porters; Shallûm, and Telem.

26. Of them of Yâshârêl, of the sons of Parôsh; Ramyâh, and Yizzîyâh, and Malkiyâhû, and Mîyâmin, and Elâzâr, and Asibias, and Benâyâhû.

27. Of the sons of Êylâm; Mattanyâhû, Zekaryâhû, and Yachîyêl, and Yarîymôth, and Êlîyâhû.

28. And of the sons of Zattû; Elyehôêynay, Elyâshîyb, Mattanyâhû, Yarîymôth, and Zâbâd, and Ăzîyzâ.

29. Of the sons of Bêbay; Yôchânân, and Chănanyâhû and Zabbay, and Athlay.

30. Of the sons of Bânîy; Meshûllâm, Mallûk, Ădâyâhû, Yâshûb, Sheâl, and Yarîymôth.

31. And of the sons of Addi; Naathus, and Maăśêyâhû, Lacunus, and Naidus, and Mattanyâhû, and Betsalêl, Binnûy, and Menashsheh.

32. And of the sons of Channâhs; Ĕlîyezer and Yishshîyâhû, and Malkiyâhû, and Sabbeus, and Shimôn Chosameus.

33. And of the sons of Châshûm; Mattenay, and Mattattâh, and Zâbâd, Ĕlîyphelet, and Menashsheh, and Shimîy.

34. And of the sons of Bânîy; Yirmeyâhû, Momdis, Omaerus, Ûêl, Maăday, and Benâyâhû, and Wanyâh, Merêmôth, and Elyâshîyb, and Mattanyâhû, Mattenay, Yaăśû, Bânîy, Binnûy, Shimîy, Shelemyâhû, Nâthân: And of the sons of Ozora; Shashai, Azarel, Azael, Samatus, Zambris, Yôsêph.

35. And of the sons of Nebô; Mattithyâhû, Zâbâd, Zebîynâ, Yiddô, Yôêl, Benâyâhû.

36. All these had taken strange women, and they put them away with their children.

37. And the Kôhên and Lêwîy, and they that were of Yâshârêl, dwelt in Yarûshâlaim, and in the country, in the first day of the seventh month: So the children of Yâshârêl were in their habitations.

38. And the whole multitude came together with one accord into the broad place of the qâdôsh porch toward the east:

39. And they spoke unto Ezrâ the Kôhên and reader that he would bring the law of Môsheh that was given of Yahuah Êlôhîym of Yâshârêl.

40. So Ezrâ the chief Kôhên brought the law unto the whole multitude from man to woman, and to all the Kôhên, to hear law in the first day of the seventh month.

41. And he read in the broad court before the qâdôsh porch from morning unto midday, before both men and women; and the multitude he gave heed unto the law.

42. And Ezrâ the Kôhên and reader of the law stood up upon a pulpit of wood, which was made for that purpose.

43. And there stood up by him Mattithyâhû, Shema, Ănâyâh, Ăzaryâhû, Ûrîyâhû, Chilqîyâhû, Maăśêyâhû, upon the right hand:

44. And upon his left hand stood Pedâyâhû, Mîyshâêl, Malkiyâhû, Châshûm, and Chashbaddânâh, and Zekaryâhû, and Meshûllâm.

45. Then took Ezrâ the book of the law before the multitude: For he sat honorably in the first place in the sight of them all.

46. And when he opened the law, they stood all straight up. So Ezrâ blessed Yahuah Êlôhîym Elyôn Êl, Êlôhîym Tsâbâ (צְבָא), Shadday Êl.

47. And all the people answered, Âmên; and lifting up their hands they fell to the ground, and worshipped Yahuah.

48. Also Yahusha, Bânîy, Shêrêbyâh, Yâmîyn, Aqqûb, Shabbethay, Hôdîyâh, Maăśêyâhû, and Qelîyṭâ, Ăzaryâhû, and Yôzâbâd, and Chănan, Pelâyâh, the Lêwîy, taught the law of Yahuah, making them withal to understand it.

49. Then spoke Tirshâthâ (תִּרְשָׁתָא) unto Ezrâ the chief Kôhên and reader, and to the Lêwîy that taught the multitude, even to all, saying,

50. This day is qâdôsh unto Yahuah; (for they all wept when they heard the law:)

51. Go then, and eat the fat, and drink the sweet, and send part to them that have nothing;

52. For this day is qâdôsh unto Yahuah: And do not be sorrowful; for Yahuah will bring you to honor.

53. So the Lêwîy published all things to the people, saying: This day is qâdôsh to Yahuah; do not be sorrowful.

54. Then they went their way, everyone to eat and drink, and make merry, and to give part to them that had nothing, and to make great cheer;

55. Because they understood the words wherein they were instructed, and for which they had been assembled.

2 Ezrâh (Esdras) & The Traditional Bible Parallels

(Dabar Yahuah Scriptures Study Guide)

Introduction – Expanded Description

2 Esdras (sometimes called 4 Ezra in Catholic tradition) is a profound apocalyptic and prophetic text that addresses Yasharel's struggles after the destruction of the First and Second Temples. It is composed of visions, dialogues, and revelations given to Ezra regarding the end times, the problem of evil, divine justice, and the hope of redemption. The book bridges wisdom literature, prophecy, and apocalyptic themes, reflecting on human suffering, divine judgment, and the ultimate restoration of Êlôhîym's people.

Key themes include:

1. Human Suffering and Divine Justice – Ezra laments the destruction of Yarûshâlaim and questions why the righteous suffer while the wicked prosper.

2. Apocalyptic Revelation – Detailed visions of the end times, the coming Messiah, and the resurrection of the dead.

3. The Problem of Evil – Explores why evil exists in a world governed by a just Êlôhîym.

4. Hope and Restoration – Despite judgment, the faithful are promised restoration, eternal life, and divine vindication.

5. Wisdom and Instruction – Includes moral instruction, reflections on divine providence, and encouragement to live righteously.

The book is structured into visions and dialogues where Ezra interacts with angels, questions Êlôhîym's justice, and receives divine explanations about the fate of Yasharel and the world. Many New Testament passages echo or reflect its themes, especially regarding resurrection, judgment, and the Messiah.

Comparison Table: 2 Esdras & The Traditional Bible

2 Esdras Passage	Biblical Parallels	Theme / Connection
2 Esdras 1:1–28 – Ezra laments Yasharel's destruction and prays for understanding.	Lam 1–5; Ps 74	Lamentation over Yarûshâlaim; seeking Êlôhîym's guidance.
2 Esdras 2:1–32 – Ezra questions why the righteous suffer.	Job 1–3; Ps 73	Problem of evil and suffering of the faithful.
2 Esdras 3:1–40 – Êlôhîym instructs Ezra through angelic vision about divine justice.	Isa 40:1–11; Dan 7	Êlôhîym's justice, ultimate vindication, and authority.
2 Esdras 4:1–50 – Vision of the end times and symbolic imagery (wilderness, storms).	Ezek 37; Dan 12	Apocalyptic symbolism; resurrection and judgment.

2 Esdras Passage	Biblical Parallels	Theme / Connection
2 Esdras 5:1–49 – Ezra receives a vision of the Messiah and future salvation.	Isa 53; Matt 24; Rev 1	Messianic prophecy and the hope of redemption.
2 Esdras 6:1–46 – Êlôhîym answers questions about the nations, the righteous, and the wicked.	Ps 37; Prov 11:31	Divine providence, justice for nations, the fate of evil.
2 Esdras 7:1–54 – Angelical instruction about Êlôhîym's plan, end times, resurrection of the dead.	Dan 12:2–3; John 5:28–29	Resurrection and eternal life of the righteous.
2 Esdras 8:1–52 – Ezra is shown a series of visions representing nations, kingdoms, and the end of the age.	Dan 2; Rev 17	Prophetic vision of historical and eschatological events.
2 Esdras 9:1–46 – Moral exhortation to seek righteousness and fear Êlôhîym.	Prov 1; Jas 4:8	Ethical guidance in the midst of calamity.
2 Esdras 11–15 – Extended visions of cosmic conflict, the end of the world, and final judgment.	Matt 24–25; Rev 20	Eschatology, judgment, resurrection, and ultimate restoration.

Summary of Key Parallels

1. Lamentation and Questioning – Ezra mirrors the Psalms and Lamentations, expressing sorrow over Yasharel's destruction and questioning Êlôhîym's justice.

2. Divine Responses – Êlôhîym responds through visions and angels, emphasizing His ultimate justice, wisdom, and plan for redemption.

3. Apocalyptic Imagery – Symbolic visions echo Dânîyêl and Revelation, providing insight into end times, resurrection, and divine judgment.

4. Messianic Expectation – Predictions of a coming savior or righteous leader, foreshadowing New Testament fulfillment in Yahuah's Messiah.

5. Moral and Ethical Instruction – Guidance for righteous living, fear of Elohiym, and avoidance of evil, paralleling Proverbs and wisdom literature.

6. Resurrection and Judgment – The righteous are promised eternal life, while the wicked face judgment, aligning with themes in Dânîyêl, Isaiah, and the Gospels.

7. Historical and Eschatological Vision – Nations and kingdoms are revealed in vision, showing Êlôhîym's sovereign control over history and the final establishment of righteousness.

2 Ezrâ - Esdras

Chapter 1

1. The second book of the Nâbîy Ezrâ, the son of Śerâyâhû, the son of Ăzaryâhû, the son of Chilqîyâhû, the son of Shallûm, the son of Tsâdôq, the son of Ăchîyṭûb,

2. The son of Ăchîyâhû, the son of Pîynechâs, the son of Êlîy, the son of Ămaryâhû, the son of Ăzaryâhû, the son of Merâyôth, the son of Arna, the son of Ûzzîy, the son of Bûqqîy, the son of Ăbîyshûa, the son of Pîynechâs, the son of Elâzâr,

3. The son of Ahărôn, of the tribe of Lêwîy; which was captive in the land of the Mâday, in the reign of Artachshashtâ king of the Pâras.

4. And the word of Yahuah came unto me, saying,

5. Go your way, and show my people their sinful deeds, and their children their wickedness which they have done against me; that they may tell their children's children:

6. Because the sins of their fathers are increased in them: For they have forgotten me, and have offered unto strange gods.

7. Am not I even he that brought them out of the land of Mitsrayim, from the house of bondage? But they have provoked me unto wrath, and despised my counsels.

8. Pull you off then the hair of your head, and cast all evil upon them, for they have not been obedient unto my law, but it is a rebellious people.

9. How long shall I forbear them, into whom I have done so much good?

10. Many kings I have destroyed for their sakes; Parôh with his servants and all his power I have smitten down.

11. All the nations I have destroyed before them, and in the east I have scattered the people of two provinces, even of Tsôr and Tsîydôn, and have slain all their enemies.

12. You speak therefore unto them, saying: Thus says Yahuah,

13. I led you through the sea and in the beginning gave you a large and safe passage; I gave you Môsheh for a leader, and Ahărôn for a Kôhên.

14. I gave you light in a pillar of fire, and great wonders I have done among you; yet have you forgotten me, says Yahuah.

15. Thus says Yahuah Shadday Êl: The quails were as a token to you; I gave you tents for your safeguard: Nevertheless you murmured there,

16. And did not triumph in my name for the destruction of your enemies, but ever to this day you do yet murmur.

17. Where are the benefits that I have done for you? When you were hungry and thirsty in the wilderness, did you not cry unto me,

18. Saying: Why you have brought us into this wilderness to kill us? It had been better for us to have served the Mitsrîy, than to die in this wilderness.

19. Then I had pity upon your mournings, and gave you mân () to eat; so you did eat angels' bread.

20. When you were thirsty, did I not cleave the rock, and waters flowed out to your fill?

For the heat I covered you with the leaves of the trees.

21. I divided among you a fruitful land, I cast out the Kenaanîy, the Perizzîy, and the Pelishtîy, before you: What shall I yet do more for you? Says Yahuah.

22 Thus says Yahuah Shadday Êl: When you were in the wilderness, in the river of the Ĕmôrîy, being thirsty, and blaspheming my name,

23. I did not give you fire for your blasphemies, but cast a tree in the water, and made the river sweet.

24. What shall I do unto you, O Yaăqôb? You, Yahûdâh, would not obey me: I will turn me to other nations, and unto those I will I give my name, that they may keep my statutes.

25. Seeing you have forsaken me, I will forsake you also; when you desire me to be gracious unto you, I shall have no mercy upon you.

26. Whenever you shall call upon me, I will not hear you: For you have defiled your hands with blood, and your feet are swift to commit manslaughter.

27. You have not as it were forsaken me, but your own selves, says Yahuah.

28. Thus says Yahuah Shadday Êl, I have not prayed you as a father his sons, as a mother her daughters, and a nurse her young babes,

29. That you would be my people, and I should be your Êlôhîym; that you would be my children, and I should be your father?

30. I gathered you together, as a hen gathers her chickens under her wings: But now, what shall I do unto you? I will cast you out from my face.

31. When you offer unto me, I will turn my face from you: For your solemn feast days, your new months, and your circumcisions, I have forsaken.

32. I sent unto you my servants the Nâbîy, whom you have taken and slain, and torn their bodies in pieces, whose blood I will require of your hands, says Yahuah.

33. Thus says Yahuah Shadday Êl, your house is desolate, I will cast you out as the wind does stubble.

34. And your children shall not be fruitful; for they have despised my commandment, and done the thing that is an evil before me.

35. Your houses I will give to a people that shall come; which not having heard of me yet shall believe me; to whom I have showed no signs, yet they shall do that I have commanded them.

36. They have seen no Nâbîy, yet they shall call their sins to remembrance, and acknowledge them.

37. I take to witness the grace of the people to come, whose little ones rejoice in gladness: And though they have not seen me with bodily eyes, yet in spirit they believe the thing that I say.

38. And now, brother, behold what glory; and see the people that come from the east:

39. Unto whom I will give for leaders, Abrâhâm, Yitschâq, and Yaăqôb, Hôshêa, Âmôs, and Mîykâh, Yôêl, Ôbadyâhû, and Yônâh,

40. Nachûm, and Chăbaqqûq, Tsephanyâhû, Chaggay, zekaryâhû, and Malâkîy, which is called also an angel of Yahuah.

Chapter 2

1. Thus says Yahuah, I brought this people out of bondage, and I gave them my commandments by menservants the Nâbîy;

whom they would not hear, but despised my counsels.

2. The mother that bare them says unto them: Go your way, you children; for I am a widow and forsaken.

3. I brought you up with gladness; but with sorrow and heaviness I have lost you: For you have sinned before Yahuah your Êlôhîym, and done that thing that is evil before him.

4. But what shall I now do unto you? I am a widow and forsaken: Go your way, O my children, and ask mercy of Yahuah.

5. As for me, O father, I call upon you for a witness over the mother of these children, which would not keep my covenant,

6. That you bring them to confusion, and their mother to a spoil, that there may be no offspring of them.

7. Let them be scattered abroad among the heathen, let their names be put out of the earth: For they have despised my covenant.

8. Woe be unto you, Ashshûr, you that hide the unrighteous in you! O you wicked people, remember what I did unto Sedôm and Ămôrâh (עֲמֹרָה);

9. Whose land lies in clods of pitch and heaps of ashes: Even so also I will do unto them that do not hear me, says Yahuah Shadday Êl.

10. Thus says Yahuah unto Ezrâ: Tell my people that I will give them the kingdom of Yarûshâlaim, which I would have given unto Yâshârêl.

11. Their glory also I will take unto me, and give these the everlasting tabernacles, which I had prepared for them.

12. They shall have the tree of life for an ointment of sweet savor; they shall neither labor, nor be weary.

13. Go, and you shall receive: Pray for few days unto you, that they may be shortened: The kingdom is already prepared for you: Watch.

14. Take shâmayim and earth to witness; for I have broken the evil in pieces, and created the good: For I live, says Yahuah.

15. Mother, embrace your children, and bring them up with gladness, make their feet as fast as a pillar: For I have chosen you, says Yahuah.

16. And those that are dead I will raise up again from their places, and bring them out of the graves: For I have known my name in Yâshârêl.

17. Do not fear, you mother of the children: For I have chosen you, says Yahuah.

18. For your help I will send my servants Yashayâhû and Yirmeyâhû, after whose counsel I have sanctified and prepared for you twelve trees laden with divers fruits,

19. And as many fountains flowing with milk and honey, and seven mighty mountains, whereupon there grow roses and lilies, whereby I will fill your children with joy.

20. Do right to the widow, judge for the fatherless, give to the poor, defend the orphan, clothe the naked,

21. Heal the broken and the weak, do not laugh a lame man to scorn, defend the maimed, and let the blind man come into the sight of my clearness.

22. Keep the old and young within your walls.

23. Wherever you find the dead, take them and bury them, and I will give you the first place in my resurrection.

24. Abide still, O my people, and take your rest, for your quietness still come.

25. Nourish your children, O you good nurse; establish their feet.

26. As for the servants whom I have given you, there shall not one of them perish; for I will require them from among your number.

27. Do not be weary: For when the day of trouble and heaviness comes, others shall weep and be sorrowful, but you shall be merry and have abundance.

28. The heathen shall envy you, but they shall be able to do nothing against you, says Yahuah.

29. My hands shall cover you, so that your children shall not see sheôl.

30. Be joyful, O you mother, with your children; for I will deliver you, says Yahuah.

31. Remember your children that sleep, for I shall bring them out of the sides of the earth, and show mercy unto them: For I am merciful, says Yahuah Shadday Êl.

32. Embrace your children until I come and show mercy unto them: For my wells run over, and my grace shall not fail.

33. I Ezrâ received a charge of Yahuah upon the mount Chôrêb that I should go unto Yâshârêl; but when I came unto them, they set me at nothing, and despised the commandment of Yahuah.

34. And therefore I say unto you, O you heathen, that hear and understand, look for your Rââh (רָעָה), he shall give you everlasting rest; for he is nigh at hand, that shall come in the end of the world.

35. Be ready to the reward of the kingdom, for the everlasting light shall shine upon you forevermore.

36. Flee the shadow of this world, receive the joyfulness of your glory: I testify my Yâsha openly.

37. O receive the gift that is given you, and be glad, giving thanks unto him that has led you to the shâmayim kingdom.

38. Arise up and stand, behold the number of those that be sealed in the Feast of Yahuah;

39. Which are departed from the shadow of the world, and have received glorious garments of Yahuah.

40. Take your number, O Tsîyôn, and shut up those of you that are clothed in white, which have fulfilled the law of Yahuah.

41. The number of your children, whom you longed for, is fulfilled: Beseech the power of Yahuah, that your people, which have been called from the beginning, may be hallowed.

42. I Ezrâ saw upon the mount Tsîyôn a great people, whom I could not number, and they all praised Yahuah with songs.

43. And in the midst of them there was a young man of a high stature, taller than all the rest, and upon every one of their heads he set crowns, and was more exalted; which I marveled at greatly.

44. So I asked the angel, and said, Sir, what are these?

45. He answered and said unto me, these are they that have put off the mortal clothing, and put on the immortal, and have confessed the name of Êlôhîym: Now they are crowned, and receive palms.

46. Then I said unto the angel, what young person is it that crowns them, and gives them palms in their hands?

47. So he answered and said unto me, it is the Bên (בֵּן) Êlôhîym, whom they have confessed in the world. Then I began greatly to commend them that stood so stiffly for the name of Yahuah.

48. Then the angel said unto me: Go your way, and tell my people what manner of things, and how great wonders of Yahuah your Êlôhîym, you have seen.

Chapter 3

1. In the thirtieth year after the ruin of the city I was in Bâbel, and lay troubled upon my bed, and my thoughts came up over my heart:

2. For I saw the desolation of Tsîyôn, and the wealth of them that dwelt at Bâbel.

3. And my spirit was sore moved, so that I began to speak words full of fear to Elyôn Êl, and said,

4. O Yahuah, who bears rule, you spoke at the beginning, when you did plant the earth, and that yourself alone, and commanded the people,

5. And gave a body unto Âdâm without soul, which was the workmanship of your hands, and did breathe into him the breath of life, and he was made living before you.

6. And you lead him into paradise, which your right hand had planted, before ever the earth came forward.

7. And unto him you gave commandment to love your way: Which he transgressed, and immediately you appointed death in him and in his generations, of whom came nations, tribes, people, and kindreds, out of number.

8. And every people walked after their own will, and did wonderful things before you, and despised your commandments.

9. And again in process of time you brought the flood upon those that dwelt in the world, and destroyed them.

10. And it came to pass in every of them, that as death was to Âdâm, so was the flood to these.

11. Nevertheless you left one of them, namely, Nôach with his household, of whom came all righteous men.

12. And it happened, that when they that dwelt upon the earth began to multiply, and had gotten them many children, and were a great people, they began again to be more ungodly than the first.

13. Now when they lived so wickedly before you, you did choose you a man from among them, whose name was Abrâhâm.

14. Him you loved, and unto him only you showed your will:

15. And made an everlasting covenant with him, promising him that you would never forsake his seed.

16. And unto him you gave Yitschâq, and unto Yitschâq also you gave Yaăqôb and Êśâw. As for Yaăqôb, you did choose him to you, and put by Êśâw: And so Yaăqôb became a great multitude.

17. And it came to pass, that when you led his seed out of Mitsrayim, you brought them up to the mount Sîynay.

18. And bowing the shâmayim, you did set fast the earth, moved the whole world, and made the depths to tremble, and troubled the men of that age.

19. And your glory went through four gates, of fire, and of earthquake, and of wind, and of cold; that you might give the law unto the seed of Yaăqôb, and diligence unto the generation of Yâshârêl.

20. And yet you did not take away from them a wicked heart, that your law might bring forth fruit in them.

21. For the first Âdâm bearing a wicked heart transgressed, and was overcome; and so are all they that are born of him.

22. Thus infirmity was made permanent; and the law also in the heart of the people with the malignity of the root; so that the good departed away, and the evil abode still.

23. So the times passed away, and the years were brought to an end: Then you did raise you up a servant, called Dâwid:

24. Whom you commanded to build a city unto your name, and to offer incense and offerings unto you therein.

25. When this was done many years, then they that inhabited the city forsook you,

26. And in all things did even as Âdâm and all his generations had done: For they also had a wicked heart:

27. And so you gave your city over into the hands of your enemies.

28. Are their deeds then any better that inhabit Bâbel, that they should therefore have the dominion over Tsîyôn?

29. For when I came thither, and had seen impieties without number, then my soul saw many evildoers in this thirtieth year, so that my heart failed me.

30. For I have seen how you suffered them sinning, and have spared wicked doers: And have destroyed your people, and have preserved your enemies, and do not have signified it.

31. I do not remember how this way may be left: Are they then of Bâbel better than they of Tsîyôn?

32. Or is there any other people that knows you besides Yâshârêl? Or what generation has so believed your covenants as Yaăqôb?

33. And yet their reward does not appear, and their labor has no fruit: For I have gone here and there through the heathen, and I see that they flow in wealth, and do not think upon your commandments.

34. Weigh you therefore our wickedness now in the balance, and their's also that dwell the world; and so shall your name nowhere be found but in Yâshârêl.

35. Or when was it that they which dwell upon the earth have not sinned in your sight? Or what people have so kept your commandments?

36. You shall find that Yâshârêl by name has kept your precepts; but not the heathen.

Chapter 4

1. And the angel that was sent unto me, whose name was Ûrîyêl, gave me an answer,

2. And said, your heart has gone too far in this world, and you think to comprehend the way of Elyôn Êl?

3. Then I said, yea, my master. And he answered me, and said, I am sent to show you three ways, and to set forth three similitudes before you:

4. Whereof if you can declare me one, I will show you also the way that you desire to see, and I shall show you from whence the wicked heart comes.

5. And I said, Tell on, my master. Then he said unto me, go your way, weigh me the weight of the fire, or measure me the blast of the wind, or call me again the day that is past.

6. Then I answered and said, what man is able to do that, that you should ask such things of me?

7. And he said unto me, if I should ask you how great dwellings are in the midst of the sea, or how many springs are in the beginning of the deep, or how many springs are

above the firmament, or which are the outgoings of paradise:

8. Peradventure you would say unto me, I never went down into the deep, nor as yet into sheôl, neither did I ever climb up into shâmayim.

9. Nevertheless now I have asked you but only of the fire and wind, and of the day where through you have passed, and of things from which you cannot be separated, and yet you can give me no answer of them.

10. He said moreover unto me, your own things, and such as are grown up with you, can you not know;

11. How should your vessel then be able to comprehend the way of Elyôn Êl, and, the world being now outwardly corrupted to understand the corruption that is evident in my sight?

12. Then I said unto him, it were better that we were not at all, than that we should live still in wickedness, and to suffer, and not to know wherefore.

13. He answered me, and said, I went into a forest into a plain, and the trees took counsel,

14. And said, come, let us go and make war against the sea that it may depart away before us, and that we may make us more woods.

15. The floods of the sea also in like manner took counsel, and said, come, let us go up and subdue the woods of the plain, that there also we may make us another country.

16. The thought of the wood was in vain, for the fire came and consumed it.

17. The thought of the floods of the sea came likewise to nothing, for the sand stood up and stopped them.

18. If you were judge now between these two, whom would you begin to justify? Or whom would you condemn?

19. I answered and said, verily it is a foolish thought that they both have devised, for the ground is given unto the wood, and the sea also has his place to bear his floods.

20. Then he answered me, and said, you have given a right judgment, but why do you not judge yourself also?

21. For like as the ground is given unto the wood, and the sea to his floods: Even so they that dwell upon the earth may understand nothing but that which is upon the earth: And he that dwells above the shâmayim may only understand the things that are above the height of the shâmayim.

22. Then I answered and said, I beseech you, O Yahuah, let me have understanding:

23. For it was not my mind to be curious of the high things, but of such as pass by us daily, namely, wherefore Yâshârêl is given up as a reproach to the heathen, and for what cause the people whom you have loved is given over unto ungodly nations, and why the law of our forefathers is brought to nothing, and the written covenants come to none effect,

24. And we pass away out of the world as grasshoppers, and our life is astonishment and fear, and we are not worthy to obtain mercy.

25. What will he then do unto his name whereby we are called? Of these things I have asked.

26. Then he answered me, and said, the more you search, the more you shall marvel; for the world hastes fast to pass away,

27. And cannot comprehend the things that are promised to the righteous in time to

come: For this world is full of unrighteousness and infirmities.

28. But as concerning the things whereof you ask me, I will tell you; for the evil is sown, but the destruction thereof is not yet come.

29. If therefore that which is sown do not be turned upside down, and if the place where the evil is sown does not pass away, then it cannot come that is sown with good.

30. For the grain of evil seed has been sown in the heart of Âdâm from the beginning, and how much ungodliness has it brought up unto this time? And how much shall it yet bring forth until the time of threshing come?

31. Ponder now by yourself, how great fruit of wickedness the grain of evil seed has brought forth.

32. And when the ears shall be cut down, which are without number, how great a floor shall they fill?

33. Then I answered and said, how, and when shall these things come to pass? Wherefore are our years few and evil?

34. And he answered me, saying, do you not hasten above Elyôn Êl: For your haste is in vain to be above him, for you have much exceeded.

35. Did not the souls also of the righteous ask question of these things in their chambers, saying, how long shall I hope on this fashion? When comes the fruit of the floor of our reward?

36. And unto these things Ûrîyêl the archangel gave them answer, and said, even when the number of seeds is filled in you: For he has weighed the world in the balance.

37. By measure he has measured the times; and by number he has numbered the times; and he does not move nor stir them, until the said measure is fulfilled.

38. Then I answered and said, O Yahuah that bears rule, even we all are full of impiety.

39. And for our sakes peradventure it is that the floors of the righteous are not filled, because of the sins of them that dwell upon the earth.

40. So he answered me, and said, go your way to a woman with child, and ask of her when she has fulfilled her nine months, if her womb may keep the birth any longer within her.

41. Then I said, no, master, that she cannot. And he said unto me, in the grave the chambers of souls are like the womb of a woman:

42. For like as a woman that travail makes haste to escape the necessity of the travail: Even so do these places haste to deliver those things that are committed unto them.

43. From the beginning, look, what you desire to see, it shall be shown you.

44. Then I answered and said, if I have found favor in your sight, and if it is possible, and if I am meet therefore,

45. Show me then whether there be more to come than is past, or more past than is to come.

46. What is past I know, but what is for to come I do not know.

47. And he said unto me, stand up upon the right side, and I shall expound the similitude unto you.

48. So I stood, and saw, and, behold, a hot burning oven passed by before me: And it happened that when the flame was gone by I looked, and, behold, the smoke remained still.

49. After this there passed by before me a watery cloud, and sent down much rain with a storm; and when the stormy rain was past, the drops remained still.

50. Then he said unto me, consider with yourself; as the rain is more than the drops, and as the fire is greater than the smoke; but the drops and the smoke remain behind: So the quantity which is past did more exceed.

51. Then I prayed, and said, may I live, do you think, until that time? Or what shall happen in those days?

52. He answered me, and said, as for the tokens whereof you ask me, I may tell you of them in part: But as touching your life, I am not sent to show you; for I do not know it.

Chapter 5

1. Nevertheless as coming the tokens, behold, the days shall come, that they which dwell upon earth shall be taken in a great number, and the way of truth shall be hidden, and the land shall be barren of faith.

2. But iniquity shall be increased above that which now you see, or that you have heard long ago.

3. And the land that you see now to have root, you shall see wasted suddenly.

4. But if Elyôn Êl grant you to live, you shall see after the third trumpet that the sun shall suddenly shine again in the night, and the moon thrice in the day:

5. And blood shall drop out of wood, and the stone shall give his voice, and the people shall be troubled:

6. And even he shall rule, whom they do not look for that dwell upon the earth, and the fowls shall take their flight away together:

7. And the Sedôm Sea shall cast out fish, and make a noise in the night, which many have not known: But they shall all hear the voice thereof.

8. There shall be a confusion also in many places, and the fire shall be oft sent out again, and the wild beasts shall change their places, and menstruous women shall bring forth monsters:

9. And salt waters shall be found in the sweet, and all friends shall destroy one another; then shall wit hide itself, and understanding withdraw itself into his secret chamber,

10. And shall be sought of many, and yet not be found: Then shall unrighteousness and incontinency be multiplied upon earth.

11. One land also shall ask another, and say, is righteousness that makes a man righteous gone through you? And it shall say, no.

12. At the same time shall men hope, but obtain nothing: They shall labor, but their ways shall not prosper.

13. To show you such tokens I have leave; and if you will pray again, and weep as now, and fast even days, you shall hear yet greater things.

14. Then I awoke, and an extreme fearfulness went through all my body, and my mind was troubled, so that it fainted.

15. So the angel that was come to talk with me held me, comforted me, and set me up upon my feet.

16. And in the second night it came to pass, that Shealtîyêl the captain of the people came unto me, saying, where have you been? And why is your countenance so heavy?

17. Do you not know that Yâshârêl is committed unto you in the land of their captivity?

18. Up then, and eat bread, and do not forsake us, as the shepherd that leaves his flock in the hands of cruel wolves.

19. Then I said unto him, go your ways from me, and do not come nigh me. And he heard what I said, and went from me.

20. And so I fasted seven days, mourning and weeping, like as Ûrîyêl the angel commanded me.

21. And after seven days so it was, that the thoughts of my heart were very grievous unto me again,

22. And my soul recovered the spirit of understanding, and I began to talk with Elyôn Êl again,

23. And said, O Yahuah that bears rule, of every wood of the earth, and of all the trees thereof, you have chosen you one only vine:

24. And of all lands of the whole world you have chosen you one pit: And of all the flowers thereof one lily:

25. And of all the depths of the sea you have filled you one river: And of all built cities you have hallowed Tsîyôn unto yourself:

26. And of all the fowls that are created you have named you one dove: And of all the cattle that are made you have provided you one sheep:

27. And among all the multitudes of people you have gotten you one people: And unto this people, whom you loved, you gave a law that is approved of all.

28. And now, O Yahuah, why you have given this one people over unto many? And upon the one root you have prepared others, and why you have scattered your only one people among many?

29. And they which did contradict your promises, and did not believe your covenants, have trodden them down.

30. If you did so much hate your people, yet you should you punish them with your own hands.

31. Now when I had spoken these words, the angel that came to me the night afore was sent unto me,

32. And said unto me, hear me, and I will instruct you; hearken to the thing that I say, and I shall tell you more.

33. And I said, speak on, my master. Then he said unto me, you are sore troubled in mind for Yâshârêl's sake: Do you love that people better than he that made them?

34. And I said, no, master: But of very grief I have spoken: For my reins pain me every hour, while I labor to comprehend the way of Elyôn Êl, and to seek out part of his judgment.

35. And he said unto me, you cannot. And I said, wherefore, master? Whereunto was I born then? Or why was not my mother's womb then my grave, that I might not have seen the travail of Yaăqôb, and the wearisome toil of the stock of Yâshârêl?

36. And he said unto me, number me the things that are not yet come, gather me together the drops that are scattered abroad, make me the flowers green again that are withered,

37. Open me the places that are closed, and bring me forth the winds that in them are shut up, show me the image of a voice: And then I will declare to you the thing that you labor to know.

38. And I said, O Yahuah that bears rule, who may know these things, but he that has not his dwelling with men?

39. As for me, I am unwise: How may I then speak of these things whereof you asked me?

40. Then he said unto me, like as you can do none of these things that I have spoken of, even so you cannot find out my judgment, or in the end the love that I have promised unto my people.

41. And I said, behold, O Yahuah, yet are you nigh unto them that be reserved till the end: And what shall they do that have been before me, or we that are now, or they that shall come after us?

42. And he said unto me, I will liken my judgment unto a ring: Like as there is no slackness of the last, even so there is no swiftness of the first.

43. So I answered and said, could you not make those that have been made, and be now, and that are for to come, at once; that you might show your judgment the sooner?

44. Then he answered me, and said, the creature may not haste above the maker; neither may the world hold them at once that shall be created therein.

45. And I said, as you have said unto your servant, that you, which give life to all, have given life at once to the creature that you have created, and the creature bare it: Even so it might now also bear them that now are present at once.

46. And he said unto me, ask the womb of a woman, and say unto her, if you bring forth children, why do you it not together, but one after another? Pray her therefore to bring forth ten children at once.

47. And I said, she cannot: But must do it by distance of time.

48. Then he said unto me, even so I have given the womb of the earth to those that be sown in it in their times.

49. For like as a young child may not bring forth the things that belong to the aged, even so I have disposed the world which I created.

50. And I asked, and said, seeing you have now given me the way, I will proceed to speak before you: For our mother, of whom you have told me that she is young, draws now nigh unto age.

51. He answered me, and said, ask a woman that bears children, and she shall tell you.

52. Say unto her, wherefore are unto they whom you have now brought forth like those that were before, but less of stature?

53. And she shall answer you, they that are born in the strength of youth are of one fashion, and they that are born in the time of age, when the womb fails, are otherwise.

54. Consider you therefore also, how that you are less of stature than those that were before you.

55. And so are they that come after you less than you, as the creatures which now begin to be old, and have passed over the strength of youth.

56. Then I said, Yahuah, I beseech you, if I have found favor in your sight, show your servant by whom you visit your creature.

Chapter 6

1. And he said unto me, in the beginning, when the earth was made, before the borders of the world stood, or ever the winds blew,

2. Before it thundered and lightened, or ever the foundations of paradise were laid,

3. Before the fair flowers were seen, or ever the moveable powers were established, before the innumerable multitude of angels were gathered together,

4. Or ever the heights of the air were lifted up, before the measures of the firmament were named, or ever the chimneys in Tsîyôn were hot,

5. And before the present years were sought out, and or ever the inventions of them that now sin were turned, before they were sealed that have gathered faith for a treasure:

6. Then I did consider these things, and they all were made through me alone, and through none other: By me also they shall be ended, and by none other.

7. Then I answered and said, what shall be the parting asunder of the times? Or when shall be the end of the first, and the beginning of it that follow?

8. And he said unto me, from Abrâhâm unto Yitschâq, when Yaăqôb and Êśâw were born of him, Yaăqôb's hand held first the heel of Êśâw.

9. For Êśâw is the end of the world, and Yaăqôb is the beginning of it that follows.

10. The hand of man is between the heel and the hand: Other question, Ezrâ, you do not ask.

11. I answered then and said, O Yahuah that bears rule, if I have found favor in your sight,

12. I beseech you, show your servant the end of your tokens, whereof you showed me part the last night.

13. So he answered and said unto me, stand up upon your feet, and hear a mighty sounding voice.

14. And it shall be as it were a great motion; but the place where you stand shall not be moved.

15. And therefore when it speaks do not be afraid: For the word is of the end, and the foundation of the earth is understood.

16. And why? Because the speech of these things trembles and is moved: For it knows that the end of these things must be changed.

17. And it happened, that when I had heard it I stood up upon my feet, and hearkened, and, behold, there was a voice that spoke, and the sound of it was like the sound of many waters.

18. And it said, behold, the days come, that I will begin to draw nigh, and to visit them that dwell upon the earth,

19. And will begin to make inquisition of them, what they are that have hurt unjustly with their unrighteousness, and when the affliction of Tsîyôn shall be fulfilled;

20. And when the world, that shall begin to vanish away, shall be finished, then I will show these tokens: The books shall be opened before the firmament, and they shall see all together:

21. And the children of a year old shall speak with their voices, the women with child shall bring forth untimely children of three or four months old, and they shall live, and be raised up.

22. And suddenly shall the sown places appear unsown, the full storehouses shall suddenly be found empty:

23. And the trumpet shall give a sound, which when every man hears, they shall be suddenly afraid.

24. At that time shall friends fight one against another like enemies, and the earth shall stand in fear with those that dwell therein, the springs of the fountains shall stand still, and in three hours they shall not run.

25. Whosoever remains from all these that I have told you shall escape, and see my salvation, and the end of your world.

26. And the men that are received shall see it, who have not tasted death from their birth: And the heart of the inhabitants shall be changed, and turned into another meaning.

27. For evil shall be put out, and deceit shall be quenched.

28. As for faith, it shall flourish, corruption shall be overcome, and the truth, which has been so long without fruit, shall be declared.

29. And when he talked with me, behold, I looked by little and little upon him before whom I stood.

30. And these words he said unto me; I am come to show you the time of the night to come.

31. If you will pray yet more, and fast seven days again, I shall tell you greater things by day than I have heard.

32. For your voice is heard before Elyôn Êl: For Shadday Êl has seen your righteous dealing, he has seen also your chastity, which you have had ever since your youth.

33. And therefore he has sent me to show you all these things, and to say unto you, be of good comfort and do not fear.

34 And do not hasten with the times that are past, to think vain things, that you may not hasten from the latter times.

35. And it came to pass after this, that I wept again, and fasted seven days in like manner, that I might fulfil the three weeks which he told me.

36. And in the eighth night was my heart vexed within me again, and I began to speak before Elyôn Êl.

37. For my spirit was greatly set on fire, and my soul was in distress.

38. And I said, O Yahuah, you spoke from the beginning of the creation, even the first day, and said thus; let shâmayim and earth be made; and your word was a perfect work.

39. And then was the spirit, and darkness and silence were on every side; the sound of man's voice was not yet formed.

40. Then you commanded a fair light to come forth of your treasures that your work might appear.

41. Upon the second day you made the spirit of the firmament, and commanded it to part asunder, and to make a division between the waters that the one part might go up, and the other remain beneath.

42. Upon the third day you did command that the waters should be gathered in the seventh part of the earth: Six parts you have dried up, and kept them, to the intent that of these some being planted of Êlôhîym and tilled might serve you.

43. For as soon as your word went forth the work was made.

44. For immediately there was great and innumerable fruit, and many and divers pleasures for the taste, and flowers of unchangeable color, and odors of wonderful smell: And this was done the third day.

45. Upon the fourth day you commanded that the sun should shine, and the moon give her light, and the stars should be in order:

46. And gave them a charge to do service unto man that was to be made.

47. Upon the fifth day you said unto the seventh part, where the waters were gathered that it should bring forth living creatures, fowls and fishes: And so it came to pass.

48. For the dumb water and without life brought forth living things at the commandment of Êlôhîym, that all people might praise your wondrous works.

49. Then you did ordain two living creatures, the one you called behêmôth, and the other Liwyâthân;

50. And did separate the one from the other: For the seventh part, namely, where the water was gathered together, might not hold them both.

51. Unto behêmôth you gave one part, which was dried up the third day, that he should dwell in the same part, wherein are a thousand hills:

52. But unto Liwyâthân you gave the seventh part, namely, the moist; and have kept her to be devoured of whom you will, and when.

53. Upon the sixth day you gave commandment unto the earth, that before you it should bring forth beasts, cattle, and creeping things:

54. And after these, Âdâm also, whom you made master of all your creatures: Of him we come all, and the people also whom you have chosen.

55. All this I have spoken before you, O Yahuah, because you made the world for our sakes

56. As for the other people, which also come of Âdâm, you have said that they are nothing, but be like unto spittle: And have likened the abundance of them unto a drop that falls from a vessel.

57. And now, O Yahuah, behold, these heathen, which have ever been reputed as nothing, have begun to be master over us, and to devour us.

58. But we your people, whom you have called your firstborn, your only begotten, and your fervent lover, are given into their hands.

59. If the world now is made for our sakes, why do we not possess an inheritance with the world? How long shall this endure?

Chapter 7

1. And when I had made an end of speaking these words, there was sent unto me the angel which had been sent unto me the nights afore:

2. And he said unto me, up, Ezrâ, and hear the words that I am come to tell you.

3. And I said, speak on, my Êlôhîym. Then he said unto me, the sea is set in a wide place, that it might be deep and great.

4. But put the case the entrance were narrow, and like a river;

5. Who then could go into the sea to look upon it, and to rule it? If he went not through the narrow, how could he come into the broad?

6. There is also another thing; a city is built, and set upon a broad field, and is full of all good things:

7. The entrance thereof is narrow, and is set in a dangerous place to fall, like as if there were a fire on the right hand, and on the left a deep water:

8. And one only path between them both, even between the fire and the water, so small that there could but one man go there at once.

9. If this city now were given unto a man for an inheritance, if he never shall pass the danger set before it, how shall he receive this inheritance?

10. And I said, it is so, master. Then he said unto me, even so also is Yâshârêl's portion.

11. Because for their sakes I made the world: And when Âdâm transgressed my statutes, then was decreed that now is done.

12. Then were the entrances of this world made narrow, full of sorrow and travail: They are but few and evil, full of perils, and very painful.

13. For the entrances of the elder world were wide and sure, and brought immortal fruit.

14. If then they that live labor not to enter these strait and vain things, they can never receive those that are laid up for them.

15. Now therefore why do you disquiet yourself, seeing you are but a corruptible man? And why are you moved, whereas you are but mortal?

16. Why you have not considered in your mind this thing that is to come, rather than that which is present?

17. Then answered I and said, O Yahuah that bears rule, you have ordained in your law, that the righteous should inherit these things, but that the ungodly should perish.

18. Nevertheless the righteous shall suffer strait things, and hope for wide: For they that have done wickedly have suffered the strait things, and yet shall not see the wide.

19. And he said unto me. There is no judge above Êlôhîym, and none that has understanding above Elyôn Êl.

20. For there are many that perish in this life, because they despise the law of Êlôhîym that is set before them.

21. For Êlôhîym has given strait commandment to such as came, what they should do to live, even as they came, and what they should observe to avoid punishment.

22. Nevertheless they were not obedient unto him; but spoke against him, and imagined vain things;

23. And deceived themselves by their wicked deeds; and said of Elyôn Êl, that he is not; and did not know his ways:

24. But his law have they despised, and denied his covenants; in his statutes have they not been faithful, and have not performed his works.

25. And therefore, Ezrâ, for the empty are empty things, and for the full are the full things.

26. Behold, the time shall come, that these tokens which I have told you shall come to pass, and the bride shall appear, and she coming forth shall be seen, that now is withdrawn from the earth.

27. And whosoever is delivered from the foresaid evils shall see my wonders.

28. For my son Yahusha shall be revealed with those that are with him, and they that remain shall rejoice within four hundred years.

29. After these years shall my son the Mâshîyach die, and all men that have life.

30. And the world shall be turned into the old silence seven days, like as in the former judgments: So that no man shall remain.

31. And after seven days the world, that yet does not awake, shall be raised up, and that shall die that is corrupt.

32. And the earth shall restore those that are asleep in her, and so shall the dust those that dwell in silence, and the secret places shall deliver those souls that were committed unto them.

33. And Elyôn Êl shall appear upon the seat of judgment, and misery shall pass away, and the long suffering shall have an end:

34. But judgment only shall remain, truth shall stand, and faith shall wax strong:

35. And the work shall follow, and the reward shall be showed, and the good deeds shall be of force, and wicked deeds shall bear no rule.

36. Then I said, Abrâhâm prayed first for the Sedôm, and Môsheh for the fathers that sinned in the wilderness:

37. And Yahusha after him for Yâshârêl in the time of Achan:

38. And Shemûêl and Dâwid for the destruction: And Shelômôh for them that should come to the sanctuary:

39. And Êlîyâhû for those that received rain; and for the dead, that he might live:

40. And Chizqîyâhû for the people in the time of Sanchêrîyb: And many for many.

41. Even so now, seeing corruption is grown up, and wickedness increased, and the righteous have prayed for the ungodly: Wherefore shall it not be so now also?

42 He answered me, and said, this present life is not the end where much glory does abide; therefore have they prayed for the weak.

43. But the day of doom shall be the end of this time, and the beginning of the immortality for to come, wherein corruption is past,

44. Intemperance is at an end, infidelity is cut off, righteousness is grown, and truth is sprung up.

45. Then shall no man be able to save him that is destroyed, nor to oppress him that has gotten the victory.

46. I answered then and said, this is my first and last saying, that it had been better not to have given the earth unto Âdâm: Or else, when it was given him, to have restrained him from sinning.

47. For what profit is it for men now in this present time to live in heaviness, and after death to look for punishment?

48. O Âdâm, what you have done? For though it was you that sinned, you are not fallen alone, but we all that come of you.

49. For what profit is it unto us, if there is promised us an immortal time, whereas we have done the works that bring death?

50. And that there is promised us an everlasting hope, whereas ourselves being wickedest are made vain?

51. And that there are laid up for us dwellings of health and safety, whereas we have lived wickedly?

52. And that the glory of Elyôn Êl is kept to defend them which have led a wary life, whereas we have walked in the wickedest ways of all?

53. And that there should be showed a paradise, whose fruit endures forever, wherein is security and remedy, since we shall not enter into it?

54. (For we have walked in unpleasant places.)

55. And that the faces of them which have used abstinence shall shine above the stars, whereas our faces shall be blacker than darkness?

56. For while we lived and committed iniquity, we did not consider that we should begin to suffer for it after death.

57. Then he answered me, and said, this is the condition of the battle, which man that is born upon the earth shall fight;

58. That, if he is overcome, he shall suffer as you have said: But if he get the victory, he shall receive the thing that I say.

59. For this is the life whereof Môsheh spoke unto the people while he lived, saying, choose you life that you may live.

60. Nevertheless they did not believe him, nor yet the Nâbîy after him, no nor me which have spoken unto them,

61. That there should not be such heaviness in their destruction, as shall be joy over them that are persuaded to salvation.

62. I answered then, and said, I know, Yahuah, that Elyôn Êl is called merciful, in that he has mercy upon them which are not yet come into the world,

63. And upon those also that turn to his law;

64. And that he is patient, and long suffers those that have sinned, as his creatures;

65. And that he is bountiful, for he is ready to give where it needs;

66. And that he is of great mercy, for he multiplies more and more mercies to them that are present, and that are past, and also to them which are to come.

67. For if he shall not multiply his mercies, the world would not continue with them that inherit therein.

68. And he pardons; for if he did not so of his goodness, that they which have committed iniquities might be eased of them, the ten thousandth part of men should not remain living.

69. And being judge, if he should not forgive them that are cured with his word, and put out the multitude of contentions,

70. There should be very few left peradventure in an innumerable multitude.

Chapter 8

1. And he answered me, saying, Elyôn Êl has made this world for many, but the world to come for few.

2. I will tell you a similitude, Ezrâ; as when you ask the earth, it shall say unto you that it gives much mold whereof earthen vessels are made, but little dust that gold comes of: Even so is the course of this present world.

3. There are many created, but few shall be saved.

4. So answered I and said, swallow then down, O my soul, understanding, and devour wisdom.

5. For you have agreed to give ear, and are willing to prophesy: For you have no longer space than only to live.

6. O Yahuah, if you suffer not your servant, that we may pray before you, and you give us seed unto our heart, and culture to our understanding, that there may come fruit of it; how shall each man live that is corrupt, who bears the place of a man?

7. For you are alone, and we all one workmanship of your hands, like as you have said.

8. For when the body is fashioned now in the mother's womb, and you give it members, your creature is preserved in fire and water, and nine months does your workmanship endure your creature which is created in her.

9. But that which keeps and is kept shall both be preserved: And when the time comes, the womb preserved delivers up the things that grew in it.

10. For you have commanded out of the parts of the body, that is to say, out of the breasts, milk to be given, which is the fruit of the breasts,

11. That the thing which is fashioned may be nourished for a time, till you dispose it to your mercy.

12. You brought it up with your righteousness, and nurtured it in your law, and reformed it with your judgment.

13. And you shall mortify it as your creature, and quicken it as your work.

14. If therefore you shall destroy him which with so great labor was fashioned, it is an easy thing to be ordained by thy commandment, that the thing which was made might be preserved.

15. Now therefore, Yahuah, I will speak; touching man in general, you know best; but touching your people, for whose sake I am sorry;

16. And for your inheritance, for whose cause I mourn; and for Yâshârêl, for whom I am heavy; and for Yaăqôb, for whose sake I am troubled;

17. Therefore I will begin to pray before you for myself and for them: For I see the falls of us that dwell in the land.

18. But I have heard the swiftness of the judge which is to come.

19. Therefore hear my voice, and understand my words, and I shall speak before you. This is the beginning of the words of Ezrâ, before he was taken up: And I said,

20. O Yahuah, you that dwell in everlastingness which behold from above things in the shâmayim and in the air;

21. Whose throne is inestimable; whose glory may not be comprehended; before whom the hosts of angels stand with trembling,

22. Whose service is conversant in wind and fire; whose word is true, and sayings constant; whose commandment is strong, and ordinance fearful;

23. Whose look dries up the depths, and indignation makes the mountains to melt away; which the truth witnesses:

24. O hear the prayer of your servant, and give ear to the petition of your creature.

25. For while I live I will speak, and so long as I have understanding I will answer.

26. O do not look upon the sins of your people; but on them which serve you in truth.

27. Do not regard the wicked inventions of the heathen, but the desire of those that keep your testimonies in afflictions.

28. Do not think upon those that have walked feignedly before you: But remember them, which according to your will have known your fear.

29. Do not let it be your will to destroy them which have lived like beasts; but to look upon them that have clearly taught your law.

30. You take no indignation at them which are deemed worse than beasts; but love them that always put their trust in your righteousness and glory.

31. For we and our fathers do languish of such diseases: But because of us sinners you shall be called merciful.

32. For if you have a desire to have mercy upon us, you shall be called merciful, to us namely, that have no works of righteousness.

33. For the just, which have many good works laid up with you, shall out of their own deeds receive reward.

34. For what is man, that you should take displeasure at him? Or what is a corruptible generation that you should be so bitter toward it?

35. For in truth them is no man among them that be born, but he has dealt wickedly; and among the faithful there is none which has not done amiss.

36. For in this, O Yahuah, your righteousness and your goodness shall be declared, if you are merciful unto them which do not have the confidence of good works.

37. Then he answered me, and said, some things you have spoken right, and according unto your words it shall be.

38. For indeed I will not think on the disposition of them which have sinned before death, before judgment, before destruction:

39. But I will rejoice over the disposition of the righteous, and I will remember also their pilgrimage, and the salvation, and the reward, that they shall have.

40. Like as I have spoken now, so shall it come to pass.

41. For as the husbandman sows much seed upon the ground, and plants many trees, and yet the thing that is sown good in his season does not come up, neither does all that is planted take root: Even so is it of them that are sown in the world; they shall not all be saved.

42. I answered then and said, if I have found grace, let me speak.

43. Like as the husbandman's seed perishes, if it does not come up, and does not receive your rain in due season; or if there come too much rain, and corrupt it:

44. Even so perishes man also, which is formed with your hands, and is called your own image, because you are like unto him, for whose sake you have made all things, and likened him unto the husbandman's seed.

45. Do not be angry with us but spare your people, and have mercy upon your own inheritance: For you are merciful unto your creature.

46. Then he answered me, and said, things present are for the present, and things to come for such as are to come.

47. For you come far short that you should be able to love my creature more than I: But I have often times drawn nigh unto you, and unto it, but never to the unrighteous.

48. In this also you are marvelous before Elyôn Êl:

49. In that you have humbled yourself, as it becomes you, and do not have judged yourself worthy to be much glorified among the righteous.

50. For many great miseries shall be done to them that in the latter time shall dwell in the world, because they have walked in great pride.

51. But you understand for yourself, and seek out the glory for such as are like you.

52. For unto you is paradise opened, the tree of life is planted, the time to come is prepared, plenteousness is made ready, a city is built, and rest is allowed, yea, perfect goodness and wisdom.

53. The root of evil is sealed up from you, weakness and the moth is hid from you, and corruption is fled into sheôl to be forgotten:

54. Sorrows are passed, and in the end is showed the treasure of immortality.

55. And therefore you ask no more questions concerning the multitude of them that perish.

56. For when they had taken liberty, they despised Elyôn Êl, thought scorn of his law, and forsook his ways.

57. Moreover they have trodden down his righteous,

58. And said in their heart, that there is no Êlôhîym; yea, and that knowing they must die.

59. For as the things before said shall receive you, so thirst and pain are prepared for them: For it was not his will that men should come to nothing:

60. But they which are created have defiled the name of him that made them, and were unthankful unto him which prepared life for them.

61. And therefore is my judgment now at hand.

62. These things I have not showed unto all men, but unto you, and a few like you. Then I answered and said,

63. Behold, O Yahuah, now you have showed me the multitude of the wonders, which you will begin to do in the last times: But at what time, you have not showed me.

Chapter 9

1. He answered me then, and said, you measure the time diligently in itself: And when you see part of the signs past, which I have told you before,

2. Then you shall understand, that it is the very same time, wherein Elyôn Êl will begin to visit the world which he made.

3. Therefore when there shall be seen earthquakes and uproars of the people in the world:

4. Then you shall well understand, that Elyôn Êl spoke of those things from the days that were before you, even from the beginning.

5. For like as all that is made in the world has a beginning and an end, and the end is manifest:

6. Even so the times also of Elyôn Êl have plain beginnings in wonder and powerful works, and endings in effects and signs.

7. And every one that shall be saved, and shall be able to escape by his works, and by faith, whereby you have believed,

8. Shall be preserved from the said perils, and shall see my salvation in my land, and within my borders: For I have sanctified them for me from the beginning.

9. Then they shall be in pitiful case, which now have abused my ways: And they that have cast them away despitefully shall dwell in torments.

10. For such as in their life have received benefits, and have not known me;

11. And they that have loathed my law, while they had yet liberty, and, when as yet place of repentance was open unto them, did not understand, but despised it;

12. The same must know it after death by pain.

13. And therefore you do not be curious how the ungodly shall be punished, and when: But enquire how the righteous shall be saved, whose the world is, and for whom the world is created.

14. Then I answered and said,

15. I have said before, and now do speak, and will speak it also hereafter, that there are many more of them which perish, than of them which shall be saved:

16. Like as a wave is greater than a drop.

17. And he answered me, saying, like as the field is, so is also the seed; as the flowers are, such are the colors also; such as the workman is, such also is the work; and as the husbandman is himself, so is his husbandry also: For it was the time of the world.

18. And now when I prepared the world, which was not yet made, even for them to dwell in that now live, no man spoke against me.

19. For then everyone obeyed: But now the manners of them which are created in this world that is made are corrupted by a perpetual seed, and by a law which is unsearchable rid themselves.

20. So I considered the world, and, behold, there was peril because of the devices that were come into it.

21. And I saw, and spared it greatly, and have kept me a grape of the cluster, and a plant of a great people.

22. Let the multitude perish then, which was born in vain; and let my grape be kept, and my plant; for with great labor I have made it perfect.

23. Nevertheless, if you will cease yet seven days more, (but you shall not fast in them,

24. But go into a field of flowers, where no house is built, and eat only the flowers of the field; taste no flesh, drink no wine, but eat flowers only;)

25. And pray unto Elyôn Êl continually, then I will come and talk with you.

26. So I went my way into the field which is called Ardath, like as he commanded me; and there I sat among the flowers, and did eat of the herbs of the field, and the meat of the same satisfied me.

27. After seven days I sat upon the grass, and my heart was vexed within me, like as before:

28. And I opened my mouth, and began to talk before Elyôn Êl, and said,

29. O Yahuah, you that show yourself unto us, you were showed unto our fathers in the wilderness, in a place where no man treads, in a barren place, when they came out of Mitsrayim.

30. And you spoke saying, hear me, O Yâshârêl; and mark my words, you seed of Yaăqôb.

31. For, behold, I sow my law in you, and it shall bring fruit in you, and you shall be honored in it forever.

32. But our fathers, which received the law, did not keep it, and did not observe your ordinances: And though the fruit of your law did not perish, neither could it, for it was yours;

33. Yet they that received it perished, because they did not keep the thing that was sown in them.

34. And, lo, it is a custom, when the ground has received seed, or the sea a ship, or any vessel meat or drink, that, that being perished wherein it was sown or cast into,

35. That thing also which was sown, or cast therein, or received, does perish, and does not remain with us: But with us it has not happened so.

36. For we that have received the law perish by sin, and our heart also which received it,

37. Notwithstanding the law does not perish, but remains in his force.

38. And when I spoke these things in my heart, I looked back with my eyes, and upon the right side I saw a woman, and, behold, she mourned and wept with a loud voice, and was much grieved in heart, and her clothes were rent, and she had ashes upon her head.

39. Then I let my thoughts go that I was in, and turned me unto her,

40. And said unto her, wherefore do you weep? Why are you so grieved in your mind?

41. And she said unto me, Sir, let me alone, that I may bewail myself, and add unto my sorrow, for I am sore vexed in my mind, and brought very low.

42. And I said unto her, what ails you? Tell me.

43. She said unto me, I your servant have been barren, and had no child, though I had an husband thirty years,

44. And those thirty years I did nothing else day and night, and every hour, but make my, prayer to Elyôn Êl.

45. After thirty years Êlôhîym heard me your handmaid, looked upon my misery, considered my trouble, and gave me a son: And I was very glad of him, so was my husband also, and all my neighbors: And we gave great honor unto Shadday Êl.

46. And I nourished him with great travail.

47. So when he grew up, and came to the time that he should have a woman, I made a feast.

Chapter 10

1. And it so came to pass, that when my son was entered into his wedding chamber, he fell down, and died.

2. Then we all overthrew the lights, and all my neighbors rose up to comfort me: So I took my rest unto the second day at night.

3. And it came to pass, when they had all left off to comfort me, to the end I might be quiet; then rose I up by night and fled, and came hither into this field, as you see.

4. And now I do not purpose to return into the city, but to stay here, and neither to eat nor drink, but continually to mourn and to fast until I die.

5. Then I left the meditations wherein I was, and spoke to her in anger, saying,

6. You foolish woman above all other, you do not see our mourning, and what happen unto us?

7. How that Tsîyôn our mother is full of all heaviness, and much humbled, mourning very sore?

8. And now, seeing we all mourn and are sad, for we are all in heaviness, are you grieved for one son?

9. For ask the earth, and she shall tell you, that it is she which ought to mourn for the fall of so many that grow upon her.

10. For out of her came all at the first, and out of her shall all others come, and, behold, they walk almost all into destruction, and a multitude of them is utterly rooted out.

11. Who then should make more mourning than she, that has lost so great a multitude; and not you, which are sorry but for one?

12. But if you say unto me, my lamentation is not like the earth's, because I have lost the fruit of my womb, which I brought forth with pains, and bare with sorrows;

13. But the earth not so: For the multitude present in it according to the course of the earth is gone, as it came:

14. Then I say unto you, like as you have brought forth with labor; even so the earth also has given her fruit, namely, man, ever since the beginning unto him that made her.

15. Now therefore keep your sorrow to yourself, and bear with a good courage that which has befallen you.

16. For if you shall acknowledge the determination of Êlôhîym to be just, you shall both receive your son in time, and shall be commended among women.

17. Go your way then into the city to your husband.

18. And she said unto me, that will I not do: I will not go into the city, but here will I die.

19. So I proceeded to speak further unto her, and said,

20. Do not so, but be counselled by me: For how many are the adversities of Tsîyôn? Be comforted in regard of the sorrow of Yarûshâlaim.

21. For you see that our sanctuary is laid waste, our altar broken down, our temple destroyed;

22. Our psaltery is laid on the ground, our song is put to silence, our rejoicing is at an end, the light of our candlestick is put out, the ark of our covenant is spoiled, our qâdôsh things are defiled, and the name that is called upon us is almost profaned: Our children are put to shame, our Kôhên are burnt, our Lêwîy are gone into captivity, our virgins are defiled, and our women ravished; our righteous men carried away, our little ones destroyed, our young men are brought in bondage, and our strong men are become weak;

23. And, which is the greatest of all, the seal of Tsîyôn has now lost her honor; for she is delivered into the hands of them that hate us.

24. And therefore shake off your great heaviness, and put away the multitude of sorrows that Elyôn Êl may be merciful unto you again, and Elyôn Êl shall give you rest and ease from your labor.

25. And it came to pass while I was talking with her, behold, her face upon a sudden shined exceedingly, and her countenance glistered, so that I was afraid of her, and mused what it might be.

26. And, behold, suddenly she made a great cry very fearful: So that the earth shook at the noise of the woman.

27. And I looked, and, behold, the woman appeared unto me no more, but there was a city built, and a large place showed itself from the foundations: Then I was afraid, and cried with a loud voice, and said,

28. Where is Ûrîyêl the angel, who came unto me at the first? For he has caused me to fall into many trances, and my end is turned into corruption, and my prayer to rebuke.

29. And as I was speaking these words behold, he came unto me, and looked upon me.

30. And, lo, I lay as one that had been dead, and my understanding was taken from me: And he took me by the right hand, and comforted me, and set me upon my feet, and said unto me,

31. What does ail you? And why are you so disquieted? And why is your understanding troubled, and the thoughts of your heart?

32. And I said, because you have forsaken me, and yet I did according to your words, and I went into the field, and, lo, I have seen, and yet see, that I am not able to express.

33. And he said unto me, stand up manfully, and I will advise you.

34. Then I said, speak on, my master, in me; only forsake me not, lest I die frustrate of my hope.

35. For I have seen that I do not know, and hear that I do not know.

36. Or is my sense deceived, or my soul in a dream?

37. Now therefore I beseech you that you will show your servant of this vision.

38. He answered me then, and said, hear me, and I shall inform you, and tell you wherefore you are afraid: For Elyôn Êl will reveal many secret things unto you.

39. He has seen that your way is right: For that you sorrow continually for your people, and make great lamentation for Tsîyôn.

40 This therefore is the meaning of the vision which you lately saw:

41. You saw a woman mourning, and you began to comfort her:

42. But now you see the likeness of the woman no more, but there appeared unto you a city built.

43. And whereas she told you of the death of her son, this is the solution:

44. This woman, whom you saw is Tsîyôn: And whereas she said unto you, even she whom you see as a city built,

45. Whereas, I say, she said unto you, that she has been thirty years barren: Those are the thirty years wherein there was no offering made in her.

46. But after thirty years Shelômôh built the city and offered offerings: And then bare the barren a son.

47. And whereas she told you that she nourished him with labor: That was the dwelling in Yarûshâlaim.

48. But whereas she said unto you, that my son coming into his marriage chamber happened to have a fail, and died: This was the destruction that came to Yarûshâlaim.

49. And, behold, you saw her likeness, and because she mourned for her son, you began to comfort her: And of these things which have chanced, these are to be opened unto you.

50. For now Elyôn Êl sees that you are grieved unfeignedly, and suffers from your whole heart for her, so he has showed you the brightness of her glory, and the comeliness of her beauty:

51. And therefore I bade you remain in the field where no house was built:

52. For I knew that Elyôn Êl would show this unto you.

53. Therefore I commanded you to go into the field, where no foundation of any building was.

54. For in the place wherein Elyôn Êl begins to show his city, there can no man's building be able to stand.

55. And therefore do not fear, do not let your heart be affrighted, but go your way in, and see the beauty and greatness of the building, as much as your eyes are able to see:

56. And then you shall hear as much as your ears may comprehend.

57. For you are blessed above many other, and are called with Elyôn Êl; and so are but few.

58. But tomorrow at night you shall remain here;

59. And so shall Elyôn Êl show you visions of the high things, which Elyôn Êl will do unto them that dwell upon the earth in the last days. So I slept that night and another, like as he commanded me.

Chapter 11

1. Then saw I a dream, and, behold, there came up from the sea an eagle, which had twelve feathered wings, and three heads.

2. And I saw, and, behold, she spread her wings over all the earth, and all the winds of the air blew on her, and were gathered together.

3. And I beheld, and out of her feathers there grew other contrary feathers; and they became little feathers and small.

4. But her heads were at rest: The head in the midst was greater than the other, yet rested it with the residue.

5. Moreover I beheld, and, lo, the eagle flew with her feathers, and reigned upon earth, and over them that dwelt therein.

6. And I saw that all things under shâmayim were subject unto her, and no man spoke against her, no, not one creature upon earth.

7. And I beheld, and, lo, the eagle rose upon her talons, and spoke to her feathers, saying,

8. Do not watch all at once: Sleep everyone in his own place, and watch by course:

9. But let the heads be preserved for the last.

10. And I beheld, and, lo, the voice did not go out of her heads, but from the midst of her body.

11. And I numbered her contrary feathers, and, behold, there were eight of them.

12. And I looked, and, behold, on the right side there arose one feather, and reigned over all the earth;

13. And so it was, that when it reigned, the end of it came, and the place thereof appeared no more: So the next following stood up. And reigned, and had a great time;

14. And it happened, that when it reigned, the end of it came also, like as the first, so that it appeared no more.

15. Then there came a voice unto it, and said,

16. You hear that have borne rule over the earth so long: This I say unto you, before you begin to appear no more,

17. There shall none after you attain unto your time, neither unto the half thereof.

18. Then arose the third, and reigned as the other before, and appeared no more also.

19. So went it with all the residue one after another, as that everyone reigned, and then appeared no more.

20. Then I beheld, and, lo, in process of time the feathers that followed stood up upon the right side, that they might rule also; and some of them ruled, but within a while they appeared no more:

21. For some of them were set up, but did not rule.

22. After this I looked, and, behold, the twelve feathers appeared no more, nor the two little feathers:

23. And there was no more upon the eagle's body, but three heads that rested, and six little wings.

24. Then I saw also that two little feathers divided themselves from the six, and remained under the head that was upon the right side: For the four continued in their place.

25. And I beheld, and, lo, the feathers that were under the wing thought to set up themselves and to have the rule.

26. And I beheld, and, lo, there was one set up, but shortly it appeared no more.

27. And the second was sooner away than the first.

28. And I beheld, and, lo, the two that remained thought also in themselves to reign:

29. And when they so thought, behold, there awoke one of the heads that were at rest, namely, it that was in the midst; for that was greater than the two other heads.

30. And then I saw that the two other heads were joined with it.

31. And, behold, the head was turned with them that were with it, and did eat up the

two feathers under the wing that would have reigned.

32. But this head put the whole earth in fear, and bare rule in it over all those that dwelt upon the earth with much oppression; and it had the governance of the world more than all the wings that had been.

33. And after this I beheld, and, lo, the head that was in the midst suddenly appeared no more, like as the wings.

34. But there remained the two heads, which also in like sort ruled upon the earth, and over those that dwelt therein.

35. And I beheld, and, lo, the head upon the right side devoured it that was upon the left side.

36. Then I heard a voice, which said unto me, look before you, and consider the thing that you see.

37. And I beheld, and lo, as it were a roaring lion chased out of the wood: And I saw that he sent out a man's voice unto the eagle, and said,

38. You hear, I will talk with you, and Elyôn Êl shall say unto you,

39. Are you not it that remain of the four beasts, whom I made to reign in my world, that the end of their times might come through them?

40. And the fourth came, and overcame all the beasts that were past, and had power over the world with great fearfulness, and over the whole compass of the earth with much wicked oppression; and so long time dwelt he upon the earth with deceit.

41. For the earth you have not judged with truth.

42. For you have afflicted the meek, you have hurt the peaceable, you have loved liars, and destroyed the dwellings of them that brought forth fruit, and have cast down the walls of such as did you no harm.

43. Therefore is your wrongful dealing come up unto Elyôn Êl, and your pride unto Shadday Êl.

44. Elyôn Êl also has looked upon the proud times, and, behold, they are ended, and his abominations are fulfilled.

45. And therefore appear no more, you eagle, nor your horrible wings, nor your wicked feathers nor your malicious heads, nor your hurtful claws, nor all your vain body:

46. That all the earth may be refreshed, and may return, being delivered from your violence, and that she may hope for the judgment and mercy of him that made her.

Chapter 12

1. And it came to pass, while the lion spoke these words unto the eagle, I saw,

2. And, behold, the head that remained and the four wings appeared no more, and the two went unto it and set themselves up to reign, and their kingdom was small, and fill of uproar.

3. And I saw, and, behold, they appeared no more, and the whole body of the eagle was burnt so that the earth was in great fear: Then I awoke out of the trouble and trance of my mind, and from great fear, and said unto my spirit,

4. Lo, this you have done unto me, in that you search out the ways of Elyôn Êl.

5. Lo, yet I am weary in my mind, and very weak in my spirit; and little strength there is in me, for the great fear wherewith I was afflicted this night.

6. Therefore I will now beseech Elyôn Êl, that he will comfort me unto the end.

7. And I said, Yahuah that bears rule, if I have found grace before your sight, and if I am justified with you before many others, and if my prayer indeed be come up before your face;

8. Comfort me then, and show me your servant the interpretation and plain difference of this fearful vision, that you may perfectly comfort my soul.

9. For you have judged me worthy to show me the last times.

10. And he said unto me, this is the interpretation of the vision:

11. The eagle, whom you saw come up from the sea, is the kingdom which was seen in the vision of your brother Dânîyêl.

12. But it was not expounded unto him, therefore now I declare it unto you.

13. Behold, the days will come, that there shall rise up a kingdom upon earth, and it shall be feared above all the kingdoms that were before it.

14. In the same shall twelve kings reign, one after another:

15. Whereof the second shall begin to reign, and shall have more time than any of the twelve.

16. And this do the twelve wings signify, which you saw.

17. As for the voice which you heard speak, and that you did not see to go out from the heads but from the midst of the body thereof, this is the interpretation:

18. That after the time of that kingdom there shall arise great strivings, and it shall stand in peril of failing: Nevertheless it shall not then fall, but shall be restored again to his beginning.

19. And whereas you saw the eight small under feathers sticking to her wings, this is the interpretation:

20. That in him there shall arise eight kings, whose times shall be but small, and their years swift.

21. And two of them shall perish, the middle time approaching: Four shall be kept until their end begin to approach: But two shall be kept unto the end.

22. And whereas you saw three heads resting, this is the interpretation:

23. In his last days shall Elyôn Êl raise up three kingdoms, and renew many things therein, and they shall have the dominion of the earth,

24. And of those that dwell therein, with much oppression, above all those that were before them: Therefore they are called the heads of the eagle.

25. For these are they that shall accomplish his wickedness, and that shall finish his last end.

26. And whereas you saw that the great head appeared no more, it signifies that one of them shall die upon his bed, and yet with pain.

27. For the two that remain shall be slain with the sword.

28. For the sword of the one shall devour the other: But at the last he shall fall through the sword himself.

29. And whereas you saw two feathers under the wings passing over the head that is on the right side;

30. It signifies that these are they, whom Elyôn Êl has kept unto their end: This is the small kingdom and full of trouble, as you saw.

31. And the lion, whom you saw rising up out of the wood, and roaring, and speaking to the eagle, and rebuking her for her unrighteousness with all the words which you have heard;

32. This is the mâshîyach, which Elyôn Êl has kept for them and for their wickedness unto the end: He shall reprove them, and shall upbraid them with their cruelty.

33. For he shall set them before him alive in judgment, and shall rebuke them, and correct them.

34. For the rest of my people he shall deliver with mercy, those that have been pressed upon my borders, and he shall make them joyful until the coming of the Day of Judgment, whereof I have spoken unto you from the beginning.

35. This is the dream that you saw, and these are the interpretations.

36. You only have been met to know this secret of Elyôn Êl.

37. Therefore write all these things that you have seen in a book, and hide them:

38. And teach them to the wise of the people, whose hearts you know may comprehend and keep these secrets.

39. But wait you here yourself yet seven days more, that it may be showed you, whatsoever it pleases Elyôn Êl to declare unto you. And with that he went his way.

40. And it came to pass, when all the people saw that the seven days were past, and I did not come again into the city, they gathered them all together, from the least unto the greatest, and came unto me, and said,

41. What have we offended you? And what evil have we done against you that you forsake us, and sit here in this place?

42. For of all the Nâbîy you only are left us, as a cluster of the vintage, and as a candle in a dark place, and as a haven or ship preserved from the tempest.

43. Are not the evils which are come to us sufficient?

44. If you shall forsake us, how much better had it been for us, if we also had been burned in the midst of Tsîyôn?

45. For we are not better than they that died there. And they wept with a loud voice. Then I answered them, and said,

46. Be of good comfort, O Yâshârêl; and do not be heavy, you house of Yaăqôb:

47. For Elyôn Êl have you in remembrance, and the Shadday Êl has not forgotten you in temptation.

48. As for me, I have not forsaken you, neither am I departed from you: But am come into this place, to pray for the desolation of Tsîyôn, and that I might seek mercy for the low estate of your sanctuary.

49. And now go your way home every man, and after these days I will come unto you.

50. So the people went their way into the city, like as I commanded them:

51. But I remained still in the field seven days, as the angel commanded me; and did eat only in those days of the flowers of the field, and had my meat of the herbs,

Chapter 13

1. And it came to pass after seven days, I dreamed a dream by night:

2. And, lo, there arose a wind from the sea, that it moved all the waves thereof.

3. And I beheld, and, lo, that man waxed strong with the thousands of shâmayim:

And when he turned his countenance to look, all the things trembled that were seen under him.

4. And whenever the voice went out of his mouth, all they burned that heard his voice, like as the earth fails when it feels the fire.

5. And after this I beheld, and, lo, there was gathered together a multitude of men, out of number, from the four winds of the shâmayim, to subdue the man that came out of the sea,

6. But I beheld, and, lo, he had graved himself a great mountain, and flew up upon it.

7. But I would have seen the region or place whereabouts the hill was graven, and I could not.

8. And after this I beheld, and, lo, all they which were gathered together to subdue him were sore afraid, and yet do fight.

9. And, lo, as he saw the violence of the multitude that came, he neither lifted up his hand, nor held sword, nor any instrument of war:

10. But I only saw that he sent out of his mouth as it had been a blast of fire, and out of his lips a flaming breath, and out of his tongue he cast out sparks and tempests.

11. And they were all mixed together; the blast of fire, the flaming breath, and the great tempest; and fell with violence upon the multitude which was prepared to fight, and burned them up every one, so that upon a sudden of an innumerable multitude nothing was to be perceived, but only dust and smell of smoke: When I saw this I was afraid.

12. Afterward I saw the same man come down from the mountain, and call unto him another peaceable multitude.

13. And there came much people unto him, whereof some were glad, some were sorry, and some of them were bound, and other some brought of them that were offered: Then I was sick through great fear, and I awoke, and said,

14. You have showed your servant these wonders from the beginning, and have counted me worthy that you should receive my prayer:

15. Show me now yet the interpretation of this dream.

16. For as I conceive in my understanding, woe unto them that shall be left in those days and much more woe unto them that are not left behind.

17. For they that were not left were in heaviness.

18. Now I understand the things that are laid up in the latter days, which shall happen unto them, and to those that are left behind.

19. Therefore they are come into great perils and many necessities, like as these dreams declare.

20. Yet is it easier for him that is in danger to come into these things, than to pass away as a cloud out of the world, and not to see the things that happen in the last days. And he answered unto me, and said,

21. The interpretation of the vision I shall show you, and I will open unto you the thing that you have required.

22. Whereas you have spoken of them that are left behind, this is the interpretation:

23. He that shall endure the peril in that time has kept himself: They that are fallen into danger are such as have works, and faith toward Shadday Êl.

24. Know this therefore, that they which are left behind are more blessed than they that be dead.

25. This is the meaning of the vision: Whereas you saw a man coming up from the midst of the sea:

26. The same is he whom Êlôhîym Elyôn Êl has kept a great season, which by his own self shall deliver his creature: And he shall order them that are left behind.

27. And whereas you saw, that out of his mouth there came as a blast of wind, and fire, and storm;

28. And that he held neither sword, nor any instrument of war, but that the rushing in of him destroyed the whole multitude that came to subdue him; this is the interpretation:

29. Behold, the days come, when Elyôn Êl will begin to deliver them that are upon the earth.

30. And he shall come to the astonishment of them that dwell on the earth.

31. And one shall undertake to fight against another, one city against another, one place against another, one people against another, and one realm against another.

32. And the time shall be when these things shall come to pass, and the signs shall happen which I showed you before, and then shall my son be declared, whom you saw as a man ascending.

33. And when all the people hear his voice, every man shall in their own land leave the battle they have one against another.

34. And an innumerable multitude shall be gathered together, as you saw them, willing to come, and to overcome him by fighting.

35. But he shall stand upon the top of the mount Tsîyôn.

36. And Tsîyôn shall come, and shall be showed to all men, being prepared and built, like as you saw the hill graven without hands.

37. And this my son shall rebuke the wicked inventions of those nations, which for their wicked life are fallen into the tempest;

38. And shall lay before them their evil thoughts, and the torments wherewith they shall begin to be tormented, which are like unto a flame: And he shall destroy them without labor by the law which is like unto me.

39. And whereas you saw that he gathered another peaceable multitude unto him;

40. Those are the ten tribes, which were carried away prisoners out of their own land in the time of Hôshêa the king, whom Shalmaneser the king of Ashshûr led away captive, and he carried them over the waters, and so came they into another land.

41. But they took this counsel among themselves, that they would leave the multitude of the heathen, and go forth into a further country, where never mankind dwelt,

42. That they might there keep their statutes, which they never kept in their own land.

43. And they entered into Perâth by the narrow places of the river.

44. For Elyôn Êl then showed signs for them, and held still the flood, till they were passed over.

45. For through that country there was a great way to go, namely, of a year and a half: And the same region is called Arsareth.

46. Then they dwelt there until the latter time; and now when they shall begin to come,

47. Elyôn Êl shall stay the springs of the stream again, that they may go through: Therefore you saw the multitude with peace.

48. But those that are left behind of your people are they that are found within my borders.

49. Now when he destroys the multitude of the nations that are gathered together, he shall defend his people that remain.

50. And then he shall show them great wonders.

51. Then I said, O Yahuah that bears rule, show me this: Wherefore I have seen the man coming up from the midst of the sea?

52. And he said unto me, like as you can neither seek out nor know the things that are in the deep of the sea: Even so can no man upon earth see my son, or those that are with him, but in the day time.

53. This is the interpretation of the dream which you saw, and whereby you only are here lightened.

54. For you have forsaken your own way, and applied your diligence unto my law, and sought it.

55. Your life you have ordered in wisdom, and have called understanding your mother.

56. And therefore I have showed you the treasures of Elyôn Êl: After other three days I will speak other things unto you, and declare unto you mighty and wondrous things.

57. Then I went forth into the field, giving praise and thanks greatly unto Elyôn Êl because of his wonders which he did in time;

58. And because he governs the same, and such things as fall in their seasons: And there I sat three days.

Chapter 14

1. And it came to pass upon the third day, I sat under an oak, and, behold, there came a voice out of a bush over against me, and said, Ezrâ, Ezrâ.

2. And I said, here I am, Yahuah and I stood up upon my feet.

3. Then he said unto me, in the bush I did manifestly reveal myself unto Môsheh, and talked with him, when my people served in Mitsrayim:

4. And I sent him and led my people out of Mitsrayim, and brought him up to the mount of where I held him by me a long season,

5. And told him many wondrous things, and showed him the secrets of the times, and the end; and commanded him, saying,

6. These words you shall declare, and these you shall hide.

7. And I now say unto you,

8. That you lay up in your heart the signs that I have showed, and the dreams that you have seen, and the interpretations which you have heard:

9. For you shall be taken away from all, and from henceforth you shall remain with my son, and with such as are like you, until the times are ended.

10. For the world has lost his youth, and the times begin to wax old.

11. For the world is divided into twelve parts, and the ten parts of it are gone already, and half of a tenth part:

12. And there remains that which is after the half of the tenth part.

13. Now therefore set your house in order, and reprove your people, comfort such of them as are in trouble, and now renounce corruption,

14. Let go from you mortal thoughts, cast away the burdens of man, put off now the weak nature,

15. And set aside the thoughts that are most heavy unto you, and haste you to flee from these times.

16. For yet greater evils than those which you have seen happen shall be done hereafter.

17. For look how much the world shall be weaker through age, so much the more shall evils increase upon them that dwell therein.

18. For the time is fled far away, and leasing is hard at hand: For now hastes the vision to come, which you have seen.

19. Then I answered before you, and said,

20. Behold, Yahuah, I will go, as you have commanded me, and reprove the people which are present: But they that shall be born afterward, who shall admonish them? Thus the world is set in darkness, and they that dwell therein are without light.

21. For your law is burnt, therefore no man knows the things that are done of you, or the work that shall begin.

22. But if I have found grace before you, send the rûach qâdôsh into me, and I shall write all that has been done in the world since the beginning, which were written in your law, that men may find thy path, and that they which will live in the latter days may live.

23. And he answered me, saying, go your way, gather the people together, and say unto them, that they do not seek you for forty days.

24. But look prepare you many box trees, and take with you Sarea, Dabria, Selemia, Ethanus, and Asiel, these five which are ready to write swiftly;

25. And come hither, and I shall light a candle of understanding in your heart, which shall not be put out, till the things are performed which you shall begin to write.

26. And when you have done, some things you shall publish, and some things you shall show secretly to the wise: Tomorrow this hour you shall begin to write.

27. Then I went forth, as he commanded, and gathered all the people together, and said,

28. Hear these words, O Yâshârêl.

29. Our fathers at the beginning were strangers in Mitsrayim, from whence they were delivered:

30. And received the law of life, which they did not keep, which you also have transgressed after them.

31. Then was the land, even the land of Tsîyôn, parted among you by lot: But your fathers, and you yourselves, have done unrighteousness, and have not kept the ways which Elyôn Êl commanded you.

32. And forasmuch as he is a righteous judge, he took from you in time the thing that he had given you.

33. And now you are here, and your brethren among you.

34. Therefore if so be that you will subdue your own understanding, and reform your hearts, you shall be kept alive and after death you shall obtain mercy.

35. For after death shall the judgment come, when we shall live again: And then shall the names of the righteous be manifest, and the works of the ungodly shall be declared.

36. Let no man therefore come unto me now, nor seek after me these forty days.

37. So I took the five men, as he commanded me, and we went into the field, and remained there.

38. And the next day, behold, a voice called me, saying, Ezrâ, open your mouth, and drink that I give you to drink.

39. Then I opened my mouth, and, behold, he reached me a full cup, which was full as

it were with water, but the color of it was like fire.

40. And I took it, and drank: And when I had drunk of it, my heart uttered understanding, and wisdom grew in my breast, for my spirit strengthened my memory:

41. And my mouth was opened, and shut no more.

42. Elyôn Êl gave understanding unto the five men, and they wrote the wonderful visions of the night that were told, which they did not know: And they sat forty days, and they wrote in the day, and at night they ate bread.

43. As for me, I spoke in the day, and I did not hold my tongue by night.

44. In forty days they wrote two hundred and four books.

45. And it came to pass, when the forty days were filled, that Elyôn Êl spoke, saying, the first that you have written publish openly, that the worthy and unworthy may read it:

46. But keep the seventy last, that you may deliver them only to such as be wise among the people:

47. For in them is the spring of understanding, the fountain of wisdom, and the stream of knowledge.

48. And I did so.

Chapter 15

1. Behold, you speak in the ears of my people the words of prophecy, which I will put in your mouth, says Yahuah:

2. And cause them to be written in paper: For they are faithful and true.

3. Do not fear the imaginations against you, do not let the incredulity of them trouble you that speak against you.

4. For all the unfaithful shall die in their unfaithfulness.

5. Behold, says Yahuah, I will bring plagues upon the world; the sword, famine, death, and destruction.

6. For wickedness has exceedingly polluted the whole earth, and their hurtful works are fulfilled.

7. Therefore says Yahuah,

8. I will hold my tongue no more as touching their wickedness, which they profanely commit, neither I will suffer them in those things, in which they wickedly exercise themselves: Behold, the innocent and righteous blood cries unto me, and the souls of the just complain continually.

9. And therefore, says Yahuah, I will surely avenge them, and receive unto me all the innocent blood from among them.

10. Behold, my people is led as a flock to the slaughter: I will not suffer them now to dwell in the land of Mitsrayim:

11. But I will bring them with a mighty hand and a stretched out arm, and smite Mitsrayim with plagues, as before, and will destroy all the land thereof.

12. Mitsrayim shall mourn, and the foundation of it shall be smitten with the plague and punishment that Êlôhîym shall bring upon it.

13. They that till the ground shall mourn: For their seeds shall fail through the blasting and hail, and with a fearful constellation.

14. Woe to the world and them that dwell therein!

15. For the sword and their destruction draws nigh, and one people shall stand up and fight against another, and swords in their hands.

16. For there shall be sedition among men, and invading one another; they shall not regard their kings nor princes, and the course of their actions shall stand in their power.

17. A man shall desire to go into a city, and shall not be able.

18. For because of their pride the cities shall be troubled, the houses shall be destroyed, and men shall be afraid.

19. A man shall have no pity upon his neighbor, but shall destroy their houses with the sword, and spoil their goods, because of the lack of bread, and for great tribulation.

20. Behold, says Êlôhîym, I will call together all the kings of the earth to reverence me, which are from the rising of the sun, from the south, from the east, and Lebânôn; to turn themselves one against another, and repay the things that they have done to them.

21. Like as they do yet this day unto my chosen, so I will do also, and recompense in their bosom. Thus says Yahuah Êlôhîym;

22. My right hand shall not spare the sinners, and my sword shall not cease over them that shed innocent blood upon the earth.

23. The fire is gone forth from his wrath, and has consumed the foundations of the earth, and the sinners, like the straw that is kindled.

24. Woe to them that sin, and do not keep my commandments! Says Yahuah.

25. I will not spare them: Go your way, you children, from the power, do not defile my sanctuary.

26. For Yahuah knows all them that sin against him, and therefore he delivers them unto death and destruction.

27. For now the plagues are come upon the whole earth and you shall remain in them: For Êlôhîym shall not deliver you, because you have sinned against him.

28. Behold a horrible vision, and the appearance thereof from the east:

29. Where the nations of the dragons of Ărâb shall come out with many chariots, and the multitude of them shall be carried as the wind upon earth that all they which hear them may fear and tremble.

30. Also the Pâras raging in wrath shall go forth as the wild boars of the wood, and with great power shall they come, and join battle with them, and shall waste a portion of the land of the Ashshûr.

31. And then shall the dragons have the upper hand, remembering their nature; and if they shall turn themselves, conspiring together in great power to persecute them,

32. Then these shall be troubled bled, and keep silence through their power, and shall flee.

33. And from the land of the Ashshûr shall the enemy besiege them, and consume some of them, and in their host shall be fear and dread, and strife among their kings.

34. Behold clouds from the east and from the north unto the south, and they are very horrible to look upon, full of wrath and storm.

35. They shall smite one upon another, and they shall smite down a great multitude of stars upon the earth, even their own star; and blood shall be from the sword unto the belly,

36. And dung of men unto the camel's hoof.

37. And there shall be great fearfulness and trembling upon earth: And they that see the

wrath shall be afraid, and trembling shall come upon them.

38. And then shall there come great storms from the south, and from the north, and another part from the west.

39. And strong winds shall arise from the east, and shall open it; and the cloud which he raised up in wrath, and the star stirred to cause fear toward the east and west wind, shall be destroyed.

40. The great and mighty clouds shall be puffed up full of wrath, and the star, that they may make all the earth afraid, and them that dwell therein; and they shall pour out over every high and eminent place a horrible star,

41. Fire, and hail, and flying swords, and many waters, that all fields may be full, and all rivers, with the abundance of great waters.

42. And they shall break down the cities and walls, mountains and hills, trees of the wood, and grass of the meadows, and their corn.

43. And they shall go steadfastly unto Bâbel, and make her afraid.

44. They shall come to her, and besiege her, the star and all wrath shall they pour out upon her: Then shall the dust and smoke go up unto the shâmayim, and all they that be about her shall bewail her.

45. And they that remain under her shall do service unto them that have put her in fear.

46. And you, Asia that are partaker of the hope of Bâbel, and are the glory of her person:

47. Woe be unto you, you wretch, because you have made yourself like unto her; and have decked your daughters in whoredom, that they might please and glory in your lovers, which have always desired to commit whoredom with you.

48. You have followed her that is hated in all her works and inventions: Therefore says Êlôhîym,

49. I will send plagues upon you; widowhood, poverty, famine, sword, and pestilence, to waste your houses with destruction and death.

50. And the glory of your power shall be dried up as a flower, the heat shall arise that is sent over you.

51. You shall be weakened as a poor woman with stripes, and as one chastised with wounds, so that the mighty and lovers shall not be able to receive you.

52. I would with jealousy have so proceeded against you, says Yahuah,

53. If you had not always slain my chosen, exalting the stroke of your hands, and saying over their dead, when you were drunken,

54. Set forth the beauty of your countenance?

55. The reward of your whoredom shall be in your bosom, therefore you shall receive recompense.

56. Like as you have done unto my chosen, says Yahuah, even so shall Êlôhîym do unto you, and shall deliver you into mischief,

57. Your children shall die of hunger, and you shall fall through the sword: Your cities shall be broken down, and all you shall perish with the sword in the field.

58. They that are in the mountains shall die of hunger, and eat their own flesh, and drink their own blood, for very hunger of bread, and thirst of water.

59. You as unhappy shall come through the sea, and receive plagues again.

60. And in the passage they shall rush on the idle city, and shall destroy some portion of your land, and consume part of your glory, and shall return to Bâbel that was destroyed.

61. And you shall be cast down by them as stubble, and they shall be unto you as fire;

62. And shall consume you, and your cities, your land, and your mountains; all your woods and your fruitful trees shall they burn up with fire.

63. Your children they shall carry away captive, and, look, what you have, they shall spoil it, and mar the beauty of your face.

Chapter 16

1. Woe be unto you, Bâbel, and Asia! Woe be unto you, Mitsrayim and Ărâm!

2. Gird up yourselves with cloths of sack and hair, bewail your children, and be sorry; for your destruction is at hand.

3. A sword is sent upon you, and who may turn it back?

4. A fire is sent among you, and who may quench it?

5. Plagues are sent unto you, and what is he that may drive them away?

6. May any man drive away a hungry lion in the wood? Or may any one quench the fire in stubble, when it has begun to burn?

7. May one turn again the arrow that is shot of a strong archer?

8. Yahuah Shadday Êl sends the plagues and who is he that can drive them away?

9. A fire shall go forth from his wrath, and who is he that may quench it?

10. He shall cast lightning, and who shall not fear? He shall thunder, and who shall not be afraid?

11. Yahuah shall threaten, and who shall not be utterly beaten to powder at his presence?

12. The earth quakes, and the foundations thereof; the sea arises up with waves from the deep, and the waves of it are troubled, and the fishes thereof also, before Yahuah, and before the glory of his power:

13. For strong is his right hand that bends the bow, his arrows that he shoots are sharp, and shall not miss, when they begin to be shot into the ends of the world.

14. Behold, the plagues are sent, and shall not return again, until they come upon the earth.

15. The fire is kindled, and shall not be put out, till it consume the foundation of the earth.

16. Like as an arrow which is shot of a mighty archer does not return backward: Even so the plagues that shall be sent upon earth shall not return again.

17. Woe is me! Woe is me! Who will deliver me in those days?

18. The beginning of sorrows and great mourning; the beginning of famine and great death; the beginning of wars, and the powers shall stand in fear; the beginning of evils! What shall I do when these evils shall come?

19. Behold, famine and plague, tribulation and anguish, are sent as scourges for amendment.

20. But for all these things they shall not turn from their wickedness, nor be always mindful of the scourges.

21. Behold, victuals shall be so good cheap upon earth, that they shall think themselves to be in good case, and even then shall evils grow upon earth, sword, famine, and great confusion.

22. For many of them that dwell upon earth shall perish of famine; and the other, that escape the hunger, shall the sword destroy.

23. And the dead shall be cast out as dung, and there shall be no man to comfort them: For the earth shall be wasted, and the cities shall be cast down.

24. There shall be no man left to till the earth, and to sow it,

25. The trees shall give fruit, and who shall gather them?

26. The grapes shall ripen, and who shall tread them? For all places shall be desolate of men:

27. So that one man shall desire to see another, and to hear his voice.

28. For of a city there shall be ten left, and two of the field, which shall hide themselves in the thick ăshêrâh, and in the clefts of the rocks.

29. As in an orchard of Olives upon every tree there are left three or four olives;

30. Or as when a vineyard is gathered, there are left some clusters of them that diligently seek through the vineyard:

31. Even so in those days there shall be three or four left by them that search their houses with the sword.

32. And the earth shall be laid waste, and the fields thereof shall wax old, and her ways and all her paths shall grow full of thorns, because no man shall travel there through.

33. The virgins shall mourn, having no bridegrooms; the women shall mourn, having no husbands; their daughters shall mourn, having no helpers.

34. In the wars shall their bridegrooms be destroyed, and their husbands shall perish of famine.

35. Hear now these things and understand them, you servants of Yahuah.

36. Behold, the word of Yahuah, receive it: Do not believe the gods of whom Yahuah spoke.

37. Behold, the plagues draw nigh, and are not slack.

38. As when a woman with child in the ninth month brings forth her son, with two or three hours of her birth great pains compass her womb, which pains, when the child comes forth, they do not slack a moment:

39. Even so shall not the plagues be slack to come upon the earth, and the world shall mourn, and sorrows shall come upon it on every side.

40. O my people, hear my word: You make ready to your battle, and in those evils be even as pilgrims upon the earth.

41. He that sells, let him be as he that flees away: And he that buys, as one that will lose:

42. He that occupies merchandise, as he that has no profit by it: And he that builds, as he that shall not dwell therein:

43. He that sows, as if he should not reap: So also he that plants the vineyard, as he that shall not gather the grapes:

44. They that marry, as they that shall get no children; and they that do not marry, as the widowers.

45. And therefore they that labor, labors in vain:

46. For strangers shall reap their fruits, and spoil their goods, overthrow their houses, and take their children captives, for in captivity and famine they shall get children.

47. And they that occupy their merchandise with robbery, the more they deck their cities, their houses, their possessions, and their own persons:

48. The more I will be angry with them for their sin, says Yahuah.

49. Like as a whore envies a right honest and virtuous woman:

50. So shall righteousness hate iniquity, when she decks herself, and shall accuse her to her face, when he comes that shall defend him that diligently searches out every sin upon earth.

51. And therefore you do not be like thereunto, nor to the works thereof.

52. For yet a little, and iniquity shall be taken away out of the earth, and righteousness shall reign among you.

53. Do not let the sinner say that he has not sinned: For Êlôhîym shall burn coals of fire upon his head, which says before Yahuah Êlôhîym and his glory, I have not sinned.

54. Behold, Yahuah knows all the works of men, their imaginations, their thoughts, and their hearts:

55. Which spoke but the word, let the earth be made; and it was made: Let the shâmayim be made; and it was created.

56. In his word were the stars made, and he knows the number of them.

57. He searches the deep, and the treasures thereof; he has measured the sea, and what it contains.

58. He has shut the sea in the midst of the waters, and with his word he has hanged the earth upon the waters.

59. He spreads out the shâmayim like a vault; upon the waters he has founded it.

60. In the desert he has made springs of water, and pools upon the tops of the mountains, that the floods might pour down from the high rocks to water the earth.

61. He made man, and put his heart in the midst of the body, and gave him breath, life, and understanding.

62. Yea and the rûach of Êlôhîym Shadday Êl, which made all things, and searches out all hidden things in the secrets of the earth,

63. He surely knows your inventions, and what you think in your hearts, even them that sin, and would hide their sin.

64. Therefore Yahuah has exactly searched out all your works, and he will put you all to shame.

65. And when your sins are brought forth, you shall be ashamed before men, and your own sins shall be your accusers in that day.

66. What will you do? Or how will you hide your sins before Êlôhîym and his angels?

67. Behold, Êlôhîym himself is the judge, fear him: Leave off from your sins, and forget your iniquities, to meddle no more with them forever: So shall Êlôhîym lead you forth, and deliver you from all trouble.

68. For, behold, the burning wrath of a great multitude is kindled over you, and they shall take away certain of you, and feed you, being idle, with things offered unto idols.

69. And they that consent unto them shall be had in derision and in reproach, and trodden under foot.

70. For there shall be in every place, and in the next cities, a great insurrection upon those that fear Yahuah.

71. They shall be like mad men, sparing none, but still spoiling and destroying those that fear Yahuah.

72. For they shall waste and take away their goods, and cast them out of their houses.

73. Then they shall be known, who are my chosen; and they shall be tried as the gold in the fire.

74. Hear, O you my beloved, says Yahuah: Behold, the days of trouble are at hand, but I will deliver you from the same.

75. Do not be afraid neither doubt; for Êlôhîym is your guide,

76. And the guide of them who keep my commandments and precepts, says Yahuah Êlôhîym: Do not let your sins weigh you down, and do not let your iniquities lift up themselves.

77. Woe be unto them that are bound with their sins, and covered with their iniquities like as a field is covered over with bushes, and the path thereof covered with thorns, that no man may travel through!

78. It is left undressed, and is cast into the fire to be consumed therewith.

Ṭôbîyâhû (Tobit) & The Traditional Bible Parallels

(Dabar Yahuah Scriptures Study Guide)

Introduction – Expanded Description

The Book of Ṭôbîyâhû (Tobit) is a deuterocanonical/apocryphal book that combines elements of wisdom literature, narrative storytelling, and theological reflection. It focuses on Ṭôbîyâhû (Tobit), a righteous Yashareliy of the tribe of **Naphtâlîy**, who experiences suffering, exile, and divine intervention. The book emphasizes **righteous living, family loyalty, prayer, almsgiving, and divine providence**. Ṭôbîyâhû (Tobit)'s story reflects themes common in canonical wisdom and historical books of the Old Testament but also introduces unique narrative elements such as angelic guidance and miraculous healing.

Key themes include:

1. Righteousness and Obedience – Ṭôbîyâhû (Tobit) exemplifies faithful observance of the Torah, prayer, and charity despite adversity.

2. Divine Providence – Êlôhîym orchestrates events through angelic intervention (Raphael) and human decisions.

3. Family and Marriage – The story of Ṭôbîyâhû (Tobit)'s son Tôbîyâh and Sarah emphasizes faithfulness, virtue, and Êlôhîym's protection.

4. Healing and Deliverance – Both spiritual and physical healing occur through prayer, angelic assistance, and adherence to Êlôhîym's instructions.

5. Wisdom and Moral Instruction – The book teaches practical ethics, piety, and the rewards of righteousness.

Ṭôbîyâhû (Tobit) is both a historical and moral narrative, combining **personal piety** with **divine guidance**, echoing lessons found in Job, Proverbs, and Psalms while offering unique episodes absent from canonical texts.

Comparison Table: Ṭôbîyâhû (Tobit) & The Traditional Bible

Ṭôbîyâhû (Tobit) Passage	Biblical Parallels	Theme / Connection
Ṭôbîyâhû (Tobit) 1:1–16 – Ṭôbîyâhû (Tobit)'s exile and his acts of righteousness (burial of the dead, almsgiving).	Deut 10:18–19; Ezek 18:5–9	Faithfulness to Êlôhîym, charity, and ethical conduct.
Ṭôbîyâhû (Tobit) 2:1–14 – Ṭôbîyâhû (Tobit) prays for death during suffering.	Job 3; Ps 38:10	Honest lamentation and despair in trials.
Ṭôbîyâhû (Tobit) 3:1–17 – Sarah prays for deliverance from her oppression.	Gen 24; Ps 34:17	Faith in Êlôhîym's help and protection; prayer as reliance on Elohiym.

Ṭôbîyâhû (Tobit) Passage	Biblical Parallels	Theme / Connection
Ṭôbîyâhû (Tobit) 4:1–21 – Ṭôbîyâhû (Tobit) instructs Ṭôbîyâh about righteousness, almsgiving, and fear of Yahuah.	Prov 3:9–10; Deut 6:5	Moral and ethical instruction; generational teaching.
Ṭôbîyâhû (Tobit) 5:1–21 – Angel Raphael guides Ṭôbîyâh to Media; Ṭôbîyâh prepares for marriage.	Gen 24; Ex 23:20	Divine guidance, angelic intervention, and trust in Êlôhîym.
Ṭôbîyâhû (Tobit) 6:1–21 – Ṭôbîyâh casts out the demon Asmodeus and marries Sarah.	Ps 91:11; Matt 12:43–45	Êlôhîym's protection, spiritual deliverance, overcoming evil.
Ṭôbîyâhû (Tobit) 8:1–21 – Ṭôbîyâh and Sarah pray before marriage; healing and blessing.	Prov 3:6; Ps 127	Prayer before action, seeking divine guidance and blessing.
Ṭôbîyâhû (Tobit) 11:1–15 – Ṭôbîyâhû (Tobit)'s sight restored; thanksgiving and recognition of Êlôhîym's providence.	Ps 34:8; Isa 35:5	Divine healing, gratitude, and faithfulness rewarded.
Ṭôbîyâhû (Tobit) 12:1–22 – Raphael reveals his angelic identity; lessons about Êlôhîym's ways.	Dan 10:13; Ex 23:20	Angels as Êlôhîym's instruments; wisdom through revelation.
Ṭôbîyâhû (Tobit) 14:1–15 – Ṭôbîyâhû (Tobit)'s final exhortation and death; blessings for family.	Deut 33; Job 42	Legacy, faithfulness, and instruction for future generations.

Summary of Key Parallels

1. Faithful Life in Exile – Ṭôbîyâhû (Tobit)'s righteousness during hardship mirrors Job and Psalms in maintaining integrity under suffering.

2. Prayer and Reliance on Elohiym – Both Ṭôbîyâhû (Tobit) and Sarah exemplify persistent prayer for protection, guidance, and deliverance.

3. Divine Intervention – Angelic assistance (Raphael) parallels Êlôhîym's guidance of Yasharel in Exodus and other historical books.

4. Ethical Instruction – Ṭôbîyâhû (Tobit)'s advice to Ṭôbîyâh emphasizes charity, obedience, and moral living, echoing Proverbs and Deuteronomy.

5. Marriage and Family – Ṭôbîyâh and Sarah's story reflects Êlôhîym's blessing and providence in family life.

6. Healing and Restoration – Ṭôbîyâhû (Tobit)'s restored sight symbolizes Êlôhîym's reward for faithfulness, paralleling Isaiah's healing imagery.

7. Angelic Revelation and Wisdom – Raphael's teaching underscores the unseen workings of Êlôhîym and the value of divine wisdom.

Ṭôbîyâhû (טוֹבִיָּהוּ) - Tobit

Chapter 1

1. The book of the words of Ṭôbîyâhû, son of Ṭôbîyêl, the son of Ananiyêl, the son of Aduêl, the son of Gabaêl, of the seed of Ăśâhêl, of the tribe of Naphtâlîy;

2. Who in the time of Shalmaneser king of the Ashshûr was led captive out of this be, which is at the right hand of that city, which is called properly Naphtâlîy in Gâlîyl above Âshêr.

3. I Ṭôbîyâhû have walked all the days of my life in the ways of truth and justice, and I did many alms deeds to my brethren, and my nation, who came with me to Nîynewêh, into the land of the Ashshûr.

4. And when I was in my own country, in the land of Yâshârêl being but young, all the tribe of Naphtâlîy my father fell from the house of Yarûshâlaim, which was chosen out of all the tribes of Yâshârêl, that all the tribes should sacrifice there, where the temple of the habitation of Elyôn Êl was consecrated and built for all ages.

5. Now all the tribes which together revolted, and the house of my father Naphtâlîy, sacrificed unto the heifer Baal.

6. But I alone went often to Yarûshâlaim at the feasts, as it was ordained unto all the people of Yâshârêl by an everlasting decree, having the first fruits and tenths of increase, with that which was first shorn; and them I gave at the altar to the Kôhên the children of Ahărôn.

7. The first tenth part of all increase I gave to the sons of Ahărôn, who ministered at Yarûshâlaim: Another tenth part I sold away, and went, and spent it every year at Yarûshâlaim:

8. And the third I gave unto them to whom it was meet, as Debôrâh my father's mother had commanded me, because I was left an orphan by my father.

9. Furthermore, when I was come to the age of a man, I married Channâh of my own kindred, and of her I begat Tôbîyâh.

10. And when we were carried away captives to Nîynewêh, all my brethren and those that were of my kindred did eat of the bread of the Gentiles.

11. But I kept myself from eating;

12. Because I remembered Êlôhîym with all my heart.

13. And Elyôn Êl gave me grace and favor before Shalmaneser, so that I was his purveyor.

14. And I went into Mâday, and left in trust with Gabaêl, the brother of Gabrias, at Rages a city of Mâday ten talents of silver.

15. Now when Shalmaneser was dead, Sanchêrîyb his son reigned in his stead; whose estate was troubled, that I could not go into Mâday.

16. And in the time of Shalmaneser I gave many alms to my brethren, and gave my bread to the hungry,

17. And my clothes to the naked: And if I saw any of my nation dead, or cast about the walls of Nîynewêh, I buried him.

18. And if the king Sanchêrîyb had slain any, when he was come, and fled from Yahûdâh,

I buried them secretly; for in his wrath he killed many; but the bodies were not found, when they were sought for of the king.

19. And when one of the Nîynewêh went and complained of me to the king that I buried them, and hid myself; understanding that I was sought for to be put to death, I withdrew myself for fear.

20. Then all my goods were forcibly taken away, neither was there anything left me, beside my woman Channâh and my son Tôbîyâh.

21. And there did not pass five and fifty days, before two of his sons killed him, and they fled into the mountains of Ărâraṭh; and Êsar Chaddôn his son reigned in his stead; who appointed over his father's accounts, and over all his affairs, Achiacharus my brother Anael's son.

22. And Achiacharus entreating for me, I returned to Nîynewêh. Now Achiacharus was cupbearer, and keeper of the signet, and steward, and overseer of the accounts: And Êsar Chaddôn appointed him next unto him: And he was my brother's son.

Chapter 2

1. Now when I was come home again, and my woman Channâh was restored unto me, with my son Tôbîyâh, in the feast of Shâbûa (שָׁבוּעַ), which is the qâdôsh feast of the seven weeks, there was a good dinner prepared me, in the which I sat down to eat.

2. And when I saw abundance of meat, I said to my son, go and bring what poor man so ever you shall find out of our brethren, who is mindful of Yahuah; and, lo, I tarry for you.

3. But he came again, and said, father, one of our nation is strangled, and is cast out in the marketplace.

4. Then before I had tasted of any meat, I started up, and took him up into a room until the going down of the sun.

5. Then I returned, and washed myself, and ate my meat in heaviness,

6. Remembering that prophecy of Âmôs, as he said, your feasts shall be turned into mourning, and all your mirth into lamentation.

7. Therefore I wept: And after the going down of the sun I went and made a grave, and buried him.

8. But my neighbors mocked me, and said, this man is not yet afraid to be put to death for this matter: Who fled away; and yet, lo, he buries the dead again.

9. The same night also I returned from the burial, and slept by the wall of my courtyard, being polluted and my face was uncovered:

10. And I did not know that there were sparrows in the wall, and my eyes being open, the sparrows muted warm dung into my eyes, and a whiteness came in my eyes: And I went to the physicians, but they did not help me: Moreover Achiacharus did nourish me, until I went into Elymais.

11. And my woman Channâh did take women's works to do.

12. And when she had sent them home to the owners, they paid her wages, and he gave her also besides a kid.

13. And when it was in my house, and began to cry, I said unto her, from whence is this kid? Is it not stolen? Render it to the owners; for it is not lawful to eat anything that is stolen.

14. But she replied upon me, it was given for a gift more than the wages. Howbeit I did not believe her, but bade her render it to the owners: And I was abashed at her. But she

replied upon me, where are your alms and your righteous deeds? Behold, you and all your works are known.

Chapter 3

1. Then I being grieved did weep, and in my sorrow prayed, saying,

2. O Yahuah, you are just, and all your works and all your ways are mercy and truth, and you judge truly and justly forever.

3. Remember me, and look on me, do not punish me for my sins and ignorance, and the sins of my fathers, who have sinned before you:

4. For they did not obey your commandments: Wherefore you have delivered us for a spoil, and unto captivity, and unto death, and for a proverb of reproach to all the nations among whom we are dispersed.

5. And now your judgments are many and true: Deal with me according to my sins and my fathers': Because we have not kept your commandments, neither have walked in truth before you.

6. Now therefore deal with me as seems best unto you, and command my spirit to be taken from me, that I may be dissolved, and become earth: For it is profitable for me to die rather than to live, because I have heard false reproaches, and have much sorrow: Command therefore that I may now be delivered out of this distress, and go into the everlasting place: Do not turn your face away from me.

7. It came to pass the same day that in Ecbatana a city of Mâday Śârâh the daughter of Reûêl (רְעוּאֵל) was also reproached by her father's maids;

8. Because that she had been married to seven husbands, whom Asmodeus the evil spirit had killed, before they had lied with her. Do you not know, said they, that you have strangled your husbands? You have had already seven husbands, neither were you named after any of them.

9. Wherefore do you beat us for them? If they are dead, go your ways after them, let us never see of you either son or daughter.

10. When she heard these things, she was very sorrowful, so that she thought to have strangled herself; and she said, I am the only daughter of my father, and if I do this, it shall be a reproach unto him, and I shall bring his old age with sorrow unto the grave.

11. Then she prayed toward the window, and said, blessed are you, O Yahuah my Êlôhîym, and your Qâdôsh and Tiphârâh (תִּפְאָרָה) name is blessed and honorable forever: Let all your works praise you forever.

12. And now, O Yahuah, I set my eyes and my face toward you,

13. And say, take me out of the earth, that I may hear no more the reproach.

14. You know, Yahuah, that I am pure from all sin with man,

15. And that I never polluted my name, nor the name of my father, in the land of my captivity: I am the only daughter of my father, neither he has any child to be his heir, neither any near kinsman, nor any son of his alive, to whom I may keep myself for a woman: My seven husbands are already dead; and why should I live? But if it does not please you that I should die, command some regard to be had of me, and pity taken of me, that I hear no more reproach.

16. So the prayers of them both were heard before the majesty of the Gâdôl Êlôhîym.

17 And Râphâêl was sent to heal them both, that is, to scale away the whiteness of

Ṭôbîyâhû's eyes, and to give Śârâh the daughter of Reûêl for a woman to Ṭôbîyâh the son of Ṭôbîyâhû; and to bind Asmodeus the evil spirit; because she belonged to Ṭôbîyâh by right of inheritance. The selfsame time came Ṭôbîyâhû home, and entered into his house, and Śârâh the daughter of Reûêl came down from her upper chamber.

Chapter 4

1. In that day Ṭôbîyâhû remembered the money which he had committed to Gabaêl in Rages of Mâday,

2. And said with himself, I have wished for death; wherefore do I not call for my son Tôbîyâh that I may signify to him of the money before I die?

3. And when he had called him, he said, my son, when I am dead, bury me; and do not despise your mother, but honor her all the days of your life, and do that which shall please her, and do not grieve her.

4. Remember, my son, that she saw many dangers for you, when you were in her womb: And when she is dead, bury her by me in one grave.

5. My son, be mindful of Yahuah our Êlôhîym all your days, and do not let your will be set to sin, or to transgress his commandments: Do uprightly all your life long, and do not follow the ways of unrighteousness.

6. For if you deal truly, your doings shall prosperously succeed to you, and to all them that live justly.

7. Give alms of your substance; and when you give alms, do not let your eye be envious, neither turn your face from any poor, and the face of Êlôhîym shall not be turned away from you.

8. If you have abundance give alms accordingly: If you have but a little, do not be afraid to give according to that little:

9. For you lay up a good treasure for yourself against the day of necessity.

10. Because that alms do deliver from death, and do not suffers to come into darkness.

11. For alms is a good gift unto all that give it in the sight of Elyôn Êl.

12. Beware of all whoredom, my son, and chiefly take a woman of the seed of your fathers, and do not take a strange woman to wife, which is not of your father's tribe: For we are the children of the Nâbîy, Nôach, Abrâhâm, Yitschâq, and Yaăqôb: Remember, my son, that our fathers from the beginning, even that they all married women of their own kindred, and were blessed in their children, and their seed shall inherit the land.

13. Now therefore, my son, love your brethren, and do not despise in your heart your brethren, the sons and daughters of your people, in not taking a woman of them: For in pride is destruction and much trouble, and in lewdness is decay and great want: For lewdness is the mother of famine.

14. Do not let the wages of any man, which has wrought for you, tarry with you, but give him it out of hand: For if you serve Êlôhîym, he will also repay you: Be circumspect my son, in all things you do, and be wise in all your conversation.

15. Do that to no man which you hate: Do not drink wine to make you drunken: Neither let drunkenness go with you in your journey.

16. Give of your bread to the hungry, and of your garments to them that are naked; and according to your abundance give alms: And do not let your eye be envious, when you give alms.

17. Pour out your bread on the burial of the just, but give nothing to the wicked.

18. Ask counsel of all that are wise, and do not despise any counsel that is profitable.

19. Bless Yahuah your Êlôhîym always, and desire of him that your ways may be directed, and that all your paths and counsels may prosper: For every nation has not counsel; but Yahuah himself gives all good things, and he humbles whom he will, as he will; now therefore, my son, remember my commandments, neither let them be put out of your mind.

20. And now I signify this to you that I committed ten talents to Gabaêl the son of Gabrias at Rages in Mâday.

21 And do not fear, my son, that we are made poor: For you have much wealth, if you fear Êlôhîym, and depart from all sin, and do that which is pleasing in his sight.

Chapter 5

1. Tôbîyâh then answered and said, father, I will do all things which you have commanded me:

2. But how can I receive the money, seeing I do not know him?

3. Then he gave him the handwriting, and said unto him, seek you a man which may go with you, while I yet live, and I will give him wages: And go and receive the money.

4. Therefore when he went to seek a man, he found Râphâêl that was an angel.

5. But he did not know it; and he said unto him, can you go with me to Rages? And do you know those places well?

6. To whom the angel said, I will go with you, and I know the way well: For I have lodged with our brother Gabaêl.

7. Then Tôbîyâh said unto him, tarry for me, till I tell my father.

8. Then he said unto him, go and do not tarry. So he went in and said to his father, behold, I have found one which will go with me. Then he said, call him unto me that I may know of what tribe he is, and whether he is a trusty man to go with you.

9. So he called him, and he came in, and they saluted one another.

10. Then Tôbîyâhû said unto him, brother, show me of what tribe and family you are.

11. To whom he said, do you seek for a tribe or family, or a hired man to go with your son? Then Tôbîyâhû said unto him, I would know, brother, your kindred and name.

12. Then he said, I am Ăzaryâhû, the son of Chănanyâhû the great, and of your brethren.

13. Then Tôbîyâhû said, you are welcome, brother; do not be now angry with me, because I have enquired to know your tribe and your family; for you are my brother, of an honest and good stock: For I know Chănanyâhû and Yahônâthân, sons of that great Shemayâhû, as we went together to Yarûshâlaim to worship, and offered the firstborn, and the tenths of the fruits; and they were not seduced with the error of our brethren: My brother, you are of a good stock.

14. But tell me, what wages shall I give you? You will a drachm a day, and things necessary, as to my own son?

15. Yea, moreover, if you return safe, I will add something to your wages.

16. So they were well pleased. Then he said to Tôbîyâh, prepare yourself for the journey, and Êlôhîym send you a good journey. And when his son had prepared all things for the journey, his father said, you go with this man, and Êlôhîym, which dwells in shâmayim, prosper your journey, and the angel of Êlôhîym keep

you company. So they went forth both, and the young man's dog with them.

17. But Channâh his mother wept, and said to Ṭôbîyâhû, why you have sent away our son? Is he not the staff of our hand, in going in and out before us?

18. Do not be greedy to add money to money: But let it be as refuse in respect of our child.

19. For that which Yahuah has given us to live with does suffice us.

20. Then Ṭôbîyâhû said to her, take no care, my sister; he shall return in safety, and your eyes shall see him.

21. For the good angel will keep him company, and his journey shall be prosperous, and he shall return safe.

22. Then she made an end of weeping.

Chapter 6

1. And as they went on their journey, they came in the evening to the river Chiddeqel, and they lodged there.

2. And when the young man went down to wash himself, a fish leaped out of the river, and would have devoured him.

3. Then the angel said unto him, take the fish. And the young man laid hold of the fish, and drew it to land.

4. To whom the angel said, open the fish, and take the heart and the liver and the gall, and put them up safely.

5. So the young man did as the angel commanded him; and when they had roasted the fish, they did eat it: Then they both went on their way, till they drew near to Ecbatana.

6. Then the young man said to the angel, brother Ăzaryâhû, to what use is the heart and the liver and the gal of the fish?

7. And he said unto him, touching the heart and the liver, if a devil or an evil spirit troubles any, we must make a smoke thereof before the man or the woman, and the party shall be no more vexed.

8. As for the gall, it is good to anoint a man that has whiteness in his eyes, and he shall be healed.

9. And when they were come near to Rages,

10. The angel said to the young man, brother, today we shall lodge with Reûêl, who is your cousin; he also has one only daughter, named Śârâh; I will speak for her that she may be given you for a woman.

11. For to you does the right of her appertain, seeing you only are of her kindred.

12. And the maid is fair and wise: Now therefore hear me, and I will speak to her father; and when we return from Rages we will celebrate the marriage: For I know that Reûêl cannot marry her to another according to the law of Môsheh, but he shall be guilty of death, because the right of inheritance does rather appertain to you than to any other.

13. Then the young man answered the angel, I have heard, brother Ăzaryâhû that this maid has been given to seven men, who all died in the marriage chamber.

14. And now I am the only son of my father, and I am afraid, lest if I go in unto her, I die, as the other before: For a wicked spirit loves her, which hurts nobody, but those which come unto her; wherefore I also fear lest I die, and bring my father's and my mother's life because of me to the grave with sorrow: For they have no other son to bury them.

15. Then the angel said unto him, do you not remember the precepts which your father gave you that you should marry a woman of your own kindred? Wherefore hear me,

O my brother; for she shall be given you to woman; and you make no reckoning of the evil spirit; for this same night she shall be given you in marriage.

16. And when you shall come into the marriage chamber, you shall take the ashes of perfume, and shall lay upon them some of the heart and liver of the fish, and shall make a smoke with it:

17. And the devil shall smell it, and flee away, and never come again any more: But when you shall come to her, rise up both of you, and pray to Êlôhîym which is merciful, who will have pity on you, and save you: Do not fear, for she is appointed unto you from the beginning; and you shall preserve her, and she shall go with you. Moreover I suppose that she shall bear you children. Now when Tôbîyâh had heard these things, he loved her, and his heart was effectually joined to her.

Chapter 7

1. And when they were come to Ecbatana, they came to the house of Reûêl, and Śârâh met them: And after they had saluted one another, she brought them into the house.

2. Then Reûêl said to Edna his woman, how like is this young man to Ṭôbîyâhû my cousin!

3. And Reûêl asked them, from whence are you, brethren? To whom they said, we are of the sons of Naphtâlîy, which are captives in Nîyneweh.

4. Then he said to them, do you know Ṭôbîyâhû our kinsman? And they said, we know him. Then he said, is he in good health?

5. And they said, he is both alive, and in good health: And Tôbîyâh said, he is my father.

6. Then Reûêl leaped up, and kissed him, and wept,

7. And blessed him, and said unto him, you are the son of an honest and good man. But when he had heard that Ṭôbîyâhû was blind, he was sorrowful, and wept.

8. And likewise Edna his woman and Śârâh his daughter wept. Moreover they entertained them cheerfully; and after that they had killed a ram of the flock, they set store of meat on the table. Then Tôbîyâh said to Râphâêl, brother Ăzaryâhû, speak of those things of which you did talk in the way, and let this business be dispatched.

9. So he communicated the matter with Reûêl: And Reûêl said to Tôbîyâh, eat and drink, and make merry:

10. For it is meet that you should marry my daughter: Nevertheless I will declare unto you the truth.

11. I have given my daughter in marriage to seven men, who died that night they came in unto her: Nevertheless for the present be merry. But Tôbîyâh said, I will eat nothing here, till we agree and swear one to another.

12. Reûêl said, then take her from henceforth according to the manner, for you are her cousin, and she is yours, and the merciful Êlôhîym give you good success in all things.

13. Then he called his daughter Śârâh, and she came to her father, and he took her by the hand, and he gave her to be woman to Tôbîyâh, saying, behold, take her after the law of Môsheh, and lead her away to your father. And he blessed them;

14. And called Edna his woman, and took paper, and did write an instrument of covenants, and sealed it.

15. Then they began to eat.

16. After Reûêl called his woman Edna, and said unto her, sister, prepare another chamber, and bring her in thither.

17. Which when she had done as he had bidden her, she brought her thither: And she wept, and she received the tears of her daughter, and said unto her,

18. Be of good comfort, my daughter; Yahuah of shâmayim and earth give you joy for this thy sorrow: Be of good comfort, my daughter.

Chapter 8

1. And when they had supped, they brought Tôbîyâh in unto her.

2. And as he went, he remembered the words of Râphâêl, and took the ashes of the perfumes, and put the heart and the liver of the fish thereupon, and made a smoke therewith.

3. The which smell when the evil spirit had smelled, he fled into the utmost parts of Mitsrayim, and the angel bound him.

4. And after that they were both shut in together, Tôbîyâh rose out of the bed, and said, sister, arise, and let us pray that Êlôhîym would have pity on us.

5. Then Tôbîyâh began to say, blessed are you, O Êlôhîym of our fathers, and blessed is your Qâdôsh and glorious name forever; let the shâmayim bless you, and all your creatures.

6. You made Âdâm, and gave him Chawwâh (חַוָּה) his woman for a helper and stay: Of them came mankind: You have said, it is not good that man should be alone; let us make unto him an aid like unto himself.

7. And now, O Yahuah, I do not take this my sister for lust but uprightly: Therefore mercifully ordain that we may become aged together.

8. And she said with him, Âmên.

9. So they slept both that night. And Reûêl arose, and went and made a grave,

10. Saying, I fear lest he also be dead.

11. But when Reûêl was come into his house,

12. He said unto his woman Edna. Send one of the maids, and let her see whether he is alive: If he is not, that we may bury him, and no man know it.

13. So the maid opened the door, and went in, and found them both asleep,

14. And came forth, and told them that he was alive.

15. Then Reûêl praised Êlôhîym, and said, O Êlôhîym, you are worthy to be praised with all pure and qâdôsh praise; therefore let your qôdesh praise you with all your creatures; and let all your angels and your elect praise you forever.

16. You are to be praised, for you have made me joyful; and that is not come to me which I suspected; but you have dealt with us according to your great mercy.

17. You are to be praised because you have had mercy of two that were the only begotten children of their fathers: Grant them mercy, O Yahuah, and finish their life in health with joy and mercy.

18. Then Reûêl bade his servants to fill the grave.

19. And he kept the wedding feast fourteen days.

20. For before the days of the marriage were finished, Reûêl had said unto him by an oath, that he should not depart till the fourteen days of the marriage were expired;

21. And then he should take the half of his goods, and go in safety to his father; and should have the rest when I and my woman are dead.

Chapter 9

1. Then Tôbîyâh called Râphâêl, and said unto him,

2. Brother Ăzaryâhû, take with you a servant, and two camels, and go to Rages of Mâday to Gabaêl, and bring me the money, and bring him to the wedding.

3. For Reûêl has sworn that I shall not depart.

4. But my father counts the days; and if I tarry long, he will be very sorry.

5. So Râphâêl went out, and lodged with Gabaêl, and gave him the handwriting: Who brought forth bags which were sealed up, and gave them to him.

6. And early in the morning they went forth both together, and came to the wedding: And Tôbîyâh blessed his woman.

Chapter 10

1. Now Tôbîyâhû his father counted every day: And when the days of the journey were expired, and they did not come,

2. Then Tôbîyâhû said, are they detained? Or is Gabaêl dead, and there is no man to give him the money?

3. Therefore he was very sorry.

4. Then his woman said unto him, my son is dead, seeing he stays long; and she began to wail him, and said,

5. Now I care for nothing, my son, since I have let you go, the light of my eyes.

6. To whom Tôbîyâhû said, hold your peace, take no care, for he is safe.

7. But she said, hold your peace, and do not deceive me; my son is dead. And she went out every day into the way which they went, and did eat no meat on the daytime, and did not cease whole nights to bewail her son Tôbîyâh, until the fourteen days of the wedding were expired, which Reûêl had sworn that he should spend there. Then Tôbîyâh said to Reûêl, let me go, for my father and my mother look no more to see me.

8. But his father in law said unto him, tarry with me, and I will send to your father, and they shall declare unto him how things go with you.

9. But Tôbîyâh said, no; but let me go to my father.

10. Then Reûêl arose, and gave him Śârâh his woman, and half his goods, servants, and cattle, and money:

11. And he blessed them, and sent them away, saying, the Êlôhîym of shâmayim give you a prosperous journey, my children.

12. And he said to his daughter, honor your father and your mother in law, which are now your parents, that I may hear good report of you. And he kissed her. Edna also said to Tôbîyâh, Yahuah of shâmayim restore you, my dear brother, and grant that I may see your children of my daughter Śârâh before I die, that I may rejoice before Yahuah: Behold, I commit my daughter unto you of special trust; wherefore do not entreat her evil.

Chapter 11

1. After these things Tôbîyâh went his way, praising Êlôhîym that he had given him a prosperous journey, and blessed Reûêl and Edna his woman, and went on his way till they drew near unto Nîynewêh.

2. Then Râphâêl said to Tôbîyâh, you know, brother, how you did leave your father:

3. Let us haste before your woman, and prepare the house.

4. And take in your hand the gall of the fish. So they went their way, and the dog went after them.

5. Now Channâh sat looking about toward the way for her son.

6. And when she espied him coming, she said to his father, behold, your son comes, and the man that went with him.

7. Then Râphâêl said, I know, Tôbîyâh, that your father will open his eyes.

8. Therefore you anoint his eyes with the gall, and being pricked therewith, he shall rub, and the whiteness shall fall away, and he shall see you.

9. Then Channâh ran forth, and fell upon the neck of her son, and said unto him, seeing I have seen you, my son, from henceforth I am content to die. And they wept both.

10. Ṭôbîyâhû also went forth toward the door, and stumbled: But his son ran unto him,

11. And took hold of his father: And he put of the gall on his fathers' eyes, saying, be of good hope, my father.

12. And when his eyes began to smart, he rubbed them;

13. And the whiteness pilled away from the corners of his eyes: And when he saw his son, he fell upon his neck.

14. And he wept, and said, blessed are you, O Êlôhîym, and blessed is your name forever; and blessed are all your qâdôsh angels:

15. For you have scourged, and have taken pity on me: For, behold, I see my son Tôbîyâh. And his son went in rejoicing, and told his father the great things that had happened to him in Mâday.

16. Then Ṭôbîyâhû went out to meet his daughter in law at the gate of Nîynewêh, rejoicing and praising Êlôhîym: And they which saw him go marveled, because he had received his sight.

17. But Tôbîyâh gave thanks before them, because Êlôhîym had mercy on him. And when he came near to Śârâh his daughter in law, he blessed her, saying, you are welcome, daughter: Be Êlôhîym blessed, which has brought you unto us, and blessed be your father and your mother. And there was joy among all his brethren which were at Nîynewêh.

18. And Achiacharus, and Nasbas his brother's son, came:

19. And Tôbîyâh's wedding was kept seven days with great joy.

Chapter 12

1. Then Ṭôbîyâhû called his son Tôbîyâh, and said unto him, my son, see that the man have his wages, which went with you, and you must give him more.

2. And Tôbîyâh said unto him, O father, it is no harm to me to give him half of those things which I have brought:

3. For he has brought me again to you in safety, and made whole my woman, and brought me the money, and likewise healed you.

4. Then the old man said, it is due unto him.

5. So he called the angel, and he said unto him, take half of all that you have brought and go away in safety.

6. Then he took them both apart, and said unto them, bless Êlôhîym, praise him, and magnify him, and praise him for the things which he has done unto you in the sight of all that live. It is good to praise Êlôhîym, and exalt his name, and honorably to show forth

the works of Êlôhîym; therefore do not be slack to praise him.

7. It is good to keep close the secret of a king, but it is honorable to reveal the works of Êlôhîym. Do that which is good, and no evil shall touch you.

8. Prayer is good with fasting and alms and righteousness. A little with righteousness is better than much with unrighteousness. It is better to give alms than to lay up gold:

9. For alms does deliver from death, and shall purge away all sin. Those that exercise alms and righteousness shall be filled with life:

10. But they that sin are enemies to their own life.

11. Surely I will keep close nothing from you. For I said, it was good to keep close the secret of a king, but that it was honorable to reveal the works of Êlôhîym.

12. Now therefore, when you did pray, and Śârâh your daughter in law, I did bring the remembrance of your prayers before the Qâdôsh: And when you did bury the dead, I was with you likewise.

13. And when you did not delay to rise up, and leave your dinner, to go and cover the dead, your good deed was not hid from me: But I was with you.

14. And now Êlôhîym has sent me to heal you and Śârâh your daughter in law.

15. I am Râphâêl, one of the seven qâdôsh angels, which present the prayers of the qôdesh, and which go in and out before the glory of the Qâdôsh.

16. Then they were both troubled, and fell upon their faces: For they feared.

17. But he said unto them, do not fear, for it shall go well with you; praise Êlôhîym therefore.

18. For not of any favor of mine, but by the will of our Êlôhîym I came; wherefore praise him forever.

19. All these days I did appear unto you; but I did neither eat nor did drink; but you see a vision.

20. Now therefore give Êlôhîym thanks: For I go up to him that sent me; but write all things which are done in a book.

21. And when they arose, they saw him no more.

22. Then they confessed the great and wonderful works of Êlôhîym, and how the angel of Yahuah had appeared unto them.

Chapter 13

1. Then Ṭôbîyâhû wrote a prayer of rejoicing, and said, blessed be Êlôhîym that lives forever, and blessed be his kingdom.

2. For he does scourge, and has mercy: He leads down to sheôl, and brings up again: Neither there is any that can avoid his hand.

3. Confess him before the Gentiles, you children of Yâshârêl: For he has scattered us among them.

4. There declare his greatness, and extol him before all the living: For he is our Yahuah, and he is the Êlôhîym our father forever.

5. And he will scourge us for our iniquities, and will have mercy again, and will gather us out of all nations, among whom he has scattered us.

6. If you turn to him with your whole heart, and with your whole mind, and deal uprightly before him, then he will turn unto you, and will not hide his face from you. Therefore see what he will do with you, and confess him with your whole mouth, and praise Yahuah Shadday Êl, and extol the

Ôlâm Melek. In the land of my captivity I do praise him, and declare his might and majesty to a sinful nation. O you sinners, turn and do justice before him: Who can tell if he will accept you, and have mercy on you?

7. I will extol my Êlôhîym, and my soul shall praise the Melek of shâmayim, and shall rejoice in his greatness.

8. Let all men speak, and let all praise him for his righteousness.

9. O Yarûshâlaim, the qâdôsh city, he will scourge you for your children's works, and will have mercy again on the sons of the righteous.

10. Give praise to Yahuah, for he is good: And praise the Ôlâm Melek, that his tabernacle may be built in you again with joy, and let him make joyful there in you those that are captives, and love in you forever those that are miserable.

11. Many nations shall come from far to the name of Yahuah Êlôhîym with gifts in their hands, even gifts to the Melek of shâmayim; all generations shall praise you with great joy.

12. Cursed are all they which hate you, and blessed shall all be which love you forever.

13. Rejoice and be glad for the children of the just: For they shall be gathered together, and shall bless Yahuah of the just.

14. O blessed are they which love you, for they shall rejoice in your peace: Blessed are they which have been sorrowful for all your scourges; for they shall rejoice for you, when they have seen all your glory, and shall be glad forever.

15. Let my soul bless Êlôhîym the Gâdôl Melek.

16. For Yarûshâlaim shall be built up with sapphires and emeralds, and precious stone: Your walls and towers and battlements with pure gold.

17. And the streets of Yarûshâlaim shall be paved with beryl and carbuncle and stones of Ôphîyr.

18. And all her streets shall say, Hâlal (הָלַל) Yâh (יָהּ); and they shall praise him, saying, Bârak be Êlôhîym, which hath extolled it forever.

Chapter 14

1. So Ṭôbîyâhû made an end of praising Êlôhîym.

2. And he was eight and fifty years old when he lost his sight, which was restored to him after eight years: And he gave alms, and he increased in the fear of Yahuah Êlôhîym, and praised him.

3. And when he was very aged he called his son, and the sons of his son, and said to him, my son, take your children; for, behold, I am aged, and am ready to depart out of this life.

4. Go into Mâday my son, for I surely believe those things which Yônâh the Nâbîy spoke of Nîyneweh, that it shall be overthrown; and that for a time peace shall rather be in Mâday; and that our brethren shall lie scattered in the earth from that good land: And Yarûshâlaim shall be desolate, and the house of Êlôhîym in it shall be burned, and shall be desolate for a time;

5. And that again Êlôhîym will have mercy on them, and bring them again into the land, where they shall build a temple, but not like to the first, until the time of that age be fulfilled; and afterward they shall return from all places of their captivity, and build up Yarûshâlaim gloriously, and the house of Êlôhîym shall be built in it forever with a

glorious building, as the Nâbîy have spoken thereof.

6. And all nations shall turn, and fear Yahuah Êlôhîym truly, and shall bury their idols.

7. So shall all nations praise Yahuah, and his people shall confess Êlôhîym, and Yahuah shall exalt his people; and all those which love Yahuah Êlôhîym in truth and justice shall rejoice, showing mercy to our brethren.

8. And now, my son, depart out of Nîynewêh, because that those things which the Nâbîy Yônâh spoke shall surely come to pass.

9. But you keep the law and the commandments, and show yourself merciful and just, that it may go well with you.

10. And bury me decently, and your mother with me; but tarry no longer at Nîynewêh. Remember, my son, how Hâmân handled Achiacharus that brought him up, how out of light he brought him into darkness, and how he rewarded him again: Yet Achiacharus was saved, but the other had his reward: For he went down into darkness. Menashsheh gave alms, and escaped the snares of death which they had set for him: But Hâmân fell into the snare, and perished.

11. Wherefore now, my son, consider what alms does, and how righteousness does deliver. When he had said these things, he gave up the ghost in the bed, being a hundred and eight and fifty years old; and he buried him honorably.

12. And when Channâh his mother was dead, he buried her with his father. But Tôbîyâh departed with his woman and children to Ecbatana to Reûêl his father in law,

13. Where he became old with honor, and he buried his father and mother in law honorably, and he inherited their substance, and his father Tôbîyâhû's.

14. And he died at Ecbatana in Mâday, being a hundred and seven and twenty years old.

15. But before he died he heard of the destruction of Nîynewêh, which was taken by Nebûkkadnetstsar and Ăchashwêrôsh: And before his death he rejoiced over Nîynewêh.

The Prayer of Menashsheh & The Traditional Bible Context

(Dabar Yahuah Scriptures Study Guide)

Introduction – Expanded Description

The Prayer of Menashsheh is a penitential prayer attributed to King Menashsheh of Yahûdâh. According to biblical history, Menashsheh was one of the most wicked kings of Yahûdâh, leading the nation into idolatry (2 Kings 21:1–18; 2 Chronicles 33:1–20). This prayer is **apocryphal/deuterocanonical** and appears in some manuscripts of the Septuagint, but is not included in the Hebrew Masoretic Text.

The prayer is a heartfelt confession, expressing **repentance, humility, and acknowledgment of Êlôhîym's mercy**. It emphasizes themes of forgiveness, divine patience, and the hope of redemption even for those who have sinned greatly.

Where it fits in the Bible:

- Historically: After Menashsheh's captivity by the Ashshûr (Assyria) (2 Chronicles 33:11–13).
- Chronologically: Between 2 Chronicles 33:10 and 2 Chronicles 33:13–20, as a reflection of his repentance before Êlôhîym restored him.
- Theologically: It complements passages on **repentance and divine mercy** found throughout Scripture, especially in Psalms, Yônâh, and Yachezqêl.

Key themes include:

1. Repentance – Confession of sins and acknowledgment of wrongdoing.

2. Divine Mercy – Appeal to Êlôhîym's enduring patience and forgiveness.

3. Humility – Recognition of human frailty and unworthiness.

4. Hope of Restoration – Êlôhîym's willingness to forgive even the gravest sins.

5. Prayer as Transformation – Personal communication with Êlôhîym leads to spiritual renewal.

Comparison Table: Prayer of Menashsheh & The traditional Bible

Prayer of Menashsheh Passage	Biblical Parallels	Theme / Connection
1–5 – Confession of sins and acknowledgment of rebellion.	2 Chronicles 33:11–13; Ps 51:1–4	Repentance, recognizing sin, and guilt.
6–10 – Plea for mercy and recognition of Êlôhîym's justice.	Yônâh 2:1–9; Ps 103:8–14	Divine mercy; Êlôhîym's compassion outweighs punishment.
11–15 – Admittance of wickedness and appeal to Êlôhîym's steadfast love.	Isa 55:6–7; Neh 1:5–6	Turning to Êlôhîym in humility and seeking forgiveness.
16–20 – Prayer for deliverance and restoration to righteousness.	Ps 34:17–19; Ezek 18:21–23	Êlôhîym hears the humble; deliverance through repentance.
21–24 – Commitment to obedience and living righteously after forgiveness.	2 Chronicles 33:13–20; Deut 30:1–10	Transformation through repentance; living according to Êlôhîym's commands.

Summary of Key Parallels

1. Historical Placement – The prayer corresponds to the time of Menashsheh's captivity in Ashshûr (Assyria) and precedes his restoration in 2 Chronicles 33:13–20.

2. Repentance and Forgiveness – The Prayer of Menashsheh emphasizes the same message as Psalm 51: a contrite heart leads to divine forgiveness.

3. Divine Mercy – Parallels Yônâh's prayer from the belly of the fish and echoes Êlôhîym's patience and compassion toward Yasharel throughout Scripture.

4. Ethical Transformation – After repentance, Menashsheh's restored life illustrates the biblical principle that repentance produces righteous living (Deuteronomy 30:1–10).

5. Liturgical Use – This prayer has been historically used in Yahûdîy and Messianic liturgies as a model of penitence, reflecting the timeless theme that no sinner is beyond Êlôhîym's mercy.

Tephillâh (תְּפִלָּה) Menashsheh (מְנַשֶּׁה) - Prayer of Manasseh

Chapter 1

1. O Yahuah, Êlôhîym Tsâbâ of our fathers, Abrâhâm, Yitschâq, and Yaăqôb, and of their righteous seed; who have made shâmayim and earth, with all the ornament thereof; who have bound the sea by the word of your commandment; who have shut up the deep, and sealed it by your terrible and glorious name;

2. Whom all men fear, and tremble before your power; for the majesty of your glory cannot be born, and your angry threatening toward sinners is importable:

3. But your merciful promise is unmeasurable and unsearchable; for you are Yahuah Elyôn, of great compassion, longsuffering, very merciful, and repent of the evils of men.

4. You, O Yahuah, according to your great goodness have promised repentance and forgiveness to them that have sinned against you:

5. And of your infinite mercies have appointed repentance unto sinners, that they may be saved.

6. You therefore, O Yahuah, that are the Êlôhîym of the just, have not appointed repentance to the just, as to Abrâhâm, and Yitschâq, and Yaăqôb, which have not sinned against you; but you have appointed repentance unto me that am a sinner:

7. For I have sinned above the number of the sands of the sea. My transgressions, O Yahuah, are multiplied: My transgressions are multiplied, and I am not worthy to behold and see the height of shâmayim for the multitude of my iniquities.

8. I am bowed down with many iron bands that I cannot lift up my head, neither have any release:

9. For I have provoked your wrath, and done evil before you: I did not do your will, neither had I kept your commandments:

10. I have set up abominations, and have multiplied offences.

11. Now therefore I bow the knee of my heart, beseeching your of grace. I have sinned, O Yahuah, I have sinned, and I acknowledge my iniquities:

12. Wherefore, I humbly beseech you, forgive me, O Yahuah, forgive me, and do not destroy me with my iniquities.

13. Do not be angry with me forever, by reserving evil for me; neither condemn me to the lower parts of the earth.

14. For you are the Êlôhîym, even the Êlôhîym of them that repent; and in me you will show all your goodness: For you will save me, that am unworthy, according to your great mercy.

15. Therefore I will praise you forever all the days of my life: For all the powers of the shâmayim do praise you, and yours is the glory forever and ever. Âmên.

Book of Bârûk (Baruch) & The Traditional Bible Context

(Dabar Yahuah Scriptures Study Guide)

Introduction – Expanded Description

The **Book of Bârûk (Baruch)** is an apocryphal/deuterocanonical book traditionally attributed to Bârûk (Baruch), the scribe of the prophet Yirmeyâhû. It was likely composed during or shortly after the Bâbel (Babylonian) exile. The book addresses **exile, repentance, wisdom, and hope for restoration**, offering moral exhortations and prayers for the return of Yasharel to Yahuah.

The book is often divided into three sections:

1. Confession and National Repentance – Reflects on Yasharel's sins and acknowledges Êlôhîym's justice (Bârûk (Baruch) 1–2).

2. Wisdom and Instruction – Exhortation to seek Yahuah's wisdom and guidance (Bârûk (Baruch) 3).

3. Prayer and Hope for Restoration – Prayer for deliverance, forgiveness, and the return to Yarûshâlaim (Bârûk (Baruch) 4–6, depending on manuscript).

Where it fits in the Bible:

- Historically: During or after the Bâbel (Babylonian) exile, contemporaneous with Yirmeyâhû's writings.
- Theologically: Complements themes of lament, repentance, and hope in Lamentations, Yirmeyâhû, and Psalms.
- Liturgically: Used in Yahûdîy and Messianic traditions as prayers of confession and supplication.

Key themes include:

- **National repentance** – Recognition of collective sin and consequences.
- **Divine wisdom** – Seeking knowledge and understanding of Êlôhîym's ways.
- **Hope and restoration** – Prayer for return and redemption.
- **Faithfulness** – Trust in Êlôhîym even in times of suffering and exile.

Comparison Table: Book of Bârûk (Baruch) & The Traditional Bible

Bârûk (Baruch) Passage	Biblical Parallels	Theme / Connection
Bârûk (Baruch) 1:1–14 – Confession of Yasharel's sins, acknowledgment of exile.	Jer 1–25; Lam 1:1–22	National repentance; recognition of Êlôhîym's judgment.
Bârûk (Baruch) 1:15–2:14 – Prayer for mercy and forgiveness.	Ps 79; Dan 9:4–19	Appeals to Êlôhîym's mercy; collective prayer and intercession.
Bârûk (Baruch) 3:1–8 – Praise of Yahuah's wisdom, exhortation to seek instruction.	Prov 2:1–6; Sirach 1:1–10	Value of wisdom; guidance for righteous living.
Bârûk (Baruch) 3:9–39 – Instruction on obedience, avoidance of sin, and hope for Êlôhîym's protection.	Deut 30:15–20; Ps 119	Moral guidance; blessings of following Êlôhîym's commandments.
Bârûk (Baruch) 4:1–5 – Call to Yarûshâlaim and exile to return to Êlôhîym.	Isa 40:1–11; Jer 31:1–14	Hope for restoration; return from exile.
Bârûk (Baruch) 4:6–5:9 – Prayer for deliverance and forgiveness.	Ps 102; Dan 9:20–27	Intercession; acknowledgment of Êlôhîym's sovereignty.
Bârûk (Baruch) 6:1–10 – Exhortation to wisdom, blessings for the faithful.	Prov 3:13–18; Sirach 4:11–16	Rewards of righteousness; adherence to divine instruction.

Summary of Key Parallels

1. National Confession – Bârûk (Baruch) emphasizes collective acknowledgment of sin, paralleling Yirmeyâhû's lamentations over Yasharel's rebellion.

2. Prayer and Intercession – The book mirrors Daniel 9's penitential prayer for Yasharel's restoration.

3. Wisdom Literature Connection – Bârûk (Baruch) 3 highlights the pursuit of divine wisdom, similar to Proverbs, Sirach, and Wisdom of Shelômôh.

4. Hope Amid Exile – Echoes themes in Yashayâhû 40–55: comfort, reassurance, and future restoration.

5. Ethical Instruction – Reinforces obedience to Êlôhîym's law, humility, and faithfulness, consistent with Deuteronomy and Psalms.

Bârûk (בָּרוּךְ) - Baruch

Chapter 1

1. And these are the words of the book, which Bârûk the son of Nêrîyâhû, the son of Maăśêyâhû, the son of Tsidqîyâhû, the son of Asadias, the son of Chilqîyâhû, wrote in Bâbel,

2. In the fifth year, and in the seventh day of the month, what time as the Kaśdîy took Yarûshâlaim, and burnt it with fire.

3. And Bârûk did read the words of this book in the hearing of Yakonyâhû the son of Yahôyâqîym king of Yahûdâh, and in the ears of all the people that came to hear the book,

4. And in the hearing of the nobles, and of the king's sons, and in the hearing of the elders, and of all the people, from the lowest unto the highest, even of all them that dwelt at Bâbel by the river Sûd.

5. Whereupon they wept, fasted, and prayed before Yahuah.

6. They made also a collection of money according to every man's power:

7. And they sent it to Yarûshâlaim unto Yahôyâqîym the high Kôhên, the son of Chilqîyâhû, son of Shâlôm (שָׁלוֹם), and to the Kôhên, and to all the people which were found with him at Yarûshâlaim,

8. At the same time when he received the vessels of the house of Yahuah, that were carried out of the temple, to return them into the land of Yahûdâh, the tenth day of the month Sîywân, namely, silver vessels, which Tsidqîyâhû the son of Yôshîyâhû king of Yâdâ had made,

9. After that Nebûkkadnetstsar king of Bâbel had carried away Yakonyâhû, and the princes, and the captives, and the mighty men, and the people of the land, from Yarûshâlaim, and brought them unto Bâbel.

10. And they said, behold, we have sent you money to buy you burnt offerings, and sin offerings, and incense, and prepare you mân, and offer upon the altar of Yahuah our Êlôhîym;

11. And pray for the life of Nebûkkadnetstsar king of Bâbel, and for the life of Bêlshatstsar his son, that their days may be upon earth as the days of shâmayim:

12. And Yahuah will give us strength, and lighten our eyes, and we shall live under the shadow of Nebûkkadnetstsar king of Bâbel, and under the shadow of Bêlshatstsar his son, and we shall serve them many days, and find favor in their sight.

13. Pray for us also unto Yahuah our Êlôhîym, for we have sinned against Yahuah our Êlôhîym; and unto this day the fury of Yahuah and his wrath is not turned from us.

14. And you shall read this book which we have sent unto you, to make confession in the house of Yahuah, upon the feasts and solemn days.

15. And you shall say, to Yahuah our Êlôhîym belongs righteousness, but unto us the confusion of faces, as it is come to pass this day, unto them of Yahûdâh, and to the inhabitants of Yarûshâlaim,

16. And to our kings, and to our princes, and to our Kôhên, and to our Nâbîy, and to our fathers:

17. For we have sinned before Yahuah,

18. And disobeyed him, and have not hearkened unto the voice of Yahuah our Êlôhîym, to walk in the commandments that he gave us openly:

19. Since the day that Yahuah brought our forefathers out of the land of Mitsrayim, unto this present day, we have been disobedient unto Yahuah our Êlôhîym, and we have been negligent in not hearing his voice.

20. Wherefore the evils cleaved unto us, and the curse, which Yahuah appointed by Môsheh his servant at the time that he brought our fathers out of the land of Mitsrayim, to give us a land that flows with milk and honey, like as it is to see this day.

21. Nevertheless we have not hearkened unto the voice of Yahuah our Êlôhîym, according unto all the words of the Nâbîy, whom he sent unto us:

22. But every man followed the imagination of his own wicked heart, to serve strange gods, and to do evil in the sight of Yahuah our Êlôhîym.

Chapter 2

1. Therefore Yahuah has made good his word, which he pronounced against us, and against our judges that judged Yâshârêl, and against our kings, and against our princes, and against the men of Yâshârêl and Yahûdâh,

2. To bring upon us great plagues, such as never happened under the whole shâmayim, as it came to pass in Yarûshâlaim, according to the things that were written in the law of Môsheh;

3. That a man should eat the flesh of his own son, and the flesh of his own daughter.

4. Moreover he has delivered them to be in subjection to all the kingdoms that are round about us, to be as a reproach and desolation among all the people round about, where Yahuah has scattered them.

5. Thus we were cast down, and not exalted, because we have sinned against Yahuah our Êlôhîym, and have not been obedient unto his voice.

6. To Yahuah our Êlôhîym appertains righteousness: But unto us and to our fathers open shame, as appears this day.

7. For all these plagues are come upon us, which Yahuah has pronounced against us,

8. Yet we have not prayed before Yahuah, that we might turn everyone from the imaginations of his wicked heart.

9. Wherefore Yahuah watched over us for evil, and Yahuah has brought it upon us: For Yahuah is righteous in all his works which he has commanded us.

10. Yet we have not hearkened unto his voice, to walk in the commandments of Yahuah that he has set before us.

11. And now, O Yahuah Êlôhîym of Yâshârêl, that have brought your people out of the land of Mitsrayim with a mighty hand, and high arm, and with signs, and with wonders, and with great power, and have gotten yourself a name, as appears this day:

12. O Yahuah our Êlôhîym, we have sinned, we have done ungodly, we have dealt unrighteously in all your ordinances.

13. Let your wrath turn from us: For we are but a few left among the heathen, where you have scattered us.

14. Hear our prayers, O Yahuah, and our petitions, and deliver us for your own sake, and give us favor in the sight of them which have led us away:

15. That all the earth may know that you are Yahuah our Êlôhîym, because Yâshârêl and his posterity is called by your name.

16. O Yahuah, look down from your qâdôsh house, and consider us: Bow down your ear, O Yahuah, to hear us.

17. Open your eyes, and behold; for the dead that are in the graves, whose souls are taken from their bodies, will give unto Yahuah neither praise nor righteousness:

18. But the soul that is greatly vexed, which goes stooping and feeble, and the eyes that fail, and the hungry soul, will give you praise and righteousness, O Yahuah.

19. Therefore we do not make our humble supplication before you, O Yahuah our Êlôhîym, for the righteousness of our fathers, and of our kings.

20. For you have sent out your wrath and indignation upon us, as you have spoken by your servants the Nâbîy, saying,

21. Thus says Yahuah, bow down your shoulders to serve the king of Bâbel: So you shall remain in the land that I gave unto your fathers.

22. But if you will not hear the voice of Yahuah, to serve the king of Bâbel,

23. I will cause to cease out of the cites of Yahûdâh, and from without Yarûshâlaim, the voice of mirth, and the voice of joy, the voice of the bridegroom, and the voice of the bride: And the whole land shall be desolate of inhabitants.

24. But we would not hearken unto your voice, to serve the king of Bâbel: Therefore you have made good the words that you spoke by your servants the Nâbîy, namely, that the bones of our kings, and the bones of our fathers, should be taken out of their place.

25. And, lo, they are cast out to the heat of the day, and to the frost of the night, and they died in great miseries by famine, by sword, and by pestilence.

26. And the house which is called by your name you have laid waste, as it is to be seen this day, for the wickedness of the house of Yâshârêl and the house of Yahûdâh.

27. O Yahuah our Êlôhîym, you have dealt with us after all your goodness, and according to all that great mercy of your,

28. As you spoke by your servant Môsheh in the day when you did command him to write the law before the children of Yâshârêl, saying,

29. If you will not hear my voice, surely this very great multitude shall be turned into a small number among the nations, where I will scatter them.

30. For I knew that they would not hear me, because it is a stiff necked people: But in the land of their captivities they shall remember themselves.

31. And shall know that I am Yahuah their Êlôhîym: For I will give them a heart, and ears to hear:

32. And they shall praise me in the land of their captivity, and think upon my name,

33. And return from their stiff neck, and from their wicked deeds: For they shall remember the way of their fathers, which sinned before Yahuah.

34. And I will bring them again into the land which I promised with an oath unto their fathers, Abrâhâm, Yitschâq, and Yaăqôb, and they shall be masters of it: And I will increase them, and they shall not be diminished.

35. And I will make an everlasting covenant with them to be their Êlôhîym, and they

shall be my people: And I will no more drive my people of Yâshârêl out of the land that I have given them.

Chapter 3

1. O Yahuah Shadday Êl, Êlôhîym of Yâshârêl, the soul in anguish the troubled spirit, cries unto you.

2. Hear, O Yahuah, and have mercy; for you are merciful: And have pity upon us, because we have sinned before you.

3. For you endure forever, and we perish utterly.

4. O Yahuah Shadday Êl, you Êlôhîym of Yâshârêl, hear now the prayers of the dead Yâshârêliy, and of their children, which have sinned before you, and do not hearkened unto the voice of you their Êlôhîym: For the which cause these plagues cleave unto us.

5. Do not remember the iniquities of our forefathers: But think upon your power and your name now at this time.

6. For you are Yahuah our Êlôhîym, and you, O Yahuah, we will praise.

7. And for this cause you have put your fear in our hearts, to the intent that we should call upon your name, and praise you in our captivity: For we have called to mind all the iniquity of our forefathers that sinned before you.

8. Behold, we are yet this day in our captivity, where you have scattered us, for a reproach and a curse, and to be subject to payments, according to all the iniquities of our fathers, which departed from Yahuah our Êlôhîym.

9. Hear, Yâshârêl, the commandments of life: Give ear to understand wisdom.

10. How it happens Yâshârêl, that you are in your enemies' land, that you are waxen old in a strange country, that you are defiled with the dead,

11. That you are counted with them that go down into the grave?

12. You have forsaken the fountain of wisdom.

13. For if you had walked in the way of Êlôhîym, you should have dwelled in peace forever.

14. Learn where is wisdom, where is strength, where is understanding; that you may know also where is length of days, and life, where is the light of the eyes, and peace.

15. Who has found out her place? Or who has come into her treasures?

16. Where are become the princes of the heathen, and such as ruled the beasts upon the earth;

17. They that had their pastime with the fowls of the air, and they that hoarded up silver and gold, wherein men trust, and made no end of their getting?

18. For they that wrought in silver, and were so careful, and whose works are unsearchable,

19. They are vanished and gone down to the grave, and others are come up in their steads.

20. Young men have seen light, and dwelt upon the earth: But the way of knowledge they have not known,

21. Nor understood the paths thereof, nor laid hold of it: Their children were far off from that way.

22. It has not been heard of in Kenaan, neither has it been seen in Têymân.

23. The Hagrîy (הַגְרִי) that seek wisdom upon earth, the merchants of Meran and of Têymân, the authors of fables, and searchers out of

understanding; none of these have known the way of wisdom, or remember her paths.

24. O Yâshârêl, how great is the house of Êlôhîym! And how large is the place of his possession!

25. Great, and has none end; high, and unmeasurable.

26. There were the nephîyl famous from the beginning, that were of so great stature, and so expert in war.

27. Yahuah did not choose those, neither he gave the way of knowledge unto them:

28. But they were destroyed, because they had no wisdom, and perished through their own foolishness.

29. Who has gone up into shâmayim, and taken her, and brought her down from the clouds?

30. Who has gone over the sea, and found her, and will bring her for pure gold?

31. No man knows her way, nor thinks of her path.

32. But he that knows all things knows her, and has found her out with his understanding: He that prepared the earth forevermore has filled it with four footed beasts:

33. He that sends forth light, and it goes, calls it again, and it obeys him with fear.

34. The stars shined in their watches, and rejoiced: When he calls them, they say, here we are; and so with cheerfulness they showed light unto him that made them.

35. This is our Êlôhîym, and there shall none other be accounted of in comparison of him,

36. He has found out all the way of knowledge, and has given it unto Yaăqôb his servant, and to Yâshârêl his beloved.

37. Afterward he did show himself upon earth, and conversed with men.

Chapter 4

1. This is the book of the commandments of Êlôhîym, and the law that endures forever: All they that keep it shall come to life; but such as leave it shall die.

2. Turn you, O Yaăqôb, and take hold of it: Walk in the presence of the light thereof, that you may be illuminated.

3. Do not give your honor to another, nor the things that are profitable unto you to a strange nation.

4. O Yâshârêl, happy are we: For things that are pleasing to Êlôhîym are made known unto us.

5. Be of good cheer, my people, the memorial of Yâshârêl.

6. You were sold to the nations, not for your destruction: But because you moved Êlôhîym to wrath, you were delivered unto the enemies.

7. For you provoked him that made you by sacrificing unto devils, and not to Êlôhîym.

8. You have forgotten Êlôhîym Ôlâm that brought you up; and you have grieved Yarûshâlaim, that nursed you.

9. For when she saw the wrath of Êlôhîym coming upon you, she said, hearken, O you that dwell about Tsîyôn: Êlôhîym has brought upon me great mourning;

10. For I saw the captivity of my sons and daughters, which Ôlâm Êl brought upon them.

11. With joy I did nourish them; but sent them away with weeping and mourning.

12. Let no man rejoice over me, a widow, and forsaken of many, who for the sins of

my children am left desolate; because they departed from the law of Êlôhîym.

13. They did not know his statutes, nor walked in the ways of his commandments, nor trod in the paths of discipline in his righteousness.

14. Let them that dwell about Tsîyôn come, and remember you the captivity of my sons and daughters, which Ôlâm Êl has brought upon them.

15. For he has brought a nation upon them from far, a shameless nation, and of a strange language, who neither reverenced old man, nor pitied child.

16. These have carried away the dear beloved children of the widow, and left her that was alone desolate without daughters.

17. But what can I help you?

18. For he that brought these plagues upon you will deliver you from the hands of your enemies.

19. Go your way, O my children, go your way: For I am left desolate.

20. I have put off the clothing of peace, and put upon me the sackcloth of my prayer: I will cry unto Ôlâm Êl in my days.

21. Be of good cheer, O my children, cry unto Yahuah, and he will deliver you from the power and hand of the enemies.

22. For my hope is in Ôlâm Êl, that he will save you; and joy is come unto me from the Qâdôsh, because of the mercy which shall soon come unto you from Ôlâm Êl our Yâsha.

23. For I sent you out with mourning and weeping: But Êlôhîym will give you to me again with joy and gladness forever.

24. Like as now the neighbors of Tsîyôn have seen your captivity: So shall they see shortly your salvation from our Êlôhîym which shall come upon you with great glory, and brightness of Ôlâm Êl.

25. My children, suffer patiently the wrath that is come upon you from Êlôhîym: For your enemy has persecuted you; but shortly you shall see his destruction, and shall tread upon his neck.

26. My delicate ones have gone rough ways, and were taken away as a flock caught of the enemies.

27. Be of good comfort, O my children, and cry unto Êlôhîym: For you shall be remembered of him that brought these things upon you.

28. For as it was your mind to go astray from Êlôhîym: So, being returned, seek him ten times more.

29. For he that has brought these plagues upon you shall bring you everlasting joy with your salvation.

30. Take a good heart, O Yarûshâlaim: For he that gave you that name will comfort you.

31. Miserable are they that afflicted you, and rejoiced at your fall.

32. Miserable are the cities which your children served: Miserable is she that received your sons.

33. For as she rejoiced at your ruin, and was glad of your fall: So she shall be grieved for her own desolation.

34. For I will take away the rejoicing of her great multitude, and her pride shall be turned into mourning.

35. For fire shall come upon her from Ôlâm Êl, long to endure; and she shall be inhabited of devils for a great time.

36. O Yarûshâlaim, look about you toward the east, and behold the joy that comes unto you from Êlôhîym.

37. Lo, your sons come, whom you sent away, they come gathered together from the east to the west by the word of the Qâdôsh, rejoicing in the glory of Êlôhîym.

Chapter 5

1. Put off, O Yarûshâlaim, the garment of mourning and affliction, and put on the comeliness of the glory that comes from Êlôhîym forever.

2. Cast about you a double garment of the righteousness which comes from Êlôhîym; and set a diadem on your head of the glory of Ôlâm Êl.

3. For Êlôhîym will show your brightness unto every country under shâmayim.

4. For your name shall be called of Êlôhîym forever: The peace of righteousness, and the glory of Êlôhîym's worship.

5. Arise, O Yarûshâlaim, and stand on high, and look about toward the east, and behold your children gathered from the west unto the east by the word of the Qâdôsh, rejoicing in the remembrance of Êlôhîym.

6. For they departed from you on foot, and were led away of their enemies: But Êlôhîym brings them unto you exalted with glory, as children of the kingdom.

7. For Êlôhîym has appointed that every high hill, and banks of long continuance, should be cast down, and valleys filled up, to make even the ground, that Yâshârêl may go safely in the glory of Êlôhîym,

8. Moreover even the woods and every sweet smelling tree shall overshadow Yâshârêl by the commandment of Êlôhîym.

9. For Êlôhîym shall lead Yâshârêl with joy in the light of his glory with the mercy and righteousness that comes from him.

Letter of Yirmeyâhû (Jeremiah) & The Traditional Bible Context

(Dabar Yahuah Scriptures Study Guide)

Introduction – Expanded Description

The **Letter of Yirmeyâhû (Jeremiah)** (sometimes called *Epistle of Yirmeyâhû (Jeremiah)*) is a short deuterocanonical/apocryphal book traditionally attributed to the prophet Yirmeyâhû (Jeremiah). It is presented as a letter sent by Yirmeyâhû (Jeremiah) to the exiled Yahûdîy community in Bâbel (Babylon), warning them **against idolatry**.

The letter emphasizes:

- The **futility of idol worship** – idols are powerless and cannot save or act.
- The **exclusive worship of Yahuah** – warning against assimilation to pagan practices.
- **Moral and spiritual exhortation** – urging the exiles to remain faithful despite foreign influence.

Where it fits in the Bible:

- Historically: Written during the Bâbel (Babylonian) exile (after 586 BCE), sent to the exiles in Bâbel (Babylon).
- Theologically: Complements Yirmeyâhû (Jeremiah) 10:1–16, which also denounces idolatry, and other prophetic calls to faithfulness during exile.
- Chronologically: Occurs after the destruction of Yarûshâlaim and the Temple, during the exile, addressing the spiritual challenges faced by the Yahûdîy community.

Key themes include:

1. Monotheism – Worship Yahuah alone; idols are powerless.

2. Faithfulness in exile – Maintain obedience despite foreign surroundings.

3. Divine judgment and justice – Idolatry leads to downfall, while Yahuah rewards faithfulness.

4. Moral clarity – Clear ethical guidance for living righteously in difficult circumstances.

Comparison Table: Letter of Yirmeyâhû (Jeremiah) & The traditional Bible

Letter of Yirmeyâhû (Jeremiah) Passage	Biblical Parallels	Theme / Connection
1:1–10 – Warning against making idols.	Jer 10:1–16; Ps 115:4–8	Idols are powerless; Yahuah is the only true Êlôhîym.
1:11–14 – Description of idols and their impotence.	Hab 2:18–19; Isa 44:9–20	Critique of idolatry; futility of worshiping created things.
1:15–20 – Call to exiles to remain faithful and not follow the customs of Bâbel (Babylon).	Ezek 20:30–32; Deut 6:5–9	Faithfulness amid exile; avoiding assimilation to pagan practices.
1:21–25 – Consequences for idol worship and rewards for faithfulness.	Jer 2:5–8; Deut 28:15–68	Obedience leads to blessing; idolatry leads to punishment.
1:26–28 – Encouragement to trust in Yahuah's power and justice.	Ps 146:3–10; Isa 45:5–7	Êlôhîym's sovereignty; do not fear powerless idols.

Summary of Key Parallels

1. Warning Against Idolatry – Directly parallels Yirmeyâhû (Jeremiah) 10:1–16; both emphasize that idols are man-made and powerless.

2. Exilic Context – Offers practical spiritual guidance for Yahûdîy living in Bâbel (Babylon), aligning with Yachezqêl's admonitions to remain faithful.

3. Moral Instruction – Reinforces the Deuteronomic principle of obedience and faithfulness leading to blessings, and disobedience leading to judgment.

4. Monotheism and Divine Justice – Affirms Yahuah's unique power, echoing Yashayâhû, Psalms, and other prophetic writings on Êlôhîym's sovereignty.

5. Ethical Guidance for the Diaspora – Encourages Yahûdîy to maintain spiritual integrity even when surrounded by pagan influences, a theme consistent in exilic prophetic literature.

Sêpher Yirmeyâhû (סֵפֶר יִרְמְיָהוּ) - Letter of Jeremiah

Chapter 1

1. A copy of an epistle, which Yirmeyâhû sent unto them which were to be led captives into Bâbel by the king of the Bâbel, to certify them, as it was commanded him of Êlôhîym.

2. Because of the sins which you have committed before Êlôhîym, you shall be led away captives into Bâbel by Nebûkkadnetstsar king of the Bâbel.

3. So when you are come unto Bâbel, you shall remain there many years, and for a long season, namely, seven generations: And after that I will bring you away peaceably from thence.

4. Now you shall see in Bâbel gods of silver, and of gold, and of wood, borne upon shoulders, which cause the nations to fear.

5. Beware therefore that you in no wise be like to strangers, neither you be and of them, when you see the multitude before them and behind them, worshipping them.

6. But you say n your hearts, O Yahuah, we must worship you.

7. For my angel is with you, and I myself caring for your souls.

8. As for their tongue, it is polished by the workman, and they themselves are gilded and laid over with silver; yet they are but false, and cannot speak.

9. And taking gold, as it were for a virgin that loves to go easy-going, they make crowns for the heads of their gods.

10. Sometimes also the Kôhên convey from their gods gold and silver, and bestow it upon themselves.

11. Yea, they will give thereof to the common harlots, and deck them as men with garments, being gods of silver, and gods of gold, and wood.

12. Yet these gods cannot save themselves from rust and moth, though they are covered with purple raiment.

13. They wipe their faces because of the dust of the temple, when there is much upon them.

14. And he that cannot put to death one that offends him holds a scepter, as though he were a judge of the country.

15. He has also in his right hand a dagger and an ax: But cannot deliver himself from war and thieves.

16. Whereby they are known not to be gods: Therefore do not fear them.

17. For like as a vessel that a man uses is nothing worth when it is broken; even so it is with their gods: When they are set up in the temple, their eyes are full of dust through the feet of them that come in.

18. And as the doors are made sure on every side upon him that offends the king, as being committed to suffer death: Even so the Kôhên make fast their temples with doors, with locks, and bars, lest their gods are spoiled with robbers.

19. They light them candles, yea, more than for themselves, whereof they cannot see one.

20. They are as one of the beams of the temple, yet they say their hearts are gnawed upon by things creeping out of the earth; and when they eat them and their clothes, they do not feel it.

21. Their faces are blacked through the smoke that comes out of the temple.

22. Upon their bodies and heads sit bats, swallows, and birds, and the cats also.

23. By this you may know that they are no gods: Therefore do not fear them.

24. Notwithstanding the gold that is about them to make them beautiful, except they wipe off the rust, they will not shine: For neither when they were molten did they feel it.

25. The things wherein there is no breath are bought for a most high price.

26. They are borne upon shoulders, having no feet whereby they declare unto men that they are nothing worth.

27. They also that serve them are ashamed: For if they fall to the ground at any time, they cannot rise up again of themselves: neither, if one set them upright, can they move of themselves: neither, if they are bowed down, can they make themselves straight: But they set gifts before them as unto dead men.

28. As for the things that are sacrificed unto them, their Kôhên sell and abuse; in like manner their women lay up part thereof in salt; but unto the poor and impotent they give nothing of it.

29. Menstruous women and women in childbed eat their sacrifices: By these things you may know that they are no gods: Do not fear them.

30. For how can they be called gods? Because women set meat before the gods of silver, gold, and wood.

31. And the Kôhên sit in their temples, having their clothes rent, and their heads and beards shaven, and nothing upon their heads.

32. They roar and cry before their gods, as men do at the feast when one is dead.

33. The Kôhên also take off their garments, and clothe their women and children.

34. Whether it is evil that one does unto them, or good, they are not able to recompense it: They can neither set up a king, nor put him down.

35. In like manner, they can neither give riches nor money: Though a man make a vow unto them, and does not keep it, they will not require it.

36. They can save no man from death, neither deliver the weak from the mighty.

37. They cannot restore a blind man to his sight, nor help any man in his distress.

38. They can show no mercy to the widow, nor do good to the fatherless.

39. Their gods of wood, and which are overlaid with gold and silver, are like the stones that are hewn out of the mountain: They that worship them shall be confounded.

40. How should a man then think and say that they are gods, when even the Kaśdîy themselves dishonor them?

41. Who if they shall see one dumb that cannot speak, they bring him, and entreat Baal that he may speak, as though he were able to understand.

42. Yet they cannot understand this themselves, and leave them: For they have no knowledge.

43. The women also with cords about them, sitting in the ways, burn bran for perfume:

But if any of them, drawn by some that passes by, lie with him, she reproaches her fellow, that she was not thought as worthy as herself, nor her cord broken.

44. Whatsoever is done among them is false: How may it then be thought or said that they are gods?

45. They are made of carpenters and goldsmiths: They can be nothing else than the workmen will have them to be.

46. And they themselves that made them can never continue long; how should then the things that are made of them be gods?

47. For they left lies and reproaches to them that come after.

48. For when there comes any war or plague upon them, the Kôhên consult with themselves, where they may be hidden with them.

49. How then cannot men perceive that they are no gods, which can neither save themselves from war, nor from plague?

50. For seeing they are but of wood, and overlaid with silver and gold, it shall be known hereafter that they are false:

51. And it shall manifestly appear to all nations and kings that they are no gods, but the works of men's hands, and that there is no work of Êlôhîym in them.

52. Who then may not know that they are no gods?

53. For neither can they set up a king in the land, nor give rain unto men.

54. Neither can they judge their own cause, nor redress a wrong, being unable: For they are as crows between shâmayim and earth.

55. Whereupon when fire falls upon the house of gods of wood, or laid over with gold or silver, their Kôhên will flee away, and escape; but they themselves shall be burned asunder like beams.

56. Moreover they cannot withstand any king or enemies: How can it then be thought or said that they be gods?

57. Neither are those gods of wood, and laid over with silver or gold, able to escape either from thieves or robbers.

58. Whose gold, and silver, and garments wherewith they are clothed, they that are strong take, and go away withal: Neither they are able to help themselves.

59. Therefore it is better to be a king that shows his power, or else a profitable vessel in a house, which the owner shall have use of, than such false gods; or to be a door in a house, to keep such things therein, than such false gods. Or a pillar of wood in a palace, than such false gods.

60. For sun, moon, and stars, being bright and sent to do their offices, are obedient.

61. In like manner the lightning when it breaks forth is easy to be seen; and after the same manner the wind blows in every country.

62. And when Êlôhîym commands the clouds to go over the whole world, they do as they are bidden.

63. And the fire sent from above to consume hills and woods does as it is commanded: But these are like unto them neither in show nor power.

64. Wherefore it is neither to be supposed nor said that they are gods, seeing, they are able neither to judge causes, nor to do good unto men.

65. Knowing therefore that they are no gods, do not fear them,

66. For they can neither curse nor bless kings:

67. Neither they can show signs in the shâmayim among the heathen, nor shine as the sun, nor give light as the moon.

68. The beasts are better than they: For they can get under a cover and help themselves.

69. It is then by no means manifest unto us that they are gods: Therefore do not fear them.

70. For as a scarecrow in a Garden of cucumbers keeps nothing: So are their gods of wood, and laid over with silver and gold.

71. And likewise their gods of wood, and laid over with silver and gold, are like to a white thorn in an orchard that every bird sits upon; as also to a dead body, that is cast into the dark.

72. And you shall know them to be no gods by the bright purple that rots upon them: And they themselves afterward shall be eaten, and shall be a reproach in the country.

73. Better therefore is the just man that has none idols: For he shall be far from reproach.

Book of Shôshannâh (Susanna) & The Traditional Bible Context

(Dabar Yahuah Scriptures Study Guide)

Introduction – Expanded Description

The **Book of Shôshannâh (Susanna)** is a short deuterocanonical/apocryphal work included as part of the Book of Dânîyêl in some traditions (Greek Septuagint). It narrates the story of **Shôshannâh (Susanna), a righteous woman falsely accused of adultery**, and how Êlôhîym delivers her through the wisdom of the young prophet Dânîyêl.

The book emphasizes:

- **Righteousness and integrity** – Shôshannâh (Susanna) remains faithful to Yahuah despite threats.
- **Divine justice** – Êlôhîym exposes the wicked and vindicates the innocent.
- **Wisdom and discernment** – Dânîyêl's discernment saves Shôshannâh (Susanna) and punishes the corrupt elders.
- **Faith under persecution** – Maintaining faith in Êlôhîym even in life-threatening trials.

Where it fits in the Bible:

- Historically: During the post-exilic period; likely set in **Bâbel (**Babylon) under Yahûdîy exile conditions.
- Theologically: Complements Dânîyêl's themes of faithfulness, divine justice, and Êlôhîym's protection of the righteous (Dânîyêl 1–6).
- Liturgically: Used in Yahûdîy and Messianic traditions as an example of righteousness, integrity, and Êlôhîym's intervention against corruption.

Key themes include:

1. Divine vindication – Êlôhîym protects the faithful and punishes the wicked.

2. Wisdom as a tool of justice – Dânîyêl acts as an instrument of Êlôhîym's judgment.

3. Faith and morality – Shôshannâh (Susanna)'s refusal to sin exemplifies moral courage.

4. Justice in society – Corruption is exposed, highlighting the need for righteous leadership.

Comparison Table: Book of Shôshannâh (Susanna) & The traditionala Bible

Shôshannâh (Susanna) Passage	Biblical Parallels	Theme / Connection
Shôshannâh (Susanna) 1–4 – The elders attempt to seduce Shôshannâh (Susanna); she refuses.	Gen 39:6–23 (**Yôsêph** and **Pôṭîyphar**'s wife); Prov 31:10–31	Faithfulness, integrity under temptation.
Shôshannâh (Susanna) 5–8 – False accusation by elders; Shôshannâh (Susanna) is sentenced to death.	Exod 23:1–8; Deut 19:15–21	False witnesses; importance of just testimony.
Shôshannâh (Susanna) 9–14 – Dânîyêl interrogates elders separately; exposes their lies.	Deut 17:6; Prov 18:17	Wisdom and discernment; Êlôhîym's justice revealed through human action.
Shôshannâh (Susanna) 15–16 – Shôshannâh (Susanna) is vindicated; elders are punished.	Ps 7:9–17; Jer 17:10	Divine justice; protection of the righteous.
Shôshannâh (Susanna) 17–20 – Conclusion praising Êlôhîym's wisdom and justice.	Dan 6:26; Ps 37:28	Praise for Êlôhîym's intervention; encouragement to remain faithful.

Summary of Key Parallels

1. Faithfulness Under Threat – Shôshannâh (Susanna) parallels **Yôsêph** (Gen 39) in resisting sexual temptation, showing unwavering integrity.

2. Divine Justice Through Wisdom – Dânîyêl functions like a divinely guided judge; the book emphasizes Êlôhîym's providence in protecting the innocent.

3. Condemnation of Corruption – The elders' downfall mirrors biblical warnings against false witnesses and unjust authorities (Deut 19:15–21).

4. Righteousness and Vindication – The story demonstrates that righteous living leads to protection and honor, consistent with Psalms and Proverbs.

5. Ethical Exemplars – Shôshannâh (Susanna)'s courage and Dânîyêl's discernment serve as moral examples for exilic communities and believers in challenging times.

Shôshannâh (שׁוֹשַׁנָּה) - Susanna

Chapter 1

1. There dwelt a man in Bâbel, called Yahôyâqîym:

2. And he took a woman, whose name was Shôshannâh, the daughter of Chilqîyâhû, a very fair woman, and one that feared Yahuah.

3. Her parents also were righteous, and taught their daughter according to the law of Môsheh.

4. Now Yahôyâqîym was a great rich man, and had a fair Garden joining unto his house: And to him resorted the Yahûdîy; because he was more honorable than all others.

5. The same year were appointed two of the ancients of the people to be judges, such as Yahuah spoke of, that wickedness came from Bâbel from ancient judges, who seemed to govern the people.

6. These kept much at Yahôyâqîym's house: And all that had any suits in law came unto them.

7. Now when the people departed away at noon, Shôshannâh went into her husband's Garden to walk.

8. And the two elders saw her going in every day, and walking; so that their lust was inflamed toward her.

9. And they perverted their own mind, and turned away their eyes, that they might not look unto shâmayim, nor remember just judgments.

10. And although they both were wounded with her love, yet did not dare to show one another his grief.

11. For they were ashamed to declare their lust, that they desired to have to do with her.

12. Yet they watched diligently from day today to see her.

13. And the one said to the other, let us now go home: For it is dinner time.

14. So when they were gone out, they parted the one from the other, and turning back again they came to the same place; and after that they had asked one another the cause, they acknowledged their lust: Then they appointed a time both together, when they might find her alone.

15. And it fell out, as they watched a fit time, she went in as before with two maids only, and she was desirous to wash herself in the Garden: For it was hot.

16. And there was no body there save the two elders that had hid themselves, and watched her.

17. Then she said to her maids, bring me oil and washing balls, and shut the Garden doors, that I may wash me.

18. And they did as she bade them, and shut the Garden doors, and went out themselves at privy doors to fetch the things that she had commanded them: But they did not see the elders, because they were hid.

19. Now when the maids were gone forth, the two elders rose up, and ran unto her, saying,

20. Behold, the Garden doors are shut, that no man can see us, and we are in love with you; therefore consent unto us, and lie with us.

21. If you will not, we will bear witness against you that a young man was with you: And therefore you did send away your maids from you.

22. Then Shôshannâh sighed, and said, I am straitened on every side: For if I do this thing, it is death unto me: And if I do not do it I cannot escape your hands.

23. It is better for me to fall into your hands, and not do it, than to sin in the sight of Yahuah.

24. With that Shôshannâh cried with a loud voice: And the two elders cried out against her.

25. Then ran the one, and opened the Garden door.

26. So when the servants of the house heard the cry in the Garden, they rushed in at the privy door, to see what was done unto her.

27. But when the elders had declared their matter, the servants were greatly ashamed: For there was never such a report made of Shôshannâh.

28. And it came to pass the next day, when the people were assembled to her husband Yahôyâqîym, the two elders came also full of mischievous imagination against Shôshannâh to put her to death;

29. And said before the people, send for Shôshannâh, the daughter of Chilqîyâhû, Yahôyâqîym's woman. And so they sent.

30. So she came with her father and mother, her children, and all her kindred.

31. Now Shôshannâh was a very delicate woman, and beautiful to behold.

32. And these wicked men commanded to uncover her face, (for she was covered) that they might be filled with her beauty.

33. Therefore her friends and all that saw her wept.

34. Then the two elders stood up in the midst of the people, and laid their hands upon her head.

35. And she weeping looked up toward shâmayim: For her heart trusted in Yahuah.

36. And the elders said, as we walked in the Garden alone, this woman came in with two maids, and shut the Garden doors, and sent the maids away.

37. Then a young man, who was hid there, came unto her, and lay with her.

38. Then we that stood in a corner of the Garden, seeing this wickedness, ran unto them.

39. And when we saw them together, the man we could not hold: For he was stronger than we, and opened the door, and leaped out.

40. But having taken this woman, we asked who the young man was, but she would not tell us: These things we do testify.

41. Then the assembly believed them as those that were the elders and judges of the people: So they condemned her to death.

42. Then Shôshannâh cried out with a loud voice, and said, O Êlôhîym Ôlâm Êl that knows the secrets, and knows all things before they are:

43. You know that they have borne false witness against me, and, behold, I must die; whereas I never did such things as these men have maliciously invented against me.

44. And Yahuah heard her voice.

45. Therefore when she was led to be put to death, Yahuah raised up the rûach qâdôsh of a young youth whose name was Dânîyêl:

46. Who cried with a loud voice, I am clear from the blood of this woman.

47. Then all the people turned them toward him, and said, what do these words mean that you have spoken?

48. So he standing in the midst of them said, are you such fools, you sons of Yâshârêl, that without examination or knowledge of the truth you have condemned a daughter of Yâshârêl?

49. Return again to the place of judgment: For they have borne false witness against her.

50. Wherefore all the people turned again in haste, and the elders said unto him, come, sit down among us, and show it us, seeing Êlôhîym has given you the honor of an elder.

51. Then Dânîyêl said unto them, put these two aside one far from another, and I will examine them.

52. So when they were put asunder one from another, he called one of them, and said unto him, O you that are waxen old in wickedness, now your sins which you have committed beforetime are come to light.

53. For you have pronounced false judgment and have condemned the innocent and have let the guilty go free; although Yahuah says, the innocent and righteous you shall not slay.

54. Now then, if you have seen her, tell me, under what tree you saw them companying together? Who answered, under a mastic tree.

55. And Dânîyêl said, very well; you have lied against your own head; for even now the angel of Êlôhîym has received the sentence of Êlôhîym to cut you in two.

56. So he put him aside, and commanded to bring the other, and said unto him, O you seed of Kenaan, and not of Yahûdâh, beauty has deceived you, and lust has perverted your heart.

57. Thus you have dealt with the daughters of Yâshârêl, and they for fear companied with you: But the daughter of Yahûdâh would not abide your wickedness.

58. Now therefore tell me, under what tree did you take them companying together? Who answered, under a holm tree.

59. Then Dânîyêl said unto him, well; you have also lied against your own head: For the angel of Êlôhîym waits with the sword to cut you in two, that he may destroy you.

60. With that all the assembly cried out with a loud voice, and praised Êlôhîym, who saves them that trust in him.

61. And they arose against the two elders, for Dânîyêl had convicted them of false witness by their own mouth:

62. And according to the law of Môsheh they did unto them in such sort as they maliciously intended to do to their neighbor: And they put them to death. Thus the innocent blood was saved the same day.

63. Therefore Chilqîyâhû and his woman praised Êlôhîym for their daughter Shôshannâh, with Yahôyâqîym her husband, and all the kindred, because there was no dishonesty found in her.

64. From that day forth was Dânîyêl had in great reputation in the sight of the people.

Prayer of Ăzaryâhû (Azariah) & The Traditional Bible Context

(Dabar Yahuah Scriptures Study Guide)

Introduction – Expanded Description

The **Prayer of Ăzaryâhû (Azariah)** is part of the deuterocanonical additions to the Book of Dânîyêl, often appearing in the Greek Septuagint between Dânîyêl 3:23 and 3:24. It is associated with the story of Shadrak, Mêyshak, **and** Ăbêd Negô **(**Chănanyâhû, Mîyshâêl, **and** Ăzaryâhû (Azariah)**)** in the fiery furnace.

The prayer emphasizes:

- **Confession and repentance** – Ăzaryâhû (Azariah) confesses the sins of Yasharel on behalf of the nation.
- **Faith and trust in Yahuah** – Despite the threat of death, the prayer expresses unwavering confidence in Êlôhîym's deliverance.
- **Divine mercy** – The prayer appeals to Êlôhîym's compassion and forgiveness.
- **Worship in adversity** – Ăzaryâhû (Azariah) praises Êlôhîym even while facing certain death.

Where it fits in the Bible:

- Historically: Set during the **Bâbel (**Babylonian) exile, when the Yahûdîy people faced persecution under Nebûkadnetstsar.
- Theologically: Fits within the **Book of Dânîyêl** narrative, showing personal and communal devotion to Êlôhîym amid trials.
- Liturgically: Provides a model of prayer, repentance, and praise for Yahû and Messianics, especially in contexts of suffering and persecution.

Key themes include:

1. Repentance for Yasharel – Ăzaryâhû (Azariah) intercedes for the sins of the nation, echoing the prophetic call to repentance.

2. Faith under persecution – The prayer highlights steadfastness in belief despite mortal danger.

3. Divine intervention – Prepares the reader for Êlôhîym's miraculous deliverance in the furnace (Dânîyêl 3:24–30).

4. Praise and worship – Even in adversity, Êlôhîym is glorified.

Comparison Table: Prayer of Ăzaryâhû (Azariah) & The Traditional Bible

Prayer of Ăzaryâhû (Azariah) Passage	Biblical Parallels	Theme / Connection
Ăzaryâhû (Azariah) 1–10 – Confession of sins by the people of Yasharel; appeals to Êlôhîym's mercy.	Dan 3:23; Dan 9:4–19; Lev 26:40–42	Confession and intercession; communal repentance.
Ăzaryâhû (Azariah) 11–20 – Praises Yahuah for His mercy, power, and faithfulness.	Ps 18:1–50; Ps 136:1–26	Worship and acknowledgment of Êlôhîym's sovereignty.
Ăzaryâhû (Azariah) 21–30 – Plea for deliverance from enemies; trust in Êlôhîym's protection.	Ps 46:1–11; Isa 43:2	Faith under threat; Êlôhîym as protector in adversity.
Ăzaryâhû (Azariah) 31–43 – Reaffirmation of Yasharel's special relationship with Êlôhîym and appeal for divine favor.	Exod 15:11; Deut 7:6–9	Covenant faithfulness; Êlôhîym's mercy on His people.

Summary of Key Parallels

1. Intercessory Prayer – Similar to Dânîyêl's own prayers (Dan 9) and national repentance found in Ezra and Nechemyâh.

2. Faith and Deliverance – Reinforces the story in Dânîyêl 3:24–30, showing Êlôhîym's miraculous protection of the faithful.

3. Praise Amid Persecution – Ăzaryâhû (Azariah)'s prayer parallels Psalms praising Êlôhîym during trials, emphasizing trust and worship under pressure.

4. National Repentance – Reflects prophetic calls in Yirmeyâhû, Yechezqêl, and Leviticus for Yasharel to confess and return to Yahuah.

5. Liturgical Use – Provides a model for prayer, confession, and praise that is often incorporated in Yahûdîy and Messianic liturgies.

Tephillâh (תְּפִלָּה) Ăzaryâhû (עֲזַרְיָהוּ) - Prayer of Azariah

Chapter 1

1. And they walked in the midst of the fire, praising Êlôhîym, and blessing Yahuah.

2. Then Ăzaryâhû stood up, and prayed on this manner; and opening his mouth in the midst of the fire said,

3. Blessed are you, O Yahuah Êlôhîym of our fathers: Your name is worthy to be praised and glorified forevermore:

4. For you are righteous in all the things that you have done to us: Yea, true are all your works, your ways are right, and all your judgments truth.

5. In all the things that you have brought upon us, and upon the qâdôsh city of our fathers, even Yarûshâlaim, You have executed true judgment: For according to truth and judgment you did bring all these things upon us because of our sins.

6. For we have sinned and committed iniquity, departing from you.

7. In all things we have trespassed, and not obeyed your commandments, nor kept them, neither done as you have commanded us that it might go well with us.

8. Wherefore all that you have brought upon us, and everything that you have done to us, you have done in true judgment.

9. And you did deliver us into the hands of lawless enemies, most hateful forsakers of Êlôhîym, and to an unjust king, and the wickedest in all the world.

10. And now we cannot open our mouths, we are become a shame and reproach to your servants; and to them that worship you.

11. Yet do not deliver us up wholly, for your name's sake, neither disannul you your covenant:

12. And do not cause your mercy to depart from us, for your beloved Abrâhâm's sake, for your servant Yitschâq's sake, and for your qâdôsh Yâshârêl's sake;

13. To whom you have spoken and promised, that you would multiply their seed as the stars of shâmayim, and as the sand that lies upon the seashore.

14. For we, O Yahuah, are become less than any nation, and be kept under this day in all the world because of our sins.

15. Neither there is at this time prince, or Nâbîy, or leader, or burnt offering, or sacrifice, or offering, or incense, or place to sacrifice before you, and to find mercy.

16. Nevertheless in a contrite heart and a humble spirit let us be accepted.

17. Like as in the burnt offerings of rams and bullocks, and like as in ten thousands of fat lambs: So let our sacrifice be in your sight this day, and grant that we may wholly go after you: For they shall not be confounded that put their trust in you.

18. And now we follow you with all our heart, we fear you, and seek your face.

19. Do not put us to shame: But deal with us after your loving kindness, and according to the multitude of your mercies.

20. Deliver us also according to your marvelous works, and give glory to your name, O Yahuah: And let all them that do your servants hurt be ashamed;

21. And let them be confounded in all their power and might, and let their strength be broken;

22. And let them know that you are Êlôhîym, the only Êlôhîym, and glorious over the whole world.

23. And the king's servants, that put them in, did not cease to make the oven hot with rosin, pitch, tow, and small wood;

24. So that the flame streamed forth above the furnace forty and nine cubits.

25. And it passed through, and burned those Kaśdîy it found about the furnace.

26. But the angel of Yahuah came down into the oven together with Ăzaryâhû and his fellows, and smote the flame of the fire out of the oven;

27. And made the midst of the furnace as it had been a moist whistling wind, so that the fire did not touch them at all, neither hurt nor troubled them.

28. Then the three, as out of one mouth, praised, glorified, and blessed, Êlôhîym in the furnace, saying,

29. Blessed are you, O Yahuah Êlôhîym of our fathers: And to be praised and exalted above all forever.

30. And blessed is your glorious and qâdôsh name: And to be praised and exalted above all forever.

31. Blessed are you in the temple of your qâdôsh glory: And to be praised and glorified above all forever.

32. Blessed are you that behold the depths, and sit upon the Kerûb: And to be praised and exalted above all forever.

33. Blessed are you on the glorious throne of your kingdom: And to be praised and glorified above all forever.

34. Blessed are you in the firmament of shâmayim: And above all to be praised and glorified forever.

35. O all your works of Yahuah, Bârak Yahuah: Praise and exalt him above all forever,

36. O you shâmayim, Bârak Yahuah: Praise and exalt him above all forever.

37. O you angels of Yahuah, Bârak Yahuah: Praise and exalt him above all forever.

38. O all you waters that be above the shâmayim, Bârak Yahuah: Praise and exalt him above all forever.

39. O all you powers of Yahuah, Bârak Yahuah: Praise and exalt him above all forever.

40. O you sun and moon, Bârak Yahuah: Praise and exalt him above all forever.

41. O you stars of shâmayim, Bârak Yahuah: Praise and exalt him above all forever.

42. O every shower and dew, Bârak Yahuah: Praise and exalt him above all forever.

43. O all you winds, Bârak Yahuah: Praise and exalt him above all forever,

44. O you fire and heat, Bârak Yahuah: Praise and exalt him above all forever.

45. O you winter and summer, Bârak Yahuah: Praise and exalt him above all forever.

46. O you dews and storms of snow, Bârak Yahuah: Praise and exalt him above all forever.

47. O you nights and days, Bârak Yahuah: Bless and exalt him above all forever.

48. O you light and darkness, Bârak Yahuah: Praise and exalt him above all forever.

49. O you ice and cold, Bârak Yahuah: Praise and exalt him above all forever.

50. O you frost and snow, Bârak Yahuah: Praise and exalt him above all forever.

51. O you lightning and clouds, Bârak Yahuah: Praise and exalt him above all forever.

52. O let the earth bless Yahuah: Praise and exalt him above all forever.

53. O you mountains and little hills, Bârak Yahuah: Praise and exalt him above all forever.

54. O all you things that grow in the earth, Bârak Yahuah: Praise and exalt him above all forever.

55. O you mountains, Bârak Yahuah: Praise and exalt him above all forever.

56. O you seas and rivers, Bârak Yahuah: Praise and exalt him above all forever.

57. O you whales, and all that move in the waters, Bârak Yahuah: Praise and exalt him above all forever.

58. O all you fowls of the air, Bârak Yahuah: Praise and exalt him above all forever.

59. O all you beasts and cattle, Bârak Yahuah: Praise and exalt him above all forever.

60. O you children of men, Bârak Yahuah: Praise and exalt him above all forever.

61. O Yâshârêl, Bârak Yahuah: Praise and exalt him above all forever.

62. O you Kôhên of Yahuah, Bârak Yahuah: Praise and exalt him above all forever.

63. O you servants of Yahuah, Bârak Yahuah: Praise and exalt him above all forever.

64. O you spirits and souls of the righteous, Bârak Yahuah: Praise and exalt him above all forever.

65. O you qâdôsh and humble men of heart, Bârak Yahuah: Praise and exalt him above all forever.

66. O Chănanyâhû, Ăzaryâhû, and Mîyshâêl, Bârak Yahuah: Praise and exalt him above all forever: For he has delivered us from sheôl, and saved us from the hand of death, and delivered us out of the midst of the furnace and burning flame: Even out of the midst of the fire he has delivered us.

67. O give thanks unto Yahuah, because he is gracious: For his mercy endures forever.

68. O all you that worship Yahuah, bless the Êlôhîym of Êlôhîym, praise him, and give him thanks: For his mercy endures forever.

Bel and the Dragon & The Traditional Bible Context

(Dabar Yahuah Scriptures Study Guide)

Introduction – Expanded Description

Bel (Baal) and the Dragon (marine or land *monster*) is a deuterocanonical addition to the Book of Dânîyêl found in the Greek Septuagint. It contains two stories highlighting **Dânîyêl's faith and Êlôhîym's judgment over idolatry.**

The book emphasizes:

- **Êlôhîym's supremacy over idols** – The futility of worshiping man-made gods is exposed.
- **Divine justice** – The punishment of the idolaters demonstrates Êlôhîym's protection of His servants.
- **Faith and courage** – Dânîyêl remains courageous, standing firm in his faith despite threats from powerful rulers.
- **Wisdom and discernment** – Dânîyêl's clever actions reveal Êlôhîym's truth.

Where it fits in the Bible:

- Historically: Set during the **Bâbel (**Babylonian**)** exile, after the main events of the canonical Dânîyêl.
- Theologically: Complements Dânîyêl's narrative by showing Êlôhîym's ongoing deliverance of His faithful servants.
- Liturgically: Encourages believers to remain faithful to Yahuah even when surrounded by idolatry and corruption.

Key themes include:

1. Judgment against false gods – Demonstrates that human-made idols have no power.

2. Faith under threat – Dânîyêl's courage inspires trust in Êlôhîym's protection.

3. Wisdom and ingenuity – Êlôhîym uses Dânîyêl's cleverness to reveal truth and punish wrongdoing.

4. Divine deliverance – Êlôhîym actively saves His faithful servants and punishes the wicked.

Comparison Table: Bel and the Dragon & The Traditional Bible

Bel and the Dragon Passage	Biblical Parallels	Theme / Connection
Bel 1–14 – Dânîyêl exposes the idol Bel (Baal); reveals that it consumes nothing, idolators are deceived.	Isa 44:9–20; Jer 10:3–5; 1 Cor 8:4–6	Idolatry condemned; Êlôhîym's supremacy; idols are powerless.
Dragon 1–12 – Dânîyêl kills the dragon worshiped by **Bâbel (**Babylonians) using a clever trick.	Ps 73:18–20; Isa 27:1; Rev 12:9	Êlôhîym defeats false gods; divine power triumphs over pagan worship.
Dragon 13–24 – Dânîyêl vindicates Êlôhîym's honor; punishes those who followed idolatry.	Deut 13:12–18; Ps 7:9	Divine justice; Êlôhîym protects His faithful; punishment of idolaters.
Conclusion – Praise to Êlôhîym for delivering Dânîyêl; idol worship shown futile.	Dan 6:26–27; Ps 33:8–9	Praise and acknowledgment of Êlôhîym's power and justice.

Summary of Key Parallels

1. Êlôhîym's Supremacy Over Idols – The story parallels Yashayâhû and Yirmeyâhû's warnings against idol worship and extends the theme in Dânîyêl.

2. Faith and Courage – Dânîyêl's bravery mirrors the steadfastness shown in Dânîyêl 3 and 6, reinforcing trust in Êlôhîym during persecution.

3. Divine Justice and Vindication – Êlôhîym's judgment on idolaters aligns with Deuteronomy's laws against false gods and mirrors the divine justice theme found throughout Psalms.

4. Wisdom as a Tool of Deliverance – Dânîyêl's clever tactics reflect Êlôhîym-given wisdom to protect the faithful and reveal the truth.

5. Liturgical and Moral Lessons – Encourages readers to trust Êlôhîym and reject idolatry, showing Êlôhîym's active protection of the righteous.

Bêl (בֵּל) Tannîyn (תַּנִּין) - Bel and the Dragon

Chapter 1

1. And king Astyages was gathered to his fathers, and Kôresh of Pâras received his kingdom.

2. And Dânîyêl conversed with the king, and was honored above all his friends.

3. Now the Bâbel had an idol, called Baal, and there were spent upon him every day twelve great measures of fine flour, and forty sheep, and six vessels of wine.

4. And the king worshipped it and went daily to adore it: But Dânîyêl worshipped his own Êlôhîym. And the king said unto him, why do you not worship Baal?

5. Who answered and said, because I may not worship idols made with hands, but the living Êlôhîym, who has created the shâmayim and the earth, and has sovereignty over all flesh.

6. Then the king said unto him, do you not think that Bêl is a living god? Do you not see how much he eats and drinks every day?

7. Then Dânîyêl smiled, and said, O king, do not be deceived: For this is but clay within, and brass without, and did never eat or drink anything.

8. So the king was angry, and called for his Kôhên, and said unto them, if you tell me not who this is that devours these expenses, you shall die.

9. But if you can certify me that Baal devours them, then Dânîyêl shall die: For he has spoken blasphemy against Baal. And Dânîyêl said unto the king, let it be according to your word.

10. Now the Kôhên of Baal were threescore and ten, beside their women and children. And the king went with Dânîyêl into the temple of Baal.

11. So Baal's Kôhên said, lo, we go out: But you, O king, set on the meat, and make ready the wine, and shut the door fast and seal it with your own signet;

12. And tomorrow when you come in, if you do not find that Baal has eaten up all, we will suffer death: Or else Dânîyêl, that speaks falsely against us.

13. And they little regarded it: For under the table they had made a privy entrance, whereby they entered in continually, and consumed those things.

14. So when they were gone forth, the king set meats before Baal. Now Dânîyêl had commanded his servants to bring ashes, and those they strewed throughout all the temple in the presence of the king alone: Then they went out, and shut the door, and sealed it with the king's signet, and so departed.

15. Now in the night the Kôhên came with their women and children, as they were wanting to do, and did eat and drink up all.

16. In the morning in good time the king arose, and Dânîyêl with him.

17. And the king said, Dânîyêl, are the seals whole? And he said, yea, O king, they are whole.

18. And as soon as he had opened the door, the king looked upon the table, and cried with a loud voice, great are you, O Baal, and with you is no deceit at all.

19. Then laughed Dânîyêl, and held the king that he should not go in, and said, behold now the pavement, and mark well whose footsteps are these.

20. And the king said, I see the footsteps of men, women, and children. And then the king was angry,

21. And took the Kôhên with their women and children, who showed him the privy doors, where they came in, and consumed such things as were upon the table.

22. Therefore the king slew them, and delivered Baal into Dânîyêl's power, who destroyed him and his temple.

23. And in that same place there was a great dragon, which they of Bâbel worshipped.

24. And the king said unto Dânîyêl, you will also say that this is of brass? Lo, he lives, he eats and drinks; you cannot say that he is no living god: Therefore worship him.

25. Then Dânîyêl said unto the king, I will worship Yahuah my Êlôhîym: For he is the living Êlôhîym.

26. But give me leave, O king, and I shall slay this dragon without sword or staff. The king said, I give you leave.

27. Then Dânîyêl took pitch, and fat, and hair, and did simmered them together, and made lumps thereof: This he put in the dragon's mouth, and so the dragon burst in sunder: And Dânîyêl said, lo, these are the gods you worship.

28. When they of Bâbel heard that, they took great indignation, and conspired against the king, saying, the king has become a Yahûdîy, and he has destroyed Baal, he has slain the dragon, and put the Kôhên to death.

29. So they came to the king, and said, deliver us Dânîyêl, or else we will destroy you and your house.

30. Now when the king saw that they pressed him sore, being constrained, he delivered Dânîyêl unto them:

31. Who cast him into the lions' den: Where he was six days.

32. And in the den there were seven lions, and they had given them every day two carcasses, and two sheep: Which then were not given to them, to the intent they might devour Dânîyêl.

33. Now there was in Yahûdâh a Nâbîy, called Chăbaqqûq, who had made pottage, and had broken bread in a bowl, and was going into the field, for to bring it to the reapers.

34. But the angel of Yahuah said unto Chăbaqqûq, go, carry the dinner that you have into Bâbel unto Dânîyêl, who is in the lions' den.

35. And Chăbaqqûq said, Yahuah, I never saw Bâbel; neither do I know where the den is.

36. Then the angel of Yahuah took him by the crown, and bare him by the hair of his head, and through the vehemence of his spirit set him in Bâbel over the den.

37. And Chăbaqqûq cried, saying, O Dânîyêl, Dânîyêl, take the dinner which Êlôhîym has sent you.

38. And Dânîyêl said, you have remembered me, O Êlôhîym: Neither you have forsaken them that seek you and love you.

39. So Dânîyêl arose, and did eat: And the angel of Yahuah set Chăbaqqûq in his own place again immediately.

40. Upon the seventh day the king went to bewail Dânîyêl: And when he came to the den, he looked in, and behold, Dânîyêl was sitting.

41. Then cried the king with a loud voice, saying, great are you, Yahuah Êlôhîym of Dânîyêl, and there is none other beside you.

42. And he drew him out, and cast those that were the cause of his destruction into the den: And they were devoured in a moment before his face.

Glossary

Previous Names	Original Restored Names	Strong Hebrew Reference
Abel	Hebel (הֶבֶל)	H1893
Achitob	Ăchîyṭûb (אֲחִיטוּב)	H285
Adath	Hădad (הֲדַד)	H1908
Aduram	Hădôrâm (הֲדוֹרָם)	H1913
Agarenes	Hagrîy (הַגְרִי)	H1905
Akrabbim	Aqrâb (עַקְרָב)	H6137
Alleluiah	Hâlal (הָלַל) YÂH (יָה)	H1984+H3068
Almighty	SHADDAY (שַׁדַּי) EL (אֵל)	H7706+H410
Amaseqa	Maśrêqâh (מַשְׂרֵקָה)	H4957
Amorites	Ĕmôrîy (אֱמֹרִי)	H567
Ananias	Chănanyâhû (חֲנַנְיָהוּ)	H2608
Anointed	Mâshîyach (מָשִׁיחַ)	H4899
Aramaean	Ărammîy (אֲרַמִּי)	H761
Ares	Ârach (אָרַח)	H733
Artexerxes	Artachshashtâ (אַרְתַּחְשַׁשְׁתָּא)	H783
Asam	Chûshâm (חוּשָׁם)	H2367
Ashur	Âshêr (אָשֵׁר)	H836
Assabias	Chăshabyâhû (חֲשַׁבְיָהוּ)	H2811
Assalimoth	Shelômîyth (שְׁלֹמִית)	H8019
Asshur	Ashshûr (אַשּׁוּר)	H804
Assyria	Ashshûr (אַשּׁוּר)	H804
Attharates	Tirshâthâ (תִּרְשָׁתָא)	H8660
Azariah	Ăzaryâhû (עֲזַרְיָהוּ)	H5838
Azbazareth	Êsar-chaddôn (אֵסַר־חַדּוֹן)	H634
Azrial	Azrîyêl (עַזְרִיאֵל)	H5837
Babylon	Bâbel (בָּבֶל)	H894
Baelunan	Baal Chânân (בַּעַל חָנָן)	H1177
Balaq	Bela (בֶּלַע)	H1106
Barad	Bedad (בְּדַד)	H911
Beliar	Belîyaal (בְּלִיַּעַל)	H1100
Benjamin	Binyâmîyn (בִּנְיָמִין)	H1144

Previous Names	Original Restored Names	Strong Hebrew Reference
Bethoron	Bêyth Chôrôn (בֵּית חוֹרוֹן)	H1032
Bethsamos	Bêyth Azmâweth (בֵּית עַזְמָוֶת)	H1041
Bilemus	Bishlâm (בִּשְׁלָם)	H1312
Boser	Botsrâh (בָּצְרָה)	H1224
Cadmiel	Qadmîy'l (קַדְמִיאֵל)	H6934
Cain	Qayin (קַיִן)	H7014
Calamolalus	Lôd (לֹד) Châdîyd (חָדִיד)	H3850+H2307
Cannan	Kenaan (כְּנַעַן)	H3667
Carchamis	Karkemîysh (כַּרְכְּמִישׁ)	H3751
Chaldees	Kaśdîy (כַּשְׂדִּי)	H3778
Cherubim	Kerûb (כְּרוּב)	H3742
Core	Qôrach (קֹרַח)	H7141
Creator	Bârâ (בָּרָא)	H1254
Creator	Bârâ (בָּרָא)	H1254
Cush	Kûsh (כּוּשׁ)	H3568
Cyrus	Kôresh (כּוֹרֶשׁ)	H3566
Danaba	Dinhâbâh (דִּנְהָבָה)	H1838
Darius	Dâreyâwêsh (דָּרְיָוֶשׁ)	H1868
Dinah	Dîynâh (דִּינָה)	H1783
Dragon	Tannîyn (תַּנִּין)	H8577
Ecbatane	Achmethâ (אַחְמְתָא)	H307
Egypt	Mitsrayim (מִצְרַיִם)	H4714
Egyptians	Mitsrîy (מִצְרִי)	H4713
Elam	Êylâm (עֵילָם)	H5867
Eliaonias	Elyehôêynay (אֶלְיְהוֹעֵינַי)	H454
Emnity	Śiṭnâh (שִׂטְנָה)	H7856
Enoch	Chănôk (חֲנוֹךְ)	H2585
Enos	Ĕnôsh (אֱנוֹשׁ)	H583
Enos	Ĕnôsh (אֱנוֹשׁ)	H583
Esdras	Ezrâ (עֶזְרָא)	H5830
Eternal	Ôlâm (עוֹלָם)	H5769
Ethiopia	Kûsh (כּוּשׁ).	H3568
Euphrates	Perâth (פְּרָת)	H6578
Euphrates	Perâth (פְּרָת)	H6576
Eve	Chawwâh (חַוָּה);	H2332

Previous Names	Original Restored Names	Strong Hebrew Reference
Eve	Chawwâh (חַוָּה)	H2332
Ezerias	Ăzaryâhû (עֲזַרְיָהוּ)	H5838
Ezias	Ăzaryâhû (עֲזַרְיָהוּ)	H5838
Father	Âb (אָב)	H1
Frankincense	lebônâh (לְבוֹנָה)	H3828
Gabriel	Gabrîyêl (גַּבְרִיאֵל)	H1403
Gamael	Dânîyêl (דָּנִיֵּאל)	H1840
Geon	Gîychôn (גִּיחוֹן)	H1521
Giants	Nephîyl (נְפִיל)	H5303
Gihon	Gîychôn (גִּיחוֹן)	H1521
Girgashites	Girgâshîy (גִּרְגָּשִׁי)	H1622
God	ĔLÔHÎYM (אֱלֹהִים)	H430
God of truth	Êl Ĕmûnâh (אֱמוּנָה)	H410+H530
Gomorrah	Ămôrâh (עֲמֹרָה)	H6017
Gomorrha	Ămôrâh (עֲמֹרָה)	H6017
Great One	Gibbôr (גִּבּוֹר) ÊL (אֵל)	H1368+H410
Groves	ăshêrâh (אֲשֵׁרָה)	H842
Ham	Châm (חָם)	H2526
Hamath	Chămâth (חֲמָת)	H2574
Head of Days	Attîyq (עַתִּיק) Yôm (יוֹם)	H6268+H3118
Head of Days	Attîyq (עַתִּיק) Yôm (יוֹם)	H6268+H3118
Heaven	Shâmayim (שָׁמַיִם)	H8064
Hebrew	Êber (עֵבֶר)	H5677
Helchiah	Chilqîyâhû (חִלְקִיָּהוּ)	H2518
Heliopolis	Ôn (אוֹן)	H204
Helkias	Chilqîyâhû (חִלְקִיָּהוּ)	H2518
Hermon	Chermôn (חֶרְמוֹן)	H2768
Heth	Chêth (חֵת)	H2845
Hivites	Chivvîy (חִוִּי)	H2340
Holy One	QÂDÔSH (קָדוֹשׁ)	H6918
Honoured	Hădar (הֲדַר)	H1922
Horites	Chôrîy (חֹרִי)	H2572
Hosts	Tsâbâ (צְבָא)	H6635
Iri	Ûrîyâhû (אוּרִיָּהוּ)	H223
Isaac	Yitschâq (יִצְחָק)	H3327

Previous Names	Original Restored Names	Strong Hebrew Reference
Ismael	Yishmâêl (יִשְׁמָעֵאל)	H3458
Israel	Yâshârêl (יִשְׂרָאֵל)	H3478
Issachar	Yiśśâśkâr (יִשָּׂשכָר)	H3485
Istalcurus	Zabbûd (זַבּוּד)	H2072
Jacob	Yaăqôb (יַעֲקֹב)	H3290
Japheth	Yapheth (יֶפֶת)	H3315
Jared	Yârad (יָרַד)	H3381
Jasub	Yôb (יוֹב)	H3102
Javan	Yâwân (יָוָן)	H3120
Jebusites	Yebûsîy (יְבוּסִי)	H2983
Jeconias	Yakonyâhû (יְכָנְיָהוּ)	H3204
Jeddu	Yadayâh (יְדַעְיָה)	H3048
Jeduthun	Yadûthûn (יְדוּתוּן)	H3038
Jerechus	Yarîychô (יְרִיחוֹ)	H3405
Jeremy	Yirmeyâhû (יִרְמְיָהוּ)	H3414
Jerusalem	Yarûshâlaim (יְרוּשָׁלַם)	H3389
Jesse	Yishay (יִשַׁי)	H3446
Jesu	Yashûa (יֵשׁוּעַ)	H3442
Jewel	Yaîyêl (יְעִיאֵל)	H3273
Jews	Yahûdîy (יְהוּדִי)	H3064
Jezelus	Yachăzîyêl (יַחֲזִיאֵל)	H3166
Joacim	Yahôyâqîym (יְהוֹיָקִים)	H3079
Joadanus	Gedalyâhû (גְּדַלְיָהוּ)	H1436
Joanan	Yahôchânân (יְהוֹחָנָן)	H3076
Johannes	Yôchânân (יוֹחָנָן)	H3110
Jonathan	Yahônâthân (יְהוֹנָתָן)	H3083
Joppa	Yâphô (יָפוֹ)	H3305
Jordan	Yardên (יַרְדֵּן)	H3383
Jordan	Yardên (יַרְדֵּן)	H3383
Josedec	Yahôtsâdâq (יְהוֹצָדָק)	H3087
Joseph	Yôsêph (יוֹסֵף)	H3130
Juda	Yahûdâh (יהודה)	H3063
Judah	Yahûdâh (יְהוּדָה)	H3063
Judea	Yahûdâh (יְהוּדָה)	H3063
Kabratan	Kibrâh (כִּבְרָה)	H3530

Previous Names	Original Restored Names	Strong Hebrew Reference
Kadmonites	Qadmônîy (קַדְמֹנִי)	H6935
Kainam	Qêynân (קֵינָן)	H7018
Kenan	Qêynân (קֵינָן)	H7018
Kenites	Qêynîy (קֵינִי)	H7017
Kenizzites	Qenizzîy (קְנִזִּי)	H7074
Kiriathiarius	Qiryath Yeârîym (קִרְיַת יְעָרִים)	H7157
Lamech	Lemek (לֶמֶךְ)	H3929
Letter	Sêpher (סֵפֶר)	H5612
Lettus	Chaṭṭûsh (חַטּוּשׁ)	H2407
Levi	Lêwîy (לֵוִי)	H3878
Leviathan	Liwyâthân (לִוְיָתָן)	H3882
Lord	Âdônây (אֲדֹנָי)	H136
Lord	Yahuah (יְהוָֹה)	H3068
Lord of righteousness	Yahuah Tsedâqâh (צְדָקָה)	H3068+H6666
Lord of Spirits	Yahuah rûach (רוּחַ)	H3068+H7307
Maitabith	Mehêyṭabêl (מְהֵיטַבְאֵל)	H4105
Maker	Âśâh (עָשָׂה)	H6213
Mamaias	Shemayâhû (שְׁמַעְיָהוּ)	H8098
Manna	mân (מָן)	H4478
Matarat	Maṭrêd (מַטְרֵד)	H4308
Medes	Mâday (מָדַי)	H4074
Media	Mâday (מָדַי)	H4074
Melca	Milkâh (מִלְכָּה)	H4435
Meremoth	Merâyôth (מְרָיוֹת)	H4812
Mesopotamia	Ărăm Năhărayim (אֲרַם נַהֲרַיִם)	H763
Metabedzaab	Mêy zâhâb (מֵי זָהָב)	H4314
Methuselah	Methûshelach (מְתוּשֶׁלַח)	H4968
Michael	Mîykâêl (מִיכָאֵל)	H4317
Might One	Gibbôr ÊL (אֵל גִּבּוֹר)	H1368+H410
Mighty One	Gâbar (גָּבַר)	H1396
Mithridates	Mithredâth (מִתְרְדָת)	H4990
Moses	Môsheh (מֹשֶׁה)	H4872
Mosollamon	Meshûllâm (מְשֻׁלָּם)	H4918
Nabuchodonosor	Nebûkkadnetstsar (נְבוּכַדְנֶצַּר)	H5020
Nahor	Nâchôr (נָחוֹר)	H5152

Previous Names	Original Restored Names	Strong Hebrew Reference
Nathanael	Nethanêl (נְתַנְאֵל)	H5417
Nineveh	Nîyneweh (נִינְוֵה)	H5210
Noah	Nôach (נֹחַ)	H5146
Ophannin	Ôphân (אוֹפָן)	H212
Osaias	Yashayâhû (יְשַׁעְיָהוּ)	H3470
Parthians	Parthos (Πάρθος)	G3934
Passover	Pesach (פֶּסַח)	H4653
Pentecost	Shâbûa (שָׁבוּעַ)	H7620
Perizzites	Perizzîy (פְּרִזִּי)	H6522
Persians	Pâras (פָּרַס)	H6539
Perversity	Êśeq (עֵשֶׂק)	H6230
Pharaoh	Parôh (פַּרְעֹה)	H6547
Phassaron	Pashchûr (פַּשְׁחוּר)	H6583
Pheresites	Perizzîy (פְּרִזִּי)	H6522
Philistia	Pelesheth (פְּלֶשֶׁת)	H6429
Philistines	Pelishtîy (פְּלִשְׁתִּי)	H6430
Philistines	Pelishtîy (פְּלִשְׁתִּי)	H6430
Phinees	Pîynechâs (פִּינְחָס)	H6372
Phinees	Pîynechâs (פִּינְחָס)	H6372
Phison	Pîyshôn (פִּישׁוֹן)	H6376
Phoros	Parôsh (פַּרְעֹשׁ)	H6551
Prayer	Pâlal (פָּלַל)	H6419
Priest (s)	Kôhên (כֹּהֵן)	H3548
Priesthood	Kehûnnâh (כְּהֻנָּה)	H3550
Prophets	Nâbîy (נָבִיא)	H5030
Qayinan	Qêynân (קֵינָן)	H7018
Raaboth	Rechôbôth (רְחֹבוֹת)	H7344
Rafa	Râphâ (רָפָא)	H7497
Raguel	Reûêl (רְעוּאֵל)	H7467
Rathumus	Rechûm (רְחוּם)	H7348
Rebecca	Ribqâh (רִבְקָה)	H7259
Rephaim	Râphâ (רָפָא)	H7497
Rich	kâbêd (כָּבֵד)	H3515
Righteous	Tsaddîyq (צַדִּיק)	H6662
Room	Rechôbôth (רְחֹבוֹת)	H7344

Previous Names	Original Restored Names	Strong Hebrew Reference
Sabbath	Shabbâth (שַׁבָּת)	H7676
Sadduc	Tsâdôq (צָדוֹק)	H6659
Salathiel	Shealtîyêl (שְׁאַלְתִּיאֵל)	H7597
Salem	Shâlêm (שָׁלֵם)	H8004
Salman	Śamlâh (שַׂמְלָה)	H8072
Salom	Shâlôm (שָׁלוֹם)	H3073
Samaias	Shemayâhû (שְׁמַעְיָהוּ)	H8098
Samaria	Shômerôn (שֹׁמְרוֹן)	H8111
Sanabassar	Shêshbatstsar (שֵׁשְׁבַּצַּר)	H8339
Saphat	Shephaṭyâhû (שְׁפַטְיָהוּ)	H8203
Satan	Adversary	H7854
Sathrabuzanes	Shethar bôzenay (שְׁתַר בּוֹזְנַי)	H8370
Saul	Shâûl (שָׁאוּל)	H4957
Saviour	Yâsha (יָשַׁע)	H3467
Sechenias	Shekanyâhû (שְׁכַנְיָהוּ)	H7935
Selo	Shîylôh (שִׁילֹה)	H7886
Semellius	Shimsay (שִׁמְשַׁי)	H8124
Sephantiphans	Tsâphnath Panêach (צָפְנַת פַּעְנֵחַ)	H6847
Seraiah	Śerâyâhû (שְׂרָיָהוּ)	H8304
Seraphin	Śârâph (שָׂרָף)	H8314
Serpent	Nâchâsh (נָחָשׁ)	H5175
Seth	Shêth (שֵׁת)	H8352
Shepherd	Rââh (רָעָה)	H7462
Simeon	Shimôn (בִּלְהָה)	H1090
Sinai	Sîynay (סִינַי)	H5514
Sisinnes	Tattenay (תַּתְּנַי)	H8674
Sodom	Sedôm (סְדֹם)	H5467
Son	Bên (בֵּן)	H1121
Son of my sorrow	Benônîy (בֶּן־אוֹנִי)	H1126
Susan	Shûshan (שׁוּשַׁן)	H7799
Susanna	Shôshannâh (שׁוֹשַׁנָּה)	H7799
Syelus	Yachîyêl (יְחִיאֵל)	H3171
Syria (Celosyria)	Ărâm (אֲרָם)	H758
Syrian	Ărâm (אֲרָם)	H758
Tabernacles	Sûkkâh (סֻכָּה)	H5521

Previous Names	Original Restored Names	Strong Hebrew Reference
Tamnatares	Timnath cheres (תִּמְנַת חֶרֶס)	H8556
Taphu	Tappûach (תַּפּוּחַ)	H8598
Tartarus	Tartaróo (ταρταρόω)	G5020
Teman	Têymân (תֵּימָן)	H8487
Tergal	Tidâl (תִּדְעָל)	H8413
Teta	Chătîyṭâ (חֲטִיטָא)	H2410
The Elect One	Bâchîyr (בָּחִיר) Êl (אֵל)	H972+H140
The Eternal King	Qedem (קֶדֶם) Melek (מֶלֶךְ)	H6924+H4418
The Great Glory	Gibbôr (גִּבּוֹר) Kâbôd (כָּבוֹד)	H1368+H3519
The Heap of Witness	Galyêd (גַּלְעֵד)	H1567
The Most High	Elyôn (עֶלְיוֹן) Êl (אֵל)	H5945+H410
The Righteousness One	Tsedâqâh (צְדָקָה) Êl (אֵל)	H6666+H140
The river of Debôrâh	Allôn Bâkûth (אַלּוֹן בָּכוּת).	H439
Theocanus	Tiqwâh (תִּקְוָה)	H8616
Theras	Ahăwâ (אַהֲוָא)	H163
Tigris	Chiddeqel (חִדֶּקֶל)	H2313
Tobit	Ṭôbîyâhû (טוֹבִיָּהוּ)	H2900
Tomas	Tâôm (תְּאוֹם)	H8380
Tyre	Tsôr (צֹר)	H6865
Tyrians	Tsôr (צֹר)	H6865
Unleavened Bread	Matstsâh (מַצָּה)	H4682
Uriel	Ûrîyêl (אוּרִיאֵל)	H222
Wife	Woman - ishshâh (אִשָּׁה)	H802
Wisdom	Chokmâh (חָכְמָה)	H2451
World	Têbêl (תֵּבֵל)	H8398
Zacarias	Zekaryâhû (זְכַרְיָה)	H2148
Zaraias	Zerachyâh (זְרַחְיָה)	H2228
Zephathite	Tsephath (צְפַת)	H6857
Zion	Tsîyôn (צִיּוֹן)	H6726
Glorious	Tiphârâh (תִּפְאָרָה)	H8597

www.ingramcontent.com/pod-product-compliance
Lightning Source LLC
Chambersburg PA
CBHW081945230426
43669CB00019B/2922